Volume III

CREATING AN EMPHASIS ON LEARNING: QUALITY CONTROL, PRODUCTIVITY, AND ACCOUNTABILITY

by

DON STEWART

SLATE Services, Publishers
Post Office Box 8769
Fountain Valley, California 92708

Copyright © 1976, by Don Stewart. All rights reserved. No part of this book may be reproduced in any form without prior written permission of the Publisher, except in the case of brief quotations embodied in critical articles, reviews, or scholarly books. For information, contact the author, Don Stewart, Director, SLATE Services, Post Office Box 8796, Fountain Valley, California 92708.

Library of Congress Card Number 75-13674
Cloth Cover ISBN 0-913448-11-7
Paperback ISBN 0-913448-12-5
Manufactured in the United States of America

First Printing January, 1976

INSTRUCTION

AS A

HUMANIZING SCIENCE

A series of three volumes to be used to increase learning by increasing the effectiveness, efficiency, and productivity in designed instruction.

Volume I — The Changing Role of the Educator: The Instructioneer

Volume II — A Behavioral Learning Systems Approach to Instruction: Analysis and Synthesis

Volume III — Creating an Emphasis on Learning: Quality Control, Productivity, and Accountability

DEDICATION

I want to dedicate this series to the thousands of teachers who during the past decade or more have indirectly helped me to develop the concepts presented in this book by challenging them and making me justify and defend these concepts over and over again.

I also want to dedicate this series to my deceased Aunt and Uncle, Birdie and Frank Christopher of Wichita, Kansas, who indirectly provided the financial resources necessary to take the time to write the series and the funds necessary to publish the series.

I want to dedicate Volume III to the thousands of administrators, school board members, trustees, regents, and legislators who will use it to make the instructional process more effective and efficient and to help all of the people involved with the instructional process to become more professional in their responses to the needs of the students and our society.

Don Stewart

Series Philosophy — "The Socratic Oath"

Most educational institutions in their charters or constitutions have stated a philosophy that is probably very much in agreement with the goals of our society. All too often these statements are so general in nature that they cannot be put into practice by the teachers and other educators whose job it is to develop a curriculum in support of the philosophy. Because the teacher's role is so critical in preparing the learner for life and even throughout life, there are many comparisons that can be made between the role of the teacher and the role of a doctor. Consequently the philosophy of the author can be succinctly stated in the following "Socratic Oath" which parallels the "Hippocratic Oath" which is taken by doctors in the performance of their role with their patients.

THE SOCRATIC OATH

You do solemnly swear, each person by whatever he holds most sacred, that you will be loyal to the profession of teaching and just and generous to its members; that you will lead your lives and practice your art in uprightness and honor; that into whatsoever educational institution you shall enter, it shall be for the good of the learner to the utmost of your power, you will set yourself up as an example to your students by constant efforts to keep abreast of the changes in your field of study, adding what is new and dropping what is obsolete; that you will endeavor to determine the knowledge level of new students and adjust the course to their needs and, if appropriate, remedial studies for some and advanced placement for others; that you will exercise your art in such a manner that every student in your classes regardless of race, creed, or economic status will progress positively through the content of your course; that you will exhaust all available methods, media, and instructional materials if necessary in order to help the student learn all of the objectives of your course; that within your power you will not allow any student in your classes to proceed to subsequent courses without achieving all of the prerequisite behaviors available in your course and necessary for a successful progress in the subsequent courses. These things do you swear. And if you will be true to this, your oath, may prosperity and good repute be ever yours; the opposite if you shall prove yourselves forsworn.

Copyright 1966 - Donald K. Stewart - all rights reserved

Parchment copies of "The Socratic Oath" ready for framing are available for purchase from SLATE Services, Publishers, P.O. Box 8796, Fountain Valley, California 92708.

TABLE OF CONTENTS*

Because the three volumes represent a series and are strongly interrelated, the Table of Contents in each volume contains the chapter and unit headings from all three volumes.

	Page No.
Preface	xxi
Introduction	xxv
Guidelines to Readers	xxxi
Summary of New Concepts	xxxix

Volume I — The Changing Role of the Educator: The Instructioneer

Chapter I — Instruction or Education: Which is the Profession? 1
- A. Educational Needs, Purposes for Schools, and Why Purposes Have Not Been Achieved 4
- B. Instruction vs. Education 15

Chapter II — Instruction or Education: Which is Humanizing? 21
- A. Need for Humanism 24
- B. Traditional Inhumanities in Our Schools 27
- C. The Tragic Results of the Traditional Inhumanities ... 36
- D. Breeding Ground of the Traditional Inhumanities 48
- E. Humanistic Solutions with Potential Inhumane Results ... 51
- F. Instruction vs. Education 62

Chapter III — Why a Behavioral Learning Systems Approach to Instruction (BLSA) 67
- A. Advantages of Applying the BLSA to the Instructional Process 70
- B. Criticisms of the Application of Systems Concepts to the Instructional Process 74

Chapter IV — Identification and Development of a Philosophy of Instruction and Theories of Instruction 79
- A. A Design for Excellence in Instruction 84
- B. A Philosophy of Instruction 91

---

*It is customary to place the Table of Contents after the front material (Preface, Foreword, etc.) and usually just before the first chapter. However, in this series, the Table of Contents is placed before most of the front material for three reasons: first, it is recognized that most potential readers skim through the Table of Contents as a preliminary appraisal of the contents of the book; second, in this book, the front material is longer than in most other books and if the Table of Contents was placed in the customary location, it could be difficult to locate; and third, the front material is considered to be important enough that it should be placed after the Table of Contents along with the rest of the book and it should be included in the Table of Contents for ease of identification and location.

			Page No.
C.	The Theories of Instruction		101
	1.	Behavioral Theory of Instruction: Cognitive and Sensory Domains	111
	2.	Behavioral Theory of Instruction: Affective Domain	115
	Chapter V — The Changing Role of the Teacher From Educator to Instructioneer		121
A.	Contemporary Role of the Teacher		128
B.	Traditional Role of the Teacher — Presenter		129
C.	The Humanizing Role for the Teacher — Instructioneer		136
	1.	What is a Learning Problem	144
	2.	Examples of Learning Problems	147
		a. What am I supposed to learn	147
		b. Decision making as a Learning Problem	151
		c. Cheating as a Learning Problem	154
		d. Cumulative ignorance as a Learning Problem	155
		e. Low correlation between Objectives and Tests as a Learning Problem	157
		f. Direction of Learning as a Learning Problem	158
		g. Reading as a Learning Problem	160
		(1) Lack of specified objectives	161
		(2) Problems in speed reading	164
		(3) Phonics and other word attack skills	166
		(4) Interest as it affects reading skills	176
		(5) Educational Malpractices in reading	177
		h. Essay Writing as a learning problem	182
		(1) Evaluation of Essays	184
		(2) The teaching and learning of writing skills	188
		i. Increased effectiveness as a potential learning problem	194
	3.	Recognition of Individual Differences in Action instead of Words	197
		a. Intelligence and Individual Differences	204
		b. Rate of learning — Traditional Situation	205
		c. Rate of Learning as affected by Amount to be learned	205
		(1) Ideal composition of amount to be learned (8 categories of objectives)	209
		(2) Compromise composition of amount to be learned	212
		(3) Contemporary efforts to recognize differences in amounts to be learned	214
		d. Rate of Learning as affected by time as a variable	217
		(1) Learning time as a variable — open entry-open exit plan	219
		(2) Compromises in using time as a variable during the transition to the ideal	221

Page No.

        (3) Contemporary efforts to allow amount to be learned and time for learning to be variables 227
    e. Rate of Learning: Traditional vs. System 232
    f. Rate of Learning as affected by Students' Intellectual and Sensory Learning Skills 234
        (1) The degree of simulation as a factor in a learning or instructional pathway 236
        (2) The method of designing instruction as a factor in a learning or instructional pathway 245
        (3) The language used for instruction as a factor in a learning or instructional pathway 247
    g. Apparent vs. Real Intelligence as affected by Students' Intellectual and Sensory Learning Skills 258
    h. Rate of Learning as affected by the Students' Emotional Tendencies 261
        (1) Motivation as it affects rate of learning 261
        (2) Interpersonal relationship (student-teacher) as it affects rate of learning 271
    i. Apparent vs. Real Intelligence as affected by Students' Emotional Tendencies 277
    j. The elusive concept of "real intelligence" 278
    k. Comparison of education, instruction, and the medical field 279
  4. Humanizing instruction by identifying and solving learning problems 281
  5. Transition from educator to *Instructioneer* 285
    a. The Humanization Factor 285
    b. Changing the number of hours spent presenting course content 286
    c. Changing the number of hours spent preparing to teach 290
    d. Changing the number of hours spent in activities not associated with measurable learning 295
    e. Changing the number of hours spent with small groups and individuals 298
    f. Developing the independent learner 299
    g. The Instructioneer's role: a limited reality already 304
D. Supporting Roles to Assist the Instructioneer 306
  1. Master Instructioneers 307
  2. Principals and Department Heads 307
  3. Substitute Instructioneers 307
  4. Graduate Students as Instructioneers 308
  5. Layman Teachers 308

		Page No.
6.	Associate Teachers	309
7.	Learners' Aids	309
8.	Practice Instructioneers	310
9.	Student Tutors	311
10.	Parents as Tutors	312
11.	Guidance and Counseling Staff	314
12.	Instructional Crisis Squad	315
13.	Curriculum Specialists	
	a. Curriculum Development	316
	b. Media Production	316
	c. Storage and Retrieval Systems	318
14.	Instructional Researchers	319
15.	Presenters in the Scholarship Function	319

Volume II — A Behavioral Learning Systems Approach to Instruction: Analysis and Synthesis

Chapter VI — Determining the Purpose of the Instructional Event: Objectives and Evaluation 321

A. Introduction 322
B. Instructional Specifications 325
   1. What is Learning 326
   2. Reasons for Specifying Objectives 327
      a. Identifies the Subject Matter Focus 328
      b. The Nature of the Behavior is Revealed 329
      c. Behaviors to be Modified are Identified 329
      d. Facilitates Instructional Planning 332
      e. The Objective can be Communicated 334
      f. Helps Students Plan Their Learning Time 336
      g. Achievement Can be Measured 338
      h. Teacher Accountability is Possible 339
      i. Facilitates the Development of Common Expectations 342
      j. Increasing Specificity, Increases Chances for Learning 343
         (1) Interaction Between SO's and Teacher's Role in Maximizing Learning 348
   3. Reasons for General Objectives 351
   4. Other Categories of Objectives 353
      a. Educational Objectives 354
   5. What is a Specific Objective? 355
      a. The Analysis of a Specific Objective 357
         (1) Specifying the Learning Environment 358
         (2) Specifying the Behavior 359
         (3) Specifying the Object of the Behavior 359

		Page No.
	(4) Specifying the Criteria for Evaluation: 100% of the Objectives vs. 100% of the Test Items	360
	(5) Increasing the Specification of the Objective	366

6. The Three Types of Learning: Cognitive Sensory, and Affective 367
   a. Mental, Emotional, and Bodily Consciousness 371
   b. Cognitive Domain 377
      (1) Taxonomy of Cognitive Objectives 381
          (a) Bloom's Taxonomy 383
          (b) Gagne's Taxonomy 391
      (2) The Cognitive Genius 393
   c. Sensory Domain 394
      (1) Introduction 395
      (2) Measurement in the Sensory Domain 397
      (3) Taxonomies of Sensory Objectives 398
          (a) Part I — The Senses in the Stimulus — Afferent Sequence 398
          (b) Part II — The Sense in the Efferent — Action Sequence 404
          (c) Part III — The Action 405
      (4) Solving Learning Problems in the Sensory Domain 408
      (5) The Sensory Genius 410
   d. The Affective Domain 412
      (1) Introduction 413
      (2) Instruction, Indoctrination, or Brainwashing 416
      (3) Measurement in the Affective Domain 417
      (4) Taxonomy of Affective Objectives 425
          (a) Acceptance and Rejection of Attitudes, Values, and Beliefs (Action-Non-Action Continuum) 427
          (b) Intensity and Direction of Attitudes, Values, and Beliefs 435
          (c) Other Factors Affecting Emotive Behaviors 437
      (5) Teaching and Learning in the Affective Domain 441
          (a) The Present Teaching and Learning of Affective Domain Objectives 441
          (b) Two Illustrative Cases: Book Banning and Religion 444
          (c) Possible Directions for Successful Teaching of Affective Domain Objectives 449
      (6) The Affective Genius 454

				Page No.
		e.	Integrated Domains: The Reality of Instruction	454
			(1) The Integrated Genius: Jack-of-all-trades	455
C.	Evaluation of the Instructional Event			456
	1.	Correlation Between Objectives and Tests		458
		a.	The Traditional View of Evaluation	459
		b.	Correlation Problems	461
			(1) Problems with "General Objectives" and "Subjective" Test Items	461
			(2) Problems with "General Objectives" and "Specific" Test Items	462
			(3) Problems with "Specific Objectives" and "Subjective" Test Items	463
			(4) Problems with "Specific Objectives" and "Specific" Test Items	469
		c.	Behavior Correlation vs. Content Correlation	469
		d.	"Don't Teach Students What You Want Them to Learn" or "Don't Teach to The Test"	474
	2.	Types of Test Items and Tests		480
		a.	Essay Items and Term Papers	481
		b.	"Objective" Type Test Items and Examinations: An Example of Insidious Subjectivity	483
		c.	Rote Memory and Thinking Test Items	495
		d.	The Best Type of Test Items	499
		e.	Functions (Purposes) of Testing	500
		f.	Formative vs. Summative Testing	502
		g.	Criterion vs. Normative Testing	504
		h.	Standardized Tests: A Designed Mirage	513
			(1) Examples of How Standardized Tests are Fraudulently and/or Mistakenly Used	518
		i.	Suggestions to Improve the Value of the Results of Standardized Tests	522
		j.	Attitudes Towards Testing	523
	3.	Teachers' Qualifications for Evaluation		524
D.	Minimum Common Core Learning			527
	1.	How to Identify Minimum Common Core Learning		532
	2.	Functions of Advisory Groups		537
	3.	The Cafeteria of Learning		538
	4.	Identifying Commonality Promotes Individuality		539
	5.	Contemporary Efforts to Establish Minimum Common Core Learning		540
E.	Justification of Instructional Objectives and/or Test Items			543
	1.	Applying the Questions to Courses		549
	2.	Applying the Questions to Non-Specific Test Items		562

		Page No.
3.	Applying the Questions to Non-Specific Objectives	563
4.	Applying the Questions to Specific Test Items Which Lack Known Specific Objectives	585
5.	Applying the Questions to Specific Test Items and Related Specific Objectives Which Have Less Than 100 Percent Correlation	608
6.	Applying the Questions to Specific Test Items Which Don't Relate to Course Objectives Implied by the Title of the Course	622

F. Guidelines for Writing and/or Obtaining Specific Objectives and/or Test Items 625
   1. Guidelines for On-Going Courses 628
   2. Guidelines for New Courses 629
   3. Utilizing Taxonomies of Objectives 631
   4. Don't Reinvent "Curriculum Wheels" 632
   5. Priorities in Writing Objectives 634
G. Freedom and Who Should Write Objectives: State, District, Teachers or Students? 635
H. The Debate: To Use or Not To Use Specific Behavioral Objectives 644
   1. Reasons Why Some educators are Against Specifying Objectives 648
I. "Do Your Own Thing": Tragedy or a Mode for Maximizing Motivation and Serendipity 651
   1. Scholarship Sessions 654

Chapter VII — A Behavioral Learning Systems Approach to the Design of the Instructional Environment 657
A. Introduction 660
B. Interrelationships Between the Elements of an Educational Event When There Are No Specific Learning Objectives 673
   1. The Teacher as the Emphasis in the Educational Event 665
   2. Technology as the Emphasis in the Educational Event 668
   3. Why Technology Hasn't Made an Impact on the Educational Event 670
   4. Technology and Accountability 672
C. Interrelationships Between the Elements of an Instructional Event When There Are Specific Objectives 679
   1. Technology: Humanizing or Dehumanizing 679
   2. Guidelines for the Utilization of Technology 683
   3. Ultimate Goal of Designed Instruction 686

			Page No.
	4.	The Physical Facilities of the Instructional Environment	690
D.	Designing the Software for the Instructional Event		694
	1.	Behavioral Analysis: The Identification of the Boundaries of the Instructional Event	697
	2.	The Instructional Process: A Form of Communication	713
		a. The Learner's Environment as a Factor in Communication	719
	3.	Behavioral Syntheses: Construction of the Instructional Event	724
		a. Instructional Models: Theories of Learning vs. Theories of Teaching vs. Theories of Instruction	728
		b. Guidelines for Development of the Instructional Event	734
		c. Sequencing the Objectives in the Instructional Event	738
		(1) The Matrix Method of Sequencing Objectives	740
		d. Development of the Instructional Event	773
		(1) Involving the Learner in Learning	776
		(2) Step Size and Reinforcement	782
		(3) Assembly and Validation	784
		(4) Potential Sources of Problems in the Development of Learning Pathways	786
	4.	Utilizing or Adapting Ready-made Software	787
	5.	Instructional Design Evaluation	791
E.	Selecting, Modifying, and/or Designing Hardware for the Instructional Event		796
	1.	Television and the "Stewart ITV" Format	802
	2.	Computers in the Instructional Event	808
	3.	The Dial-Access Concept in the Instructional Event	812
	4.	Selection of Hardware and the Use of Consultants	817
	5.	Questions to be Considered When Planning for an Instructional Information Retrieval System (IIRS)	825
		a. Software Considerations	826
		b. Hardware Considerations	829
Volume III — Creating an Emphasis on Learning: Quality Control, Productivity, and Accountability			
Chapter VIII — Quality Control, Productivity, and Accountability			835
A.	Introduction		838
	1.	Accountability Alone is Not Sufficient!	847
	2.	Accountable for What? (The Effects of a Critical Principle of Evaluation	855
	3.	Who is Accountable and for What?	858
		a. "Youth-anasia" (School Violence and Push-outs)	860

				Page No.
	b.	Is Learning Measurable		866
	c.	The Affective Domain and Accountability		869
	d.	New Curriculum Areas for Accountability		872
	e.	Accountability and Commercially Prepared Instructional Materials		875
4.	Teacher's Fear of Accountability			876
5.	Entropic Drift and the Transposition of Controlling Influences			888

B. Evaluation of Students 901
    1. Testing and Grading 902
    2. Grading and Cumulative Ignorance 914
        a. Pass—Fail grading 916
        b. "F" Grades: Coffin Nails in the Educational System .. 918
        c. Social Promotion 923
        d. Elimination of Evaluation 926
    3. Evaluation and Discipline 929
        a. Cheating 935
    4. Systems Evaluation and Grading 937
        a. Testing Under a Behavioral Learning Systems Approach 938
        b. Grading Under a Behavioral Learning Systems Approach 942
        c. The ABI Alternative 946
        d. Student Errors 950
    5. Students' Rights in the Evaluation Process 951
        a. Instructional Grievance Committee 954

C. Evaluation of Teachers 956
    1. The Traditional Teachers' Role and Evaluation 959
        a. Student Evaluation of Teachers 965
    2. Teachers as Individuals 967
    3. The Teachers' Role and Evaluation Under the Behavioral Learning Systems Approach 971
        a. Pre-service Training for Teachers 972
        b. Teachers' Role and Evaluation 980
            (1) Hiring Practices 986
        c. In-service Training and the Instructional Crisis Squad 987
        d. Class Size 989
        e. Teaching Load 994
        f. The SLATE Criteria for Remuneration 997
            (1) Cost per Student and Teacher Salaries: Cause or Effect? 1000

		Page No.
	(2) An Example and Other Comments	1011
g.	Teacher Surplus or a Shortage of Students and Learning?	1014
4.	Professionalism vs. Unionism	1018
a.	Affective Learning as Affected by the Teaching Environment	1020
b.	Professional Responsibilities	1023
c.	Part-time and Substitute Teachers	1036
d.	Professionalism vs. Unionism: A Comparison	1036
e.	Additional Benefits of Accountability and Professionalism	1040
D. Evaluation of Administrators		1042
1. The Administrators' Role and Evaluation Under BLSA		1047
2. Counseling and Guidance Staff: A New Role and Evaluation		1050
E. Evaluation of Local School Boards, Regents, etc.		1052
F. Evaluation of State Boards and Offices of Instruction		1055
1. The Role and Evaluation of State Offices of Instruction Under the Behavioral Learning Systems Approach		1057
G. Evaluation of the U.S. Office of Instruction		1058
1. The Role and Evaluation of the U.S. Office of Instruction Under the Behavioral Learning Systems Approach		1059
Chapter IX — Instructional Research: A New Role		1061
A. Science vs. Non-Science or Why Educational Research has Failed!		1064
1. The Identification of Research Problems		1068
2. The Ignoring of Individual Differences		1069
3. Media and Method Research		1071
4. Tests: The Critical Hidden Variable (GIGO)		1075
a. Correlation Problems in Constructing Evaluation Instruments		1076
b. The Use of Subjective "Objective" Type Test Items		1078
c. Percentage of Test Items Correct Not Necessarily Equal to Percentage of Objectives Achieved		1079
d. The Invalidity of Standardized (Normed) Tests		1083
B. The Role of Instructional Research in the Behavioral Learning Systems Approach to Instruction		1090
1. Modes of Research		1093
a. Theories of Instruction and Instructional Research		1095
2. Instructional Design Evaluation: A New Tool for Research		1096
a. Evaluating Examples of Educational Research		1101
C. Priorities for Instructional Research		1108

Page No.

    1. The National Institute of Education: Traditional Research
Hidden Under System's Concepts and Terminology 1111
       a. The Actual Direction of NIE Research and
Subsequent Reductions in Funding 1118
    2. The Need for Regional, State, and Local Institutes
for Instructional Research 1120
D. Teaching, Research, and the Role of the Teacher 1121
Chapter X — Changing From Traditional (Chance) Education to
Designed Instruction 1125
A. Bringing About the Change 1131
    1. Do You Need to Change 1131
    2. System's Plan for Change 1134
    3. General Guidelines for Planning Change 1139
    4. In-service Training to Bring About Change 1147
    5. In-service and Pre-service Training: An Advertisement ... 1151
       a. Publications 1152
       b. Using the Series as Textbooks for Pre-service
Training 1154
       c. Consulting Services 1161
          (1) An Example of Contract Seminars —
Washington State Community Colleges 1162
          (2) Alternate Pathways to Change Available 1169
B. Implications of the System's Concepts as Applied to
Education and Educational Innovations 1174
    1. Educational Innovations from the System's Point-of-View 1177
       a. Bilingual Education 1180
       b. Alternative Schools 1181
       c. Open Education 1183
       d. Value Clarification 1187
       e. Early Childhood or Pre-School Education 1188
       f. Other Systems Approaches to Instruction 1190
       g. Career and Vocational Education 1192
       h. Community Colleges 1195
       i. Adult Education 1197
       j. Irregular Students 1199
       k. Racial Integration in Schools 1200
       l. Year-round Schools 1203
       m. Parochial and Private Schools 1204
C. Questions and Answers About Utilizing the Behavioral
Learning Systems Concepts 1205

PREFACE

or

Why Be Concerned About the Role of the Educator?

Almost one out of every three people in the United States is either a full or part-time student, a teacher, or an educational administrator and at some time in every person's life in the United States, they are directly involved and affected by the educational process. Although the 1974-75 enrollment of almost 59 million students gave evidence of a continued slight decline of less than one percent, the total cost of education of almost $108 billion gave evidence of a continued increase of over eleven percent and accounts for eight percent of our gross national product. There is no other facet of our society that involves so many people and has such a critical affect on the future lives of the people (students) who are the consumers of these educational services. Therefore, the purveyors of these services take on a very critical role in our society. Ideally, this role should be performed in such a manner that the consumers are positively affected by these services. In fact, this is not the case. That is why I wrote my first book *Educational Malpractices: The Big Gamble in our Schools* in which I identified forty-one (41) educational malpractices that are commonly found in most educational institutions and being practiced by a majority of the teachers and administrators. This first book was primarily written for students and parents of students to make them aware of the malpractices being perpetrated on them and to give them some practical suggestions (including actual dialogues) which can be used to alleviate or eliminate these malpractices. Secondarily, this book was also written for teachers as a summary of the solutions to the problems as presented in this three volume series. Ironically, the very same educators who are performing the malpractices against students basically want students to have success in learning. The major problem is the strength of the loyalty that most educators hold for the traditions of education which have been handed down through generations of teachers. The strength of these traditions, even though they are malpractices, gathers support from two areas. Since *teachers tend to teach the way they are taught not the way they are taught to teach*, as long as most of the teachers at all levels of education carry on most of the malpractices, their students who become teachers will tend to do the same. However, the major support for the continuation of these malpractices comes from most of the teacher-training institutions which not only practice the malpractices, but they preach them and demand that their students also perform these malpractices in order to graduate.

If education is a critical aspect of our society and the teachers and administrators in education perform a critical role in the educational process, I can't possibly imagine a more critical role in our society than those faculty in higher education who are teachers of students who are planning to be teachers. In any other discipline at a college or university, the faculty members may affect hundreds of students each semester or quarter and over a lifetime they may affect thousands of students, but teachers of students who are planning to be teachers, indirectly affect millions of students. Because of this, it is critical that teacher-training institutions make the necessary changes to eliminate the malpractices in their own teaching and in how they teach others to teach. As a result, the major motivation behind the writing of this book is to prepare a text that could be used by students who are preparing to teach. *Notice though*, at the present time, only teachers who are planning to teach at the elementary or secondary level are required to take any special training in *how to teach*. All that is needed at most institutions of higher education is an advanced degree. The assumption is made that to require graduate students or non-education faculty to take some education courses or training on *how to teach* and/or *how to test* would not be of much value because it can be easily pointed out that teachers who have had these education courses and the faculty who teach the courses typically don't actually behave much differently in the classroom than teachers who have never had any of these courses.*

Consider for a moment the seriousness of the existing problem in which thousands of higher education faculty are involved in the teaching and testing of millions of students and they are not in the least qualified to perform this critical role of *teaching* and *testing*. Yet, their actions and decisions are permanently affecting the future lives of their students. Therefore, a secondary audience for this book are the teachers who have never had any courses or formal training on *how to teach* and/or *how to test*, but would like to help more of their students learn more and would like to be more honest with students in their instructional evaluation situations. A third group for which this book could be of value are the administrators and teachers who have been trained through the traditional education courses to carry on the malpractices

---

* A recent study funded by the U. S. Office of Education as part of its Targeted Research and Development Program found little research evidence to show that teachers having teacher preparation courses have any greater effect on students' performance than teachers who haven't had these courses.

described in my first book.

Although the titles of the series and each volume were selected to communicate to potential readers the emphasis which I have placed in the series and within each volume, it is possible because of differences in the prior experiences of the reader to misinterpret this emphasis. To minimize possible misinterpretation, the primary emphasis throughout the series is on increasing learning — student learning! In changing the emphasis in the instructional setting from *what teachers do* to *increasing student learning*, two traditional concepts become obsolete: the classroom itself and the teacher's role as a presenter of content in that classroom. Almost every educational institution has somewhere in its charter or constitution the statement *to develop each student to the maximum of his or her ability*. Notice, the statement does not say to develop the *average* student or *most* students or a *curve's worth* of students. The statement specifies EACH student. In other words, the majority of educational institutions are legally committed to the concept and practice of individualized instruction. Since it is practically impossible to have a class of students who are all at the same level and who all learn at the same rate, it is also impossible to individualize instruction on a mass or class basis. Hence, the concept of classes of students is obsolete and since under the concept of individualized instruction it would be rare to gather a group of students together for an instructional experience, the concept of the teacher's role as a presenter of course content to a group of students also becomes obsolete.

As pointed out in my first book, the two major problems in traditional education are the evaluation process throughout education (from evaluating students all the way up to the evaluation of the U.S. Office of Education) and the teacher-training institutions. The reasons that the teacher-training institutions have become a major part of the problem in education instead of being a part of the solution are that most of them are practicing the malpractices, are teaching the teachers-to-be to practice the malpractices, and are training the students for an obsolete role as presenters of course content. Although some of the schools of education think they are being very modern by individualizing their instructional program, the content of the individualized program still emphasizes the traditional role of the teacher as a presenter of course content rather than teaching the teachers-to-be on how to individualize instruction for their students. The new role of the teacher as an instructioneer is the one that should be taught by the teacher-training institutions and should be *practiced by teachers at all levels of education.*

Among traditional educators, there has been a belief for decades that elementary school teachers teach differently and should be trained differently than either secondary school teachers or higher education faculty and that secondary school teachers teach differently and should be trained differently than either elementary school teachers or higher education faculty. The new role of the teacher and the process of designing instruction as described in this series is essentially the same role and involves the same basic behaviors for teachers at all levels of education from pre-school to graduate or continuing education.

The National Field Task Force on the Improvement and Reform of American Education has called for a new leadership to bring about increased effectiveness and inefficiency. In their report, the Task Force states that:

> *The welfare of this nation requires that schools attain new levels of success, and that this attainment be more inclusive of the population. Although a larger proportion of American youth is enrolled in school than at any other time in our national history, many thousands leave school with inadequate sustaining learning skills — and with insufficient preparation for the transition from school to the work force and effective participation in other aspects of the society.*

Although their report calls for administrators to take on the leadership role, I believe successful change can best be brought about by cooperative leadership on the part of both teachers and administrators. Teachers should take the lead in accepting and performing their new role and encourage administrators to accept and perform their new role. Administrators should take the lead in accepting and performing their new role and encourage teachers to accept and perform their new role. Because of the transposition of authority as discussed in Chapter IX, Volume No. 3, it is actually more important that teachers be the first to institute changes which increase student learning. Whereas it is possible for teachers to improve student learning without administrative leadership and cooperation, it is almost impossible for administrators to improve student learning without the leadership and cooperation of teachers.

An important point to remember is that regardless of the teacher's feelings towards behavioral objectives, systems approaches, humanism, etc., practically every teacher evaluates their students and assigns some kind of evaluation mark. Realizing that not all desirable objectives lend themselves to measurement, the intent of this series is to maximize the learning of whatever it is that teachers are presently using as a basis to evaluate students and then to improve the quality, quantity and relevance of the learning objectives for each course.

INTRODUCTION

I expect to hear repeatedly three particular comments about this series. First, I expect to hear comments about the reading level of this series or that it is not very *scholarly*. Second, I expect some traditional oriented educators to be upset because I haven't quoted from or referred to the works of the many *big wheels* in education often enough (name-dropping) or at all. Third, in looking at this series in its present form, some readers will charge that I have not practiced what I am preaching.

With reference to the use of *scholarly* language, I would like to describe an experience which I had about five years ago. I had just completed a two-day seminar at a university when one of the faculty participants approached me and said, *I really liked the Seminar, but one thing has bothered me throughout the Seminar. What is that?,* I asked. *Your language,* said the professor. I asked him, *What is wrong with my language?* He replied, *It was not very scholarly.* I asked him, *What do you mean by saying that my language was not very scholarly?* The participant replied, *I understood everything you said!!!* Particularly in higher education, there is a tendency among faculty to select textbooks that will impress members of an accrediting team or most visiting colleagues even though the textbook may be so *scholarly* that even the teacher has trouble understanding what the author is saying (not to mention the fact that many of the students can't read or learn from it).

The name-dropping syndrome which is found in most *acceptable* papers, articles, and books is supposed to indicate that the author is acquainted with the work done by others in the field. By careful selection of references and quotes from the publications of *big wheels* in almost any major field of study, it is possible to support almost any point of view via inference. This is because in the process of developing a particular point-of-view, many of the *big wheels* have changed their ways of looking at certain concepts. As a partial result of the *publish or perish* dictum in higher education, a trend has developed which at best is questionable. This trend is the writing of articles and books which are primarily built on quotations and references from other writers with little, if any, new contributions actually being made by the person writing the article or book except the collecting of the quotations and references. Under certain conditions, this type of article or book could be of value particularly when it is one of the first in its field. After that, most of the articles and books in this category are just a rehash of one another. Since I have been conducting seminars and classes for over a decade on the topic of this series, the vast majority of the material in this series is original. In fact, the beginning of this series goes back to a 74-page paper entitled *A Behavioral Learning Systems Concept as Applied to Courses in Education and Training* which I wrote in 1964. Over 5,000 copies of this paper and revised editions of this paper have been sold. I have also written a number of articles during the past decade on various aspects of the same basic concept and these have been published in a wide variety of journals, magazines, and books.

There have been a number of publications which have been written about various aspects of developing objectives or developing instructional units which have been written in a format which would illustrate that the author was *practicing what he was preaching.* This would be very laudable if all the readers of the publications had the same needs. Rarely is this a realistic assumption. Although it is possible that some publications will only be read by one type of reader, the majority of publications are read by readers with differing needs. Therefore, the design of this series has been based on an analysis of reader needs and hopefully has built in sufficient flexibility that most of the many reader needs can be satisfied.

A majority of the initial users of this series will probably use this book as a reference source and many of the learners who use this series as textbooks for formal courses will probably also want to use this series as reference sources after they have completed the courses. Since most reference books are of the traditional format, I decided to write this series in the traditional format except for the following:

1. The general objectives (GO) and some of the specific objectives (SO) for each chapter will be listed at the beginning of each chapter.
    NOTE: The GO's and SO's at the beginning of each chapter are those which I believe are particularly important. A teacher who may want to use one or more of the volumes as a textbook for a course, may want to add more GO's and SO's and/or may want to delete some of the GO's and SO's which I have listed.
2. Following this Introduction, there is a list of six categories of readers who might read this book with directed guidelines for each type as to how they might locate what is most relevant for them.
3. Following the list of potential readers and their prescriptions is a list of fifty-one critical new concepts which are suggested in this book with the page numbers where these concepts are discussed in more detail.
4. For those learners who have problems in reading this series because of the reading level and for those learners who learn better from an audio-visual source or like an audio-visual reinforcement, films

covering most of the major topics and accompanying Active-Involvement Forms will be available by late 1975 or in 1976.

As mentioned in the Preface, the primary purpose of my first book, *Educational Malpractices: The Big Gamble in Our Schools,* was to point out to students, parents and educators, specific problems in the traditional approach to the instructional process which interfere with learning and to present a summary of the solutions to these problems which is presented in this series in much greater detail and are designed to eliminate the educational malpractices and to maximize student learning. To accomplish this task, I have divided the series into three volumes.

Volume I   Changing Role of the Educator: The Instructioneer
Volume II   A Behavioral Learning Systems Approach to Instruction: Analysis and Synthesis
Volume III Creating an Emphasis on Learning: Quality Control, Productivity, and Accountability

In order to help most educators to accept the changes suggested in this series, I have found that it is necessary to present the rationale or reasons which support the need for the changes. Chapters I-III, Volume I, have been written with this view in mind. Chapter I, *Education vs. Instruction: Which is the Profession,* points out some of the major problems in education today and how they conflict with the alleged functions of education in our society. Chapter II, *Instruction or Education: Which is Humanizing,* takes a very critical problem which is of concern to educators, students, parents, and almost every citizen in our country and points out how the present instructional approach in most schools is not very humane and how by changing the teacher's role and by instituting a Behavioral Learning Systems Approach in the instructional process not only makes the process more humane, but can contribute significantly towards developing students who are more humane in their relationships with other people. Chapter III, *Why a Behavioral Learning Systems Approach (BLSA) to Instruction?,* describes various definitions of *systems* and how the application of the systems concept can help to eliminate many of the problems found in the present educational process without being as rigid and inhumane. Chapter IV, *Identification and Development of a Philosophy of Instruction and Theories of Instruction,* describes the six steps to be taken in achieving excellence in instruction and then continues on to develop the first step, identification of a philosophy of instruction and the theories of instruction. Chapter V, *The Changing Role of the Teacher from Educator to Instructioneer,* is the major and last chapter of the first volume and describes the second step in the process of designing effective and efficient instruction. A comparison is made of the new role with the traditional role of the teacher with an emphasis on how the new role helps the teacher and the whole instructional process become more humane in dealing with students. Major differences between the traditional philosophy and the philosophy of the Behavioral Learning Systems Approach (BLSA) to instruction are pointed out particularly as these differences affect the role of the teacher, i.e., whereas tradition considers student errors as a normal student or genetic problem which requires little, if any, follow up, the philosophy of the BLSA considers student errors as a learning problem brought about by student learning differences or problems in the learning environment, both of which can be solved. The Chapter ends with a description of a number of supportive roles which can help the teacher be more effective and efficient.

Volume II, *A Behavioral Learning Systems Approach to Instruction: Analysis and Synthesis,* concerns the next two steps in the process of designed instruction: the identification and specification of learning objectives and matching test items and the development of the instructional environment such that it will facilitate the achievement of the desired objectives. Chapter VI, *Determining the Purpose of the Instructional Event: Objectives and Evaluation,* is the first chapter in Volume II and is primarily concerned with the specifying and evaluation of instructional objectives in all three domains of learning: cognitive, sensory, and affective. In addition, reasons for specifying objectives, and guidelines for writing specific objectives, and the questions to be asked to justify the students' need to learn the objectives are discussed in detail. One of the most important concepts covered in this chapter is the need for and how to identify the minimum common core specific objectives in each course. Another important concept presented in this chapter concerns the need for a high correlation between the statements of what should be learned (specific objectives) and the test items or criteria for evaluation used to evaluate whether or not the desired learning has been achieved. As discussed in the chapter, this need for a high correlation between objectives and evaluation makes most traditional evaluation procedures and formats inappropriate and obsolete including standardized and normed tests and the so-called objective type test items (multiple-choice, true-false, and matching).

Chapter VII, *A Behavioral Learning Systems Approach to the Design of the Instructional Environment,* is the other chapter in Volume II of the series. The Chapter starts out with a comparison between the development of learning environments with and without specific objectives. Next, the development and selection of instructional software and hardware is discussed in detail.

Volume III, *Creating an Emphasis on Learning: Quality Control, Productivity, and Accountability,* concerns the necessity for making learning the major emphasis in our schools rather than the traditional emphasis which may have little relationship with learning. Chapter VIII, *Quality Control, Productivity, and Accountability,* starts out by discussing three important concepts: a critical principle of evaluation, the effects of a problem called *entropic drift,* and an evolutionary (some might call it revolutionary) transposition of authority which takes student learning from the bottom of the authority pyramid and puts it at the top of an inverted pyramid of support functions. Then the evaluation of students, teachers, administrators, etc., are discussed from the point of view of their affect on student learning. Of particular importance is the discussion of the evaluation of teachers as professionals rather than as artists or laborers.

Chapter IX, *Instructional Research: A New Role,* describes the last step in the designing of effective and efficient instruction. Traditionally, educational research has had little, if any, affect on what actually happens in the classrooms of our schools. The reasons for this waste of energy, time, and educational dollars are identified and then, the chapter concerns itself with methods by which instructional research can become a critical partner in designed instruction.

Chapter X, *Changing From Traditional (Chance) Education to Designed Instruction,* concerns the various steps that can be taken to bring about the change in the instructional environment. Included are comments on the implications of the Behavioral Learning Systems Approach on a variety of contemporary innovations in education.

By the time many readers reach this point in the last volume of the series, they will have questions which they want answered. For other readers who want to implement some of the suggestions I have made in this book, their colleagues may have challenged them with some questions about various aspects of the systems concept or about the imagined results of implementing some or all of the systems concepts. Therefore, the last part of Chapter X consists of a number of questions (and my answers to these questions) which typically arise at the Seminars which I have conducted with faculty from a variety of schools, colleges, and universities throughout the United States and Canada.

GUIDELINES TO READERS

In order to minimize the learning time involved in going through this book, I will identify six categories of readers. Categories II and III are further divided into sub-categories. After each grouping there are brief guidelines as to how readers in that grouping can get the most out of this series in the shortest time. (Those readers who have already read my book, *Educational Malpractices,* or have attended one of my seminars, see footnote below.)

I. *Description:* Learners who are planning to be teachers in preschool, elementary, secondary, higher education, or continuing adult education (this also includes people who are planning to teach in training programs in business and industry, military programs, and private schools).

Prescription: In reading through this series, pay particular attention to the general objectives (GO's) and specific objectives (SO's) found at the beginning of each chapter. If one or more of these volumes are being used as a textbook for a course, it would be particularly helpful if the teacher of the course followed some of the guidelines suggested in the series. Although most of the SO's are rote memory, the major process objective is described in Chapter X, Volume III, under pre-service training. It is very important that you get involved in solving a learning problem such that 90 percent or more of the students learn 100 percent of your SO's as the process will convince you of the practicality of the instructional design process. Also, be sure to use a pretest and post-test of your attitudes towards the four basic concepts of the whole series. This attitudinal instrument is described under the affective domain in Chapter VI, Volume II.

II. *Description:* Teachers who are already teaching and would be

---

My book, *Educational Malpractices,* and my seminars have both emphasized the problems to be found in traditional education and have presented a summary in 68 pages of the book or in two days or more of the seminars what is contained in about 1000 pages in this series. Consequently there is an overlap which is spread throughout the series. Therefore, in addition to the guidelines suggested for the reader category that you fit into, try to program yourself through the reading. Every time you come to a familiar concept, section, paragraph, or sentence which you recognize comes from *Educational Malpractices* or from one of my seminars, skip ahead by skim reading until you encounter new material and then slow down your reading speed to your usual level.

interested in trying out some new ideas and/or approaches to the instructional process. This category can be divided into six subgroups.

A. *Description:* Teachers who are already trying some aspects of the systems concepts and want to either double check their present approach or expand their application of the systems concept to their instructional activities.

Prescription: Before reading any of this book, readers in this group should read through the list of fifty-one critical new concepts which follows this section. Any concept which is of interest can be pursued by reading the reference pages listed at the end of each concept. In addition to these specific references, here are some general guidelines. For this group, the first three chapters of Volume I can probably be skipped. You should read through Chapter IV and those parts of Chapter V dealing with learning problems and individual differences. In Volume II, depending upon your experience in specifying objectives and developing matching test items, you may find it best to skim read over those parts you already know and practice and read a little more carefully those parts that are new. You may also find that Volume II will be a very good reference source as you develop and/or select instructional materials. In Volume III, that part of Chapter VIII dealing with the evaluation of students should be of interest and you might want your administrators to read that part of Chapter VIII dealing with teacher evaluation. If your use of various systems concepts is being challenged by your colleagues, you may find the last part of Chapter X useful as it concerns questions and answers about various systems concepts.

B. *Description:* New teachers who have not had any formal training on *how to teach* or *how to test* and also haven't been teaching long enough that they are committed to a particular technique or approach to instruction.*

Prescription: Readers in this group can probably skim over the first three chapters in Volume I. Because teachers in this group

---

* Quite often, teachers in this group feel guilty about not having any special training or courses on *how to teach and test*. Since few education courses are relevant to the needs of teachers-to-be, not having any formal training actually becomes a benefit. In other words, they haven't been tainted yet!

will have a tendency to teach *as they were taught*, Chapter IV and particularly Chapter V will be very important. All of Volume II will also be very important. That part of Chapter VIII in Volume III dealing with student evaluation is of importance, but the rest of Volume III may not be appropriate at the moment.

C. *Description:* New teachers who have had formal training on *how to teach and test*, but haven't been teaching long enough to be considered as being in the traditional teaching rut.

Prescription: The first three chapters in Volume I will probably be very important for these readers as they may have difficulty in accepting the rationale for the need to change the teacher's role and in accepting the new role itself. Chapters IV and V and all of Volume II will also be of importance to this group of readers. Again, only that part of Chapter VIII dealing with student evaluation is of particular importance; however, all of Volume III could be of value in helping the reader to accept and put into action the Behavioral Learing System Approach (BLSA) to instruction.

D. *Description:* Teachers who have been teaching for a long enough period of time to develop a pattern or style of teaching that is fairly consistent, but haven't had any formal training on *how to teach or test*.

Prescription: Teachers in this group will generally take a little longer to make the transition from the traditional approach to the Behavioral Learning Systems Approach. Because of this, readers in this group should pay particular attention to Chapters I—III in Volume I. Depending upon how traditional your pattern of teaching is (if you fit into this group), it may be useful to read Volume III before finishing Volume I or starting Volume II. The more traditional you are, the more important it may be to read Volume III. After Volume III, it may be best to read through Volume II and then come back to read Chapter IV and V in Volume I. After reading Chapter V on the new role of the teacher, it may be useful to review those sections in the rest of the series which you found most difficult to accept. It would also be useful if you could follow up the reading by attending a seminar dealing with these concepts in order to meet and talk with other teachers who are in a similar situation and some person(s) who is well acquainted with the systems concept.

E. *Description:* Teachers who have been teaching for a long enough period of time to develop a pattern or style of teaching that is fairly consistent and have had formal training on *how to teach and test.*

Prescription: The more traditional the teacher's pattern of teaching the more difficult it may be to make the transition from the traditional approach to the Behavioral Learning Systems Approach. However, an ameliorative factor is that many or maybe even most traditional teachers basically want students to have successes in learning and want to be at least partially involved in helping the students achieve their successes. I sincerely believe that once the traditional teacher is convinced that the concepts suggested in this series will actually help more students learn more that the teacher will be motivated to make the change and will try to be as loyal to the systems approach as the teacher was to the traditional approach. Given this situation, readers from this group should read Chapters I—III in Volume I, skip over Chapter IV, read Chapter V and then read Chapters VIII and X in Volume III. If, at this point, the reader is convinced of the need for specific objectives and matching test items in designed instruction, read Chapter IV and then all of Volume II. If the reader still has doubts about the need for specific objectives and matching test items, it may be best to try to attend a seminar on the systems concepts; to try to meet with some fellow teachers who are applying some of the systems concepts in their courses; and/or identify a learning problem in one of the reader's own courses and while trying to develop a solution to the problem read through Chapter IV in Volume I and all of Volume II.

III. *Description:* This category of readers are involved in trying to help teachers to make the changes and/or to implement some of the suggestions made in this book through in-service sessions which probably include large and small group meetings and individual conferences.

A. *Description:* This subgroup of readers are ones whose primary task is the conducting of in-service professional development sessions.

Prescription: For this group, Chapter X of Volume III will probably be the most important preparation and should be read first. In addition, Chapters I—III in Volume I and the malpractice dialogues at the end of my book, *Educational Malpractices,* should be very useful in answering the faculty questions of the type *Why I shouldn't change!* I assume that if the in-service sessions are to be about the systems concepts, that Chapters IV through VIII will be read very thoroughly. It would be very useful for this person if before any in-service sessions he or she worked with an interested teacher and identified a learning problem and solved it in accordance with the systems concepts. This would not only be a good experience for the in-service trainer, but the problem and solution could be used as a model for similar efforts by other teachers attending the in-service session.

B. *Description:* This subgroup are administrators who have responsibilities for the instructional program but have never had any formal training on *how to teach or test.*

Prescription: During the past decade, this group has been trying to think of themselves as *instructional leaders.* At the present time, this particular group of readers may be hesitant to lead in a direction in which they have not had any formal training. Since most formal courses on *How to Teach and Test* are irrelevant, not having them can actually be considered a benefit. For this group it would probably be best to read Chapters I–III in Volume I and all of Volume III. Before trying to encourage teachers to change, it might be very useful to read through the malpractice dialogues at the end of my book, *Educational Malpractices,* and then to read Chapters IV and V of Volume I. Because the administrator will probably not be as involved in the instructional process as the teacher, it isn't as necessary that he or she knows the contents of Volume II as well as the teachers. However, administrators should be acquainted with the concepts if only to be in a better position to understand what the teachers are doing. Those administrators who want to think of themselves as *instructional leaders,* should know Volume II as well or better than the teachers and since these administrators usually don't have classes of students upon which they could practice the application of the systems concepts, they should work frequently with teachers in their efforts to identify and solve learning problems and to develop instructional materials in accordance with the systems concepts (as presented in Volume II).

C. *Description:* This subgroup are administrators who have responsibilities for the instructional program and have had formal training on *How to Teach and Test.*

Prescription: The main difference between the last subgroup and this one is that the administrators who have been trained as traditional teachers will have a greater tendency to evaluate teachers in accordance with traditional criteria which in turn will tend to keep teachers in their traditional role despite efforts by the administrators to get them to change. As a result, readers in this group may have to pay particular attention to Chapter VIII in Volume III. Otherwise, the prescription would be the same as the last group. If you are a reader in this group and you feel that you are quite progressive and that your faculty have been and are involved in many instructional innovations, you may find that the Exhibits (pp. 143—244) in Part II of my book, *Educational Malpractices: **The Big Gamble in Our Schools**,* and Chapter X in Volume III of this series may be important in evaluating prior and present innovations. In case your time for reading is limited and particularly if you feel your faculty are already using some aspects of the learning systems concept, you may want to look through the following section on the *Summary of New Concepts* (as suggested in this series) and pick out the concepts which you feel most relevant for you and your faculty and read up on those.

IV. *Description:* This category of readers are in many ways the most important because they are the teachers of students who are learning to be teachers and what they do or don't do with these students will indirectly affect millions of other students that these students will be teaching.

Prescription: This category breaks into two subgroups. The largest of the two subgroups concerns those teachers of teachers-to-be that are teaching any of the subjects these students might take *but not* actually courses on *How to Teach and/or Test.* These readers can follow the prescriptions outlined for them under category II with the following added reminder: students will go out as teachers and they will teach the way they were taught not necessarily the way they were taught to teach (particularly when the way they were taught to teach doesn't match the way they were actually taught)!

The other subgroup, although smaller, is the most critical group of all. These readers are the ones who will decide whether or not to use this book as a textbook in their course(s) on *How to Teach and/or Test.* In previewing this book, look through the following section on the *Summary of New Concepts* (as suggested in this series). Then, you should read Chapter X, Chapter V, and Chapter VIII. If you can accept the concepts and particularly the new teacher's role as an instructioneer, then you might read Chapters I—IV, skim read through Chapter V again, and then read Chapters VI and VII. Of critical importance in the design of a successful course involving the concepts presented in this series, would be the practicing of what is preached and the course project in which each student identifies and solves one or more learning problem units.

V. *Description:* This particular group of readers are primarily interested in doing research which might affect what happens in instructional situations.

Prescription: For this group, Chapters IV and IX will be the most important. Then the reader may want to look through the following section on the *Summary of New Concepts* (as suggested in this series) and also Chapter V for some ideas on what research they might want to do. The balance of the book could be read in any sequence desired.

VI. *Description:* This last category of readers consists of parents of students and students themselves who want to find out in more detail how to go about improving the instructional process so as to be more conversant on the topic when talking with professional educators or when trying to evaluate teachers or schools as to their effectiveness and efficiency.

Prescription: The readers in this group should first read my other book, *Educational Malpractices: The Big Gamble in Our Schools.* Having read that book, these readers might want to read Chapters IV, V, VIII, and X in this series and then whatever concepts in the following section, *Summary of New Concepts* (as suggested in this series, which are of interest to them.

SUMMARY OF NEW CONCEPTS

I consider the following 51 concepts to be essentially new and different from instructional concepts found in most other books of a similar nature. Not all of these concepts are new from the point-of-view that no one has ever heard or thought of them before; but they are new in that most educators, particularly traditional educators, have not come in contact with them before. Even though some of the more innovative educators have thought of and maybe even practiced some of these concepts, the major contribution I think I can make in addition to the concepts themselves, which may be new to even these innovative educators, is that all of these 51 concepts fit together in a package and constitute the Behavioral Learning Systems Approach to Instruction.

Volume I. *The Changing Role of the Educator: The Instructioneer.*

1. As a profession, education is the only one that commits malpractices on its clients by design and tradition. (See pages 27-36).

2. Actually education, as traditionally practiced, is not a profession in accordance with the three primary criteria for evaluating a profession: the existence of a specialized knowledge and skills; high standards of achievement and conduct; and a prime purpose of public service. (See pages 7-20).

3. Although the humanization or dehumanization of the instructional process is a critical issue in our society, most of the teachers of the courses which are claimed to be the major vehicles for humanization actually teach and test in a manner which is not very humane! (See pages 26, 29-31).

4. Given that humanism is concerned with positive interrelationships with other people and the respect for the rights of others, to interpret humanism as the freedom to *do your own thing* is to develop selfism, an emphasis on self regardless of effects on others, which is anti-humanism. (See pages 57-60).

5. Regardless of whether or not a teacher likes the concept of a *system's approach to instruction*, each teacher and each student is already an integral part of one or more systems and these systems

will continue to exist and function as systems. Therefore, the question *is not* do we or don't we want to use a systems approach, but given we are already in an instructional system, do we want to maximize the potential positive benefits and minimize any negative aspects. (See pages 69-78).

6. Although many educators, psychologists, and others have written about and tried to develop a theory of instruction, there hasn't been one which has proved itself in application. There is a theory of instruction, in fact, two theories of instruction: one for teaching and learning in the affective domain and one for teaching and learning in the other domains of learning. (See pages 101-120).

7. Once an educator accepts the concept and need for actually individualizing instruction instead of just talking about it, the classroom concept becomes obsolete along with all of the teacher behaviors associated with the classroom concept, i.e., the teacher as a presenter of content, the topic of classroom management, micro-teaching, practice-teaching (as practiced in most teacher-training institutions, etc. (See pages 129-136).

8. The humanistic role is that of an Instructioneer who helps each student achieve success by identifying his or her learning problems and solving them. (See pages 136-144).

9. Most teachers already practice this role but not in the right place. Notice the following conflict in most traditional teachers' behavior. If a student came up to a teacher in the hallway and said, *I don't understand what you were just saying in class,* not a single teacher in the tens of thousands that I have ever talked with would even think of taking out their gradebook and grade the student down for asking that question. Almost all of the teachers I know would try to solve the student's learning problem. However, in the classroom, when most traditional teachers give tests and students make mistakes which indicate that *they don't know or understand,* most teachers will mark the mistake as wrong and record the score in the gradebook without solving the learning problems. The instructional process can be significantly improved, if teachers will only bring their behavior in the hallways of *trying to solve learning problems* into the classroom and solve learners' learning problems instead of recording grades. (See pages 304-306).

10. In almost all areas of our society, it is an accepted common sense practice to diagnose first and design the appropriate treatment

second. Only in the traditional approach to education is this process reversed. The treatment is given to the students first and then the students are given the test. Not only is the common sense sequence reversed, but the data revealed in the diagnosis (test) is usually ignored except for some kind of score which is recorded. I refer to this behavior of the traditional educators as evidence of the *Backwards Ostrich Philosophy*. Tests should be given first and the treatments designed to fit the needs of the learner as evidenced by the results of the tests. At the end of the treatment, a duplicate test should be given and depending upon the results of that test, subsequent treatments should be revised to facilitate the learning of whatever was missed. (See pages 88,187-188).

11. A learning problem is basically any situation in which a student is expected to learn, but for one reason or another the student hasn't achieved the desired learning (student errors on tests, essays, etc.) As a learning problem, it is something to be solved, not just recorded in a gradebook. (See pages 144-196).

12. When a student leaves a unit of a course or a course not knowing some of the objectives of that unit or course which are a prerequisite for success in subsequent units or courses, his or her chances for success are significantly reduced. This condition is referred to as *cumulative ignornace*. It is not the fault of the learner. The teacher and our present system were the ones that allowed the student to leave the unit or course not knowing the critical objectives. *Cumulative ignorance* is a malignant disease associated with the traditional teacher-oriented educational system and it should be eliminated or at least reduced. (See pages 36-39, 42-43, 64,73).

13. A very common and hence popular misconception among educators and psychologists is the use of the words *ability* and *capacity* as synonyms when referring to intelligence. As a result, evidence of differences in ability and particularly evidence of different levels of ability are reported in such a manner as to indicate that these same differences apply to *capacity* (limits) as well. Most research that is used to suggest or prove that one race or culture has more intelligence than another is based on this popular misconception. As far as I have been able to find out, no one has ever identified the 100 percent full capacity (limits) of the human mind. Therefore, at this point in time, it is not valid to even hypothesize, let alone prove, that there are differences in capacity (limits). Probably the most acceptable hypothesis of the capacity (limits) of the human mind is that it has infinite capacity (limits). Can you imagine a situation in

which the healthy mind stops accepting any further input because it is full? On the other hand, I can't imagine anyone not agreeing that there are individual differences in ability of which part of this difference is genetic and part of it is environmental or learned. Just because there are differences in ability does not in any way affect the concept of capacity (limits). Ability may very well affect how the capacity *is filled* given certain situations but not the capacity (limits) itself. Differences in ability are clues which indicate the need for different learning materials, techniques, and pathways in order for the same learning to occur. For example, most IQ tests tend to be based on verbal ability. Therefore, students who score low on IQ tests have low verbal ability at that point in time. In order to bring about learning, a teacher could either teach verbal ability or use learning techniques that are less verbal and more appropriate for the learner's abilities. You do not have to compromise or change what they learn only how they learn. (See pages 31-35, 75, 88, 92-100).

14. Intelligence is frequently equated to *rate of learning* such that the slower learner is considered to be not as *intelligent* as the faster learner. Given that students learn best in different ways, to compare students intelligence (rate of learning) in a situation where these differences are ignored is unfair and the student's *apparent* rate of learning is not equal to the student's *real* rate of learning. (See pages 204-279).

15. Given that a teacher performs the role of the Instructioneer such that students' learning problems are identified and solved, at least 90 percent or more of the students can learn 100 percent of specified learning objectives. (See pages 111-120).

Volume II. *A Behavioral Learning Systems Approach to Instruction: Analysis and Synthesis*

16. An addition to the two domains of learning, cognitive and affective, the third domain is not the psychomotor domain as is popularly believed. The third domain of learning is the *sensory* domain. (See pages 394-412).

17. All cognitive, sensory, and affective domain objectives are nonmeasurable on a direct basis and, as such, they are all general objectives. (See page 104, Volume I, and pages 351-353).

18. When one specifies a specific behavior which is supposed to signify

indirectly the achievement or existence of a cognitive, sensory, or affective domain objective, the achievement is by inference only and, as such, the specific measurable objective is only a part of the more general non-measurable objective. (See pages 343-348).

19. The measurement of the achievement of specific learning objectives in the three domains of learning refers to different student behaviors: cognitive learning is inferred from psychomotor behavior, sensory learning is inferred from sensomotor behavior, and affective learning is inferred from emotive behavior. (See pages 103-104, Volume I and 367-370).

20. Instead of hiding from students what they should be learning which is traditional, students should know at the beginning of a unit or course what cognitive and sensory learning they will be expected to achieve. (See pages 105, 147-151, Volume I, and pages 336-338).

21. Affective domain objectives are not generally given to the learners ahead of time nor should the achievement or non-achievement of affective domain objectives be used to arrive at grades for learners. The achievement or non-achievement of affective domain objectives by learners is primarily a measure of the effectiveness of the teaching design rather than being a measure of learning. (See pages 105-110, Volume I, and pages 413-424).

22. In contrast to the teaching and learning of cognitive and sensory learning which is done directly, the teaching and learning of affective learning has to be done indirectly. You cannot demand the achievement of an affective objective. If you do, you are liable to develop beliefs, attitudes, and values which are opposite from what you want. (See pages 105-110, Volume I, and pages 413-424).

23. In contrast to cognitive and sensory learning which is achieved best when it is done intentionally and is achieved least when ignored, affective learning goes on all the time regardless of whether or not teachers want to do anything about the development of beliefs, attitudes, and values through the use of a designed systematic approach to instruction. At the present time, most beliefs, attitudes, and values are developing by chance and, as such, some of these emotional tendencies are not necessarily in the best interests of the students, the schools, the community, or our country. (See pages 416-417).

24. Despite the fact that some educators are against the concept of

behavioral objectives, almost every teacher depends on *behavioral test items* for evaluation. In other words, almost every teacher evaluates their students and bases their evaluation on something the student is doing (behavior) or has done (the result of a behavior). (See pages 456-57, 644-648).

25. The learner behaviors which are required to indicate achievement of an objective have to match as close as possible the behavior specified in the unit or course objectives, i.e., objective type test items are inappropriate because rarely does an objective specify the exact behaviors which take place in the objective type test situation. (See pages 458-468).

26. The purpose of most tests which are given in traditional educational settings is to obtain a score of some kind which later can be used as a basis for assigning a grade or can be manipulated in a variety of ways using various statistical instruments in order to generate more data. The purpose of tests under the learning systems concept is to identify student learning problems. If any score is given to a student, it would be when the student has achieved 100 percent of the test. (See pages 461, 490, 500-2).

27. The test items, papers, performances or whatever else a teacher uses to evaluate students' achievement are actually the real objectives of a course or instructional unit. If there is any difference between the learner behaviors described in the professed objectives for the course and the learner behaviors necessary to successfully pass the evaluation instrument (test, paper, etc.), students will generally try to learn whatever is on the evaluation instrument and will ignore the stated objectives. As a result, if there are stupid or irrelevant test items and/or criteria in the evaluation instrument, students end up learning stupid and irrelevant things. (See pages 500-502).

28. It is good to *teach to the test*. In fact, that is what teachers should be doing! If a test actually tests for the achievement of something a teacher wants students to learn, then why not teach what you want the students to learn (the test). If a test doesn't test for the achievement of something a teacher wants students to learn then of course a teacher shouldn't teach to *that* test nor should the teacher use *that* test. (See pages 474-480).

29. There is no place in designed instruction for *normal* or standardized tests because they are not based on a standardized list of specific objectives and the distribution of scores is built into the tests, i.e., a

professional test item writer can take any multiple-choice item and by holding the stem and the correct choice constant and by varying the distractors in the wrong choices can get almost any percentage the writer wants of the people who are answering the test item to answer it correctly or incorrectly. In addition, in *normed* tests, test items are selected primarily because they are good discriminators rather than because they measure the achievement of important learning. A good discriminator is a test item that 50 percent of the students will miss whereas a good test item should be one that is first considered important and desirable. (See pages 513-523).

30. When dealing with rote memory objectives and test items, 100 percent achievement of the objectives is equal to 100 percent achievement of the matching test items because they are on a one to one basis. However, when dealing with process objectives and test items where almost every objective is tested by more than one test item, the percentage achievement of the objective is rarely equal to the percentage achievement of process test items. 100 percent achievement of process objective may be equal to 80 percent achievement of process test items. (See pages 360-365, 495-499).

31. Most innovations in education and instruction are concerned with different methods of doing something. As long as teachers don't know specifically what they want their students to learn, any method should be acceptable. However, once a goal is defined, there may be certain methods which will be more successful in facilitating learning in certain students than other methods. (See pages 662-670).

32. Similarly, as long as teachers don't know specifically what their students should be learning, almost any materials can be selected, particularly for a learning resource center and open classrooms. Under these conditions, learning is by chance and is biased in the direction of the person(s) who selects the materials. Once the desired objectives are specified, there will be certain materials which will be more successful in facilitating learning for certain students than other materials. (See pages 672-679).

33. Instead of having every teacher reinvent their course objectives as if no one else had ever taught the course before and given that the vast majority of students are going to live in the same society, there has got to be something in common in every course with the same name that is considered desirable to learn, regardless of where in the country the course is taught. These minimum common core

objectives can be identified. (See pages 527-537, 632-4).

34. Students may know best how they learn and what they are interested in, but they do not know best *what* they should learn. (See pages 635-643).

Volume III. *Creating an Emphasis on Learning: Quality Control, Productivity, and Accountability*

35. In all evaluation of humans, there is a psychological principle in operation. *Human beings tend to do those things that the person whom they allow to evaluate them wants them to do!* What this means is that as long as teachers are evaluated on a variety of things not including learning, then teachers will tend to be concerned about a variety of things not including learning. When teachers are at least partially evaluated on the basis of the student learning they have helped facilitate, then they will tend to be concerned about facilitating learning. (See pages 855-858).

36. Whenever the goals are unknown or fuzzy, there is a tendency to make the means to the goals the objective or goal. This situation can be referred to as *Entropic Drift*. As long as we don't really know what students should be learning, the process or method becomes the most important. When a teacher doesn't know what students should be learning from reading a book, reading the book (the vehicle for learning) becomes the objective, rather than learning. (See pages 888-890).

37. When identified student learning becomes the focus of schools, there can and will be a transposition of control. Whereas at the present time student learning is at the bottom of the authority pyramid and important (often critical) decisions concerning student learning are being made by people who rarely work with or even see the students, under the Behavioral Learning Systems Approach (BLSA), student learning is at the top of an inverted support pyramid, and everyone's role is designed to support the one above and indirectly to help facilitate student learning. (See pages 890-900).

38. Whereas quality control is a familiar concept in many fields, it is long overdue in the instructional process. Whereas the traditional approach is satisfied with a normal curve's worth of achievement wherein the average student learns about "C" worth or about 75 percent which causes designed cumulative ignorance, under the

Behavioral Learning Systems Approach (BLSA), 90 percent or more of the students have to learn 100 percent of the required specific objectives. Whereas in the traditional approach, time, methods, and materials are constant and learning is a variable, under the BLSA, learning is kept as constant as possible and time, methods, and materials are all variables. (See pages 852-855, 914-916).

39. In talking with thousands of teachers, I find that they want quality control such that all students should be learning 100 percent of the specified objectives and/or test items instead of the 80-90 percent suggested by many *systems* consultants or the 65-75 percent (or less) which has been considered *normal* under the traditional approach to instruction. If you are a teacher or plan to be a teacher, consider the following situation, the question and your answer to the question:

> You have given your class a test in which there were 50 points possible and 40 points (80 percent) was identified as passing. The question is *If 40 points is passing, which 10 points are not important?* If your answer is that you think all 50 points are important, then you actually want the students to achieve 100 percent. If your answer is that there are 10 points that aren't important, then why are you testing for student achievement of unimportant things and why are you grading a student down for not learning something you now admit is not important! (See pages 914-916).

40. Just as teacher organizations and other employee groups demand the right to have a grievance committee to give them recourse as protection against administrative decisions which are unjust and capricious, and with negative effects on the teachers; students need and should have the same right as protection against teacher decisions, grading, and educational procedures which are unjust and capricious and with negative effects on the students. (See pages 951-955).

41. Once teacher training institutions accept the concept of individual differences in bringing about quality control in student learning, and that tests are diagnostic in nature, the present test and measurement course as offered in most teacher training institutions becomes obsolete. Unless a student is going into research, there is no need for the teacher-to-be to learn how to do statistical gymnastics with students' scores. Even if a student may plan to do educational research, there is no need to teach the student how to

use *distractors* in order to trick students into answering tests in such a way that the test maker obtains the curve of results he wants regardless of what students actually know or don't know. The emphasis in test and measurement courses from the systems point-of-view will be how to write objectives and test items that have a 100 percent correlation and on how to solve learning problems. Whereas in the traditional test and measurement course the best test items are ones that 50 percent of the students who are answering them will answer them wrong, under the learning systems concept the best test items are ones that are first considered important and secondly the ideal situation would be where 100 percent of the learners learn 100 percent of these important items. (See page 1085).

42. Since the traditional courses in test and measurement are essentially useless, a critical condition exists in that not only are those teachers who have not had any training in testing not qualified to do testing and evaluation (about 50 percent of elementary and secondary teachers and almost 90 percent of higher education faculty), but even those teachers who have had training in tests and measurement are also not qualified to perform such a critical task in education and particularly in designed instruction.

43. Given an educational situation in which the average student only has to learn 75 percent of the course and a normal or *chance* distribution of learning is acceptable, it is not very necessary for the teacher to know much about teaching and/or testing. In addition, given that the teachers role is to present course content rather than to facilitate learning and that tests can be manipulated to give almost any desired results without affecting student learning, there is even less reason to know anything about teaching and testing. In contrast, in a society where learning has become very important, teaching-learning effectiveness also becomes important. As the costs of education increase, efficiency also becomes a critical issue. Under the BLSA where 90 percent or more of the students have to achieve 100 percent of the required SO's, it is necessary for teachers to know what they are doing. It takes specialized knowledge to be an effective and efficient teacher not only at the elementary and secondary levels, but also in higher education. (See pages 907-913).

44. Individual differences as a concept applies to teachers as well as to students. Teacher negotiations and/or contracts which ignore indi-

vidual differences among teachers are unreal, and inappropriate, i.e., all teachers in a given institution should have the same size class, same teaching load, and paid about the same amount of money. (See pages 997-1014).

45. Given that the individual differences in teachers can be recognized and the teachers are performing the role of an instructioneer, teachers will be able to teach multiple levels of the same course and/or multiple courses simultaneously. This would be very similar to the old one-room school concept. No one ever heard of a teacher in a one-room school canceling fourth grade because there wasn't enough students enrolled. This concept becomes more important in view of decreasing enrollments. (See pages 996-997).

46. Given that most teachers have not been taught how to teach as defined in terms of facilitating student learning, nor on how to develop and use diagnostic tests and that very few teachers have ever been hired on the basis of their ability to facilitate student learning, then it is not fair to hold a teacher accountable for student learning unless schools and administrative bodies provide appropriate systematic in-service training first. (See pages 986-987).

47. Given a situation where a teacher is having trouble solving student learning problems, the administrative structure should include an *Instructional Crisis Squad* that could work with the teacher and help solve learning problems such that both the students and the teacher have success. (See pages 987-989).

48. Although teacher salaries were in need of improvement and the teacher union movement has done a great deal to increase teacher salaries and to improve other working conditions, continued emphasis of teacher organizations on the teacher as a laborer rather than as a professional will be at the detriment of the teaching-learning situation. Professionalism and unionism are almost antithetical in their goals and concepts and teachers will have to decide which way they want to go. (See pages 1036-1040).

49. Educational research has also been affected by entropic drift in that since we don't know what students should be learning (the goals of education), the emphasis of educational research has been on the process of education, i.e., methods, materials, techniques, etc. As such, educational research is a non-science because it deals with man-made phenomenon. In contrast, instructional research is primarily concerned with learning and is a science becuase learning

is a natural phenomenon. (See pages 1064-1068).

50. Given that there is little commonality in what is being learned in courses with the same title, that tests can be manipulated to give any desired results, and that standardized tests don't match any known lists of specific learning objectives, not only is most educational research irrelevent and useless, most of it is invalid because the data is invalid. Regardless of the power of the statistical instruments used and the validity of the methods used, if the data is *garbage* to begin with, the results are still *garbage*. (GIGO — garbage in — garbage out!). (See pages 1075-1090).

51. There is a method of evaluating the design of an instructional situation on the basis of three factors: potential boredom factor, the instructional effectiveness factor, and the instructional efficiency factor. Using this technique, it can be shown that *Seasame Street*, which has been heralded as the model for future instructional television, although entertaining, has a high potential for boredom and is not very effective nor efficient from the point-of-view of learning. (See pages 1096-1108).

CHAPTER VIII

QUALITY CONTROL, PRODUCTIVITY, AND ACCOUNTABILITY

General and Specific Objectives

GGO — To understand that if facilitating *learning* is the primary purpose of schools, then the evaluation of everyone involved in or affecting the instructional environment should be evaluated directly or indirectly on the basis of their contribution to the facilitation of learning.

    GO — To understand that present methods of assessment are not valid.

        SO — List any three of the five problems with standardized tests.

        SO — List any four of the six instances of fraud being perpetrated by the National Assessment of Educational Progress (NAEP).

        SO — Differentiate between positive and negative evaluation and cite at least two examples of each from your own experience.

    GO — To understand the effects of the principle of evaluation.

        SO — State the principle of evaluation and cite at least two examples from your own experience (outside of schools) which substantiate the existence of this principle.

    GO — To realize that *learning* can only be measured indirectly.

        SO — Cite three or more instances in other courses in which you were graded down (less than an "A" or 100 percent) on a test or other evaluation experience for not *learning* what you were supposed to.

GO — To understand what the various contributors to the learning event are accountable for.

    SO — State what students should be held accountable for from the point of view of quality control in instruction and contrast this to what students are traditionally held accountable for.

    SO — State what teachers should be held accountable for from the point of view of quality control and their role in instruction and contrast this to what teachers are traditionally held accountable for.

    SO — State what administrators should be held accountable for from the point of view quality control and their role in instruction and contrast this to what administrators are traditionally held accountable for.

    SO — Define *entropic drift* and describe how it affects what is being evaluated and describe two or more examples of entropic drift (other than those listed in this book).

    SO — Contrast the traditional pyramid of controlling influences with the inverted pyramid of supportive influences.

    SO — List at least ten of the 18 paired statements used to contrast the Behavioral Learning Systems Approach which has minimum entropic drift with the traditional educational approach with maximum entropic drift.

GO — To understand that in order to evaluate students, one needs to have criteria for evaluation and if the emphasis is to be on *learning*, then the criteria should reflect *learning* (learning objectives).

    SO — List the six variables to be considered when discussing the traditional evaluation of students and write a description of each to explain its variability (include two or more examples which illustrate the variability).

- SO — Given the concepts of quality control, cumulative ignorance, and positive evaluation, describe how the traditional approaches to grading and promotion (curve grading, pass-fail grading, the "F" grade itself, social promotion, and no evaluation at all) actually interfere with subsequent learning.

- SO — With reference to the six variables to be considered when discussing the evaluation of students, write a statement about each one which explains how under the Behavioral Learning Systems Approach the variability is eliminated, minimized, and/or kept positive.

- SO — List the ten basic rights of students which parallel the ten basic rights of teachers.

GO — To understand that proper evaluation of teachers should reflect their role as an *Instructioneer* and the results of their efforts in terms of facilitating student learning rather than on their performance regardless of student learning.

- SO — Given that student learning should be our primary concern and given two or more traditional criteria used to evaluate teachers (discussed in this chapter) show how the traditional criteria are almost irrelevant with reference to the primary concern of *learning*.

- SO — Describe two or more ways in which individual differences among teachers are ignored with potentially negative effects on student learning.

- SO — List the seven steps for a successful practice teaching experience as described in this chapter.

- SO — Actually perform the seven steps such that 90 percent or more of the students learn 100 percent of the required SO's.

- SO — List the eight areas of accountability for teachers.

- SO — List the three sets of data used in evaluating a teacher's performance and describe how this data can be used to evaluate the teacher.

SO — With reference to the Instructional Crisis Squad, describe its purpose and the make up of its membership.

SO — List the nine SLATE criteria for increased remuneration and describe each criterion in terms of its variability and effects on learning.

SO — List at least ten of the fifteen comparisons between teaching-learning situations where *professionalism* is the emphasis in the role of the teacher and where *unionism* is the emphasis in the role of the teacher.

GO — To understand that proper evaluation of administrators, school boards, regents, and state and national offices of education should reflect their roles of directly and indirectly helping teachers facilitate student learning.

SO — List the four comparisons between School Management by Objectives (SMBO) and the Behavioral Learning Systems Approach (BLSA).

SO — List the sixteen tasks which should be performed by administrators in their supportive role as an *instructional leader*.

SO — List the seven tasks which should be performed by school boards and regents.

A. INTRODUCTION

In my book, *Educational Malpractices: The Big Gamble in Our Schools* (February, 1971), and also in my newsletter, *DAIRS and Systems for Instruction* (January, 1970), I wrote an article entitled *Accountability: A Mole Hill that is going to become a MOUNTAIN*. At that time, I commented on how I had first heard the word *accountability* in reference to the educational process at a conference in 1960. As of January, 1970, forty or more companies were willing to help educators become more accountable through the use of performance contracts and at least five or more publishers were willing to guarantee learning as a result of using their materials or the purchaser could get a complete refund. As of this writing, not only has the concept of *accountability* become a mountain, it has become an active volcano spreading from coast to coast, tormenting many educators at all levels with its minor eruptions, and threatening the whole educational profession with potential major eruptions.

During the past seven or eight years, most school districts have gone through two, three, four, or more teacher-administrator-taxpayer confrontations in which the costs of education were increased under the banner of increased *quality* of instruction. So far, neither the administrators, the taxpayers, the parents, nor even the teachers' have been able to observe, let alone even measure, this increased *quality*. This academic year will see approximately 100 billion dollars spent for public and private education and on all sides, the public is being bombarded with headlines about the financial crises in education and with demands for ever increasing funding from all sources: local, state, and federal. At the same time, the only accountability seems to be: baby-sit the very young, keep the young people off the streets and out of the labor market, and spend all of the money while doing these things. It would be an extremely rare event for any teacher to be fired or not rehired because his or her students weren't learning, for any administrator to be fired or not rehired because he or she did not help their teachers to facilitate student learning, or for any school district to be closed down by taxpayers as being instructionally bankrupt.

This past year, as in almost each of the previous years since about 1965, an ever increasing number of property tax bills and school bond issues have been defeated. Most educators continue to view these defeats as a rebellion by the taxpayers against paying more property taxes and as a mandate by the public for the state and federal governments to take on a greater share of the burden of supporting the increasing costs of operating our educational institutions.

Is this interpretation of the mandate correct? Is it possible that the voters are NOT asking for greater state and federal sharing of the costs of education because they realize that regardless of whether the money is obtained locally, from the state, or from the federal government *all of the funds are obtained from some form of taxes.* After all, does it really matter from which pocket you take money to pay a bill as long as you have to pay it one way or the other? Are the people who are asking directly and openly for more state and federal help the voters and taxpayers or the educators?

Consider for a moment the possibility that the growing tide of defeats for school bond issues is really a mandate for change in the way our schools are being run. Although university, college, high school, and even junior high school students have reacted physically (riots and other forms of protest) to the way the schools are being run, the only way the voters (both parents and nonparents) can react is via the ballot box. It is tempting to believe that parents can comment on the school program either directly to the teachers or indirectly through PTA groups, but most parents are afraid of retaliation against their children in the classroom by the teacher or administrator. Among the thousands of teachers involved in the SLATE Seminars, it is very common to have even teachers, who are parents of school children, voice their reluctance to criticize their children's teachers for fear of retaliation against their children.

Another major problem in criticizing the schools is that neither the students nor the parents can identify exactly what is wrong, but they know they are dissatisfied with the schools. An examination of student demands will reveal the superficiality of most of the demands in comparison to the devotion and passionate strength of the students' protest efforts. The violence is a reaction to deeper feelings than those expressed by the lists of student demands. Consider the psychological violence on the minds of millions of students who have to sit and listen to a teacher regardless of any learning that may take place (at all levels of education, punitive action can be taken against students if they are absent from the classroom). Almost every person has suffered mental anguish in the classrooms because of tests, grades, or other forms of *educational* abuse, i.e., talk to many ex-students who have gone through some of the frustrations of working with graduate committees.

Is it not possible that if the students are unhappy about what is happening in the schools that they have communicated this to their parents (who also were students and felt the same kinds of frustrations)? It is no longer possible to convince the parents and students that the *failure to learn* is something natural and normal. Too many parents and students are starting to reject the concept of *failure* as a fault of the students and are asking, *Why shouldn't teachers and schools be responsible for what they do (or don't do) to children?* At the present time, the only way parents can comment on what is happening is through silent violence at the ballot box — voting No on school bond issues.

The mistake that many schools are making is to try *mass blackmail* on the public. This *educational malpractice* is expressed in several ways. The most common form of *mass blackmail* has recently been referred to as the *Youngstown syndrome*. This form is identified by the following four steps: first, a school district bond election is defeated one or more times; second, the district continues spending at the normal or increased rate (deficit financing) on the pretext that a future election will be won or that needed funds will come from state or federal sources; third, the district announces that all funds will be exhausted by a certain date and the schools will have to be closed unless funds are found someplace; and fourth, a new bond election is scheduled in which now if the voters vote NO, it will be their fault that the schools have to close. Notice in this form of *mass blackmail*, the school districts, colleges, or universities start out assuming that whatever they are doing can only be improved with more money and that the public does not have any other option but to succumb to the pressure.

The public does have another option! As I pointed out in my DAIRS Newsletter (Issue No. 8, December 1967) business and industry may step into public education and contract with taxpayers to operate their schools. Besides being able to do it cheaper, business and industry would be able and willing to guarantee learning which is something few, if any, schools will do at the present time. Since business and industry are spending more and more each year to teach reading, writing, and arithmetic to their employees and also publishing materials to be used in schools, it would be an easy step for several of the large corporations to compete with public schools at a local election. The non-taxpayers will want this alternative because of the guaranteed results, the taxpayers will want this alternative because of the guaranteed results at lower costs, and even many educators who are not afraid of *accountability* will want this alternative because of the higher salaries offered by private business. Since ineffective education, lack of education, and the negative aspects of traditional educational malpractices have a definite relationship with unemployment, welfare, and rehabilitation programs (juvenile delinquency, prisons, etc.), then as the state and federal governments pay more and more for both education and the results of bad education, the state and federal legislators are also going to be in favor of any alternative which will make education more effective and efficient and consequently help reduce the costs of bad education.

> NOTE: Junior high schools have remedial programs in which students successfully learn what they should have learned in elementary school. Senior high schools have remedial programs in which students successfully learn what they should have learned in junior high school. Colleges and universities have remedial programs in which students successfully learn what they should have learned in high school. Schools, hospitals, and other professional institutions have in-service programs in which graduates successfully learn what they should have learned in their college or university studies. (If the instructional process could be made more effective and efficient, then the redundancy from grade to grade and the remedial and in-service programs could be eliminated or significantly reduced in cost and time.)

As many readers know, the Office of Economic Opportunity (OEO) and other groups have come out with negative evaluations of the performance contracting concept. Since almost all performance contracts are evaluated on a pretest and posttest basis using standardized tests, it is important to consider these negative results from the point of view of the following five major problems with the use of standardized achievement tests. These same five problems are also present in national and state assessment programs.

1. Most of these tests utilize objective type test items (multiple-choice, true-false, and matching) which involve tricking and deceiving the students by use of distractors.

2. Test items are selected primarily because the items are able to discriminate between students and are easy to grade or score. The test items are not primarily selected because they are testing important things or concepts.

3. In the process of standardizing tests, a test is considered valid when after trying the test out on a sample of the intended audience, the resultant distribution of scores fits or closely approximates the desired curve (normal curve, positive skewed curve, negative skewed curve, the triple hump curve of the National Assessment, etc.). As a result, the distribution of scores at any time is more affected by the makers of the test then by what the students know or don't know about what is on the test!

4. To have national or state tests, assumes that there are also national or state instructional objectives which are accepted as common in all of the classes and schools in which the tests are used. Since this is not the case and teachers, administrators, and school districts have not agreed on any common specific or general objectives, then any results (regardless of the first three problems) are also an indication of the correlation between the local specific and general objectives and the national or state specific and general objectives. For example, schools whose students score below average are also schools whose objectives may be more different than average from the assumed national or state objectives. Schools whose students score above average may be schools whose objectives are less different than average or closer to the assumed national or state objectives.

5. Because the process of standardizing tests involves a great deal of work to select the best discriminating items and to arrive at the right placement of distractors such that the *correct* curve of results occurs, standardized tests are hidden from teachers and students and a whole mythology has developed into the traditions of education that it is *wrong to teach to the test!* Obviously, if teachers taught students what was on the test, the items wouldn't discrimi-

nate and the results of using the test would no longer fit the *correct curve* — hence, the test would be invalid and would have to be reworked. Consider the conclusion *don't* teach what is on tests from the point-of-view of logic. In order to arrive at this conclusion, it would have to be the result of the following two premises:

   a. *don't teach* what you want students to learn and

   b. *what is on tests* is what you want students to learn.

It should be obvious to every reader that premise (a) is false which of course then makes the conclusion, *don't teach what is on tests*, also false. If this isn't sufficient evidence, consider the implied parallel conclusion, *teach what is not on tests*. If teachers can't teach what is on tests then it must be that they are supposed to teach what is not on tests. In order to arrive at this conclusion, it would have to be the result of the following two premises:

   c. *teach* what you want students to learn.

   d. *what is not on tests* is what you want students to learn.

Again, it should be obvious that premise (d) is false which of course makes the implied conclusion also false.

There is nothing wrong with teaching what is on a test if what is on the test is what you want students to learn. If what is on the tests, you don't want the students to learn, then you should not teach what you don't want students to learn and you should also not test what you don't want students to learn — the standardized tests.

It shouldn't be necessary for the public to exercise the option of making education a commercial enterprise. Even though business and industry could probably make student learning more effective and efficient, sooner or later dollar profit may be more important than learning. A much better action would be for the present school systems to become more effective and efficient. Many state and national legislators and educators have selected this option and are involved in trying to bring about increased accountability through a variety of legislative action.

Of particular importance in the growing trend of accountability are the assessment efforts at the national and state levels. If this trend continues throughout the country, the fifty states could be spending as high as 400 million education dollars per year on statewide versions of the NAEP (National Assessment of Educational Progress). In a country where there is supposed to be a financial crisis in education, we cannot afford to divert potentially billions of education dollars over the years to a program which is fraudulent. Not only is it a shame to waste the money, but its tremendous negative effect on the image of students, teachers, schools, etc. in the eyes of the public and educators alike will be unmeasurable and will probably result in the defeat of more bond issues and tax increases which were designed to help education. The results may even further alineate the youth of our country from our schools.

Let me point out again that the concept of a national assessment is valid and badly needed as will be pointed out later, but the NAEP program as it is presently being perpetrated on the educational scene is a fraud because it is purposely misleading the public, educators, and even state governors who are on the Education Commission of the States (ECS) as to the value of the program, (NOTE: ECS is administering the NAEP program and as such indicates their approval of this fraud against the public). The fraud involved is discussed in detail in my book, *Educational Malpractices,* and concerns the following instances of fraud:

1. NAEP knowingly did not carry out the specification of the goals and objectives to the point of being specific and measurable — ala Mager — as is the current emphasis throughout the country. Why did NAEP do this? Because once an objective becomes specific and measurable, the actual behavioral test item is identified — ala Stewart — and it would be impossible or obviously fraudulent to change the format or content of the test item to obtain certain preplanned results.

2. NAEP knowingly designed the results of the assessment into the assessment by constructing test items that could only be answered by predetermined percentages of students. As a consequence, the millions of dollars are really being spent to find out whether or not their test item writers can prepare test items ahead of time that will have predetermined results. NAEP has denied this accusation by admitting the inability of their test item writers to *armchair* the difficulty level of test items which invalidates the assessment even under traditional test making criteria. However, the literature of NAEP states that they plan to use test items that only 10 percent can answer, some that only 50 percent can answer, and some that 90 percent can answer. At least, if the writers were accurate and a 10 percent item was answered by 18 percent of the students in a particular region, the educators there would know that their schools were doing well. If the 10 percent item was answered by only 2 percent of the students in a particular region, the educators would know that their schools were not doing so well (assuming that the items were behavioral test items — ala Stewart — and really tested the actual desired behavior of a specified behavioral objective). As it

is, no one, including the writers, knows the designed level of a test item so the actual results cannot be evaluated. Remember, when an item is designed for a certain result, the evaluation is dependent upon the comparison of the actual result with the designed result. In the absence of a reliable designed result *you can NOT assume that the designed result was 100 percent.* In other words, if the actual result in the assessment for a particular test item was 46 percent, do not assume that 100 percent of the students were supposed to be able to answer the item. If the test item had been originally designed as a 10 percent item, the students are going great. If the item was a 50 percent item, the students are doing average. If the item was a 90 percent item, the students aren't doing so good.

3. The results of the NAEP were supposed to be used as guidelines to educators for instructional emphasis and in the spending of educational dollars. In the absence of any reliable data as to what the designed results of the test items were supposed to be, the interpretation of the results is next to impossible. Hence, the NAEP staff and the ECS staff avoid any interpretation of the data. Thus, leaving it up to the unknowing educators and the naive laymen (naive in that they aren't aware of the deception and trickery built into traditional educational testing) to make their own interpretations of the NAEP results. In that way, at a later date if the changes in curriculum and the changes in the allocation of financial and human resources that are made because of the interpretations of the results of the NAEP (by the educators and laymen) do not achieve the increases in learning that was expected, then the NAEP and ECS staffs can claim immunity from the blame for any losses caused by the changes or any lack of gains made by the changes because they didn't make the interpretations.

4. NAEP used a large number of multiple-choice test items in the assessment in spite of the fact that they knew that the multiple-choice items didn't really test directly the behavior they wanted which contradicts their original statement concerning the need for high correlation between objectives and test items. This use of multiple-choice items was also in spite of NAEP staffs' knowledge that the format of the item utilizes *distractors* to affect the percentage of students answering the item correctly without affecting the subject matter content of the item. Because of this, the percentage of the students answering a multiple-choice item is more affected by the *distractors* used then by whether or not the students know the correct answer. This fact in itself practically nullifies the value of any of the NAEP results.

5. By maintaining a continued process of re-evaluation, the National Assessment program hopes that it can attain its goal of providing information on the correspondence between what our educational system is attempting to achieve and what, in fact, it is achieving. From the point of view of NAEP's own statement, *the purpose of NAEP is to take a reading of... and then to reassess the same attributes several years later in order to measure progress over time. Otherwise, changes that take place over time are neither correct nor incorrect, desirable nor undesirable and tell nothing about the extent to which an objective of education is being attained.* In contrast, a major feature of NAEP is the release of 40-50 percent of the test items in each recycle of the assessment. How is it then possible to measure increases or progress in achievement for the specific items that were released for public information as these items will not be used in subsequent assessments? If 40-50 percent of the items in the reassessment are different, then in NAEP's own words, almost half of the reassessment will *tell nothing about the extent to which an objective of education is being attained.*

6. Of the remaining 50-60 percent of the items that will remain in the assessment, they of course are not revealed nor will the data concerning them be revealed so educators will not be able to make any changes concerning half or more of the assessment. This in effect constitutes another point of fraud in the original design of the NAEP program because half or more of the supposedly valuable data resulting from the assessment is purposely being withheld from the public. If the assessment was an honest effort and the results of the hidden 50-60 percent of the items identified critical areas of needed change, then to keep them hidden would cause the schools to continue ignoring the needed changes for at least another three years or more (depending on when the data was finally released). If the criteria for selecting items for release concerned whether or not the data was critical for educators to know and the most critical items were represented by the items and data released to the public, then subsequent assessments for NAEP would not measure any increases or progress in those critical areas. This constitutes a fraud on the intent of the program and is in direct violation of their own statements. Consider the following three situations:
    a. Given the criteria for revealing items is because they are critical and then these items are dropped and new items are developed then the reassessment would be a fraud as just indicated above by their own statement;
    b. Given the criteria for revealing items is because they are least critical, then to have educators base educational

changes on those least critical items would make the assessment a fraud; and

c. Given any mixture of the two ("a" and "b") will result in varying degrees of fraud of both types.

In order to have valid instructional accountability, there are two critical prerequisites: first, it is necessary to know specifically what it is that is being instructed (objectives) and secondly, any test items that are used to evaluate students' achievement of the objectives should have a very high if not a perfect correlation with the objectives. Test items used in accountability are not selected because they are easy to grade or because they are good discriminators (between 35% and 65% of the students miss them), they are selected because they test for the achievement of important objectives. Under the concept of accountability, test results that approximate a normal curve are unacceptable. The best results would be to have 100% of the learners learn 100% of the objectives.

1. ACCOUNTABILITY ALONE IS NOT SUFFICIENT

To measure the level of student achievement of some nebulous, vague, non-specified objectives by the use of tests which have the results designed into the tests regardless of student achievement constitutes exercises in futility. To use the results of such tests to arrive at some estimates of the effectiveness and efficiency of a student's learning, of a class or group of students' learning, of a teacher's ability to teach, and/or of a school's ability to facilitate learning, is to not only delude or deceive anyone who reads or hears about the false estimates but also creates false *whipping posts* for the problems in traditional education. As identified in Chapter II (Vol. I), there are two major causes of our problems in traditional education: the process of evaluation of everyone concerned with the educational process from the student up to and including the U.S. Office of Education, and the teacher training institutions which continue to practice and to pass on the traditional educational malpractices and inhumanities to successive generations of teachers-to-be! These two factors are very closely related in that the faculties of the teacher training institutions generally determine or strongly affect how the process of evaluation is carried out at all levels of education. However, in some cases such as the national and state assessment efforts, the evaluation process is affected by people outside of education. Even then, educators are called in to advise and design the evaluation or assessment instruments with all of the problems just discussed.

The first thing that has to be agreed upon is that the primary function of schools is to facilitate student learning and that schools are not primarily established and maintained in order to give teachers, administrators, school board members, etc., a place in which they can do their *thing*. Once it has been established that schools are there to facilitate student learning, then it is not too big of a step to identify and accept that a school's most important product is student learning! As such, any concept relating to the effectiveness and efficiency of the educational or instructional event has to affect or involve learning.

The second thing to realize and accept is that accountability and assessment are not one and the same even if many traditional educators think of them interchangeably. In a traditional educational environment where it is normal not to have specific objectives (SO's), it becomes easy to think of accountability in terms of an assessment because tests are manipulated to get desired distributions of scores rather than manipulating student learning and it is not necessary that the tests have any relationship with objectives (GO's and/or SO's). This makes the reliability of the assessment very tenuous at best. The results could be raised to make whoever is being held accountable look good even though the real learning achievement levels could be very low. On the other hand, the results could be lowered to make whoever is being held accountable look bad even though the real learning achievement levels could be very high. Accountability can only be valid when the assessment instruments indicate real achievement levels and when the assessments results can only be changed if and when the real learning achievement levels change. It is very unfair and non-professional to hold anyone accountable for learning achievement levels when the assessment instruments have little, if any, relationship with the stated or implied SO's being taught and learned in the classrooms.

A third and very critical point to be remembered is that schools and teachers can make a difference in the instruction of the learners despite the rash of contemporary articles which suggest that schools and teachers don't make a difference. This situation may be true in a traditional environment, but it does not have to be that way. The reasons why the research results in the traditional setting end up with no significant differences in test results is that:

— without any SO's, it is practically impossible to make a difference;
— the use of curve grading practically guarantees chance learning (no difference);
— the use of standardized tests which have little or no relationship to existing or non-existing standardized lists of SO's; and
— it is considered bad to teach what is on a test because if a teacher does, he or she might make a difference.

In addition to the traditional assessment of educational efforts being designed to show that teachers and schools don't make a difference, many psychologists and particularly educational psychologists have convinced themselves and many educators that the genetic and other external (to the school) factors have much more affect on student learning than the teacher and schools could possible have. Given that traditional assessment procedures are followed, the psychologists are correct in that little can be done to change the assessment results. In a 1970 conference sponsored by the U.S. Office of Education and later in a report of that conference, Alexander Mood, University of California at Irvine, reported that in reviewing research on the effects of teachers on student achievement that:

> We can only make the not very useful observation that at the present moment we cannot make any sort of meaningful quantitative estimate of the effect of teachers on student achievement.

The point to remember in reading the above statement by Mood is that it is an unfinished statement. At the beginning or end of the statement should have been the following:

> Given that the present teachers' role emphasizes the presenting of course content regardless of learning, that most teachers have not identified specifically what they want their students to learn, and that the tests or assessment instruments are designed to indicate chance learning (curve grading or normed tests) and have little relationship to what is taught (can't teach what is on the tests!) . . . .

In 1972, Christopher Jencks of Harvard's School of Education reported in his study *Inequality: A Reassessment of the Effect of Family and Schooling in America* that teachers and schools have such an insignificant affect on student achievement that instead of wasting time trying to teach anything, teachers and administrators should concentrate on making schools a pleasant place to be for 12 years or more of ones life! If there was no way to get schools to be more effective, I would agree with Jencks and at least the traditional educational malpractices would be eliminated if the schools were to be pleasant places. However, I do not agree with Jencks and in particular, I do not agree with his conclusions.

As pointed out earlier, any data resulting from standardized tests is for most practical purposes *useless* because the test items are selected because they discriminate and are easy to score or grade, not because they test important concepts. Because most standardized tests make use of objective type items, the most important thing to remember is that a professional test item writer (by holding the stem of a multiple-choice item constant and by just varying the distractors in the wrong choices) can get any percentage of persons taking the test item to miss it or to get it correct almost regardless of what the persons taking the test know or don't know about the concept or fact involved in the test item. In other words, the distribution of scores resulting from an objective type standardized test is more affected by the author of the test than by the persons taking the test. If it can be assumed that the teacher-training schools and the school administrators have convinced a majority of teachers that it is wrong to teach what is on the standardized tests, then obviously any differences between students indicated by the tests (even assuming that the tests were useful and honest) would surely have to be a result of *out of school* learning. But these results can't be used to evaluate what schools can or could contribute unless the tests test what is considered important and the teachers were directed to teach what is important.

Jencks also concluded that if all schools were made equally effective, the inequality among sixth graders as measured by standardized tests would decline by only three percent. Assuming that *equally effective* means that *all sixth graders would learn what is taught in sixth grade,* then it is obvious that Jencks agrees with me that standardized tests are so unrelated to what is happening in the real classroom that even though great changes in learning occurred in the classroom, any changes in the results of the standardized tests would be very minor.

Jencks points out that success in *cognitive learning* has little relationship with subsequent earning power. Again, when *cognitive learning* is measured by standardized tests, it is no wonder that Jencks came to his conclusion. After all, where in the real world outside of testing situations will anyone meet with multiple-choice items on a piece of paper. No doctor in doing surgery has ever found a multiple-choice item inside a patient. No pilot has ever run into an emergency in flight and found a multiple-choice item on the windshield telling him what to do. No dentist has ever found a multiple-choice item in the bottom of a cavity in a tooth. Yet, professionals are certified on the basis of their ability to answer these irrelevant so-called *objective* type standardized tests!

Jencks points out that the school budget, educational policies, and teacher characteristics have a minor or almost an irrelevant effect on cognitive learning. This conclusion has the same problems as the previous conclusions because the data comes from standardized tests. In addition, since few schools have ever specifically identified what it is that students should be learning, it would be highly unusual for the school budget, educational policies, and teacher characteristics to be related to learning. This does not mean that these factors couldn't have an effect on learning. If schools and teachers specified what students were to learn and that became the overall goal of all participants in the teaching-learning process, it would be easy to prove that these factors could significantly affect learning — IF the tests which were used were related to the learning objectives the students were supposed to learn and the teachers were allowed to teach what the students were supposed to learn.

Another conclusion from Jencks study is that luck and personality account for 75 percent of the variations in incomes. With reference to *luck*, remember that in standardizing tests, the normal probability curve or variations of the curve are used to validate most of these tests and since the normal probability curve can be generated by throwing dice or flipping coins it shouldn't be unusual that tests based on *chance* are highly correlated with *luck!* With reference to personality, Jencks states that such traits as the ability to persuade a customer, to look a man in the eye without seeming to stare, to synthesize large quantities of information, to *psych out* the boss, etc., have much more effect on earning power than what is learned in schools. Again, if teachers haven't specified the learning objectives for their students, chances are fairly good that unidentified objectives could be irrelevant. Also, if these other traits are that important, why not teach these in schools rather than leaving it up to chance that students will pick up these critical traits outside of schools.

Jencks believes that his report debunks the widely held belief that integration, compensatory and preschool programs which teach the children of the poor to read, write and use numbers well will help them get higher paying jobs. The first problem with this conclusion is that few of the compensatory and preschool programs are associated with specific measurable learning objectives and as such it is difficult to defend them in terms of learning under any circumstances. Second, the continuing problem of conclusions based on data from standardized tests are not honest and valid. Third, if the traits identified in the last prargraph really make the difference, then obviously, in compensatory programs, the children of the poor should be taught those critical traits.

As pointed out in all of my books, our greatest problem in our society is a *people* problem. In business and industry, there are more people who are fired because they can't get along with their fellow workers than there are people who are fired because of incompetence. Because *getting along with your fellow man* is essentially the *christian ethic* or religious related, this critical behavior has been left up to the churches and homes to develop. However, neither the churches nor the homes have been very successful in teaching this critical concept, so it is time for the schools to do it. In conflict with Jencks overall conclusion that schools should concentrate on just being a pleasant place for teachers and students to spend time, I believe that schools are more important than ever, but the importance is only in relationship to the degree that schools and teachers identify what is important for learners to learn in order to be successful in an occupation and to be able to be successful in life away from their work and then to be accountable for the students achieving these critical behaviors.

In creating an emphasis on learning in the instructional event, it is not enough to associate accountability only with the results of a valid assessment without considering accountability for doing something about the results. Once the assessment instruments match the desired SO's such that the results indicate the real learning achievement levels of the students and valid accountability is possible, then procedures and measures should be available to increase the effectiveness of the learning environment. In business and industry and in most other scientific or systematic endeavors, procedures and measures which are used to increase and maintain effectiveness in a process are usually referred to in terms of *quality control.* One hundred percent achievement would be similar to *zero defect* quality control. In order to institute quality control measures and procedures, it is necessary to change from the traditional negative evaluation to positive evaluation. Negative evaluation is where the assessment results are used to grade students down, to chastise or ridicule students, or to fail, suspend or eliminate students. The emphasis in negative evaluation is on what has not been achieved and there are generally no follow-up activities except the recording of a score or grade. Negative evaluation of teachers or administrators is similar in that the emphasis is on what the teacher or administrator is not doing correctly and this data is used to threaten or eliminate the teacher or administrator.

Positive evaluation is where the emphasis is on what hasn't been achieved in order that different methods, materials and/or strategies can be identified which will help the student learn what he or she missed. In the case of teachers and administrators, the emphasis in positive evaluation is on the identification of problem areas in their performance of their roles so that subsequent training will help the teachers and administrators solve their problems and improve their performance. A very important point to remember is that in many educational institutions, teachers and administrators have been and are being evaluated on a positive basis in accordance with this definition of positive evaluation. However, the resultant improvements in role performance have little or nothing to do with student learning. In other words, the criteria for evaluation of the teachers and administrators performance is in reference to their traditional roles and have not been tied directly to student learning on a cause and effect basis.

In bringing about *quality control* in instruction, it is critical that all of the people in the instructional process be evaluated on a positive basis from the point-of-view of student learning. The *quality control* goal would be to get at least 90 percent or more of the students to learn 100 percent of the required SO's in the units and courses they are enrolled in. The activities carried on by students, teachers, and administrators under this form of *quality control* are such that those activities, methods, materials, etc., which don't result in increased learning, are replaced by other activities, methods, materials, etc., which will facilitate the desired learning. The emphasis is on up-grading the instructional process by recognizing and responding to individual differences while trying to maximize learning. Traditionally, the emphasis on *quality control*, if any, is on the input to the instructional process rather than on the process itself. Such efforts as being more selective in admitting students and hiring faculty; building more modern school buildings; having a greater selection of books, materials, films, etc.; higher teacher salaries and lighter teaching loads; are typical of traditional educational efforts at quality control. If the instructional process is left constant, improving the quality of the students admitted to the process should result in a similar increase in the output of the process. However, this assumes that the process can't be improved and probably doesn't make much difference. All too often, the bringing about of *quality* in traditional education (particularly in secondary and higher education) means that more students are failed. This is achieved by raising the level (quality?) of the presentations such that fewer students can understand and learn and/or to increase the difficulty level (quality?) of the tests such that fewer students can pass the tests. The effect of this false quality and negative discrimination is to make sure that the few who do make it through this traditional process at the 100 percent level stand out like talented artists. The *art* of teaching emphasizes the elimination of students rather than as in the *science* of teaching where the emphasis is on success for all or most of the students.

Under the present traditional approach where the majority of students get grades of "C" or less and assuming that a "C" is equivalent to about 75 percent achievement, the majority of students are graduating from high school with nine years or less cumulative achievement (12 years x .75 = 9 years). The majority of students graduating from junior colleges are only achieving 10.5 years or less (14 years x .75 = 10.5 years). The majority of students graduating from a four year college or university course are only achieving 12 years or less (16 years x .75 = 12 years) which is equivalent to a high school graduate who got all A's. Obviously, the present system is not only ineffective and lacks real quality control, but a lot of time is wasted and the costs to our students and the taxpayers is staggering. Henry Levin of Stanford, in a study for the U.S. Senate Committee on Equal Educational Opportunity, concluded that an inadequate education of 3.1 million men between 25 and 34 years of age has cost the country about $200 billion in lost income and that crime and welfare costs attributable to an inadequate education add about $6 billion annually.

Bringing about *quality control* as suggested in these three volumes changes the process to fit the variable needs of students that are the input to the process such that high quality levels of learning output are facilitated for all students (in contrast to a *normal curve's* worth of students).

Whereas the emphasis under *quality control* is on increasing the effectiveness of the instructional process, another factor becomes important once the desired effectiveness is achieved. This factor is efficiency or *productivity*. The emphasis under *productivity* is on achieving the same high levels of learning but achieving them faster, at lower costs, using fewer materials, using less space, etc. Frequently, a mistake is made in that efforts to make the instructional process more efficient are imposed before the instructional process can be made effective. Given the two concepts *effectiveness* and *efficiency*, there are four combinations which could occur. A situation could be both ineffective and inefficient which describes the present traditional educational process in that most students are not learning what they should be learning (100 percent of the stated or implied SO's) and the process is very costly, involves a lot of duplication and is essentially non-directional. Because the dollar costs are easy to measure, the usual first step is to tighten up the efficiency. This creates a situation where the ineffective educational process becomes more efficient at being ineffective. PPBS (Programming, Planning and Budgeting Systems) have been and are being implemented in many educational institutions in order to make them operate more efficiently. Although students don't learn any more under PPBS controls, at least the ineffective educational process doesn't cost as much. The problem with this situation is that once the situation is efficient at being ineffective it may be even more difficult to affect the effectiveness of the situation.

A much better approach would be to increase the effectiveness of the situation even though the situation is still inefficient. Actually, in making the instructional process more effective and by eliminating duplication, the process automatically becomes more efficient. Once the process has become effective (90 percent or more of the students learn 100 percent of their courses), that is the best time to worry about becoming more efficient. However, as long as most teachers have not specified what it is they want their students to learn, then effectiveness is very difficult to measure and the educational process becomes ineffective by default and also inefficient.

Because of the individual differences among students in reference to how they learn and what they need and/or want to learn and also because of the individual differences among teachers in reference to how well they can teach, who they can teach, and how many they can teach, maximizing effectiveness is not enough and the cost of maximizing the effectiveness may be prohibitive for some instructional institutions, if effectiveness is all that is desired. In order to facilitate achievement of maximum effectiveness and at a cost that is well within the financial capabilities of most instructional institutions, it is critical to bring about maximum effectiveness in a step-by-step fashion which will tend to also maximize efficiency of learning. In other words, as a technique is developed which will increase learning at an increased cost of instruction, it will be necessary to identify a technique for increased efficiency which will offer a corresponding decrease in the cost of instruction. At the present time, there are so many educational practices which produce a minimum of learning, if any, for a high investment in instructional costs, that by eliminating or changing some of these practices the need for major increases in instructional budgets could be delayed for a long time, if not eliminated. The major changes necessary to bring about maximum efficiency involve the recognition of individual differences in ACTION as well as in theory and includes not only the recognition of individual differences among students, but also the recognition of individual differences among teachers and the utilization of instructional technology and instructional facilities to take maximum advantage of these differences.

The major trend in traditional education at the present time is to reduce productivity (decrease efficiency). This is occurring as the costs of education are increasing significantly while the effectiveness of education is remaining at the same levels and in some schools is actually decreasing. When class size is reduced and teachers' teaching load is reduced without any accompanying increase in the effectiveness of student learning, productivity is decreased.

Therefore, in creating an emphasis on learning, it is not enough to just talk about accountability. It is necessary to identify what is desired (required SO's), make sure that the assessment instruments are matched to the SO's, evaluate all concerned from a positive point-of-view, institute quality control until at least 90 percent or more of the students are achieving 100 percent of the required SO's, and then examine the process in order to increase the efficiency or productivity without losing any of the effectiveness of the process. Not only will this emphasis on learning benefit students, the process will increase the professionalism of the teachers and administrators involved.

2. ACCOUNTABLE FOR WHAT? (THE EFFECTS OF A CRITICAL PRINCIPLE OF EVALUATION)

People have a tendency to be involved in activities and to acquire and perform those behaviors which are used as criteria for evaluation by those in a position to evaluate us.

Not everyone accepts evaluations of themselves by others. Some people will accept evaluations from some people and not from others. For example, some teachers may accept evaluations by their peers or administrators, but not from their students. Some teachers could be just the opposite in which they care more about what their students think of them than what their colleagues or administrators think of them. In reference to this principle of evaluation, remember this does not only refer to obvious and specified criteria used for evaluation but also to hidden and unspecified criteria. For example, in some schools in addition to the usual specified criteria for evaluation, a teacher may also be evaluated on the basis of hidden criteria, i.e., manner of dress, religious or political affiliations, extra time spent at school, etc.

What makes this principle so critical is that in trying to create an emphasis on learning, it is critical that everyone concerned with the instructional process be evaluated on the basis of their direct or indirect affect on student learning or learning will not have priority in their activities as is the case in the traditional approach to evaluation of the educational environment. Most students try to find out what teachers want in addition to what is specified in order to get good grades from the teachers. For example, some teachers want to see long bibliographies at the end of student papers, some teachers evaluate student papers by weight, some teachers are favorably impressed by students who do extra study in the teacher's favorite topics, some teachers are favorably impressed by students who talk a lot in class or after class. When teachers don't specify what they want in terms of SO's, students are then generally evaluated on the basis of criteria which are not related to student learning.

The most influential groups and people affecting the educational process via the evaluation principle are accrediting associations, state and national education agencies, and administrators. Typically, accrediting associations and agencies evaluate the input factors of the educational process, i.e., the classrooms, the library and other resources, the degrees of the faculty, courses offered and required, class sizes, curve grading (have to have *educational quality* which means some students have to fail by design), etc. As a result, and in accordance with the evaluation principle, schools are concerned about the physical facilities; the number of books, films, etc., in their library; the degrees of their faculty, their course and program offerings, class sizes, that they have a normal curve of results; etc. It would be a rare event if accrediting associations and agencies evaluated a school on the basis of what students learned. Consequently, schools are not that concerned about learning.

Conspicuously absent from accrediting association forms are questions and observations concerning the effectiveness and efficiency of the learning situation, such as, *What specifically are the students supposed to be learning?* and *What have they learned?* It may be very possible for students to be learning everything they are supposed to learn and still not have some of the educational *artifacts* which the accrediting commission deems necessary. On the other hand, it is very possible that an educational institution with all or most of the educational *artifacts* is not able to facilitate even a minor portion of the learning that is supposed to be taking place.

Some state agencies are planning to accredit teacher training programs on a competancy basis. In other words, the students have to be able to perform in certain ways in order to pass their courses and to get their degrees. This appears to be in line with the systems concept except that the required performances are inappropriate for the new role of the teacher. Competancy Based Teacher Education (CBTE) training programs are using systems concepts in the teaching of the traditional role of the teacher. They are an individualized approach to the teaching of how to teach classes where the emphasis is on the teacher as a person who presents course content to classes and works with groups of students. Notice, by having each teacher-training student perform in the same way, the concept ignores individual differences in teaching styles. In a program where learning is the emphasis, the teacher-training students would be evaluated on the basis of the results of their performance (Did the students being taught by the teacher-training student learn what they were supposed to learn?) which allows the teacher-training student to use whatever style he or she finds successful as long as the students they are teaching learn all of the required SO's.

Few administrators are evaluated on the basis of how much they help their teachers facilitate learning. Traditionally, most administrators are evaluated on the basis of such criteria as: were they able to operate the school within their budget, did they maintain good public relations, not too many parents complained to the school board members, were they able to obtain some outside funds for special projects, how well did they minimize vandalism, how well disciplined were the students, etc. As a result and again in accordance with the evaluation principle, most administrators tend to be more concerned with these criteria which have little relationship with student learning than with whether or not students are learning and whether or not the teachers are helping or hindering students learning.

The same principle affects all groups involved and affecting the instructional process including state and federal education agencies. Rarely are state and particularly federal education agencies evaluated on the basis of how much student learning they have directly or indirectly facilitated. In most of these agencies it is more important to placate the members of the legislative bodies that control the agencies' budget than it is to worry about specific student learning.

Knowing that this principle is in operation and critically affects all concerned with the instructional process, the guideline or objective to follow is to change the emphasis in evaluation activities at all levels of education from the present criteria which have little, if any, relationship to learning to an emphasis on student learning and how one's activities directly or indirectly affect achievement. Of course, to do this, is to critical to identify specifically what it is that students should be learning (SO's).

3. WHO IS ACCOUNTABLE AND FOR WHAT?

If student learning is really the most important product of our schools, then for anyone to be held accountable for things which do not result directly or indirectly in student learning or may even actually inhibit or decrease student learning is worse than no accountability at all. To institute accountability without knowing what the person or persons are to be held accountable for is to promote fear and distrust and to practically guarantee the uselessness and ultimate failure of the concept.

In California, where each individual teacher decides what they will be held accountable for in terms of class progress during a period of time, there is a tendency to state objectives in general terms and to underestimate the predicted achievement levels. This continues the traditional educational environment in which there is little planned relationship in learning from class to class and from school to school and as such is a *closed system.* As relationships between the *real* world and the *academic* world are identified and established and relationships between schools and between classes are identified and established, the instructional system can be opened up. Obviously, open instructional systems lend themselves to accountability procedures, but what is more important is that the accountability can now be shared with others who are also responsible for promoting student learning. Even more important than accountability, in an open instructional system there can also be a sharing in the cost and effort to solve common student learning problems and a sharing of the solutions which will benefit all concerned.

Our society has a responsibility to the members of our society and in particular to the young people in our society such that they will be able to obtain sufficient and effective instruction in order to participate fully in our society, i.e., being able to take advantage of the benefits of our society, contributing to our society for the benefit of others in our society, etc. As a result of this responsibility, our society through legislative bodies, taxes, fees, and direct voting has set up and maintains instructional institutions whose responsibility it is to fulfill the responsibility of our society. As professional educators or instructors, our responsibility is to identify those things that students should be learning in order to exist fully in our society and in order to contribute to our society, and then to make sure that all or almost all of the students learn 100 percent of these things. For maximum effectiveness and efficiency, the instructional process should reflect the individual differences of the students and the teachers.

Under the traditional approach to education where the needs of the students have not been identified and individual differences in students and teachers are ignored, it has been common to use time as a measure of progress, i.e., elementary school takes six years, bachelor's degree takes four years, two years of English, four years of mathematics, students have to stay in school until 18 years old, etc. Because of individual differences in rates of learning and levels of cumulative ignorance (unlearned prerequisites, knowledge and skills), whenever time is treated as a constant, levels of achievement have to be varied and it becomes impossible for educators to fulfill their responsibility to society or to the students. Also, under the traditional approach, the teacher's role emphasizes the presenting of course content regardless of individual differences of students and teachers, and, as pointed out, the evaluation of students and educators is not necessarily related to effective and/or efficient instruction and frequently is irrelevant and may actually interfere with effective or efficient instructional activities.

Under current *pseudo-humanistic* or *modern* approaches to education where the emphasis is on letting students and teachers *do their own thing* and/or on *keeping the students busy*, the responsibility of society and educators is ignored. In fact, since the *do your own thing* movement emphasizes self (selfism) over a responsibility to others (humanism), these so-called *modern* approaches to education create attitudes, values, and beliefs (not to mention the lack of necessary knowledge and skills) which tend to make the students a potential or actual liability rather than an asset to our society as a result of juvenile delinquency, vandalism, adult crime, unemployment, and/or welfare. Many educators use the *pseudo-humanist* approaches because they are honestly convinced that allowing students to *do their own thing* is the humane way to go; however, they are unaware that they are developing selfism which is in conflict with humanism and ignores the responsibility that our society and professional educators have to our young people. Many other educators use the *pseudo-humanist* approaches because they hope that the *do your own thing* movement will help them escape accountability and responsibility to the students and society. Sad to say, there are some educators who use the *pseudo-humanist* approaches because they know that they are creating conflict and turmoil for our society by indoctrinating the students with attitudes, values, and beliefs which are contrary to the ideals and goals of our present forms of family, society, and government. Yes, there are problems in our society which need correction (like our present traditional form of education); but these problems are not problems with our ideals and goals. The problems are generally created by individuals and groups who misinterpret the ideals and goals of our society in such a manner that *self* becomes not only more important than *others*, but at the expense of *others*.

    a.   *YOUTH-ANASIA* (SCHOOL VIOLENCE AND PUSH-OUTS)

Another aspect of the *pseudo-humanist* approach are the efforts by some educators who want to eliminate students who are having trouble learning. Most of the problem students are problems because the present traditional approach ignores their instructional needs. In many cases the problem students are eliminated by directly or indirectly pushing them out of school and calling them *drop-outs*. Some times the students are labeled as being mentally retarded rather than educationally retarded which places the blame on the parents via genetics. There are some efforts to lower the age requirement for compulsory schooling[1] in order to allow students to *drop-out* sooner. A growing demand by some teacher groups is for the right to eliminate the non-achieving student who also happens to be a behavioral problem. This trend should be very disturbing to other professional teachers as it is analogous to a doctor saying that he or she only wanted to work with well patients and those patients who could get well by whatever treatment the doctor selected for them regardless of what their needs were.

NOTE: Euthanasia is the practice of painlessly putting to death persons suffering from incurable conditions or disease. *Youth-anasia* is the practice of painlessly (to the teachers and schools) putting students out of schools who are suffering from incurable learning conditions (supposed limited learning abilities) and who are involved in vandalism and bored with school.

Given that a major portion of new learning is based in part on prior learning, students who don't achieve the prior learning (cumulative ignornace) will have problems in achieving the new learning. In a typical teaching-learning situation where the teacher is teaching to the *average* student, up to half of the students who are below average are going to

---

[1] Eventually, compulsory schooling will refer to minimum learning requirements in order to exist and contribute to our society rather than the current emphasis on age.

slowly, but surely, fall behind. When they get far enough behind, there is little, if any, chance that they will be able to learn. Not because they are genetically incapable of learning, but because they were allowed to progress through school without learning what they needed to know to be successful in subsequent learning experiences (discipline in learning).

Imagine for a moment that you are sitting in a classroom where the language of instruction is one that you don't understand but you still had to sit there five or six hours per day, five days a week, for 36 weeks a year, year after year. How long could you stand to be still and suffer in that kind of learning environment which is a design for non-achievement? Most adults would probably react negatively and actively against that type of a situation in a matter of hours and some in minutes. They would get up and leave! However, if they were forced to stay in the negative environment, it wouldn't be long before violence and vandalism would occur. If these negative behaviors resulted in getting them released from the negative environment, the release (or suspension) would be considered a reward and as such, there would be a tendency to repeat the negative behaviors. By expelling, or in some way getting rid of the students who are behavioral problems, it may make the schools a better place and be easier on teachers, but the *push-outs* are now out in our society believing that negative behaviors (violence and vandalism) will bring them rewards! In addition, the non-achievement history of the students also suggests that they probably will not have the necessary skills to obtain work and even if they did get work, their negative attitudes, values and beliefs (negative acts bring rewards) will soon get them into trouble on the job.

If these ex-students (who were pushed out of school to make it easier for teachers and schools) end up in some type of correctional institution, the costs to society could easily exceed $5,000 per year. Not to mention the fact that in a time of increased costs of education, each student who is pushed out of school reduces the school's income by over $1,000 per year in most areas of the country.

> NOTE: The negative behaviors of the student are symptoms of a *problem the student has.* Doing something about eliminating the symptoms (or the student) may solve the problem the student has caused for the school, but it doesn't solve the *problem the student has* and causes greater and more costly problems for society and the student.

Judge John Toner of Cuyahoga County (Ohio) Juvenile Court told a House of Representatives educational subcommittee hearing on school violence that keeping students in school until they were 18 forces students who are deficient and *unable to learn* to endure continued failures which results in frustration and hostility (towards teachers, schools, students who have success, and most of our society).

Believing that these students are genetically incapable of learning, Judge Toner wants these students to be released from school at a younger age than 18. Although the idea may be *innovative*, it is based on traditional beliefs and doesn't solve the students' problems and causes more problems for society.

In California, a similar solution has been enacted such that beginning this fall, 16 year old students will be able to get out of school by passing a special equivalency test of *survival skills* (for surviving in society). Of interest is the fact that there is no accompanying requirement that schools teach these survival skills which hopefully will be very relevant. As a *face-saving* gesture, community colleges in California are required to accept these *equivalency diplomas* even though the equivalency test does not test for the achievement of *survival skills* needed to succeed in college, nor are the schools required to teach these skills. A result which should be expected is that the *open door* policy of the community colleges will become more of a *revolving door* in which more students will be going out the *back door* because they haven't learned the necessary *survival skills* (for college survival). This should also result in more push-outs with negative attitudes towards schools, teachers, other students who succeed, and most of society.

Even without this added problem of reducing the *quality* of entering college students by design, the students who are entering colleges and universities on the basis of the regular diplomas are coming to college with fewer of the *survival skills* needed to make it. More and more colleges and universities are having to have special classes to help students learn to read and write better and to enable them to do basic arithmetic functions. In those colleges and universities where they don't have these special classes, the so-called marginal student probably won't survive through the first year. It is bad enough to say to a marginal student (and particularly a minority student from a disadvantaged background), *You can't go to college!* But it is even worse to say to a marginal student, *Yes, start college with all the others* and then have an academic design (curve grading) which forces the student out as a failure. If educators supposedly care enough to *open* the college door to students with marginal college survival skills, they should also care enough to teach these students the necessary skills in order to have success in college courses. Of course, it would even be better if the students were taught and they learned these skills back in elementary and secondary schools, rather than wait until they are in remedial classes at a college or university. This duplication of effort is an example of the high costs of ineffectiveness in the traditional educational teaching environment with all its malpractices!

According to a recent study on *Dropout Prevention* by the National Advisory Council on Supplementary Centers and Services, potential dropouts (push-outs) are fairly easy to identify, although once identified, they are not sure what to do about them. The *early warning signs* are as follows:

- *The student is usually two or three years behind grade level.* As cumulative ignorance develops, the success ratio decreases and failures increase. Any student who wouldn't want to drop out under these conditions would have to be a masochist. If the educational system is operating properly by recognizing that students are individually different, no student would be that far behind. By the time a student's cumulative ignorance builds up to three years, it is pretty late to change the negative attitudes which have been developed even though the student could be successfully helped academically.

- *A record of high absenteeism.* Given the negative, non-learning environment the student is in, any sane person would try to absent themselves as much as possible. Any failing student who says, *I want to go to school because they fail me almost every day and make me feel so dumb*, has got to be mentally sick!

- *Disruptive behavior.* First of all, potential push-outs may be disruptive because at least they find they can be successful at something by making teachers as frustrated as the students are. Second, potential push-outs may get rewarded for their disruptive behavior and be suspended or allowed to quit. Third, given the negative environment they are in (from the students' point-of-view), being disruptive is a coping behavior of a normal person. The passive sufferer is the one to watch.

- *Has failed one or more grades.* First, failure is negative and indirectly creates negative attitudes. Second, failure is an indication of critical cumulative ignorance if the student is passed on in spite of the failure. Third, failure is an indication of critical boredom if the student has to repeat a whole grade or course even when the student already knows parts of the course and/or has passed in other courses.

NOTE: In Santa Ana, California, beginning fall 1975, students who fail in reading will have to repeat the whole grade just as if they didn't learn anything at all! A sure design for boredom, potential violence, and more absenteeism which has already cost the district about $800,000 in state funds for this past school year. At the same time, the Santa Ana School Board wants to hold their teachers responsible for truancy. A situation in which compliance with one rule creates problems in the compliance of the other rule.

- *A lack of motivation and interest in school.* Again, only mentally sick people like to be in places which are continually associated with negative experiences.
- *Lack of participation in extracurricular activities.* Increased participation comes with increasing positive experiences — decreased participation comes with increasing negative experiences.
- *Poor marks in school subjects, work habits, and cooperation.* These are symptoms of student learning problems which, if not solved, leads to the other symptoms listed here as early warning signs. If the learning problems are solved so the students' marks improve, other positive signs will develop.

It continues to amaze me how the traditional educator steeped in the traditional lore of education can overlook obvious problems and solutions and perceives the symptoms of a problem as the problems to be dealt with, rather than the problem itself. For example, although every educator will admit intellectually that students learn at different rates (need different lengths of time to learn), educational lore (and entropic drift) states that formal education occurs within set limits of semesters, quarters, etc. When differences in achievement are observed, rather than admit that it is the result of ignoring individual differences in rates of learning, educational lore helps the educator blame these differences on genetic or environmental limitations which are beyond the educator's control. Therefore, the symptoms (differences in achievement) of the problem (ignoring individual differences) become the problems to be dealt with. As a result of not dealing directly with the first level symptoms (differences in achievement) because it is believed nothing can be done, the low achievers and non-achievers develop secondary symptoms (behavioral problems, i.e., absenteeism, low grades, lack of motivation and participation, disruptive behaviors, vandalism, etc.) Now, these secondary symptoms can be solved (for the schools) by the traditional educator via discipline in behavior and *youth-anasia* designed to eliminate the students and in the process creating more problems for the students and society. The Instructioneer in utilizing concepts from the Behavioral Learning Systems Approach would have solved the basic problems via honesty and discipline in learning designed only to eliminate ignorance and barriers to successful living and in the process to facilitate the solving of other problems for the students and society.

If one can think of our young people as a natural resource, just as it is considered wrong to throw away or waste our other natural resources, it should also be wrong to throw out or waste our students. In addition, just as many groups are demanding ecological impact reports before anyone can disturb our natural resources, shouldn't it be reasonable that teachers should prepare an instructional impact report for each student as part of their responsibility?

Many teachers claim that they shouldn't be held accountable for student learning because they cannot force students to learn. Once learning becomes the primary emphasis of the instructional process, students should be held accountable for learning and teachers should be held accountable for solving the students' learning problems and facilitating learning. Traditional methods of promotion where students are promoted because of their age (social promotion) or because of attendance and other non-learning activities convince students that attendance is more important than learning. The systems approach is designed such that students are only promoted or get credit for courses when they learn 100 percent of the required SO's. More and more teachers and parents are saying that discipline is the most critical problem in our schools. What is needed is not more physical and mental punishment which is the traditional view of *discipline;* but intellectual discipline where students have to learn 100 percent of the required SO's before being promoted or given credit for a course. Students can be held accountable for learning with resultant benefits for all concerned.

Some educators believe that if students are held accountable for learning, some students will be in a course for years. That might be true for certain rare cases. However, if students were required to learn 100 percent of the required SO's before going on, there would be a savings in time, effort, and money because there would be no duplication of SO's in subsequent courses to overcome non-learning in prerequisite courses. Also, if students were fully prepared for learning by having to learn 100 percent of prerequisite SO's, they would learn much faster and would have a more positive attitude.

By instituting accountability in learning (quality control), our diplomas and degrees would begin to take on *real academic meaning.* Instead of only referring to the completion of so many hours or years regardless of any learning, our diplomas and degrees could stand for specific minimum standards of achievement. Efforts in this direction have already begun in some states. However, the achievement of the required levels of learning are apt to be measured by some standardized tests which are irrelevant to the required achievement levels.

As more and more state and federal funds are being used in our schools and as more and more state and federal funds are being used to correct the ineffectiveness and inefficiencies of our schools (via welfare, unemployment, crime, etc.), it should be expected that state and federal education agencies will be under increasing pressure to be held accountable for certain minimum levels of learning. This means that the federal office of education will have to identify the minimum common core of SO's in a variety of courses taught nationally and they will also fund research to identify and solve learning problems associated with the national minimum common core SO's. In a similar manner, the state education agencies will be primarily concerned with those minimum common core SO's which are unique to that state and are above and beyond the national level of minimum common core SO's. The state will also fund research to identify and solve learning problems associated with the state minimum common core SO's. This increased responsibility and accountability is in contrast to the current suggestions and demands by many educators that the state and federal education agencies hand out more funds for education with no strings attached (no accountability).

The same areas of responsibility and accountability should affect school districts in that they should be responsible for identifying those additional minimum common core SO's which are above and beyond those required by the state and federal agencies. School districts should also fund research to identify and solve learning problems associated with the district minimum common core SO's.

b. IS LEARNING MEASURABLE?

If learning is to be the emphasis in instruction and accountability utilizes assessment, then learning should be measurable. Yet, many educators claim that you cannot measure learning. They are right in that for most practical purposes, learning is not directly measurable. However, learning can be measured indirectly. The most important point to remember is that almost every teacher is presently measuring something when they evaluate their students. In fact, I have never met a teacher who didn't evaluate his or her students in one way or another. For some teachers they may be evaluating their students with tests, essays, and/or papers. Some teachers may evaluate their students on the basis of the students' products or physical performance. Other teachers may evaluate their students on the basis of their personality or other non-measurable criteria. The very same teachers who may claim that you can't measure learning turn around and grade students down from 100 percent, an "A", a *superior*, or other symbols indicating top grades because the students didn't *learn as much* as some other students. If learning is not measurable, then millions of students at all levels of education are being unjustly treated in receiving lower grades than other students. Admittedly, what some teachers are measuring at the present time may not be related to learning, but that doesn't mean that learning can not be indirectly measured.

In measuring learning, it is important to remember that there are three domains of learning: (discussed in detail in Chapter VI, Volume II and also in Chapter IV, Volume I): cognitive, sensory, and affective.[2] Although each domain of learning is usually discussed as if it was completely separated from the other domains, in actuality, all three domains of learning are involved in the learning of an objective in any one of the domains. Objectives in all three domains are general objectives (GO's) and are non-measurable on a direct basis. They can only be measured on an indirect basis when stated in terms of some specific actions or behaviors (SO's) of the students.

Although more and more states are getting involved with the concept of accountability, most of them are using various forms of standardized tests similar to the National Assessment tests which are practically useless because the tests are related to vague, non-measurable GO's and most of the test items are designed to give predetermined results regardless of the knowledge and skill levels of the students. In some states, they have gone to a great expense in time, effort, and dollars, to identify district and/or state educational goals. Frequently, these goals are in terms of what the educators should be doing (the traditional approach) not what the learners should be learning (see the following examples):

1. To provide an educational program which encourages each student to learn how to think and develop modes of inquiry in order to adapt to any of life's challenges with confidence and effective behavior.

2. To provide the opportunity for each student to acquire the basic skills, information, and concepts in order to be intellectually curious; to develop habits of listening, observing, and reasoning effectively; and to think and work creatively.

3. To provide each student the opportunity to develop both verbal and non-verbal skills in communication.

---

[2]*THE COGNITIVE DOMAIN* is concerned with the development of intellectual skills and other activities, i.e., thinking, knowing, understanding, comprehending, analyzing, synthesizing, problem solving, etc.

THE SENSORY DOMAIN is concerned with the development of sensomotor skills in the input senses of hearing, seeing, touch, taste, and smell and the output sense which is the muscle sense. (Although most educators and educational psychologists believe that the third domain is the *psychomotor domain*, rather than the sensory domain, it is a common misunderstanding. The term psychomotor behavior is defined as a physical movement or observable behavior resulting from some mental activity and as such is the behavior from which one can infer cognitive learning.)

THE AFFECTIVE DOMAIN is concerned with the development or change of emotional tendencies, i.e., attitudes, values, beliefs, guiding philosophies, feelings, etc.

4. To provide each student the opportunity to develop skills in intelligent, constructive, critical, and creative thinking so that he or she may develop the ability to analyze situations, recognize resources, evaluate alternatives, make judgements, accept responsibility, and take intelligent action.

5. To provide each student the opportunity to recognize the value of developing intellectual curiosity and of acquiring a positive attitude toward learning as a life-long process by engaging in educational experiences which are relevant to his present and future needs.

However, these objectives can be converted into student objectives by changing the beginning of the statements to *the students will learn how to think and develop..., the students will acquire the basic skills..., the students will develop both verbal...*, etc.

Some school districts and states have identified goals for student learning which are very similar to the previous list of goals for educators (when these goals are converted into student goals), i.e.

1. Each student should learn to reason independently.
2. Each student should understand the moral and ethical values, goals and processes of our society.
3. Each student should acquire fundamental skills in listening, speaking, reading, spelling, writing and arithmetic.
4. Each student should develop pride and appreciation for good workmanship and skills in performance.

These two lists of objectives are similar in that they indicate very important objectives which most parents, teachers, students, and other members of our society would be in agreement that students should learn them; BUT, they are all general, non-measurable objectives. In order for these objectives to become measurable, they would have to be broken down into a sufficient number of statements of specific student behaviors from which an inference can be drawn that the general objective has been achieved. Then, it would be critical that the evaluation (or tests) of the students' achievement be correlated very highly or exactly with these specific statements.[3]

---

[3] This is the point at which the ultimate usefulness of the test results is determined. If the actual formation of the test items are manipulated to affect the results of the tests such as in standardized or *normed* tests, the results are useless, tell you nothing about what the students know about the SO's, and cannot be used to guide subsequent instruction. If the correlation between the SO's and test items is very high or exact, the results can be used for accountability purposes, they indicate actual achievement levels of each student, and can be used to guide subsequent learning activities.

Some teachers, school districts, and states are now beginning to realize the need for specific statements and are listing specific skills that students should attain before getting credit for courses and/or before getting a diploma. Pennsylvania's Citizens Commission on Basic Education has done a very good job in this area. Some of their *specific* skills are still not specific enough to be directly measurable, but the statements are much more specific than those being prepared by other state groups. (A much more detailed discussion of general and specific objectives and the measurement of them can be found in Chapter VI, Volume II).

There has been and will probably continue to be a lot of discussions on the pros and cons of specifying instructional objectives. The most common misunderstanding on both sides is that general objectives and specific objectives are two separate and unrelated concepts. Actually, both types of objectives are necessary. The general objectives (GO's) are critical because they are the wellhead or source of the SO's and because they usually represent the *real* desired objective in that they indicate the domain or domains of learning to be emphasized, i.e., to have an understanding (cognitive), to know (cognitive), to see (sensory), to taste (sensory), to appreciate (affective), to value (affective), etc. Since the GO's are usually what is actually desired, they should be identified first and then the SO's generated from the GO's. If learning is important and instruction is to take place by design rather than by chance, it is also critical to have the measurable SO's. Frequently, however, the advocates of specifying objectives downgrade the GO's and say *if you can't measure the objective, throw it out.* In using only SO's, it is easy to lose organization and relatedness and end up with a fragmented unit of study. Also, without the GO's, it becomes difficult to replace or reword unsatisfactory SO's.

Among some educators, the major objection against SO's is that they are called specific *behavioral* objectives and the word *behavioral*, to these educators, suggests something akin to animal psychology with its rat mazes, cages, etc. The use of the word *behavioral* in behavioral objectives is used to indicate that the objective has to describe an observable and measurable event and should not be confused with behavioral psychology. If the word *behavioral* is a serious hang-up and delays the development and use of SO's, don't use it. Use any other term you want, just as long as you remember that SO's (or whatever word or term you use for them) have to be observable and measurable.

c. THE AFFECTIVE DOMAIN AND ACCOUNTABILITY

Just as there are two different theories or strategies of instruction in reference to the three domains of learning, there are two different views of accountability. Students can be held accountable for the learning of SO's in the cognitive and sensory domains. Teachers and other educators involved in the instructional process can be held accountable for helping the students learn the SO's in the cognitive and sensory domain. Notice that the accountability is concerned with the learning of positive things. Also notice that the SO's to be learned in the cognitive and sensory domains are generally the ones that would be most likely learned in school which also helps identify who is accountable.

The key difference between the cognitive and sensory domains and the affective domain is that students can control whether or not they learn cognitive and sensory SO's as they are taught and learned directly; whereas, students can not control whether or not they learn affective SO's as they are taught and learned indirectly.

Also, the learning of affective SO's can occur almost anyplace, i.e., at home, in school, with peer groups, etc. Consequently, as long as students are learning attitudes, values, and/or beliefs which are commonly held in the home, school, and community, it would be practically impossible to pinpoint who contributed the most or least to the learning of those emotional tendencies. On the other hand, if students are developing attitudes, values, and/or beliefs which are in conflict with those commonly held in the home and community, it becomes easier to identify the person or persons who are accountable for developing these conflicting emotional tendencies. Therefore, accountability in the affective domain is more concerned with SO's which are not really the ones specified for learning and, as such, are generally not the ones desired by the family and community. In that sense, educators could be held accountable for the development of emotional tendencies which were not wanted and are considered negative.

Parallel with the growth of interest by administrators and legislators in the accountability concept has been a growth of concern by teachers for teaching affective domain objectives (mostly GO's). In part, the concern of teachers about affective domain objectives could reflect a sincere desire to help students develop those attitudes, values, and/or beliefs which are commonly held and considered desirable by the home, community, and other educators. As such, there would be no accountability problems because accountability in the affective domain is only concerned with the development of negative emotional tendencies. Hopefully, teachers who are sincere about students developing positive emotional tendencies are also concerned about students learning the required SO's in the cognitive and sensory domains. There are some teachers who either know or suspect that they are not very successful teachers in the cognitive and sensory domains. To avoid accountability, they try to claim that affective learning is much more important than the other domains and concentrate their efforts in teaching affective learning which they hope is less amenable to measurement. If affective learning is really more important, then the sad part is that these teachers who are not very effective in teaching cognitive and sensory objectives now want to teach in the affective area. Even if these teachers are ineffective in teaching affective objectives, as long as they don't develop negative emotional tendencies, they may escape accountability.

> NOTE: Since affective SO's are created indirectly as a result of experiences, students who are having trouble learning cognitive and sensory SO's will probably develop negative attitudes and values. Students who are successful in learning cognitive and sensory SO's will probably develop positive attitudes and values. Therefore, teachers who run into accountability problems because they are ineffective in helping students learn cognitive and sensory SO's may also run into accountability problems in the affective domain because their students will probably develop negative emotional tendencies.

Another small group of teachers want to teach in the affective domain because they want to inculcate the students with their own ideas which may be in conflict with those commonly held by the students' family and community. When a child is born, he or she does not have any preset bundle of attitudes, values, and beliefs. Whatever emotional tendencies a child has have been acquired since birth. It is relatively easy to establish certain attitudes, values, and beliefs when there are no previous ones to interfere with the learning event. Once a person develops certain attitudes, values, and beliefs, it is much harder to change them. As such, if teachers could get students early enough, they could develop in their students almost any combination of emotional tendencies. This is what makes accountability in the affective domain very critical. If a child is taught affective objectives which are in conflict with those held by his or her parents, peer groups, community, and/or country, the child will be destined for trouble.

The greater the degree of heterogeneity with respect to emotional tendencies between students and their families and community, the greater the potential for internal conflict and destruction of the family unit, the community, and eventually our society. The greater the degree of homogeneity between students and their families and community, the greater the potential for internal strengthening of the family, community, and our society. The greater the differences between the commonly held emotional tendencies of one group and those of a surrounding or nearby group, the greater the potential for conflict between the two groups and the greater the internal strength of each group. To let teachers develop emotional tendencies in students that are in direct conflict with those of their parents and community is to let teachers have the potential of destroying our society as we know it. To purposely teach conflicting emotional tendencies is to purposely develop unhappiness for all concerned and as such is an educational malpractice and the teachers should be held accountable for creating the problem.

This does not mean that everyone should have the exact same set of emotional tendencies. However, if our families, communities, and nation want to survive, it is critical and necessary that there be some commonality of values. In other words, there must be a minimum common core of affective SO's at the national level, a few more in common at the regional or state level, and a few more in common at the community level. Beyond that minimum common core level, there may be some emotional tendencies held by others, and there may be some emotional tendencies which are in conflict with those held by others. To minimize conflict, students should be taught how to cope with situations where conflict of emotional tendencies could cause problems.

Since parents and society have a responsibility to their children and to support the schools that teach their children, it should be reasonable to expect the children and schools to have a responsibility to the parents and society and support some common set of emotional tendencies and not to purposely bring about internal conflict and destruction of the family and/or society.

d. NEW CURRICULUM AREAS FOR ACCOUNTABILITY

Not only is it important for students to learn how to cope with other people who have different emotional tendencies, but it is important for each student to learn how to guide the development of emotional tendencies the student might want. Some of the guidelines (objectives) are:

1. to be able to identify efforts by *others* to instill emotional tendencies or to change existing emotional tendencies;

2. to be able to identify what emotional tendencies the *others* are trying to instill or change;

3. to be able to evaluate the desirability of the emotional tendencies that *others* are trying to instill or change in them, i.e.,

    a. how will having that emotional tendency affect my life, my relationship with friends and others?

    b. is the emotional tendency in conflict with an existing emotional tendency?

1) (the greater the internal conflict in emotional tendencies, the greater the probability for internal stress affecting the person's intellectual, physical, and emotional being.)

2) (the greater the internal agreement in emotional tendencies, the greater the probability for internal strength and stability.);

4. to be able to make decisions about emotional tendencies based on self evaluation; and

5. to be able to resist efforts by *others* to instill undesirable emotional tendencies or to change existing emotional tendencies which are desirable and compatible with a persons' social community into emotional tendencies which are undesirable and non-compatible with the person's social community.

As the working person's work week is reduced, as more and more labor saving devices are utilized in the home, and as people are starting work later in life and retiring earlier, it is also becoming more important for people to learn by design how to best utilize their leisure time. This suggestion should not be construed to mean that I am suggesting everyone should do the same thing during their leisure time. Everyone should be free to select their own leisure time activities. However, if a person has never heard of a certain activity, he or she would never try it. Also, for most people, if they can't do something well, they probably won't want to do it. Therefore, the objective of leisure time training should be to introduce each student to a variety of activities in a variety of categories and then let the student select activities that he or she wants to become proficient in. Every person should have one or more leisure time activities that he or she can enjoy and do well. Too often music, the arts, and sports are only taught to those students who are gifted and only to a minority of any one student body. In addition to the usual activities in this category, landscaping could be taught, as many men and women enjoy working around their homes during their leisure time. The problem is that most people learn landscaping by trial and error rather than by design.

Another area that is critical concerns the raising of a family. It is fantastic to think of the millions of young families that have to learn independently what it is like to raise a child. There is no need for this and it is a tremendous waste of time, effort, and emotional energy to have each couple reinvent the *wheel* of how to raise a child. This does not mean that some teacher should tell students that there is only one way to raise a child. However, it is reasonable to acquaint students with the probable results of different types of techniques and how these techniques may interact with different personality types and environments.

A recent area to be introduced into some schools concerns consumer education. A portion of this area (or in another course) should be devoted to a person's legal rights as a consumer. Everyone needs to know some things about their legal rights and responsibilities as a citizen in our society because everyone becomes involved in legal oriented situations throughout life.

However, the most important area may well be learning how to get along with your fellow person. If the homes and/or religious groups can do it, great! But if they are not successful, then professional instructors have the responsibility to help each student learn how to get along with others. During the past decade in business and industry (as stated earlier) more people have lost or quit their jobs because they couldn't get along with their fellow workers than have lost or quit their jobs because they were incompetent on the job. Although, a good part of this area concerns cognitive and sensory objectives, a major part is in the affective domain and as such, this area has to be taught differently than the usual academic subjects. Remember, the affective domain has to be taught and learned indirectly. A critical part of this course would have to include a study of self and a study of interaction with others. As a part of learning how to best interact with others, it should be basic to learn about *internal politics*. This term does not refer to political parties, but does refer to the internal politics of almost every social group, public or private institution, and practically every working situation where there are two or more people working. Millions of people have lost their jobs or have become unhappy with their job because they didn't understand the internal politics of the organization they were working for.

A possible area to be considered is the concept of *futurizing* in which teachers use historian type methods to identify existing trends in their subject area and then predict changes in their fields. In light of these possible changes, the teachers would teach SO's which might be appropriate and would avoid the students having to learn obsolete things. Students should also be taught to *futurize* about their own life directions based on a maximum of facts and a minimum of emotional opinions. As a part of this area, every career oriented program should be required to keep students posted as to the future employment possibilities in that particular career field. As it is now, any efforts in this direction usually result in opening up or closing down the sizes of the entering classes. Under the above proposal, there would be no limitation on the number of students wanting to major in a particular field, but the students would know ahead of time what their chances would be for employment in their chosen field. If a student wanted to study in a field in which the employment possibilities were low, he or she may decide to take a double major: one that he or she hopes to ultimately work in and the other to earn a living until opportunities in the preferred field open up.

e. ACCOUNTABILITY AND COMMERCIALLY PREPARED INSTRUCTIONAL MATERIALS

The training divisions of many business and industrial companies have used and are using high *quality control* instructional materials in their own instructional activities and as such, it should not be surprising that commercial companies should want to get into the $100 billion dollar educational market. At the same time, many educators who have not specified their own course SO's are asking companies that produce educational materials to produce evidence that the materials have been *learner verified* (tried out and perfected on samples of students from the potential audience of the materials). Surveys of various teacher groups as to what their major problems are in the teaching-learning environment, indicate that near the top of any list is the need for more effective and efficient instructional materials. In an effort to aid this problem, the Educational Products Information Exchange (EPIE) Institute was funded to test out educational materials and equipment. Their efforts have reached the same conclusion that various teacher groups have and that is that there is a shortage of *learner verified* materials and as the teacher groups have done, EPIE has blamed the companies that produce these materials. The problem is serious enough that it should be discussed.

Consider for a moment, the paradox facing these companies. They could all identify SO's for all of their educational materials and they could all go through the learner verification process to maximize the learning of *their SO's*. But, what if *their SO's* don't match the identified or implied SO's and/or GO's of the states, school districts, and teachers who might adopt or use their materials? When teachers and curriculum groups really don't know specifically what they want students to learn, it is easier to reject materials which have specified objectives. There are hundreds of SO's that could be listed for almost any set of materials depending upon what is wanted (the GO's). Therefore, once a company lists some SO's which could be learned and then proves that the materials are effective and efficient in teaching those SO's, the company also limits the market for the materials.

A common complaint of educators who are anti-systems and against the use of commercially prepared materials which have a list of SO's and are learner verified is that they object to any company dictating what the teachers should teach and the students should learn. They are right, it is the responsibility of teachers and curriculum groups to identify what should be taught and learned particularly in reference to the minimum common core SO's. Once the teachers identify the minimum common core SO's to be learned nationally, state wide, and/or district wide, I'm sure companies will be glad to develop materials and verify their effectiveness and efficiency with students because the *learner verification* process will now qualify their materials for purchase.

For those companies that distribute nationally, they will probably develop basic instructional materials for a variety of courses which will be designed to teach the national minimum common core SO's in those courses and then a series of supplemental instructional materials which will teach the extra SO's in the various state minimum common core SO's for those courses and even for the extra SO's for those courses in large school districts (colleges or universities). Companies should be held accountable for the effectiveness and efficiency of their materials, *BUT* only in reference to the SO's identified by teachers and/or curriculum groups as being the minimum common core SO's for that particular course or unit. Teachers, not the companies, have the primary responsibility.

4. TEACHERS' FEAR OF ACCOUNTABILITY

Teachers who fear accountability generally fall into one or more of seven categories even though they may use similar arguments in their attacks against the accountability concept. Therefore, I will discuss first the five types of teachers who appear to fear accountability and then some of the major or most often cited reasons for being against accountability. An important point to keep in mind is that many teachers welcome the accountability concept and many others are so busy helping students learn and are sufficiently confident of their ability to teach that they are unconcerned about whether or not the accountability concept is part of the instructional scene. Of those teachers who fear accountability, they range from being slightly fearful of the concept to those who have developed almost a paranoic attitude towards the concept of accountability. Some of the teachers in the latter group exhibit some tendencies towards megalomania in which they put forth fantastic amounts of energy in research projects and/or in writing articles and books trying to evade the inevitable day of accountability. Over 30 states have already passed legislation concerning educational accountability and almost all of the other states are studying or preparing similar legislation.

The first category of teachers who fear accountability are those who are afraid that the results will show that they are unable to teach (as measured in terms of student learning instead of the traditional view which would be in terms of their ability to present course content, degrees earned, publications, seniority, etc.). As pointed out in my book, *Educational Malpractices: The Big Gamble In Our Schools,* one of the two major sources of most of the problems in present day education are the teacher-training institutions. The major emphasis in the vast majority of these institutions is on *teaching* as measured by ability to present course content, to control or manage the classroom, and to manipulate groups. In a few institutions, there is a minor and once in awhile a major emphasis on *teaching* as measured by whether or not students are learning — accountability. In the seminars and workshops which I have conducted, I have asked over 200,000 teachers, *How many were evaluated during their practice teaching experience on the basis of whether or not the students they were teaching were learning successfully the objectives of their practice teaching unit?* In groups ranging from 20 to 6,000 teachers, from zero to about five percent have indicated that they had been evaluated on the basis of student learning. Once student-teachers graduate and become professional teachers in elementary and secondary schools, it is even rarer that any teacher is evaluated by an administrator on the basis of whether or not their students are learning. No wonder that many teachers are afraid. The rules of the game (evaluation) are being changed in the middle of the game.

In the case of college and university teachers, the problem is even more fearful because most of them haven't even had any training at all in teaching and testing. Their main hope is to maintain the superior air as if they knew what they were doing and hope that no one pushes the concept of accountability in higher education. After all, if accountability makes sense in elementary and secondary education, why not in higher education.

> NOTE: Actually, there are a number of teachers in higher education who are already trying to be accountable for student learning. For most of these teachers, it has been an asset rather than a detriment not to have had any professional education courses because too many of these courses promote negative teaching practices. Yet, many of these teachers feel guilty because they haven't had any specialized training in how to teach (help students learn) and test (diagnose learning problems).

Compounding this problem is a very basic fault in education today which is that few teachers have identified what it is they want students to learn — specific and general objectives. Teachers who have never been taught how to help students learn and have never previously been evaluated on the criterion of student learning, also realize that they don't really know what it is their students should be learning or how administrators are going to evaluate this unknown learning. This situation would frighten almost anyone.

As a part of the problems associated with this category, for a teacher to find out that an ineffective teaching-learning situation is primarily the result of an ineffective teacher ends up putting a heavy load of responsibility on the teacher's shoulders. No longer will the teacher be able to place the blame solely on the students. For the humanist teacher, a heavy burden of guilt develops the realization that most or all of the students that the teacher had graded low or failed over the past years could have made it through with higher achievement levels and grades if the teacher had known how to teach (help students learn). It is so much easier to blame the students, their parents, their environment, the school administrators, etc. For some teachers, finding out that they can't teach (help students learn) as well as some of their colleagues will be a shock to their ego.

Actually most teachers do have specific objectives — their test items. Since test items, criteria for evaluating essays, etc. are what affect grades, they are the objectives which students want to learn. If teachers can accept this fact, then half of the problem is solved. Admittedly, many test items and criteria for grading essays and projects may not be very good, but once teachers recognize that their testing and evaluation items are the true objectives of their courses, they'll eliminate the trash.

Concerning the second part of the problem, since most teachers are not trained or hired on the basis of their being able to help students learn, it is the duty and responsibility of administrators to provide help and training for the teachers who need it. This can be done through in-service sessions and the development of an *Instructional Crisis Squad* which would consist of a librarian, audiovisual specialist, counseling and/or guidance person, reading specialist, and one or more teachers who are or have been successful in helping students learn. When an administrator identifies that a particular teacher is having trouble in teaching (helping each student learn), then the administrator sends the *Instructional Crisis Squad* to help the teacher. Just as students need successful learning experiences to develop a positive self-image, so do teachers need successful teaching experiences (helping students learn) in order to develop positive self-images which are free from the fear that they are not able to teach!

A second category of teachers who fear accountability are those that believe that some or most students' learning levels are predetermined and there is nothing that a teacher can do about it. One of the most serious inhumanities committed against students by educators at all levels concerns the definitions of two words: ability and capacity. *Ability* is easily defined as the quality or state of being able to perform (Physically or mentally) or the natural talent or *acquired proficiency (learning)* to perform. The problem comes in the definitions of capa-

city. The primary definition concerns the concepts of limit and volume. The secondary definition tends to make *capacity* a synonym for *ability*. As a result, in many situations, *ability* and *capacity* are used interchangeably because of the similarity in the general definition for *ability* and the secondary definition for *capacity*. But in reading these words and also in using these words, most people tend to think of the two words as synonyms from the point of view of the primary definition of *capacity*. In other words, whereas *ability* refers to a natural or *learned* quality (level of ability can be increased by learning), *capacity* refers to a limit (a point beyond which it is impossible to go — one can't put six gallons in a five-gallon can). As a result of this confusion, once educators, psychologists, and others identify that certain students have or don't have certain abilities, this is interpreted as indicating different capacities (limits — no further learning possible) instead of different capacities (abilities — able to increase by learning). To help clarify this problem, think of *ability* as referring to how children learn and *capacity* as referring to how *much* children can learn. With reference to the latter, it will also be helpful to know that I do not know of anyone anywhere in our world that has succeeded in identifying the 100 percent full capacity of the human mind and neither does anyone of the over 100,000 educators I have talked to. In short, educators, psychologists, or anyone else who uses the word *capacity* has to be referring to abilities which are in part natural talent and in part learned abilities. Since no one knows what the full capacity (limits) of the human mind is, no one can say and defend that any one person or group (racial or otherwise) has less capacity (limits) than some one else with out falling into the semantic trap of measuring capacity (abilities) and then refer to the results in terms of capacity (limits).

As an example of an extension of this confusion in definitions, consider the *nature-nurture* controversy which has been debated for decades. The *nature-nurture* theory states that heredity sets the absolute capacity (limits) as to what it is possible for one to do or become, while the environment sets the capacity (limits) as to what one actually does with the inborn equipment that he or she received through biological inheritance. Obviously, this theory is based on the primary definition of capacity (limits) and as such indicates that it is possible to reach a static state mentally and physically in which no more learning can take place — an extremely inhumane point-of-view and improbable situation. From the point-of-view of the secondary definition of capacity (abilities) the nature-nurture theory sounds dynamic, exciting, and humane, i.e., the theory states that heredity gives a person certain natural talents or capacity (abilities), while the environment controls which of these abilities are developed and utilized and which other abilities are learned and developed.

Intelligence tests are often defined as mental capacity (limits) tests, yet in actuality, these tests are only testing the individual's capacity (ability) to answer or perform the intelligence test at that particular time. Many intelligence tests are primarily testing verbal ability (not limits) and as long as schools don't really teach verbal ability by design, the I.Q. scores will remain essentially constant (when corrected for chronological age) and consequently were believed to represent natures contribution. During the late 1950's and throughout the 1960's, many different projects have been conducted in which verbal ability has been taught directly or indirectly and I.Q. scores for individual student participants have been raised as high as 30 points. Obviously, the verbal ability which is being tested includes not only nature's contribution but also nurture's contribution. In line with the definition of capacity (limits) in I.Q. testing, notice the static categories: genius, superior, average, educable, trainable, high-grade moron, etc. Using the definition of capacity (ability), regardless of whether it is ability based on nature, nurture, or both, the concept of limits will have to be deleted from the achievement categories. The new categories might be genius ability (can help others learn), superior ability (independent learner), average ability (needs some help from teacher), below average ability (needs frequent help from teacher), low ability (needs constant help from teacher), etc. Under the concept of capacity (ability) rather than capacity (limits), students in lower achievement categories can move up into higher categories.

Most teachers make statements concerning whether or not students are learning to capacity. Are these teachers talking about *limits* or *abilities?* If they are referring to limits, remember that no one knows what these limits are, so in a way, no one is working or learning up to his or her limit. If these teachers are referring to abilities, are these a result of nature, nurture, or both? If nurture or both, maybe the reason why a student isn't learning to capacity (ability) is because the teacher isn't nurturing (teaching)!

This same confusion in definitions has also put Arthur Jensen of the University of California at Berkeley and William Shockly of Stanford University in the newspaper headlines. Both of these men are claiming that there are racial differences in intelligence and these claims are backed up by tests that supposedly measure capacity (limits). What is interesting, but very sad and inhumane in its effects, is that Jensen and Shockly are saying publicly what a majority of educators and psychologists also believe by their actions with students. In many schools throughout the United States and Canada, there are efforts to group students according to ability in which the educators are equating ability to capacity (limits). In addition, at every single seminar, conference, workshop, or class which I have conducted or attended, sooner or later one or more educators have made statements regarding their students which indicate their belief in racial differences in mental capacity (limits). The slight difference between what Jensen and Shockly are saying and what most other teachers are saying is that Jensen and Shockly are very open in their use of the word *racial* in talking about these differences whereas other educators are not quite that open in their use of the word *racial* but somehow in setting up the various *ability* groupings based on standardized tests, these groupings all too often follow *racial* lines. Almost anyone who has been exposed to other cultures beyond a brief glimpse, should be willing to attest to the fact that different cultures *nurture* different abilities. It should follow then that on intelligence tests which test capacities (abilities) that certain cultural or racial groups would score consistently higher or lower than other groups. If the identified abilities could be defended as desirable and necessary to be successful in our society, then it also follows that arrangements should be made to *nurture* by design any inadequate abilities until they are adequate. One should keep in mind that almost every cultural or racial group have nurtured certain abilities which may be very useful to everyone in our society. If anyone in reading or listening to Jensen's or Shockly's statements would substitute the word *ability* every time they use the word capacity (limit), then what they are saying is not so radical.

From the point of view of educators, it is so much easier on their conscience to believe that a student's inability to learn is a problem of capacity (limits) because there is nothing that they or anyone else can do. To accept that a student's inability to learn is a problem of capacity (ability), then conscientious educators would be bothered by the possibilities that maybe they didn't *nurture* the inadequate abilities sufficiently for learning to take place or that maybe they should have tried other instructional methods and materials that were more in tune with the learner's present abilities such that the same objectives could have been learned. The percentage of students that learn and the percentage of objectives that the students learn is determined by the willingness, persistence, and capacity (ability) of the teacher to solve students' learning problems. [It is assumed that teachers don't have a problem with capacity (limits) in solving learning problems.]

What complicates this problem is a concept developed by Merton and others, *the self-fulfilling prophecy*, in which if teachers, parents, the students themselves, and others believe that certain students are capable (limits) of only learning so much, that is about as much as the students will learn. If teachers-to-be are taught that they will get only a normal curve's worth of learning in their classrooms, this is what will happen and when it does, the teachers believe it is normal that most students can't achieve "A" or "B" worth of their courses. Curve grading has been used for decades in education and almost all teachers use some form of curve grading — a design for non-learning! Under the concept of accountability, it will no longer be acceptable for a majority of the students to learn 75 percent or less of a course ("C". "D". or "F's" worth of a course).

> NOTE: Under the traditional approach to education, in which tests were designed specifically so that only a few students could get an "A" or "B", Phi Beta Kappa assumed that tests were honest and actually tested learning capacity (limits). Under the accountability concept and as more and more educators recognize that identified learning capacity (abilities) can be changed, probably 90 percent or more of the students can become "A" or "B" students. Of interest is that officials of Phi Beta Kappa look on this new trend as lowering the standards of academia. It is a sad commentary on our society when an honorary educational organization dedicated to excellence in learning is upset because more students are becoming successful by learning more of what they are supposed to be learning in their courses. This elitist attitude is fostered and maintained by the belief in learning capacities (limits).

To make sure that readers do not misunderstand what I am saying, I am not saying that students don't have different abilities. What I am saying is that different abilities to learn dictate how a student learns most effectively and efficiently. Different abilities to learn *do not dictate* WHAT or HOW MUCH a student can learn. Since any one ability is part nature and part nurture, what is lacking in nature, can in most cases, be made up by nurture — if teachers are willing to nurture (teach) by design. Consider the following analogy. In any family of three or more children, the children have different abilities to get well. The children do not all get well from the same prescription, the same treatment, and in the same amount of time. It would be the rare parents that when one of their children got sick that they would try one remedy and if it didn't work, they would assume that the child couldn't get well and that nothing else would work either so the child would just have to remain sick or die. It is standard practice in the medical field if one treatment doesn't work, for the doctor to try another one and if that doesn't work, the doctor tries another one, etc. Different abilities to get well only dictate the need for a variety of treatments to fit the different abilities.

In education, teachers have to start assuming that students can learn and non-learning is treated as a learning problem which can be solved. As educators, if we really believe in individual differences, then we will have to stop expecting all students to learn the same way, using the same materials, and in the same amount of time.

NOTE: Throughout educational research, there is a preoccupation with trying to find one method that will work for everyone which completely contradicts the avowed belief in the existence of individual differences.

There is no need to be afraid of accountability from the point of view that the students' learning levels are predetermined and there is nothing that a teacher can do about it. There is no such thing as a limit to learning and there are many things a teacher can do to facilitate and increase learning.

A third category of teachers who tend to fear accountability are those who not only believe that teachers can't affect learning and that students have predetermined learning levels regardless of teacher efforts but they also accept the belief that the whole school environment is of little value. This category usually cite Illich's *Deschooling Society,* one or more authors such as Holt & Postman who have ideas similar to Illich, and/or Christopher Jencks whose research has indicated that schools have little effect on student learning. Illich wants to get rid of all schools as they presently exist and set up centers of resource materials and people in which students can learn what they want to rather than what and when society wants them to. The problems with this point of view is that Illich's solution assumes:

1. That trial and error self-learning is the best way. He feels that there is a value in reinventing the *wheel* and that there are no values, knowledge, etc. that is of sufficient value to hand down to the next generation and to make sure they learn it.

2. He assumes that there is no one thing that anyone should learn — like reading, speaking, basic math, telling time, communicating to others, how to get and hold a job, how to get along with other human beings, etc.

3. Although he says that *learning is the human activity which least needs manipulation,* he in turn wants to set up resource centers and have resource people available. Since it would be impossible to make everything in the world available and make each concept and thing equally accessible, even Illich would have to select which things and masters to make available and in so doing he himself is manipulating *learning* by making some things and people available and others not so available.

4. He assumes that all students are able to learn on an independent study basis at his resource centers, like how to use books, computers, films, etc. if he doesn't assume this and someone is expected to teach the students how to read, how to use computers, etc. then Illich himself is manipulating learning.

5. If learning is going to take place by chance, if at all, and there is nothing specific that is worth learning, where is the money going to come from to pay for all the materials? I can't believe that taxpayers will support Illich's form of self-selected learning without wanting some kind of results as a return for their investment.

6. In Illich's solution, where the young learner is assumed to know more about his or her learning needs to exist in our society than adults do, this also assumes that we are born all intelligent and slowly regress until we die ignorant. I can't accept this point-of-view. To accept this view would mean that instead of self-learning, the students would actually be involved in self-unlearning because to learn means to most people that a learner has gained something he or she didn't know before. In any series of learning events whether by trial and error, out of school, or in school, the one who has successfully learned whatever was available to learn in all of the learning events knows more than the one who is just starting.

Although Holt, Postman, and others in this category want to get rid of all objectives, tests, classes, courses, and administrators, they don't want to get rid of teachers and their salaries — only all of the teachers' responsibilities (hence no chance for accountability). This is the *do your own thing* group where not only students do what they feel like doing, but the teachers also are free to do anything or nothing. It is a nice dream and I'm sure a lot of people would love getting paid $10,000 to $30,000 and not have to do anything to earn it. This group also includes teachers who may just be lazy and don't want to work or to be held accountable (hopefully few in number). Any efforts to analyze, organize, or synthesize the instructional process for these teachers will be met with resistance as these efforts make responsibility and accountability possible. As mentioned before, teachers who promote the *Do your own thing* philosophy, are self-oriented and are doing a disservice to the students by implying that selfism is more important than thinking of others. As might be expected, almost all of the educators who are anti-specific objectives (also anti-accountability) actually describe objectives in their own articles and books which they think all students should learn, i.e., *all students should learn the inquiry method* (Postman).

A fourth category of teachers who fear accountability consists of those who have been indoctrinated by their colleagues, peer groups, and/or teacher groups that accountability is wrong. These teachers accept the opinions of their colleagues without further thought of their own. Both the National Education Association (NEA) and the American Federation of Teachers (AFT) have come out against accountability. As members of either organization, many teachers may accept the statements of their fellow members and/or of the union officials because they believe in them and because they are possibly looking for an excuse to escape accountability too. In teacher associations where the official position is to be against accountability, teachers who may be in favor of it would tend not to say too much in favor of accountability. Both NEA and AFT have referred to accountability as a business — industrial model and as such is not appropriate for education. (Note that the union model also comes from business and industry — sort of a *pot calling the kettle black.*) A NEA report in 1973 referred to the current approaches to accountability as being simplistic and results in victimization of pupils and teachers through punitive, ill-conceived and probably inoperative legislation. The NEA report stated that a continuation of the trend towards accountability can lead to a closed system and educational fascism by compelling, constraining, and coercing educators and students to comply with inhumane, arbitrarily set requirements! (Notice the emotional content of this last statement.)

Consider for a moment, the present situation in most classrooms where students are *compelled, constrained, and coerced into complying with arbitrarily set requirements* in order to pass their courses. Whereas the present course and unit requirements are generally hidden from the students, at least under accountability, students, parents, teachers, and administrators would know what should be learned.

Consider for a moment the situation in which teachers are striking on a *if you don't give us what we want — no school* basis where parents, taxpayers, and administrators are *compelled, constrained, and coerced into complying with arbitrarily set requirements!*

> NOTE: Webster's Dictionary defines *fascism* as any program for setting up a centralized autocratic national regime with severely nationalistic policies, exercising regimentation of industry, commerce, and finance, rigid censorship and forcible suppression of opposition. Also, any tendency towards or actual exercise of severe autocratic or dictatorial control (as over others within an organization).

If NEA and AFT merge such that the one person who leads the union has control over what millions of teachers do, what tens of millions of students learn, and what all the taxpayers have to pay without any responsibility to the students, parents, or taxpayers. I wonder which group is operating closer to fascism; the other-oriented group who through accountability wants the teachers to show responsibility towards their students, parents, and taxpayers or the self-oriented group who wants the teachers to only show responsibility towards themselves, their fellow members, and the central union office.

Of interest is that in spite of the fact that multi-millions of dollars have been added to costs of education throughout the country in order to *improve the quality of instruction* via smaller classes, lighter teaching loads, increased salaries, etc., 150 representatives of NEA and AFT in a meeting with the U.S. Office of Education and CAP (Cooperative Accountability Project) agreed that standardized test scores should not be used to evaluate teacher competence because there are too many factors affecting learning which are external to the school and beyond control! If *improvement of instructional quality* can be defined as *helping more students learn more*, then this meeting of NEA, AFT, USOE, and CAP have agreed that teachers can't be held accountable for levels of student learning or instructional quality because *the factors affecting learning are beyond their control.* If teachers can't control instructional quality or student learning (as stated by the teacher organizations, USOE, and CAP) then it should seem reasonable that teachers shouldn't request nor be granted changes which are claimed to affect instructional quality, i.e., smaller classes, lighter teaching loads, etc. It does not stand the test of reason and logic to request changes in teaching conditions because the changes will improve (control) levels of instructional quality and learning and then when the changes are made, to claim that levels of instructional quality and learning are beyond the teachers control and that they should not be held accountable!

Among the teachers in this group are some who may or may not be personally against accountability. Their anti-accountability statements are made more for political reasons to influence other teachers than for personal reasons. These are teachers who are more interested in the teacher organizational or union movement than they are in student learning.

When accountability is used negatively to fail students, to fire teachers, or to replace administrators, I would have to be cautious about utilizing the concept. On the other hand, when accountability is used positively such that it is used to diagnose, prescribe, and reward, I find it hard to understand why anyone would be against it. The concept can be used to help learners learn more; help teachers be better teachers, earn more money, and be more professional; help administrators be better administrators; and help the whole instructional process become more effective and efficient. Actually, once the desired and required learning is specified, and that becomes the primary basis for positive accountability, teachers will have a freedom like they have never had or ever imagined. As long as the teachers can prove that their students have learned what they are supposed to, both students and teachers shoud be free to *do their thing.* Under positive accountability, the present arbitrary criteria for teacher evaluation which is non-related to student learning will be eliminated. Teachers and administrators will have opportunities under positive accountability to become truly professional.

The fifth category of teachers who fear accountability or are more likely just anti-accountability are teachers who honestly feel that the concept would have a negative effect on education. These teachers are usually very traditional and anything that tends to change educational traditions should be resisted. There are a number of reasons which are referred to by these teachers, but there are only a few that are most commonly cited.

The most common argument equates accountability with mechanism, engineering, the business-industrial model, and/or the behaviorist model. Since the definition of mechanism among other things refers to a process or technique for achieving a predesigned result through a cooperative effort, the association of mechanism with accountability may not be so bad at all! Engineering refers to the designing or production of something using reasonable, rational, and/or scientific methods. In contrast to a random or chance approach to something as important as learning (education), engineering or designing the instructional process can't be that bad if it helps the learning process be more effective, efficient, and less random such that more students are more successful in achieving what is necessary to live fully and enjoy the *good life* in our society!

At the present time, where students get the same treatment for the same amount of time, the teachers are already in sort of a factory model. Negotiations and teacher contracts want teachers to be paid the same, to have the same teaching load, to teach the same number of students regardless of the individual differences of the teachers. However, because of the individual differences in the students which are presently ignored, the results of the present educational process are very un-factory like. In fact, if any business or industry was as ineffective and inefficient as the educational process, the company would go out of business in a very short time. Whereas *quality control* and *zero defect* are common terms in reference to the products of factories, the average traditional school turns out students where the majority have learned "C" worth or less of what they were supposed to learn. If applying the *industrial model* helps more students learn more, can it be bad?

NOTE: Because of individual differences, in order to get all or most students to learn 100 percent of the required SO's, the teachers will have to be very flexible and creative and very few students will learn from exactly the same treatment and for the same length of time. Actually, under accountability, there will be much less uniformity than there is now under the traditional approach.

As mentioned earlier, just because the only way to measure learning is indirect and is based on what students *do* or how they *behave*, it should not be assumed that a behavioristic model was used. Actually, under positive accountability, the process of how a student learns is very open. If a teacher uses a behavioristic model and it works, great. If a teacher uses a process model which is in direct opposition to the behavioristic model and it works in helping students learn, then it is also a great situation. If a teacher hangs upside down from the ceiling and chants mystical sounds and this somehow helps students learn what they need to learn, this method is also great (for that teacher). The behavioral emphasis is on how learning achievement is demonstrated and is not concerned with the process of how something is learned unless learning the process is the objective to be learned.

Another common complaint is that accountability will narrow and limit learning and creativity. Actually, by making sure that all students learn the minimum common core SO's of basic courses, students will be able to learn much more. Many of the anti-accountability teachers look on chance and serendipitous learning as something good. If true, it should be remembered that chance and serendipitous learning occurs most frequently and with higher probability in the *prepared mind.*

5. ENTROPIC DRIFT AND THE TRANSPOSITION OF CONTROLLING INFLUENCES

I think Robert Hawley originated the term *entropic drift*. I found it to be very descriptive of a critical problem in education and hence useful in communicating about the problem. My definition for *entropic drift* may be slightly different from Hawley's definition, but my use of the term is in the same sense as Hawley used it in his booklet, **Human Values in the Classroom.** Hawley illustrates *entropic drift* as occurring when certain aspects of the man's values become false end values. For example, consider the desirable end value that religious expression is an important part of human existence. The means for this is usually achieved by attending some sort of church or temple. Entropic drift occurs when the false end value or objective becomes *attend church or a temple* regardless of the religious expression which may or may not occur. For another example, consider the desirable end value that everyone should understand your fellow man. One of the means for this could be to read literature. Entropic drift occurs when the false end value or objective becomes *read a specific novel, short story, or poem* regardless of whether or not you understand your fellow man any better as a result of the reading.

Entropic Drift refers to a situation where there is a relatively high level of uncertainty (entropy). In human beings, this condition results in efforts to reduce the uncertainty. In the process, means values are substituted for ends values.

In educational situations where the goals or ends values are GO's (non-measurable) and there are few, if any, SO's which are measurable, there is a strong tendency to invert the goals and means such that the means becomes the goals or ends. Sociologists refer to this situation as *goal displacement.*

In general, there are three types of evaluations in education: presage (predictors), process, and product evaluations. As long as the descriptions of the product remain in terms of GO's and are non-measurable, there will be a continued emphasis on the means or process and to a degree on presage or input evaluation. As mentioned earlier, presage or input measurements include grades in previous courses, ACT and SAT scores, IQ scores, degrees, years of experience, etc. In the traditional approach towards the educational process, evaluative descriptions emphasize time in school, in programs, and in courses, i.e., two years of English, four years of mathematics, three years of a foreign language, etc. To keep track of multiple courses, the concept of credits and/or units becomes useful, i.e., a high school diploma represents about twelve years during which so many units of English, mathematics, science, etc. are taken; degrees represent a certain number of credits of which a certain number have to be in certain areas.

Since the assumed and/or implied goal of education is learning and it is rather obvious that using descriptions of the educational process i.e., two years of English, as an evaluation tool doesn't indicate individual differences in achievement, teachers who are in charge of the process make up tests, projects, essays, etc. (which may or may not have any relationship with the unspecified goals of the process) in order to try to relate the process to learning and to indicate differences in achievement. Again, since the goals are not specified, uncertainty arises as to the meaning of the results of the tests used during the process in reference to the GO's. As a result of this uncertainty, some teachers reduce or eliminate any testing, or downgrade the importance of the tests (even though the results of the tests affect students' grades). Other teachers look at presage evaluation as predictors of how students will achieve and design tests which parallel the presage evaluation (curve grading) so that when the results are similar, the teachers can reduce their uncertainty about the relationship between the process evaluation and the goals of the process. A common problem in this is the effect of the *self-fulfilling prophecies* of presage evaluation, i.e., if the student is about average according to presage evaluation instruments, then *obviously* the student should only be an average or "C" student according to process evaluation instruments.

NOTE: Even those teachers who have or want to eliminate any evaluation or who downgrade the importance of the results of any evaluation, still want the students to go through the process. So the process has still become the objective for these teachers. For some of these teachers, eliminating all evaluation actually increases uncertainty and as such the next step becomes one in which *deschooling* becomes the only way to reduce uncertainty. However, deschooling is in conflict with the teachers' desire to make a living. The easiest way to solve this dilemma is to stop worrying about student learning and concentrate on self: increase salary and fringe benefits, decrease workload and student contact (as it concerns learning), and avoid any accountability for student learning as it increases uncertainty.

With an emphasis on time rather than specific learning and with no requirements as to levels of learning, students have been able to obtain diplomas and degrees with wide variations in knowledge and skills ranging from practically nothing to very high levels. Since in most schools, the learning associated with certain courses has never been specified, it has become difficult to defend the need for many courses particularly in a society where premissiveness has become almost the norm. As a result, fewer and fewer courses are required. The whole situation in education has been and is developing more and more uncertainty (entropy), so it should be expected that many parents, taxpayers, and non-educators would be in favor of some sort of accountability in terms of the product of the educational process. Particularly, when it is so obvious that the costs of a faulty educational process, i.e., unemployment, welfare, crime, etc., are borne by the same sources that support the process (a fact supported by the reports of various national study groups). A reduction of uncertainty will occur when certification carries with it guaranteed levels of competancy.

As a result of entropic drift, another more serious problem occurs in the transposition of the dominating or controlling influences. In an ideal instructional situation, it should be easily agreed upon that the learners' needs should be the dominant influence controlling the instructional process. However, in the traditional situation where learning has not been specified and entropic drift has changed the emphasis from the product to the process, the controlling influence has changed almost from the start from the students who would have benefited from the product to the teachers who control and dominate the process. Whereas originally, teachers were hired to serve the needs of the students, entropic drift and the accompanying transposition of the controlling influence changed the situation around such that the students are serving the teacher and doing whatever the teacher decides should be in the educational process (regardless of whether or not the process activities related to the non-specified goals).

In a like manner, in schools where two or more teachers were teaching, administrators were originally hired to help the teachers facilitate student learning. However, since the desired learning was not specified, entropic drift changed the emphasis from student learning to the process and the environment within which the teachers were teaching. The accompanying transposition of controlling influences put the administrator in charge such that instead of the administrators serving the teachers to facilitate the teachers helping students learn, the teachers ended up serving the administrators who controlled the environment within which the teachers were teaching. As the number of teachers and schools increased, there was an increasing number of administrators and levels of administration within which the same entropic drift and transposition of controlling influences occurred such that the lower levels of administrators were serving the higher levels of administrators.

Originally, school boards were set up to serve as a communication link between the educators and the taxpayers who were financially supporting the schools. They would indicate to the educators the needs of the students in order to exist in society as determined by the members of our society and then would also communicate back to society what was happening in the schools. Although society played their part by setting up the GO's, the teachers did not further define them into SO's. As a result, entropic drift and the transposition of controlling influences occurred. Whereas the school boards should have been serving the public and the educators in order to maximize student learning and the relevance of that learning to the real world, the educators ended up serving the school boards by carrying out their demands and the public ended up serving the school boards by paying the bill for the educational process with little input as to what should be in the process or in the results of the process.

Similarly, where state and national departments of education and regional accrediting associations should be serving the school districts, colleges, and universities, due to entropic drift and the transposition of controlling influence, the school districts, colleges, and universities are subservient to these agencies.

As a result of not really knowing specifically what should be learned in our schools, entropic drift and the accompanying transposition of controlling influences have established a traditional hierarchy of decision making similar to Figure 122. A similar pyramid of controlling influences could be constructed for colleges and universities and even for single private schools. The shape of the pyramid is to symbolize the number of people involved at each level. It is a situation in which the decisions of a few at the top of the pyramid can affect hundreds, thousands, and even millions of students on the bottom level.

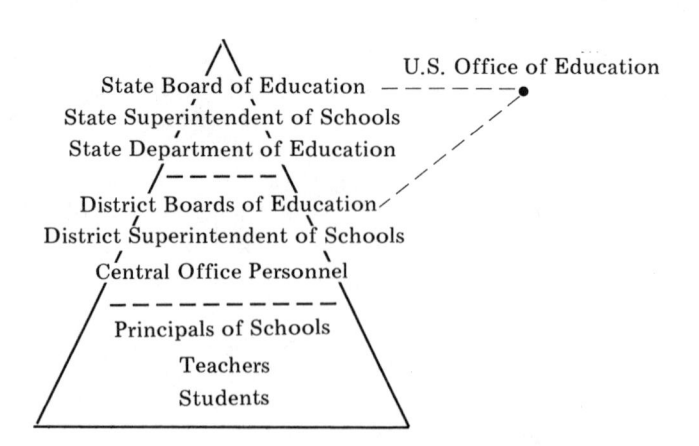

```
                    /\              U.S. Office of Education
          State Board of Education ──────•
         State Superintendent of Schools        /
         State Department of Education        /
             /─────\                         /
          District Boards of Education
         District Superintendent of Schools
             Central Office Personnel
          /──────────────\
         /  Principals of Schools  \
        /       Teachers            \
       /        Students             \
      /_____\
```

Figure 122 — The Traditional Pyramid of Controlling Influences

In large school districts and in large colleges or universities, there are attempts to decentralize the decision making such that the critical decisions are being made closer to the students. The point that is overlooked is that the decisions are still being handed down without regard to the learning problems of the individual students and as such the process still carries with it the problems of traditional education.

Many teachers feel that the traditional pyramid of controlling influences is wrong and are requesting or demanding greater control in the decision-making. However, as long as the teachers still haven't identified what should be learned by the students, their increased decision-making still is without regard to the individual learning needs of the students and tends to reduce what the teachers have to do (productivity), increases the number of people involved in the process, and increases the costs of the educational process.

One of the most important advantages of the Behavioral Learning Systems Approach and accountability is that it is possible to *flip-flop* the pyramid of controlling influences such that learning can be the most important product of our schools and at each level, the people can make those decisions which best facilitate learning (see Figure 123). In the process of inverting the pyramid, the controlling influences of the traditional approach to education become the supportive influences of the systems approach to instruction. Since learning is what is important, the problem is not who controls who, but who is supporting who in order to facilitate student learning.

In placing student learning at the top of the inverted pyramid, this does not mean that *students* control the whole thing, it is to symbolize that *student learning* is the most important and when it is identified, *student learning* can be the primary emphasis in our schools. In a sense,

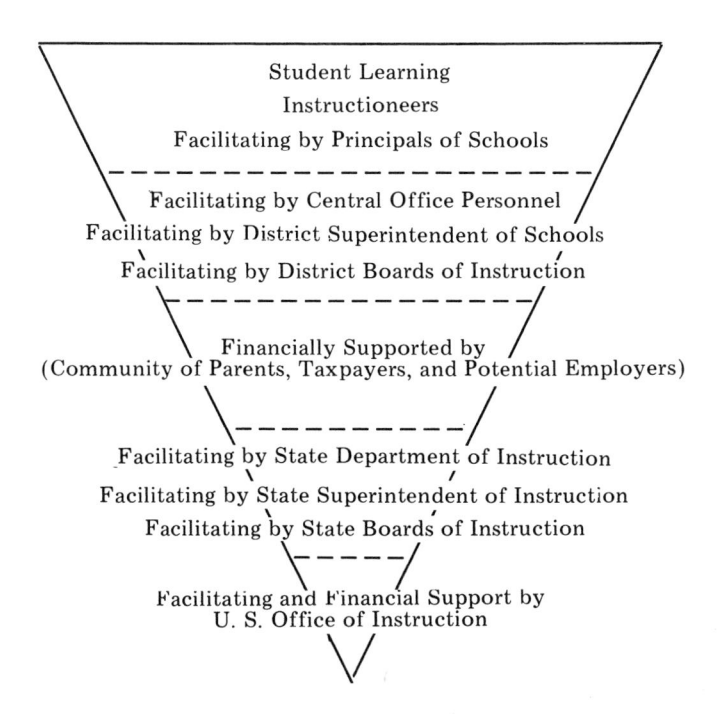

```
         Student Learning
         Instructioneers
      Facilitating by Principals of Schools
   ─────────────────────────────
      Facilitating by Central Office Personnel
    Facilitating by District Superintendent of Schools
     Facilitating by District Boards of Instruction
     ─────────────────────────
              Financially Supported by
    (Community of Parents, Taxpayers, and Potential Employers)
         ──────────────
    Facilitating by State Department of Instruction
     Facilitating by State Superintendent of Instruction
       Facilitating by State Boards of Instruction
            ──────
         Facilitating and Financial Support by
              U. S. Office of Instruction
```

Figure 123 — The Systems Pyramid of Supportive Influences

student learning can control the whole system because everyone is committed to improving the effectiveness and efficiency of the instructional process. Notice in the present traditional pyramid (Fig. 122), the emphasis is on people and the positions who are in control of those in lower positions, whereas in the systems pyramid (Fig. 123), the emphasis is on what people *do* (learn, teach, facilitate) and how each level supports the higher levels in achieving the learning goals of students.

In placing *Instructioneers* at the second level, this does not mean that the teachers as instructioneers should control and tell the lower levels what to do. The placement of *instructioneers* in second place symbolizes that teachers as instructioneers will have a primary effect on student learning and as such should have a major decision-making power over student learning (with open accountability). These decisions should be capable of being defended in terms of specifically what students will or won't be learning. The transposition of teachers from the second to the bottom level in the traditional pyramid (Fig. 122) to the second from the top level in the systems pyramid (Fig. 123) elevates their importance in the instructional process and also elevates the need for accountability.

The placing of administrative positions at lower levels on the pyramid in Fig. 123 does not mean that administrators are necessarily below anyone. The placement indicates reality in that the administrators are further removed from the teaching-learning event than are the students and teachers. The placement also indicates the importance of their supportive services. A closely parallel situation would be the role of the administrators in hospitals in which they don't tell the professional doctors what to do, but their services are invaluable in supporting the doctors with necessary facilities, equipment, and services to maximize the doctors opportunities to help their patients get well. Also, as in the hospitals, the administrators in schools would keep watch to make sure that the students' (in the hospitals — the patients') welfare is kept foremost in the minds of all concerned. This change in position for administrators may be best accomplished if there are two distinct types of administrators: those who are primarily concerned with being supportive of the instructional event and have had the instructional training and background to be proficient in this role, and those who are primarily concerned with the typical business type of supportive role and have had the business training and background to be proficient in this role.

The placement of school boards (regents, etc.) beneath the students, teachers, and administrators in Fig. 123 does not mean that they are controlled by them. The placement indicates the reality of their distance from the instructional event. However, the placement also indicates the importance of their position as a communication link between the professional educators in the local situation and the people in the community who are served by the instructional system and who also financially support the instructional system. In addition to the role as a communication link from the community to the educators and vice versa, the school boards' major *watch dog* role would be to make sure that the educators are accountable for what occurs in the instructional event as the event may benefit the individual students and the community and as the instructional event may be harmful to the individual student and the community. This includes supporting and facilitating the learning of those minimum common core SO's which have been agreed upon by the teachers in their particular school district, college, or university.

The placement of state and national instructional agencies at the bottom of the pyramid does not indicate that the local communities control or dictate what these agencies do; however, it should indicate that the state agency is supportive of all the local school districts, colleges, and universities in the state. The primary concern of the state agency is in supporting and facilitating the learning of those minimum common core SO's in all subject areas which are commonly taught throughout the state and in which the teachers have indicated statewide agreement. In a like manner, the U.S. Office of Instruction should be supportive of all the school districts, colleges, and universities in the nation. The primary concern of the national agency is in supporting and facilitating the learning of those minimum common core SO's in all subject areas which are commonly taught throughout the country and in which the teachers have indicated nation-wide agreement.

Too often at the present time, state and federal funds are used to identify and hopefully solve local problems which have little or no transference to other schools in the state and/or nation. This should be considered a misuse of state and federal funds. The emphasis has to be on the minimum common core SO's which have been identified as having statewide or national application. In this manner, problems and solutions dealing with these SO's will have maximum transference and benefits throughout the state for the state minimum common core SO's and throughout the nation for the national minimum common core SO's.

Most state education agencies are accustomed to working with local school districts and making efforts to establish some sort of uniformity in the curriculum. The major change in their activities will be to stop trying to make the teachers' presentations and textbooks uniform regardless of student learning needs and concentrate on making sure that all students learn at least the statewide minimum common core SO's and leave the presentation decisions and instructional materials selection up to the teachers who are in a position to identify and solve individual students' learning problems.

A missing function at the state and national level is an agency that works with institutions of higher education to identify common problems, common curriculum, or any other commonality except maybe a common need for money. The traditional supposition is that faculty in the institutions of higher education with their advanced degrees (in their specialty areas) don't need any coordination and help in the instructional event and any efforts to coordinate teaching or learning would be considered an infringement on their academic freedom. The critical point to remember is that the two approaches are very different. Under the traditional approach to education where *chance* learning (curve grading) was considered to be the norm, teachers in higher education without any training in teaching could teach as well by *chance* as the teachers who took education courses and were taught how to teach by *chance*. In fact, some faculty in higher education might actually be able to facilitate student learning better than those teachers who took the education courses because they weren't taught the bad habits which interfere with student learning. In contrast, under the Behavioral Learning Systems Approach where designed learning is the emphasis, all teachers will need special training in order to be effective and efficient in the instructional event. An advanced degree in a specialty field other than teaching is not sufficient to qualify as an Instructioneer. If advanced degrees in subject areas other than teaching were really indicative of increased teaching abilities in addition to the supposed increased knowledge and skills in the primary subject area, then faculty in higher education should be more successful in bringing about student learning than the faculty in elementary and secondary schools. Obviously, this is not the case, as there is a greater dropout rate in higher education than in secondary schools and the grading curves in freshmen and sophomore classes are even more negatively skewed and yet the students and faculty are supposed to be better. For example, in California, the universities get the students who are in the top 13 percent of their high school classes. With such high quality students and faculty, it should be a norm that the students would certainly be all straight "A" students and they should be able to learn more in the same time as other college students or learn the same amount in less time. As can be easily observed, the same time schedules and about the same grading curves exist at all three levels of higher education in California.

In order to have quality control in learning such that 90 percent of more of the students learn 100 percent of the required SO's, the students and faculty in the university system should be able to achieve the equivalent of the bachelor's degree in about three years for the average student. In the state (university) college system where the students come from the top third of their classes, the average student might complete the bachelor's degree (100 percent of the required SO's) in the present four years. In the community colleges with supposedly less qualified students and faculty, the average student might complete the bachelor's degree (100 percent of the required SO's) in five years. Actually, since advanced degrees are rarely associated with any guarantee of increased ability to help students learn, and since most teachers at all levels of education have not really specified what students are supposed to learn, the differences in time for learning based on the inferred quality of students and faculty is more likely an unreal supposition.[4]

There is a strong need for a state and national coordinating agency that will get involved with helping colleges and university faculty identify the minimum common core SO's of subjects commonly taught in the colleges and universities.

---

[4] Because most community colleges are not as old as other colleges and universities, they are more innovative and probably have more faculty (still few in number) who are working with SO's and systematic approaches to instruction than the four year colleges and universities.

NOTE: This does not mean that all students will complete courses with the same amount of learning (maximum). They will complete common courses with a common base of learning. The maximum would be different for every student and would reflect the demands of the institution, the departments, the faculty member, and the needs and desires of the individual student. At the present time, the only commonality in common courses are the names of the courses and the length of time spent in the courses.

Under the present approach to education, where the primary product of schools should be *learning* but the *learning* has not been specified, the educational environment is restrictive and negative. As a result, the financial supporters of the schools (the taxpayers), the recipients of the educational services (the students), the emotional supporters of the recipients (the parents), and the emotional recipients of the results of our schools (our society) are liable to call for accountability on a variety of criteria which may or may not have any relationship with student learning and will probably take the form of constraints and limitations handed down from above in which each persons freedom is affected negatively by those above in the traditional pyramid (Fig. 122). As an example, the first pages in most student handbooks and college and university catalogs list all the different ways a student can be failed out of school and all of the rules which have to be followed — few of which actually relate to specific learning.

On the other hand, the Behavioral Learning Systems Approach to instruction wherein the primary product is student learning and the required learning is specified, the instructional environment is facilitative and positive. The emphasis is on creating more freedom rather than limiting freedom. As a student learns all of the required SO's and then as much more as the student wants to, the student is increasing his or her freedom to act as an independent decision-maker in our society. The teacher's job is to help the student learn to be an independent decision-maker by making sure that all of the students at least learn the necessary basic knowledge and skills. In achieving this goal, the teacher should be free to use whatever techniques, materials, and/or resources that he or she finds useful in helping the students learn. As the teacher identifies and helps solve the students' learning problems, the teacher is freeing the student for more learning time. The administrator's job is to facilitate the teachers' efforts to help students learn which gives teachers more free time to work with students. The school board's job is to facilitate the administrator's efforts to help the teachers which in effect gives the administrator more free time to do his work. The state and national instructional agencies' job is to facilitate the school boards in their work facilitating the administrators job.

NOTE: The less able people are in making good decisions about themselves, the more dependent they will be on others and the more restrictive the others will be on them. The more able people are in making good decisions about themselves, the less dependent they will be on others and the more facilitative the others will be with them.

NOTE: This last concept could be misconstrued as being supportive of the *do your own thing* approach. I am in favor of the *do your own thing* concept AFTER the students have learned the required SO's in their courses so they will know how to use their freedom in a responsible manner such that they don't interfere with the freedoms of others.

A student who has learned the necessary knowledge and skills in order to get a job and to get along with his or her fellow person has a lot of freedom to do *his or her own thing* without affecting the freedom of others. A student who hasn't learned enough to get a job or to get along with others because he or she was allowed to do *his or her own thing* regardless of learning does not have much freedom. Without a job, there are many restrictions placed on a person's life style. In not knowing how to get along with other people, there will be many restrictions placed on the person by others who don't understand him or her. In addition, in being dependent upon others for support and shelter and in not knowing how to get along with others in our society, the person is interfering with the freedoms of other people.

A better understanding of the results of the *flip-flop* of the decision-making process can be had by making a comparison of a number of points in the instructional event as found in the traditional approach in which the goals are not specified so there is maximum entropic drift (substitution of means for goals) and in the Behavioral Learning Systems Approach in which the goals are specified so there is minimum entropic drift.

Behavioral Learning Systems	Traditional Education
Minimum Entropic Drift	**Maximum Entropic Drift**
1. Emphasis on students and student learning (Individualized)	1. Emphasis on teachers and teaching (Classes)
2. Maximum cooperation among teachers to identify common SO's so each teacher only has to invent new SO's.	2. Minimum cooperation among teachers to identify common SO's so each teacher reinvents the whole curriculum wheel on his or her own.

Behavioral Learning Systems **Minimum Entropic Drift**	Traditional Education **Maximum Entropic Drift**
3. Teachers' load defined in terms of the number of students, the students' present abilities, and what they have to learn.	3. Teachers' load defined in terms of number of classes — regardless of the number of students.
4. Class size relevant to learning but dependent on the teachers' ability to facilitate learning.	4. Class size irrelevant to learning and ignores individual differences in teachers.
5. Teaching considered as a science — students learn by design.	5. Teaching considered as an art — students learn by chance.
6. Emphasis is on professionalism where the teacher is an independent decision-maker.	6. Emphasis is on unionism where the teacher is a laborer and depends on group decisions.
7. Teachers evaluated on the results of their performance (student learning) regardless of how achieved.	7. Teachers evaluated on their performance regardless of the results (learning).
8. Instructional process consists of diagnosis first and treatment second and the treatment is dependent upon the diagnosis.	8. Educational process consists of treatments first and diagnosis second where the treatments seldom are affected by the diagnosis.
9. Learning is more affected by factors internal to the instructional process (by design).	9. Learning is more affected by factors external to the educational process (chance).
10. Course objectives made up of interrelated GO's and SO's and criteria for achievement.	10. Course objectives, if any, made up of non-measurable GO's and a few unrelated SO's.
11. Tests are designed to match the SO's and criteria and reflect actual learning (no *objective* type test items as they are subjectively written and don't match objectives).	11. Tests are designed to give desired results regardless of actual learning levels (normed tests) or are designed for ease of scoring regardless of correlation to objectives (use of *objective* type test items).

Behavioral Learning Systems **Minimum Entropic Drift**	Traditional Education **Maximum Entropic Drift**
12. Because the tests reflect desired objectives, teachers teach to the test and students learn what is to be tested (tests are open to students, teachers, parents, etc.)	12. Because tests have only a chance relationship with unknown course objectives and because the desired results might be affected, teachers are not supposed to teach what is on tests and students can only learn what is on tests by guessing (tests are hidden from students and in the case of standardized tests they are also hidden from teachers).
13. Individual differences among students and teachers taken into consideration in the instructional process.	13. Individual differences among students and teachers ignored during the educational process.
14. Minimum common core SO's a constant regardless of time and materials needed to achieve.	14. Time and materials held as a constant regardless of learning.
15. State and federal money tied to individual student needs and learning.	15. State and federal money tied to average daily attendance and external factors such as poverty level, federal impact, etc.
16. An instructional environment which is positive and freeing.	16. An educational environment which is negative and restrictive.
17. Characterized by unity in direction by all concerned — student learning.	17. Characterized by each group in conflict with other groups for their own benefits regardless of any effect on student learning.
18. The major goal is to develop students who can participate fully in society, can obtain and hold a job, and can get along with his or her fellow persons.	18. The major goal is to develop students who can only participate in society by chance, may or may not be able to obtain and hold a job, and taught either to be dependent on others for decisions or to make independent decisions without regard for others.

B. EVALUATION OF STUDENTS

In considering the concept of student evaluation, there are two groups that have to be thought of. The major group by far are those educators who consciously or unconsciously do evaluate students. A minor group are those who at least vocally claim that the students should not be evaluated. This latter group is representative of the *do your own thing* group who are also usually in favor of *deschooling* as long as they can somehow keep receiving their salaries. Most of these educators are trying to avoid any responsibility (accountability) or are trying to be radical in order to gain attention from their colleagues. If they really believed in everyone doing *their own thing*, there wouldn't be anyone left who would be willing to pay taxes for their salaries as they would be too busy doing *their thing*. Actually, I have never met an educator who didn't suggest in his or her written or vocal statements that there were certain things he or she thought students should learn. Even the most free thinking English or art teacher has some criteria for evaluation. Therefore, in practice, there is really only one group as all educators evaluate students in one way or another.

The key to the whole concept of evaluation is that in order to evaluate, one has to have something to evaluate the student on. I would call this something *objectives*, although, some educators may prefer other terms i.e., goals, outcomes, etc. Given that there is something that an educator may wish to evaluate a student on, there are five more variables to consider? Is the something actually taught?; How is the something evaluated?; If grades are to be given, how are the grades arrived at?; Are there any follow up activities as a result of the evaluation?; and, What are the effects on the student? Given these six variables, there are an infinite number of combinations which could occur in any classroom. Therefore, I will discuss each of the variables and then give some examples of persent usage along with the preferred combination.

The first variable concerns what *it* is that educators want students to do. Within this variable, there are two sub-categories, each of which can be further divided into two sub-sub-categories. The main division is whether or not what is wanted is learning. Frequently, all teachers really want are activities regardless of the learning which may or may not take place. For example, some teachers may say *If you just attend class everytime, you'll at least get a "C" grade*, or *If you turn in each essay (project, paper, etc.) you'll at least get a "C" grade*. This approach is found in some humanities courses and many shop courses. The sub-divisions of this category concern whether or not the activities are specific or general. General activities might be to *participate* in class activities, *to develop good citizenship*, or in other ways indicate attitudes similar to the teacher's. Notice that these activities tend to fall into the affective domain and as such, it is important to remember that they may or may not have learned these attitudes, values, and/or beliefs in the class. (Affective domain objectives have to be measured on a pretest and postest basis in order to find out whether or not the change in attitudes or learning, if any, occurred during the course.) The other division of this category concerns learning and the sub-divisions concern whether or not the objectives are general and non-measurable or specific and measurable. At the present time, most educational objectives or goals either concern non-learning activities or non-measurable learning objectives (GO's). In reference to the GO's, it is important to remember that the degree of generality (or specificity) is a sort of continuum (see Figure 124) in which at point A the objectives are specific and measurable. In moving towards point B, the objectives get more and more generalized and also more and more non-measurable.

```
                                                        specific
B                    General Objectives                 A
very
general                                                 objective
```

Figure 124 — Continuum of Generality (or Specificity) of Objectives

The second variable concerns whether or not the teacher teaches the objectives of the course. It should be obvious that even if given a list of SO's, a teacher could decide to teach something else. However, if a teacher is given or has developed a list of SO's for a course (particularly if the SO's represent the consensus of many teachers as being the minimum common core of the course), hopefully, the teacher will teach those SO's first. After all of the students have learned the required SO's, the teacher could teach whatever else he or she, or the students want. A major problem develops when the objectives for the course are GO's. The more general and non-measurable the course objectives, the more varied the teaching is apt to be and consequently, the more varied will be the learning in both quality and quantity.

1. TESTING AND GRADING

The third variable concerns the actual evaluation and/or testing. In using the word *testing*, some educators will say that they don't test (with paper and pencil) but they do evaluate. In my use of the word *test*, I am referring to any mode of evaluation, i.e., paper and pencil, oral, performance, the evaluation of a project, etc. The first division of this category concerns whether or not the testing or evaluation matches the desired goals or objectives of the course. Since most teachers work from GO's, it is difficult to establish a direct relationship between the objectives and the tests. As a result, the results of the testing may or may not reflect achievement of the desired objectives. A compounding factor concerns the second variable and its relationship with the first and third variables. The evaluation may match the objectives, but if the teacher didn't teach the desired objectives, the students wouldn't achieve very well and it really wouldn't be the students fault. In another situation, the evaluation and what the teacher taught might not correlate very highly with the course objectives; but the evaluation might correlate highly with what the teacher taught. In this case the students would probably do well, but not in terms of the course objectives. Of course, the worst situation would be one in which there would be little, if any, correlation between the course objectives, what the teacher taught, and what was evaluated. As bad as it seems, this is the current situation in many courses which are evaluated by standardized tests. The course objectives are very general, what the teachers teach is varied and yet all students take the same standardized test which was hidden from teachers and students (after all the teachers might teach it and the students might learn it!). Typically, the standardized tests are designed to obtain a certain curve of results regardless of the course objectives, what was taught, or what students learned and the tests contain a lot of so-called *objective* type test items which are very subjective in preparation and rarely represent real world or even classroom situations. In the use of the so-called *objective* type test items (multiple-choice, true-false, and matching), it is critical to remember that a professional test item writer can hold constant the stem and correct choice of a multiple-choice item and by just varying the words in the wrong choices can get almost any percentage of students to get the item correct or to miss it regardless of what the students actually know. When a non-professional test item writer (which includes most teachers) makes up their own test items, the percentage of students who will get an item right or wrong is almost chance (giving a curve of results) and again almost regardless of what the students actually know.

A fourth variable concerns the grading of the students. Although most final grades may be an *objective* composite of all the grades given during a course, many of the grades given during a course may contain subjective evaluations. For example, many teachers may start out a course by saying something like the following: 40 percent of your final grade is based on the unit tests, 40 percent on the final examination, and 20 percent on class participation. The first two parts of the grade sound objective, but if part of the tests are essays, then the grade is part subjective.

NOTE: Although a teacher may be able to grade an essay objectively in reference to specified criteria for evaluation, the actual assignment of a grade becomes subjective because the total number of possible errors or correct responses is usually not identified so a grade which indicates any percentage or ratio of mistakes to possible correct responses has to be subjective.

The third part of the grade (20 percent on class participation) is extremely subjective and is primarily in the affective domain and as such is more dependent upon the teacher doing the evaluating than on the students. Although students can put on phony attitudes and values to please a teacher (to get a good grade), if the teacher is concerned about the REAL attitudes and values over which the student has limited, if any, control, than any grade given should really be given to the teacher, parents, peer groups, and community rather than to the student. I am not against teachers expressing their feelings towards a student. However, I am against the hiding of these subjective feelings in a grade which others assume was arrived at objectively. There should be a place in any student's record for the teacher to put personal comments. In that way, a student who achieves all of the requirements of a course and is disliked by the teacher should get an "A" instead of being graded down to a "C" or less because of the personal feelings of the teacher and some other student who hasn't learned much of the course but is liked by the teacher would be graded accordingly instead of getting an inflated grade.

Most teachers grade according to some kind of curve (normal or skewed) which really indicates more about how a student learned in comparison to his classmates rather than how a student learned in comparison to the objectives of the course. If you are teaching at the present moment, consider the list of percentage scores in Figure 125 as resulting from a test that you have just given in whatever subject matter you teach. If you are not teaching at the present time, role-play for a

Percentage of Test Items Correct	Number of Students
* 60	* 1
55	4
50	8
45	15
40	3
35	2
30	1
25	1

Figure 125 — Percentage Test Results

moment, and consider the percentage test scores in Figure 125 as resulting from a test that you have given in the subject that you either have taught or plan to teach at some future date. Remember, the scores listed in Figure 125 are percentage scores.

Consider the student at the top of the list in Figure 125 who is able to answer 60 percent of the test items correctly on a test. What letter grade would you give to this student (write this letter grade on a slip of paper)? Pick the letter grade from among the following: "A", "B", "C", "D", "F", "I" (incomplete), or "TOT" (through out the test). *Be sure that you have written down this letter grade before you go on reading.* Now, in examining the teaching-learning situation which resulted in the figures given in Figure 125, it turned out that the same test was given to more students in other classes. The composite results of all the classes for that test are listed in Figure 126. Again, look at the one

Percentage of Test Items Correct	Number of Students
100	11
95	16
90	31
85	62
80	104
75	75
70	25
65	15
* 60	* 1
55	4
50	8
45	15
40	3
35	2
30	1
25	1

Figure 126 — Percentage Test Results

student who got 60 percent of the test items correct on the test. Under this new situation, what would his grade be now? (Stop and decide on your response before continuing to read.) If you changed the letter grade that you wanted to give this student, or if, in fact, you even thought of changing the letter grade that you gave to the student under the situation in Figure 125, you have a tendency to mark on a curve. You tend to mark a student relative to the achievement of his classmates, rather than relative to the objectives of the test (represented by the collective test items).

One of the big problems with curve grading is that (see Figure 127) if Group 1 represents the students in a class during one particular year and they were not very good, the "A" students may only be achieving

COURSE GOALS OR OBJECTIVES

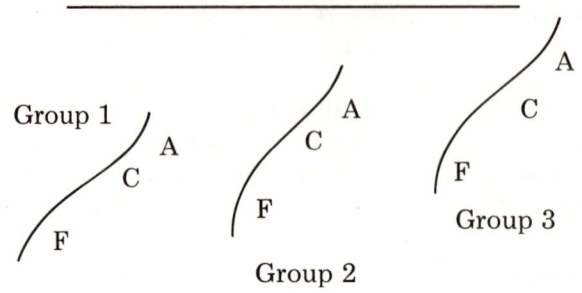

Group 1
  A
  C
  F

Group 2
  A
  C
  F

Group 3
  A
  C
  F

Starting Point of Course

Figure 127 — Curve Grading of Same Course Content by Different Student Groups

little more than half of the course content. The next year, the teacher has a little better class, and now the "A" students are achieving about three-fourths of the course content, and in the third Group, the students are really pretty smart, and so the best student now is achieving almost 100 percent of the course content. But notice, the failing student in Group 3 has learned as much as the "A" student in Group 1, so given that a student would learn say 60 percent of a course, the letter grade he gets depends on which year he went to school. In the first Group he'd get an "A". In the second Group a "C" and in the third Group he'd fail. What makes this even more serious is when Group 1 is in Room 101 and Group 2 in Room 102 and Group 3 in Room 103, right next to each other, and a student's grade depends on which room he was assigned to and the other students in the room, rather than on what the student learned.

In the traditional educational situation, educators have been under the impression that their role in society was to separate the students into groups which could later be identified with various levels of occupations or professions in our society. Curve grading was a very convenient method of grading to support this philosophy because regardless of how the students performed on a test, only a certain percentage of the students will get "A's", another larger percentage will get "B's", the majority of the students will usually get "C's", about the same percentage who got "B" will get a "D", and about the same percentage who got "A" will fail. This type of *curve grading* is usually referred to as regular or *normal* curve grading. In certain instances, teachers may alter the percentages of students who get "A's", "B's", "C's" "D's" or "F's", in such a way that the percentage of students getting "A's" and "B's" is increased, and consequently, the percentage of students getting "C's", "D's", and "F's" are decreased. This method of assigning grades usually makes students and parents happy because it appears that *increased learning has taken place*. The teacher may increase the percentage of students who are getting "D's" and "F's" and consequently reduce the percentage of students who are getting "A's" and "B's" and "C's". This method of assigning grades usually indicates to students and other teachers that *the students aren't capable of achieving the high standards of the course*. The important point to notice is that it is the type of curve that the teacher uses for assigning grades that determines what letter grade the student receives, rather than what the student has or hasn't learned determining the letter grade.

TABLE I — CURVE GRADING OF A CLASS OF 30 STUDENTS

Type of Curve	Number of Students Receiving Grade[5]				
	A	B	C	D	F
"Normal curve grading where average students get "C"	1	4	20	4	1
Curve grading where average students get "B"	5	12	10	2	1
Curve grading where average students get "D"	1	2	10	12	5

The numbers in Table I for *normal* curve grading are derived from a normal probability curve. The numbers in Table I for the curve grading with the "B" emphasis and the curve grading with the "D" emphasis were selected to represent a point. The actual numbers of students

---

[5] The numbers given may vary considerably from teacher to teacher, but the emphasis on more students getting "C". "B", or "D" correlates with the teacher's or school's philosophy on grading, not necessarily on the students' ability or lack of ability to learn.

receiving "A", "B", "C", "D", or "F" could vary considerably from teacher to teacher and from class to class. Although most curve grading refers at least in part to the normal curve, there are so many variations from the actual normal curve that the term *curve grading* can not be defined in terms of the normal curve. The best definition of curve grading is as follows:

> Curve grading relates to the practice of evaluating students with a major emphasis on what a student learns relative to his classmates, and a minor, if any emphasis on what a student learns in comparison to the defined content of the course.

Many school districts, colleges, and universities utilize and encourage some form of curve grading. In fact, among the tens of thousands of teachers that I have worked with, probably 80 to 90 percent of the teachers use some form of curve grading in their evaluation procedures. Of interest is the fact that if normal curve grading is based on the normal probability curve, which in turn is based on the concept of *chance*, then this evaluation system is essentially saying that learning which takes place in our educational institutions takes place by *chance*. If any educator, school district, college, or university is willing to state that any learning that takes place in its classrooms or institutions takes place by chance, then normal curve grading may be appropriate. But, if the educators have been hired to help students learn and the school buildings have been built and the facilities have been provided to facilitate learning, then the use of normal curve grading is not appropriate. The major defense for using curve grading is based on the results of intelligence, or I.Q. tests, which are designed to separate students into groups such that the numbers of students in any one group happen to fit this normal, bell-shaped curve. As a consequence, in a classroom, it is assumed that whatever learning takes place will fit the results of the standard intelligence tests. In other words, the same percentages of students in the various groups or levels of the intelligence tests should be the same percentages of students that you will find in groups receiving "A's", "B's", "C's", "D's" and "F's". Since students are not normally taught how to pass the intelligence tests, the results of the intelligence tests indicate what the students know about that test at that time, without any additional help. In the classroom, when all of the students have essentially the same learning experiences, individual differences among students will affect what they can or can't learn from the common experiences. As a result, the achievement of these students may actually fit a curve *as long as the teacher doesn't try to teach the students who need help.* Once teachers start helping students who need help, then the whole concept of the curve has to be thrown out. It has been proven in many projects that with help for those students who need help, they can learn almost anything that can be measured, if given sufficient time and appropriate materials.

Because of the widespread use of curve grading, a unique situation has developed in education. Consider the picture (Figure 128) showing

Figure 128

students coming to school. If this picture was taken at the beginning of the year, semester, or quarter, teachers wouldn't know who the students are and what their abilities or problems will be. But, based on previous years, semesters, or quarters, the teachers can predict *according to the curve* the percentages of grades these students will receive (see Figure 129). Of special interest is that in high schools and colleges, failing and "D" students see what is going to happen and they drop out of school. Technically, the effect of the students' dropping out of school should reduce or eliminate the "F" category, but this is generally not the case, as the curve of grades is applied to the students who remain (see Figure 130). In effect, if the students who dropped out had

Figure 129 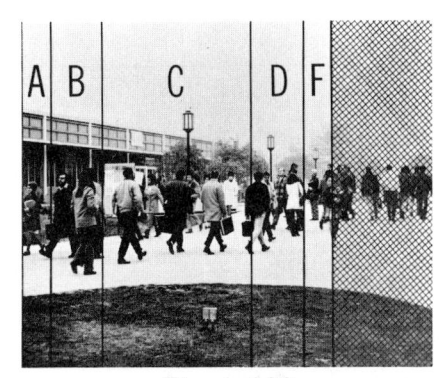   Figure 130

stayed in school, the students who actually received "D" and "F" might have received a "C". Because of the design of the curve grading method, some students have to fail which makes *education the only profession that fails its clients by design!!* Consider the following statements:

> What would you think of an aircraft designer who would design airplanes such that five percent would crash!

> What would you think of a structural engineer who designed buildings so five percent would crumble!

> What would you think of a doctor who in looking at the 40 people in his reception room planned on killing at least two of them!

> What would you think of a pastor, priest, or rabbi who in looking out at his congregation of 200 people planned on sending at least ten or more to hell!

If these statements seem wild, unreal, and nightmarish, then consider the following statements which are describing real situations that are actually happening in education, but no less nightmarish:

> Almost every student in higher education has had a teacher who said to a new class,
>
> > *Look to the right and then look to the left, one of your neighboring classmates won't be here at the end of this semester!*

> At a technical college in Colorado which has a reputation for *high quality*, it is common talk among the freshmen that when you are standing in line to register that either the student in front of you, yourself, or the student behind you will not last out the first semester.

If you have wondered why some of the *disadvantaged* students are causing trouble in our high schools, colleges, and universities, consider how it might feel to finally have an opportunity to obtain an education, but because of curve grading the so-called disadvantaged student is practically predestined to failure. The schools, colleges, and universities that brag about their *open-door* policy rarely talk about their *open-back-door* policy of grading that gets rid of the disadvantaged students almost as fast as they enter.

A unique situation in higher education is that many schools and many faculty in higher education equate high and low standards with high and low failure rates. In other words, the school that has a low failure rate has low standards; a school that has a high failure rate has high standards. Consequently a teacher who fails a lot of students has high standards in his course and a teacher who has a low failure rate in his course has low standards. In view of the fact that a teacher can design a test to fail as many students as he wants, this becomes really an arbitrary level and really has no relationship with standards at all because regardless of what is taught, the test can be designed to fail as many students as you wish. Every year millions of students have to change their educational and vocational goals because they have been in the classroom of some teacher who wanted to give evidence of high standards by having a higher percentage of failure, which doesn't really mean that the students couldn't learn the subject they failed in. What it does mean is that the kinds of learning experiences that they were exposed to in the course were not appropriate to pass the kinds of test items that were designed to test achievement in the course.

As an example of the affect of years of curve grading in higher education, in 1970, at the University of California at Santa Barbara, a professor gave more than 1200 "A's" in an introductory course. W. Glenn Campbell, a Regent of the University of California, stated that the action of awarding that many "A's" was *outrageous and indefensible* and demanded a study of the University's grading system in order to identify if there had been a decline in grading *standards* in recent years. A statewide faculty group had just completed such a study and found no evidence of declining *standards.*

> Can you imagine a member of a hospital board publically saying that it was *outrageous and indefensible* that most of the patients in the hospital were getting well!

Even a primitive analysis of the above situation indicates a rather grave situation, but a situation much different than the regents or faculty seemed to be concerned about. Assuming that the differences being the letter grades "A", "B", "C", "D", and "F" indicate differences in achievement (learning) and that these differences are measurable, then a teacher who can maximize learning ("A" worth) for all or most of his students is a very good teacher.

However, if the letter grades do not relate to achievement (learning) or if the differences between the letter grades are not measurable, then there is a serious problem. How does the teacher arrive at any grade and how does the teacher differentiate between who gets an "A" and who gets any other grade. A subjective basis is certainly not consistent with rational, reasonable, and humane behavior. But, oddly enough, this is not the problem as seen by W. Glenn Cambell and the statewide faculty group. The problem they are concerned with is associated with the traditional concept of *curve grading* and *high standards!* Remembering that when the results, (grades) of a class approximate a *normal curve*, it is evidence that the degree of learning which took place in the course occurred by *chance* (the teacher neither tried to facilitate learning nor to inhibit learning). Assuming that anything important enough to grade a student down for not learning is also important enough for a teacher to try to teach, then when students are getting more "A's" and "B's" than *normal*, this indicates that a teacher is trying to *improve* learning beyond mere chance. Conversely, when students are getting more "D's" and "F's" than *normal*, this indicates that a teacher is trying to *inhibit* learning beyond mere chance.

Of interest, is the fact that the vast majority of the students attending the University of California represent the *cream of the crop* and *do not* represent a *normal distribution* of student ability. Therefore, the use of a *normal curve* for grading these students would be highly inappropriate and the use of a negatively skewed curve (more "D's" and "F's" than *normal)* should be indicative of a catastrophe in the teaching-learning situation.

In accord with the belief that *high standards* of teaching are equated to high percentages of "D's" and "F's", the University of California like most other institutions of higher education will fail or push out from 25-40 percent or more of their freshman classes. With over a $1000 taxpayer investment in each of the students who are pushed out, this ineffectiveness in teaching wastes over $100 million annually of the investment in higher education made by the taxpayers of California (not to mention the irrepairable damage done to our young people) and close to a billion dollars nationally. To force faculty to continue such ineffective teaching in California is the problem that W. Glenn Campbell and the rest of the regents should be concerned about. Consider also the results of the statewide faculty study which indicated no change in grading *standards* (effectiveness) over the years. What with the reduction in class size, a reduction in the number of classes to teach, and increased salaries (tripling the cost of higher education), doesn't even the *normal* taxpayer have the right to expect some small increase in teaching effectiveness???

As mentioned earlier, Phi Beta Kappa, an organization which is usually associated with excellence in achievement, has also become upset with the increasing percentages of "A's" in some institutions of higher education. Assuming that there is some relationship between learning and grades, Phi Beta Kappa is in the unusual position of being against students learning more than the usual *curve's* worth.

Many teachers will insist that they do not grade on a curve because they equate certain achievement levels to grades even before the test. However, many of these teachers are probably designing their tests to give a curve of results before the test is even taken by the students. Although there are many different methods of grading, a 1973 survey of the nation's high schools by Educational Testing Service (ETS) found that about 68 percent of the teachers in these schools still use letter grades and 16 percent use percentages for grades. The point to remember is that regardless of what letters, numbers, or words are used for grades, there is a strong tendency for traditional educators to assign the grades according to some preconceived curve of expected results and one or more of the following criteria:

1. The student's achievement relative to what other students achieved (curve grading);
2. the student's achievement relative to what the teacher thinks the student's achievement should have been (or was capable of achieving);
3. the students achievement according to the teacher's subjective opinion (few, if any, tests given); and/or
4. the student's achievement relative to the results of the tests and other evaluations given during the course (generally designed to give a curve of results).

Under the traditional point of view, teachers are measured by their ability to complete the presentation of the content and all students, in spite of individual differences, are assumed to start where the content of the course starts and finish at the end of a specified length of time. Thus, most grading systems are based on the assumption that all learners are the same, and then the grades represent the amount of effort put forth by the learner. As a consequence, learners who start a course and are either approximately at the place where the teacher starts, knows part of the course or all of the course, will be the students who get the good grades in the course. Students who do not have the appropriate entry behaviors to start the course and particularly if they are two, three and four years behind, will get the low grades in the course. Therefore, given the kind of background experiences the learners have and the kinds of learning experiences they are exposed to in the class, what the grades really measure is all they are able to learn in the time provided for this learning to take place. Knowing that students aren't all at the same place at the beginning of a course and knowing that students learn best in different ways, it should be at least recognized that if given more time and different materials, most or all of the students would be able to learn whatever it is that teachers consider important enough to grade students down for not learning it. However, a problem that has been present for many years is that, if teachers don't specifically know what the content of a course is, then how can they possible say that a student has achieved "C" worth of the course if they don't really know what "C" worth is. Within the next few years, students who receive a "C", "D" or "F" in a course and/or their parents may ask the teacher how much is "C" worth of the course — is it 70 percent or 80 percent? How much is "D" worth of the course — is it 60 percent or 75 percent? In order to answer these questions the teacher is going to have to know what is 100 percent of the course, and if they don't know what 100 percent of the course is, then they are going to find it very difficult to explain to students and parents what 60 or 70 percent of the course is.

2. GRADING AND CUMULATIVE IGNORANCE

Although many teachers can equate a certain percentage of achievement to a certain letter grade, i.e., a "C" is 70-85 percent, a "B" is 86-93 percent etc., a question that few teachers ask themselves when allowing students to leave their courses with "C's", "D's", or 70 percent, 83 percent, etc. is what 15, 20, or 30 percent of the course is not important! In allowing a student to get credit for a course and yet leave the course with a "C" or 75 percent is the same as saying that the other 25 percent is not important. If the missing *learning* is important, then the student shouldn't be given credit for the course until he or she learns the missing important *learning*. As pointed out in Chapter V (Volume I), allowing students to leave a course or even a unit of a course without learning what is necessary for successful learning in subsequent courses or units fosters cumulative ignorance[6] and is an educational malpractice.

If students are not learning everything they are supposed to learn at each grade level (represented by students getting "C's", "D's", and "F's") as they proceed from kindergarten through college, it should not be the least bit surprising when we identify students who are one or two years behind their classmates in elementary school and they never seem to be able to catch up with their classmates; in fact, they get further and further behind. It is very possible that years of cumulative ignorance can build up to the point where a learner is unable to perform adequately in the learning situation. At present, students' inability to learn is blamed on a variety of causes, such as genetics, home environment, motivation, etc., rather than on the fault of an ineffective and inefficient teaching-learning situation which cumulatively makes it impossible for the students to learn.

Although cumulative ignorance may be a problem in all subject matter areas, it is of particular significance in course sequences in which the achievement of basic course content is necessary in order for the student to have satisfactory achievement in subsequent courses. Cumu-

---

[6] Cumulative ignorance is the cumulative effect of nonlearning which affects subsequent learning, and is created in a situation where a learner is permitted to leave a course or unit without achieving the critical objectives which are necessary in order for the student to have success in subsequent units or courses (or out in the real world).

lative ignorance can be most easily demonstrated in courses such as mathematics, English, foreign languages and science. Depending on the number of courses in the sequence, this process of *cumulative ignorance* may continue until either the student drops out of the course sequence because he feels uncomfortable in a situation where he does not understand what is being presented, or the student is forced out of the sequence because of failing grades, e.g., very few "C", "D", and "F" students in ninth grade algebra complete four years of high school mathematics. The effects of cumulative ignorance are very easily observed in foreign language, in that almost any student who is a "C" student in the first year of a foreign language will experience a great deal of difficulty during the second year of a foreign language, because the "C" achievement in the first year indicates that there were a number of learning objectives which were not learned during the first year, but are very necessary for successful achievement during the second year of the foreign language. All teachers are very familiar with the effects of cumulative ignorance in English grammar, in which students, during the very early years of elementary school are allowed to pass on with "C" and "D" achievement in English grammar, spelling, vocabulary, essays, etc., and as a result, English grammar is taught almost every year all through the twelve grades of elementary and secondary education, and when the students start college, the freshman year at college also devotes a certain amount of time to English grammar and writing essays. Cumulative ignorance is also very apparent in reference to the disadvantaged students who start school anywhere from one to three years behind the average advantaged student. Because this difference is never really eliminated, the difference affects the ceiling of what the disadvantaged student can learn in each of the subsequent grade levels such that, if they go on to high school, they will be five and six years behind the average advantaged student.

If cumulative ignorance can develop when students receive a grade of "C", consider how quickly the cumulative ignorance can develop when students are only achieving "D" or "F" worth of a unit or course. Of course, when the concept of cumulative ignorance is associated with the concept of curve grading, it is very possible for students who are even achieving "A" or "B" worth of a course to be developing cumulative ignorance. Almost every student has had the experience of being in the class where the results of a test were so low that even the "A" or "B" student achieved only half or less of the test items. Students who are suffering from cumulative ignorance are generally referred to as potential dropouts or noncollege material. A number of educators around the country are beginning to recognize the existence of cumulative ignorance, and in recognizing the causes, refer to these students as potential *pushouts*.

One particular aspect of the evaluation process which appears on the outside to be a very positive concept, but underneath it has very negative consequences. This is in reference to the situation in which teachers know that the student has not learned what he needs to know to be successful in subsequent courses, but they are trying to be nice to the student, and so they give the student what is called a *soft "D"* or they may just like the student and may give the student a "B" or a "C" when actually the student didn't learn that much of the course. A slightly different situation, but with the same effects, occurs in many classrooms in which there are *disadvantaged* or minority group students and a teacher who either does not like the students or doesn't believe that they are capable of learning the course objectives. It is common for these teachers to give students passing grades so as not to be identified as being discriminatory, even though the teachers know that the students have not learned the course objectives. The common result of both of these situations is that the student is passed on with varying degrees of cumulative ignorance. Over a period of time, what may have been intended as an act of friendship actually reduces the student's chances for success. As far as cumulative ignorance is concerned, it is just as bad for a student to progress to the next course with a "C" or a "D" as it is for the student to progress to the next course with an "A" or a "B", but still knowing only a "C". "D", or "F" worth of the objectives.

In order to avoid fostering cumulative ignorance, students who are given "C", "D" and "F", or any other grade indicating less than 100 percent achievement, should then be given an opportunity to learn whatever they didn't learn, and once they have shown that they have learned 100 percent, then the students should be given an "A" (if a grade is necessary at all). Currently, throughout the country, students with "D's" and "F's" are allowed or required to take a course over again, but they have to take the entire course over again, not just the 30, 40, or 50 percent that they didn't learn. As a consequence, the students end up being so bored by having to learn over again that which they already knew, that they are not very attentive to the objectives which they don't know, and as a consequence, end up knowing less than they knew at the end of the first time through the course. Also, they end up with antagonisms towards the teachers, the educational insitiutions, and society.

a. PASS — FAIL GRADING

During the last few years, an increasing number of elementary and secondary schools, and colleges and universities, have been utilizing the grading concept of pass or fail, in addition to or rather than the traditional "A", "B", "C", "D", or "F" grades. The rationale behind the pass-fail grading concept is that it encourages students to take courses that they wouldn't normally take, because they would be afraid of endangering their grade point average, and second, it is supposed to eliminate the worry about what grade the student will receive.

The first thing to point out in reference to this grading concept is the statement that the student will not take a chance on lowering his grade point average. Since "C" and "D" students make up the greatest percentage of students in our schools, to get another "C" or "D" wouldn't affect their grade point averages at all. the only students that might be affected by getting a "C" or a "D" would be those who generally get "A" or "B" grades. It is rather obvious right from the beginning that the pass-fail grading concept is biased in favor of the "A" and "B" students. A much more serious criticism of the grading concept is that the passing grade does not affect the students' grade point average, but the *failing grade does.*

The *pass-fail* method places achievement into a dichotomy, rather than into some kind of a continuum which would range from the point where the student learns nothing to where he learns everything. The value, if any, of the pass-fail concept depends quite a bit on where the dividing line is between *pass* and *fail*. If the student, in order to get a passing grade, has to learn all of the objectives of the course, then the *pass* grade is good. If the student is allowed to pass with essentially what used to be called a "C" or "D" achievement of the course, then the pass-fail concept is contributing to cumulative ignorance. From a learning systems point of view, the two major criticisms of the pass-fail concept is first of all, the pass-fail concept of grading tends to allow even sloppier teaching in reference to specifying objectives than the old method of "A" "B" "C" "D" and "F". At least under the multiple-letter grade approach the teacher had to identify varying degrees of achievement and to do this, had to identify at least some semi-measurable differences in achievement, whereas under the pass-fail concept the achievement level of *pass* tends to become extremely subjective.

In reference to the desire to encourage students to explore other courses, a passing grade in most courses is the equivalent of a "C" or "D" grade. In asking hundreds of students and teachers what their collective opinion is concerning all of the courses in which they received "C's" or "D's", their response is generally almost a neutral response! On the other hand, when these same students and teachers were asked to think about all the courses in which they received "A's" and "B's" and what they collectively thought about these courses their response was (with a few exceptions) that they generally liked them.

If we truly want to let students have an opportunity to explore other courses and to get excited about them, "C" or "D" worth of a course will not get the student very excited. Typically, "C" or "D" worth of a course is rote memory worth which can be obtained by cram studying the night before final examinations. On the other hand, if the students are required to go into sufficient depth in the course to earn an "A" or "B", the chances for the student to become excited about the subject are greatly increased. For this reason, if educators truly want students to explore other courses without endangering their grade point averages and maybe with the possibility of increasing their grade point averages, the grading concept of "A", "B", or Incomplete would be much more compatible with the rationale for the pass-fail concept than the pass-fail concept itself. (The "A", "B", Incomplete concept is discussed in more detail on page 946).

Another potential problem that could arise is that if a student should become interested in the subject matter area of the course in which he received a *Pass* ("C" or "D") and decided to take a second or third course in a sequence of courses, it is very possible that *passing* work in the first course might be low enough so as to develop cumulative ignorance which would cause the student to have learning problems in subsequent courses and the fragile interest would be extinguished.

Another major objection to the pass-fail grading concept is the grade of "F". It would be very difficult for a teacher to identify exactly what it was the student did not learn, because there are not many courses that utilize the pass-fail grading concept in which the teachers have also specified all of the learning objectives in the course.

b. "F" GRADES: COFFIN NAILS IN THE EDUCATIONAL SYSTEM

One of the most serious aspects of the evaluation of students by teachers is the failing grade, regardless of the letter used to indicate this failure, if it is "F" or "E" or "U" or the word *Fail*. All of these symbols indicate a rather terminal situation, and when these grades are placed on a student's record, they remain there throughout his lifetime.

Teachers have the right and obligation to indicate to students that they have not learned everything important in their courses by giving the student an "I" (incomplete), but teachers do not have the right to fail students, nor is the giving of an "F" in accordance with the concepts of professionalism. By giving an "I" until such time as a student learns everything important in a course, the responsibility for learning is given to the student and also allows for individual differences in rate, amount, and mode of learning. In giving an "I", the student has to learn what he hasn't learned. In giving an "F", the student has to repeat the course not only to learn what he hasn't learned but to sit through the presentation of everything he has learned. The boredom resulting from sitting through the whole course a second time generally results in losses in learning, rather than any increases in learning. In many schools, an "I" automatically becomes an "F" after a certain period of time. Is it possible that after the administrative deadline that something that was once worthwhile learning is now worthless?????

What would you think of a doctor who said, to his patients who were not getting well fast enough,

> *If you don't get well or show some signs of improvement by June 10, I'm going to give you arsenic and get rid of you.*

What would you think of a clergyman who said, to members of his church who were not changing from their sinful ways fast enough,

> *If you don't repent or show signs of changing by June 10, I'm going to pray that you all go to hell.*

What would you think of a clinical psychologist who said, to his patients who were not getting well fast enough,

> *If you don't get well or show some signs of improvement by June 10, I'm going to put you back in the "snake pit" and forget you.*

What would you think of an educator who said, to his students who were not learning fast enough,

> *If you don't learn what I want you to learn or show some interest in what I'm teaching by June 10, I'm going to fail you.*
> (In case you doubt this, consider the following quote of a University of Miami faculty member and reported in the Saturday Review, March 15, 1969):
>> *Let those kids come in their Ferraris. We'll take their money and flunk 'em out.* And flunk out they do. Three-fourths of Miami's entering freshmen don't survive through graduation (at that time).

Although millions of students throughout the country will receive one or more "F's" every time grades are reported, the grade "F" tells more about their teachers and the philosophy of the system than it does about the students. Just as easily as teachers can say that the students *are not able to learn or will not learn*, others could say that the teachers *are not able to teach or will not teach.*

In solving learning problems with teachers at all levels of education and in all subjects, it is very common to find teachers giving certain students materials to learn from, knowing that the students can't learn from them — and sure enough — when the students can't learn, the teachers fail the students. In a similar situation, many teachers start teaching their courses at a point (usually page 1 of the textbook) regardless of whether or not the students are ready to start the course at that point. *Generally, most teachers feel it is more important that they complete the presentation of the content of the course, rather than identify where learners are and start from there. Even if most of the class fails, at least the teacher finished the course!*

How long is a student supposed to remember whatever it is that is taught in a course? All teachers and almost everyone who has ever been a student realizes that people forget. In fact, many teachers have discovered that if they give a test or final exam to students three months, six months, or a year later, that there is a certain amount of deterioration in the learning. In view of this, consider the following statement:

> Do teachers really have the right to fail a student at the end of a quarter or semester for not knowing *something* that a certain percentage of his classmates who passed will not know three months, six months, nine months, or a year later?

Are schools really only interested in students remembering information for a very short time, in some cases just long enough to pass the test? If the learning that the tests test is important, it should be important that the students take this learning with them when they go out into the *real* world. Maybe we should be giving comprehensive examinations to our students prior to their graduation from any sequence of courses and based on the results of this comprehensive test teach the students whatever they were unable to answer correctly. If the learning represented by these test items is not that important, then maybe we shouldn't be testing it in the first place, and particularly not failing the students for not knowing something that is not that important.

Very few teachers will state that they want their students to learn facts, yet an examination of the tests that most teachers are giving will reveal that students are being failed for not learning what the teachers say are not important — FACTS. This is because teachers have not specified what they want students to learn and do not know how to specifically test for the achievement of desired behaviors which they can't identify or specify. Therefore, in order to have some kind of tests upon which to base a grade, many teachers test for the easiest things to make up test items for — FACTS!

Teachers should not be permitted to fail students for not learning something that the teacher is not able to specify or identify what it was the student did not learn. Testing and grading situations which exemplify this statement can be found in almost all teaching-learning situations, in which the teacher is unable to specify what it is exactly the students were supposed to learn, yet they are able to assign some kind of grade which is supposed to indicate the student's achievement or lack of achievement of something which has never been defined or identified.

If a student who is given an "I" decides not to complete the work and leaves the "I" on his record, *that is the student's decision* and any time he wants to complete the course the opportunity should be open. When a teacher or school gives a student an "F", that is the teacher's or school's decision and that decision may drastically change the student's future life by:
- affecting whether or not the student can stay in school.
- affecting the educational or vocational goals of the student,
- predetermining the types of education and employment the student can go into,
- affecting the success of the student in subsequent courses because of the influence on future teachers' subjective judgment,
- affecting whether or not the student will get a job because of the influence on future employers,
- affecting the students' self-image and subsequent relationship with the rest of society, and
- alienating the student sufficiently from the majority of society that the student becomes a social misfit, delinquent, and potential criminal.

Nothing breeds success like success and nothing breeds failure like failure!

The concept of being a *failure* is not acceptable to the healthy human mind. Therefore, a student who receives a series of "F's" and "D's" will sooner or later reject the concept of being a *failure* and in doing so will have a strong tendency to reject the society that supports the point of view that he or she is a *failure*. Quite often parents become a part of the group which considers the student a *failure*, and as such, also become a part of the group rejected by the student. In rejecting the majority of society, the student too often finds the only alternatives open are to join a segment of society which also has rejected the majority of society or a group which the majority of society has rejected. In either case, the results tend to lead eventually into juvenile delinquency and crime. This conclusion has been supported by a number of committees, commissions, research projects, individuals, etc. Somerset Maugham stated:

> *The common idea that success spoils people by making them vain, egotistical, and self-complacent is erroneous; on the contrary; it makes them for the most part, humble, tolerant and kind. Failure makes people bitter and cruel.*

Clyde Cambell, in his article, *The Effect of Failure on Learning*, states that

> *... failure is the germ bed for arson, pillaging, looting, and not the surface reasons frequently stated,* (for arson, pillaging, and looting).

Arthur W. Foshay in his *Curriculum for the 70's: An Agenda for Invention* states that

> *The schools, one may say, are organized around the presumption of ultimate failure. If a child isn't held back early in his career (and about 20 percent of all American children repeat a grade during the first three years of schooling), he is nevertheless ultimately defeated by the system. He fails to finish high school, or to gain entrance to college, or to make graduate school, or to win a doctorate, or to publish his dissertation to general acclaim. Sooner or later, he loses. Eventually, the system excludes almost everyone. It is not so much that the schools foster the pursuit of excellence. Rather, they pursue the excellent. The others are rejected.*

No educator is justified in giving a student a failing grade. Nevertheless, in working with thousands of teachers at all levels of education, it is quite obvious that there are teachers that resist very strongly the giving up of their power to condemn a student for life by placing the "F" grade on the student's transcript, rather than giving the student an opportunity to learn what the student has to learn in order to get an acceptable grade. Failure as it is commonly used in the traditional educational process is negative, degrading, and destructive. Non-achievement where there are no other ways to try to achieve is frustrating, but, if there is a potential for success of the same goals (SO's) via other pathways, temporary non-achievement can be a positive experience. Nonachievement where compromises are made by permanent lowering of the goals such as in ability grouping, streaming, etc. based on some imagined *capacity* of the students mind is also destructive and negative.

Some people claim that there are positive aspects of failure in school because in real life there may also be failure. If our educational goal is to help learners face the concept of *failure* and somehow benefit from the experience then the teaching-learning situation should be designed accordingly — to be able to derive benefits from failure or to cope with failure. In other words, if the concept of *failure* is important, then let's teach all students "A" or "B" worth of *coping with failure.*

There are a variety of alternate methods to failing. The major criteria of any alternate methods should be that the student is allowed to continue learning whatever it is he hasn't learned in order to get a passing grade or to achieve whatever degree of achievement that is considered necessary. What is the difference if it takes one semester or two semesters or more to learn whatever is supposed to be learned in a course? If our objective is that the student learn, does it really make that much difference how long it takes him to learn? Given the concept or philosophy that all learners can learn, when a learner doesn't learn, it is because we haven't found the right solution to the student's learning problem. In other words, we have failed, not the student.

c. SOCIAL PROMOTION

One of the oldest efforts to do something about individual differences in our elementary education is the concept of *social promotion*. This concept to varying degrees is also practiced in many junior high schools and even in a number of senior high schools. Essentially, *social promotion* refers to the practice of allowing students to pass who have previously failed in a given course. In other words, a student who fails in a particular grade, if he repeats this grade a second year, then regardless of whether he learns anything additional or even tries to learn anything, he is passed at the end of the second year. In many elementary schools, they have a policy of promoting a student even if the student is failing in two or three subject areas.

Social promotion in several different forms is practiced in almost every school district in the United States. It is justified on the basis that you can't have 17 and 18-year old students in elementary grades, and also, theoretically, the supporters of the social promotion concept claim that some students who are *late bloomers* will sooner or later start learning and will very quickly catch up to their class. In actual practice, social promotion is probably one of the worst concepts and one of the most detrimental practices found in education today. If students know that they are going to be passed on to the next grade, regardless of learning, there is no motivation to learn. When they have to repeat the same course that they have already taken, instead of learning those things which they did not learn the first year during the course, they are forced to try to learn the entire course from scratch, as if they had never been in the course in the first place. So when you combine the fact that the student knows he is going to pass, regardless of whether he learns or not, with the fact that the student is probably bored sitting through the same thing a second time around, you create about as negative a teaching-learning situation or environment as can possibly be developed. If cumulative ignorance develops when students only achieve "C" worth of a course, it should be very easy to demonstrate how rapidly cumulative ignorance can develop when students get "D's" or failing grades in courses and are passed on anyway. Therefore, if a student is socially promoted through two gardes (two years in each grade) the student is already so far behind due to cumulative ignorance that it is impossible for the student to learn what he is supposed to learn, and he is almost predestined to a series of failures throughout his academic career.

My boy, he pass to fifth grade this year and he can't hardly read at all. That just not right. Why they pass him when he don't know how to read? That school, it just not doing the job it ought.

A Negro Mother in Washington, D.C.
Saturday Review, November 18, 1967

If students had to stay in first grade until the student learned 100 percent of the required SO's, the traditional educators would visualize a single 17 or 18 year old student in first grade along with 30 five and six year old students. This would not be the case. If there was such a situation that the first grade SO's were so difficult that a student had to take 12 years to learn them, then because of the distribution of abilities (learned and inherited), there would also be several 15 and 16 year old students, four or five 13 and 14 year old students, eight or nine 11 and 12 year old students, etc. In such a situation, the 17 year old student wouldn't feel so out of place. Actually, no such situation would occur. Either the student would get tired of the teacher and the SO's and would learn them to get away from them or the teacher would get so tired of the student he or she would solve the student's learning problems to get rid of the student.

A common misunderstanding is that the student has to stay in the same physical facilities until he or she learns the required SO's. If it is deemed better, a student could pass on with other students to a different class, but the critical point is that the student has to continue on learning where the student stopped in the previous class. A traditional myth particularly in elementary schools is that the following teacher will pick a student up where the previous teacher stopped. Notice that the emphasis is on *where the teacher stopped* not *where the student stopped!* In the traditional educational process, where the teacher's role is to present the content of the course, a teacher may finish Chapter XI in a book and the next teacher starts out on Chapter XII. But this is where the teacher was in presenting the content of the course not where the students were in reference to their individual learning achievement (an examination of the differences in grades given in almost any class proves that the students are at different levels of achievement. In a situation where the teachers are working with GO's, it is impossible to have the next teacher help the student continue on where the student stopped in a previous class because GO's are not specific enough to measure where the student is at the end of one course or at the beginning of a subsequent course. If the teachers and students are working with SO's, it is relatively simple to have continuous progress for a student as he or she goes from one class to another.

Many so-called *modern* elementary schools claim to be practicing the concept of *continuous progress* in which the students are supposedly progressing at their own pace. If it is actually occurring, then some students should be completing sixth grade almost every day of the school year. Rarely is this the case. Usually what happens is that students may be progressing at their own pace in one or two subjects from September to June. The faster students who might finish the regular materials by April are giving busy work to keep them occupied until June or are sometimes given the next years materials. The slower students may only be half way through the materials by June. In September all students are promoted to the next grade and start at the same place. The faster students of the year before may now be bored because they are repeating some of the advanced material they had the previous year. The slower students are suffering from cumulative ignorance (the one-half of the previous year they didn't learn) and will probably progress even slower the following year with subsequent increased cumulative ignorance for the next year.

The whole issue appears to be a debate between which situation is the most important. To be promoted socially (affective domain) regardless of the cognitive and sensory learning levels or to be promoted because of cognitive and sensory learning regardless of the social and emotional growth. Evidence indicates that changes in the affective domain occur indirectly as a result of something else occurring. To promote students into a situation where they can't learn and are made to appear ignorant develops negative attitudes and actually regresses their social and emotional growth. When students are promoted because of cognitive and sensory achievement, they are not considered ignorant and their success will build positive attitudes towards school and the community.

If you are an adult, consider how you try to avoid boring situations which may only take a half-hour or an hour of your time. Consider the situation of the youngster who has been socially promoted through several grades even though the student learned less than half of what should have been learned and from that time until he is old enough to either drop out of school or be kicked out of school, the student sits in classes seven hours a day, five days a week, 36 weeks a year, year after year, without the slightest possibility of any learning taking place. As adults, we wonder why these students come back at night and vandalize our schools by shooting out the windows, setting fire to the schools, beating up on teachers, etc. If adults were placed in their position, having to endure what these students endure over the length of time that they are forced to be in school, adults would probably do the same things, but much sooner than the students do. Any time a teacher allows a student to leave his or her course or grade without learning what the student should have learned in the course or grade, they are fostering cumulative ignorance, which will eventually push the student out of school. One of the side effects of this procedure is to alienate the youngster from society, because society supported the institution that subjected the student to many years of negative experiences.

In response to the supporters of social promotion who want to prevent having 17 and 18 year old students in early elementary grades, it has been the experience of numerous projects throughout the United States that if educators will take the trouble to identify where the learner is and then take him from there at his own rate towards whatever the goals of the course are, that the student will learn and he can progress. It has also been the experience of many teachers that it is the nonlearning student that is the troublesome student. When a student is learning, he doesn't have time to get into trouble, or does not want to get into trouble. Under a program in which learners are able to progress at their own pace, starting from wherever they are and continuing on through the various objectives of the courses that they are taking, the problem is not going to be one of what to do with the students who takes too long to get through. The problem that will develop under a continuous progress plan based on specified learning objectives is that some students will complete our normal 12 years of elementary and secondary education in about six or seven years. Of course, if we can't identify specifically what it is the students are supposed to learn in our classes, then it may take students up to ten years or more to try to guess what it is the teachers are trying to teach.

d. ELIMINATION OF EVALUATION

There are small but growing groups of educators who are in favor of eliminating all forms of evaluation. Some of these teachers are conscious of the damage done to the students by bad grades and low test scores and as such want to eliminate any evaluation. To me, the obvious solution to this problem is to teach the students and solve their learning problems so they will have success; however, the teachers in this group assume that the students probably couldn't learn anymore anyway (based on the existence of a limit to intelligence which is a false assumption). Another group of teachers suspect or recognize that most tests used in the traditional educational process are faulty and useless so they also want to eliminate any evaluations. To me, the obvious solution should be to change the tests and make them fit the SO's and as such, the tests will be more relevant. Some teachers want to eliminate any evaluation because they may be forced to individualize instruction when they see differences in achievement. It is a lot easier to assume that all students are alike. Some teachers want to eliminate any evaluation because it allows accountability and they may find out that teachers are different in their ability to help students learn. It is a lot easier to assume that all teachers are alike also. Under the traditional approach, it seems acceptable to identify differences in student achievement which could cause cumulative ignorance problems and blame it on genetics but it is not acceptable to identify differences in the teaching ability of teachers as it might lead to differences in pay and/or teaching load.

There are a number of elementary school teachers who are in favor of eliminating all grading as far as evaluation is concerned, and there are also faculty in higher education who would like to eliminate any form of evaluation. The major bases which are stated for this concept are to reduce the emphasis on the letter grade itself and to reduce or eliminate the anxiety and fear associated with receiving low grades. First of all, if there was a high correlation between letter grades and learning, then an emphasis on getting a good grade (high level of learning) should be an acceptable teaching behavior. Secondly, if students were receiving low grades because of low levels of learning, eliminating the letter grade may reduce the students' anxiety and fear, but it doesn't affect the fact that the students still aren't learning what they are supposed to learn in order to have success in subsequent courses because of cumulative ignorance.

In schools where they have experimented with elimination of any form of evaluation, there appears to be a strong tendency towards even more ineffective and more inefficient teaching than existed before. There are a number of elementary schools and a few total school districts which have eliminated the letter grade type of evaluation in favor of parent-teacher conferences and written reports. Too often, under this approach, the teachers cut down on the number of tests or cut them out all together. Because of this, the teacher's evaluation of the student is more than ever based on *subjective* opinions which at its best is non-scientific and affected by chance, interpersonal relations, and the teacher's point-of-view of whether or not the student *can learn*. The reason that giving letter grades at the present time in most schools is bad, is that the grades are based on a lot of questionable educational practices. Eliminating letter grades or evaluation only eliminates the symptoms, it does not affect the questionable practices except possibly those affecting grading and testing.

Frequently, after a school or school district has eliminated letter grades and has turned to conferences and/or written reports to communicate to parents about their child's progress, parents become dissatisfied and ask for a return to letter grades. The problem is that the teacher conferences or the written reports don't really communicate how a child is progressing particularly when a teacher hasn't identified the SO's of the courses and/or has reduced the frequency of testing. What is being communicated is that even the teacher doesn't really know whether or not the student is progressing. I don't think parents are as concerned about how their child compares on a grading curve with other specific students as they are about whether or not their child is learning what they need to know and whether or not the rate of learning is above or below average. If their child's rate of learning is above average, that is okay. If their child's rate of learning is below average, parents want to know if they can help and they want to be assured that the school and teachers are doing what they can as professional educators to help their child. It is very frustrating for parents to observe that their child has trouble reading, writing, and doing arithmetic; never brings home any homework; and yet in the teacher conferences, the teacher continues to assure the parents that the child is doing fine!

There are two major unstated reasons behind the elimination of letter grades. First, with the number of student and parent protests increasing throughout the country, educational administrators are trying to reduce sources of student-school and community-school irritations wherever possible. Second, with the advent of the concept of *instructional accountability*, letter grades not only can be used to evaluate students, but they can also be used to evaluate the ability of teachers to teach and the effectiveness of the system within which the students and teachers are supposed to interact. Also, there will be no way of knowing the degree of *cumulative ignorance* the students may have developed before going to subsequent courses and the elimination of evaluation decreases the need to **know what the student should be learning** (the specification of learning objectives).

NOTE: A guiding philosophical statement found in many military classrooms back during World War II was *If the student hasn't learned, the teacher hasn't taught.*

Ideally, I would agree with the elimination of letter grades provided that the following three conditions are met:

1. Teachers have identified the content of their courses by specifying all of the important learning objectives in each course.
2. Teachers have developed tests that test for the achievement of all the important learning objectives on a one-to-one basis.
3. The design of the instructional system is such that almost every student learns *all* of the objectives of each course. (90% or more of the students will be "A" or "B" students.)

There will always be a need to evaluate whether or not the students have learned in order that the teachers will know what to teach. If it is not important enough to evaluate whether or not the students have learned, then it probably isn't important whether or not the teacher teaches and whether or not the students attend the classes. A senior at a very well-known university which had experienced a number of student strikes from 1965-1973 said to me, *During the past several years, I don't think I've really learned anything, because the teachers have stopped giving tests and don't seem to care about whether or not students learn.*

3. EVALUATION AND DISCIPLINE

In the beginning of this unit on Evaluation of Students, I pointed out that there were six variables and their interrelationships to consider in discussing the evaluation of students: the presence or absence of measurable objectives, whether or not the teacher taught the SO's, whether or not the tests tested for the achievement of the SO's, whether or not the grading was objectively related to the achievement of the SO's, whether or not there were any follow-up activities after the evaluation, and the effects on the student.

Positive and negative evaluation refers to what happens after the evaluation event (the fifth variable). Negative evaluation is when the results of the evaluation are used to do negative things to the student, i.e., assign low grades, assign negative labels (dumb), cause parent-student conflict because of low grades, etc. Negative evaluation usually refers to traditional evaluation and is typically done at the end of a unit or course (finals, mid-term, etc.) when it is too late to do anything about the diagnostic information revealed by the test. Positive evaluation is when the results of the evaluation are used to do positive things to the student, i.e., identify and solve learning problem, start the student where he or she is with minimum gaps and overlaps in learning, etc. Positive evaluation is the only type of evaluation used in the Behavioral Learning Systems Approach to instruction and is typically done at the beginning and during an instructional unit or course to determine the appropriate materials for the students.

To the traditional educator, there may not seem to be much of a relationship between the concepts of *evaluation* and *discipline.* However from the systems point of view, the two terms are related concepts. The relationship becomes more apparent as one examines positive and negative evaluation (the fifth variable) and positive and negative discipline (the sixth variable). Just as teachers don't like to be evaluated when they think the results might be used to fire them, students don't like to take tests if the results might be used to fail them. Conversely, teachers won't mind evaluation (as much) if the results are used to help the teacher be a better teacher and students won't mind evaluation if the results are used to help the students to be better students and have more successes.

Negative evaluation can have a positive effect on students if they are identified as being at the top of the class and the test shows that they have learned most or all of what they were supposed to learn.

Obviously, under the traditional curve approach to evaluation and grading, the number of students who react positively to negative evaluation are a small minority. For the majority of students, negative evaluation results in negative feelings. For the students who receive "D" and "F" grades, the negative feelings are felt almost immediately. For these and other students who are passed on with varying degrees of cumulative ignorance, the negative feelings may be delayed until the lack of knowledge and/or skills causes the student to have learning problems.

Positive evaluation should have a positive effect on all students. However, some students who are accustomed to academic permissiveness and social promotion (being promoted without having to learn) may feel negative at first when they find out that they have to learn all of the SO's in order to be promoted. As these students have successes in learning, their negative feelings will be softened or eliminated.

Whereas positive evaluation indicates what students need to know in order to complete a unit or course, positive discipline is the demanding that the students learn all of the required SO's before being promoted. Positive discipline is generally associated with increasing the learning of desired SO's which in turn indicates that the teachers are concerned about the students, the learning that should occur, and their responsibility to society. Positive discipline which forces students and teachers to be successful, ultimately involves intrinsic and/or positive extrinsic motivation. On the other hand, negative discipline usually results in the development of negative feelings and anti-establishment attitudes and values and indicates that the teachers and schools are not very interested in the students, in their learning, nor in the results of their actions on society.

For six years, the Gallup Poll has found in their annual survey of adults (non-students) and students that the lack of discipline was felt to be the most critical problem in our schools. Surveys of teachers have come out with the same results. In response to these feelings, there has been an increase in courses and emphasis on classroom management from the point of view of negative discipline. Quite typically, increases in negative discipline (which is punishment oriented) results in the development of negative attitudes and values which in turn results in more student actions which requires more negative discipline. This sequence of events is a downward negative spiral and can eventually get out of control and result in violence and destruction of property and people particularly when associated with permissiveness in learning which fosters cumulative ignorance.

Teachers, and particularly principals, spend a significant portion of their time being concerned about discipline in our schools. In fact, at many teacher's and/or administrative meetings, a common subject of concern is discipline in the schools. Admittedly, discipline is a very critical problem, but our present approaches or solutions to this problem are in error from two points of view. First, the solutions are in error because too often the punishment vs. reward concepts are all mixed up. Second, the emphasis of discipline is in an area which tends to indicate that educators are hypocritical in reference to what we say is important vocally and what we indicate is important by our actions.

As an example of the confused concept of punishment, consider the case of hundreds of students across the nation who skip school because they don't want to be in school. A common punishment for truancy if the student is beyond the age where they have to be in school, is to suspend the student from school. This is really what the student wanted all along. What the educational establishment is essentially saying is, *That poor student, he won't be able to sit hour after hour and listen to us any more and he is going to be sorry.* Meanwhile, the student is happily leaving the school grounds. He has finally achieved what he wanted — to be away from an environment he hated. We actually end up rewarding the student for skipping school What is important to point out is that the concept of punishment and reward has to be a receiver-oriented concept, in which in order for something to be punishing, the person who is being punished has to think of it as punishment. The same with the concept of reward. A person who is going to be rewarded has to think of the reward as a reward.

As a result of the confusion between punishment and reward, consider the change in attitude of students who are attending school as they progress from the first grade through the twelfth grade. Generally speaking, most first-grade students are very positive towards coming to school. By the time students get into fifth or sixth grade, the general feeling is almost neutral, with some students still liking school and some students now developing a dislike for school. By the time the students are in twelfth grade, the general feeling is on the negative side, with many students only attending school because they know they have to. Education has become a necessary evil in their lives rather than a positive influence. What causes this change in attitude?

Since this change in attitude occurs even during elementary school, it would tend to indicate that something must be happening in the elementary schools to effect this change in attitude. In examining the kind of punishment often given in second, third, fourth, and fifth grades, etc., it is easy to find teachers who are assigning extra homework problems, extra essays, writing drills, i.e., write 200 times *I won't chew gum.* Since doing problems and writing essays are the types of student behaviors which most teachers want, it is not surprising that when these activities are used as punishment, it doesn't take students very long to be convinced that doing educational activities is punishing. This student reaction then carries over into changing their attitude so that by the time students are in fifth or sixth grade and the teacher announces the homework assignment, the students complain either vocally or subvocally by saying, *What did we do wrong to deserve such a punsihment?* Consider a similar situation when physical education instructors are asked, *Why should students take physical education courses and of what value will physical education be for later life?* Almost all physical education personnel will claim that their major objective is to develop in the student a positive attitude towards keeping the body physically fit throughout his like. If this is really our objective in physical education, it is rather odd, that in almost all physical education courses when students do something wrong, they are punished by being made to do physical exercise, i.e., *Run ten laps around the gym, do ten pushups, etc.* The most common punishment is to make the student stay after school. It doesn't take too long before students are convinced that staying in school even during the daytime is punishment.

In some ways, the problems of discipline, student strikes, and teacher strikes overlap. For example, both students and teachers who are for striking and also against striking, talk about the need for freedom to teach and freedom to learn. Academic freedom is often defined as a freedom from coercion. Are the students really free to learn? Are they really free from coercion? How about the thousands and thousands of students who face failure daily in the classroom; not only failure in terms of learning, but failure because they don't attend class, wear their hair too long, wear the wrong clothes, smoke cigarettes, etc. Although the educational establishment claims that learning is our most important goal, by our actions we are saying that the most important thing is how students look and the maintenance of the status quo. We need to increase our *discipline in learning* by holding both students and teachers accountable for what happens in the learning process.

Of particular interest in the area of discipline is the fact that those very teachers whose subjects are concerned with the scientific methods, critical analysis, etc., in which the records of performance, research, etc., are very strict, are all too often the teachers who tend to resist the most in instituting discipline into the learning situation, by demanding that all students learn "A" or "B" worth of the course. For some reason, many of these teachers tend to believe that to have high standards they have to give a high percentage of their students "D's" and "F's".

In a recent college graduating class, of approximately 400 bachelor's degrees that were awarded, only 80 or 20 percent of these degrees candidates, had done "B" or better work, which meant that 80 percent of the graduating students were suffering from varying degrees of cumulative ignorance. Is that the best that the teaching staff of that particular college can do? If what there is in the college to be learned is worth learning, then why not make all students learn it, regardless of the amount of time it takes?

Although thousands of students are dropped from school or failed because of nonlearning, very few teachers are fired or dropped because of their inability to teach. In the very same schools where students are penalized for wearing long hair or the wrong clothes, nothing is done to the teacher who lets the majority of the students leave a course only learning "C", "D", or "F" worth of the course. Discipline in education has to be defined in terms of learning, such that every student has to learn or he can not go on to the next unit. Not only should students be held accountable for learning, but also their teachers. Not only should teachers be free of negative coercion in their teaching, but students should be free of negative coercion in learning. In other words, when learning does not take place, students should not be punished by giving them "F's" and "D's". They should be encouraged or helped to keep working at it until such time as they learn either "A" or "B" worth of a course. If the student decides to take the Incomplete and not finish a course, then this should be the student's choice and his freedom to do so.

There is an organized movement headed up by the American Civil Liberties Union (ACLU) to get rid of any corporal punishment in the schools. In opposition to this movement are many teachers, parents, and even students who feel the need for more discipline in the schools not less discipline. Actually, these two groups are not in opposition if you consider discipline in terms of positive and negative. The ACLU is against negative discipline and certainly wouldn't be against students learning more. The educator, parents, and students want different things: the educators want more order and less vandalism; the parents want the students to learn more; and the students want the teachers to show that they care about the students and what they are teaching. Positive discipline can help all three groups. Students will be more orderly and develop more positive feelings when they start having positive experiences. Students will be learning more under positive discipline (90 percent or more of the students have to learn 100 percent of the required SO's) and as the teachers work more individually with the students, tailoring the materials and experiences to fit the needs of the students in learning the required SO's, students will know that the teachers care about them.

Consider for a moment several excerpts from an article, *The Crisis In Our Schools*, written by Dr. Donald Hair, Acting Superintendent of

Schools in Kansas City and published in the February, 1970, issue of *Town Squire*. Parts of the *Crisis* were defined as follows:

— *violence in the schools is accelerating (197 incidents within a five-week period, 500 disruptive students suspended, $100,000 spent for security guards, $400,000 spent to repair vandalism, etc.),*

> Notice the emphasis on eliminating the symptoms while not treating the cause.

— *teachers who have been trained to teach are so involved in disciplinary activities that they don't have time to teach and principals don't have time for instructional leadership,*

> First of all, most teacher training institutions in our country do not train students to *teach* as measured by helping students learn. Most of these institutions train students to *present course content*. Maybe if the teachers and administrators concentrated on improving learning, the disciplinary problems would start to decrease. Of course, to place an emphasis on learning, the teachers would have to know what the students are supposed to be learning (specific learning objectives) and they would have to use tests that test these objectives (specific behavioral test items).

— *absenteeism is alarming (15-20 percent of the students are not coming to some high schools which cuts down the support money from the state which is based on average daily attendance).*

> Why should a student want to go to a school or classroom to incur further negative experiences? Notice, the problem is that the *absenteeism is affecting the budget* not that the students may or may not be learning. When schools can not identify or account for what is happening in our schools in terms of learning, then the next best thing is to count bodies and the number of hours and days the bodies are in a classroom in front of a teacher. Once schools specify the learning that should be taking place, then the accountability for state support can be in terms of whether or not students are learning instead of whether or not the students are in school — regardless of learning!

Dr. Stanley Coopersmith in his studies of self-esteem, found that children who had high self-esteem also had parents who were strict and consistent in their discipline and relied on rewards (positive discipline) rather than punishment. He also found that children who had low self-esteem had parents who were generally permissive but inflicted harsh punishment (negative discipline) when the children got into trouble. Dr. William Glasser found similar results in working with *deprived* children, that lax standards are interpreted as not caring while firm standards are interpreted as showing interest and caring.

Even Dr. Benjamin Spock who used to preach permissiveness stated in February, 1974, issue of *Redbook* that our *inability to be firm is the commonest problem of parents*. Although these specialists didn't bring it out, the key is to be firm in your area of concern, i.e., educators should be firm and strict in learning, employers should be strict in areas connected to employment, parents should be strict in areas connected to the home, etc.

In 1971, American College Testing Program (ACT) questioned a cross section of students and found that the two characteristics mentioned most often as being typical of a *best* teacher were *demanding* and *caring*. The *demanding* was in reference to learning.

A very real situation which indicates the lack of discipline in the learning process is that few, if any, principals or superintendents are willing to guarantee that their high school diploma stands for any specified list of learning achievements. All they are willing to guarantee is that the student has been in the school system for twelve or more years. Surely, the taxpayers supporting the schools have the right to expect something more to occur then just the required physical presence of the students in schools for twelve years. With all the talk of increased taxes, bond issues, higher salaries for educators, increased programs, smaller classes, etc., can the taxpayers, parents, and students continue to give *carte blanche* to the educators without some accountability in the area of learning? Hopefully, learning is more important than whether or not a student sat in a classroom, had long hair, sideburns, smoked cigarettes, etc.

a, CHEATING

The concept of cheating has been considered as a very negative form of behavior and has resulted in a wide variety of disciplinary actions ranging from a simple reprimand by a teacher who may pick up the students test paper and tell him or her to start over again, to a very serious formal charge which could result in actions affecting the students entire lifetime (particularly in the military academies). I don't believe that students innately want to cheat. I believe that students have to be pressured into cheating for the first time. If it turns out to be a positive experience, the student may turn to cheating a little easier the next time. What the traditional educators don't realize is that they are the ones who set up the conditions which pressure the students into cheating. The guiding principle is that:

> anytime a person is put into a situation where the outcome of the situation can have a serious and lasting affect on him or her and the person has little more than chance control over the outcome, the person will tend to do anything possible to have more control over

the outcome. (The more critical the outcome, the more effort will be expended in trying to affect the outcome).

When teachers set up any of the following situations, they should expect some form of cheating: the use of curve grading; the teaching of one thing but the testing of something else; say you are going to teach one thing (objectives), teach a second thing, and then test a third thing; the use of hidden objectives and hidden tests; the use of external standardized tests which probably have little to do with what happens in the classroom; and/or the requiring of a course which the students see as irrelevant to their goals. Putting a time limit on the test increases the tendency to cheat and skewing the grading curve such that more students fail also increases the tendency to cheat. If the evaluation is negative such that there is only one chance to pass and the score is your grade, students will be tempted to cheat. If teachers are honest and open with the course objectives such that the SO's are taught and tested and the students have an option to take the test over again as many times as necessary to prove achievement of the test items (which should match the SO's of the course), students will not be tempted to cheat. Therefore, cheating should be considered a symptom of an educational process in which the teacher is not being completely honest with the students. Instead of punishing the students who cheated, the administrator should find out why the teacher tried to hide from the students what the students were supposed to learn!

For example, there have been several cheating *scandals* at the military academies involving many students. Those who are found guilty of cheating are kicked out and discharged under other than honorable circumstances. These actions no doubt affected the students entire lifetime. It is not the students fault, it is the fault of the traditional education system which supports dishonesty and unfairness on the part of teachers but condemns students for trying to improve their chances for success. Not knowing what the teacher will be testing, some students prepare hidden notes to prepare them for surprise test items that teachers may spring on them. This is similar to the Navy's use of radar to improve their chances for success in the event of hidden surprises from an enemy. Compare the offenses on both sides!

STUDENTS	TEACHERS
1. Used one or more techniques to improve their chances for success.	1. Probably did not give the students the SO's they were supposed to learn.
	2. Probably did not test the SO's, if any, nor what was taught.

3. Teachers probably were not trained in teaching or testing and hence not qualified to make up the test or interpret the test results.
4. Probably used a curve approach to grading such that some students had to fail regardless of what they learned.
5. Probably used so-called *objective* type test items in which the distractors are purposely put in the test items to trick students.
6. The evaluation was probably negative in that the scores were used to eliminate students or to punish them rather than as diagnostic instruments.
7. Because of the negative evaluation at the end of the units, the students were allowed to go into the final examination with cumulative ignorance which the teacher knew would affect the students' performance.

4. SYSTEMS EVALUATION AND GRADING

With reference to the six variables which could be involved in student evaluation, the Behavioral Learning Systems Approach to instruction suggests that the unit and course objectives consist of interrelated GO's and SO's and that the minimum common core SO's be identified; that the teacher has primary responsibility to teach the required SO's to all students; that the tests are designed to test for the achievement of the required SO's; that the grading is such that the student's achievement is compared to himself or herself in previous tests and/or to the required SO's; that the evaluation is positive in that the purpose of the testing is diagnostic in nature and the students are taught whatever they miss on the tests until at least 90 percent or more have learned 100 percent of the required SO's; that the instructional process recognizes the individual differences in the students and teachers such that the process is a positive experience for the students and hopefully for the teachers too.

The most basic criteria for the Behavioral Learning Systems Approach to evaluation is that the teachers and students are working from a list of interrelated GO's and SO's for each course and that the SO's are measurable and represent the required SO's which have been agreed upon by the teachers who teach the course. The approach is open in that teachers, students and parents have the lists of GO's and SO's available at all times and as such, they all know exactly where the student is and what he or she should be learning. (A much more detailed discussion of GO's and SO's is in Chapter VI, Vol. II).

In teaching under the Behavioral Learning Systems Approach, the new role of the teacher is concerned with the results of the teachers' performance rather than the traditional concern for the teachers' performance regardless of the results. In maximizing the results, the teacher actually teaches to the test either directly in small groups of students with common learning problems or indirectly via a variety of instructional materials. The ultimate objective is to develop students who can learn on their own and can solve their own learning problems. Therefore, the majority of the teachers' time is spent with students who can't learn independently and can't solve their own learning problems. Whereas time and materials were kept constant under the traditional approach and learning was treated as a variable, under the Learning Systems Approach, minimum common core learning will be held as a minimum constant and the time and materials could vary as needed by the students and teachers.

One of the defenses often used to support the use of curve grading and the use of A, B, C, D, and F letter grades is that these concepts facilitate the development of a competitive spirit which is needed to survive in a capitalistic environment. Just because most or all students will now learn 100 percent of the required SO's, doesn't mean that competition is no longer there. There will be differences in how much time it will take different students to learn the required SO's. There will be differences in the materials used (and therefore the costs) by different students in order to learn the required SO's. There will be differences in the extra SO's that students will elect to learn. There will be differences in the number of hours, days, and maybe weeks that different students will put in helping other students learn. There will also be differences in the number of times students will put on presentations (scholarship sessions) for other students, teachers, and members of the community.

a. TESTING UNDER A BEHAVIORAL LEARNING SYSTEMS APPROACH

The basic key to testing is that the test items have to reflect the SO's with a high if not perfect correlation. If the test items are even slightly different, it is difficult to interpret the results in terms of any achievement of the required SO's. The tests should not be *normed* as this involves the manipulation of the test items to get whatever results the teacher or educator wants regardless of actual learning levels. In one situation, the *norm* which splits those above and those below could be say 50% of what should be learned in which the smartest student might only learn 60-70% of what should have been learned. In another instance, all the students could learn 90% or more of what they were supposed to learn, but in order to have a *norm* it could be any student between 90-95 would get the "C's", "D's", and "F's". Typically, the manipulating of the test items to affect the results of the test invalidates the test results as being of any value in reference to the achievement of the required SO's.

Under a system where mastery of all SO's is expected and the development of cumulative ignorance has to be minimized, several testing problems occur. The first problem concerns the frequency of testing. The rule to follow is that the student should be tested as often as necessary to identify any cumulative ignorance which may interfere with the next learning task. In a situation where no SO is dependent upon another SO for learning to occur, tests can occur whenever the student needs reinforcement that he or she is learning successfully. Whenever the achievement of a SO is necessary in order to achieve a subsequent SO, then the student should be tested as soon as possible after the prerequisite SO has been learned to verify achievement or to identify a learning problem.

In a situation where students can take tests over and over again, there are some students who want to learn by taking the tests rather than to study. This usually results in making a lot of work for the teacher. In order to avoid this problem, insist on some evidence of work between tests.

If there are rote memory SO's to be learned, a teacher can ask for an increasing repetition or drilling of the items missed between tests. For example, if there are 20 items to be memorized (facts, rules, spelling words, etc.), a teacher may tell the students to write the items five times as homework. If after the first test, a student misses 10 of the items, ask the student to write each of the 10 items 10 times. If after the second test, a student misses five of the items, ask the student to write each of the five items at least 20 times. If after the third test, a student misses three of the items, ask the student to write each of the three items at least 40 times, etc. The same process can be used with the learning and testing of process objectives (addition, subtraction, writing a sentence, applying a formula, etc.) in which the student has to do an increasing number of applications of each process objective missed every time the student has to repeat the test (only the objectives missed).

Another common problem when mastery learning is expected is that in the testing of all SO's for each student, there could be a lot of work for the teacher. Under the traditional approach, teachers usually compromise on the way they test and also on what they test. As indicated earlier, the sampling techniques typically used are very unscientific and usually fall into the category of teachers saying to themselves, *I guess I'll test the students on this and that* while the students are saying to themselves, *I guess the teacher is going to test us on this and some other things.* If the guesses match, the students get an "A". If the guesses don't match, the size of the deviation is traditionally blamed on genetics.

Of course, the primary basis for the guessing game in the traditional approach is that the teachers don't really know what they want the students to learn anyway. When teachers have their SO's to work from, the urge to sample in order to lessen the work is still there, but some teachers will decide to compromise on the way they test rather than sample what they test. Typically, these teachers will use multiple-choice or true-false test items because they are easy to grade. Ironically, in order to have test items which are easy and fast to grade some teachers will spend many hours and even days to make up that test rather than taking minutes to make up test items from the SO's and use the hours to diagnose and prescribe for student learning problems as identified by the results of the test. If a teacher had 100 SO's and felt compelled to lessen the work load, it would be better for the teacher to sample 10-20 of the SO's and test them right rather than to compromise on the format of the test items and test all 100 SO's wrong.

There are two more systemized ways to solve this problem. First, it is possible to test with a sample of the total population of SO's under certain conditions. The best sampling technique would be the use of test items which represent all of the terminal SO's. For example, if there are 40 SO's in a particular unit or course, maybe 10 of them are terminal objectives and the other 30 SO's have to be learned in order to learn the 10 terminal objectives. By testing for the achievement of the 10 terminal objectives, you are also indirectly testing for the achievement of the other 30 SO's because they have to be learned in the process of learning the 10 terminal objectives.

Another sampling procedure which would be acceptable is where the students are given the total list from which the sample will be taken. The guideline in order to indicate mastery is that if the student gets 100 percent of the random sample the teacher will assume that the student has mastered the total population of items. If the student misses one or more from the sample, the student will have to take the total test in order to identify what other SO's were not learned.

NOTE: Remember, in this type of sampling, if the student misses one or more of the sample, he or she probably will miss others in the population of required SO's that were not in the sample. It is not sufficient to just teach the items missed in the sample. The whole test has to be given in order to identify which SO's were not learned in order to teach them.

If only a fourth or a half of the students achieve a 100 percent on the sample and are given credit for having achieved all of the SO's, this still saves the teacher a lot of time.

A second method to reduce the amount of work involved in testing where there are a lot of SO's to be tested and a lot of students to be tested, involves letting the students use self-tests and to test one another. In the traditional situation where the average student only achieves about 70 percent of what should be learned, most teachers would be reluctant to take one student's word about the achievement of another student. However, under the Behavioral Learning Systems Approach, a student has to achieve 100 percent and so a teacher can have more confidence in a situation where a student who already has achieved 100 percent of the unit SO's is the one who is testing another student. In trying to develop students who are independent learners, it is good to let students assume responsibility for part of the testing. In instructional units, it would be useful to let the students have one or more self-tests which should match the lists of SO's given with the unit and are similar to the actual tests to be given at the end of the unit.

If you are planning to give sort of a final examination to check for mastery at the end of a course or after several units of instruction, it is reasonable to let the students check their own unit tests. Be sure to impress on the students that if they don't really achieve 100 percent of all the unit objectives, they could have trouble in subsequent units because of cumulative ignorance and if they aren't able to achieve all of the SO's by the time they take the final examination, they will still have to go back and learn all of the SO's they missed. If the students are convinced that they will have to learn all of the SO's, most of them will correct the self-tests honestly.

In giving diagnostic tests at the beginning of a course or unit, have the students do the paper and pencil part of the tests in duplicate using carbon paper or NCR type treated paper. When the students finish the test, they turn in the copy to the teacher who in turn gives them a special type of an answer sheet. After each answer on the answer sheet is a prescription on how to learn the SO related to the test item in case the student missed it. The prescription could include the name of a book, page numbers, and exercises to do, or it could include a reference to an independent study unit, a programmed instructional unit, etc.

Within minutes after each student has completed the test, each student also has an individualized prescription for his or her learning needs. Any student that has achieved mastery or 100 percent can ask the teacher to verify it by checking the copy of the test which the student turned in.

b. GRADING UNDER A BEHAVIORAL LEARNING SYSTEMS APPROACH

Under the traditional approach, grades are usually given to represent how one student achieved in reference to other students based in part on objective data and in part on subjective data. The ratio of objective data to subjective data may or may not be identified. However, in the case of the A, B, C, D, and F letter grades, percentage grades, or other numerical grades, the combined objective — subjective data is forced into interval data called *grade points* and *grade point averages*. One of the more serious hypocritical malpractices in higher education and particularly in the sciences and in graduate education is the insistance by the teachers on the use of the scientific method and principles by the students and yet in grading, it is a very common practice to force subjective evaluation data into interval data which in turn is used as a basis for considerable statistical manipulation and research which affects the progress and future of students.

Ideally, under a Behavioral Learning Systems Approach, there shouldn't be any grade given since all students are to learn 100 percent of the required SO's and all students then would eventually get "A's". More appropriate grading terms would be the use of *pass — not pass* or *go — no go* because the student doesn't leave a unit or course until he or she has learned all of the required SO's. The function of grades would be to indicate where the student is in reference to the achievement of the required SO's of a unit, course, or program. There is no need for the negative aspects of grading, so students wouldn't fail a unit or course. They would stay in the course or unit until it was completed. Students would not repeat a course in which they had to relearn SO's they had already learned, they would only learn the SO's they did not learn previously.

Hopefully, in the near future all schools will be *nongraded*, but nongraded as defined by students who continuously progress in the achievement of defined specific objectives in their various courses, which are being taught by teachers who look on learning as a continuum and are concerned about quality control in learning. In a situation like this, instead of a student receiving a report card at various times during a course or at the end of a course, each student will have a continuing achievement profile that indicates where the student is at any one time as he progresses through the various subjects in his course (see Figure 131).

Learning Objectives by Grade Level

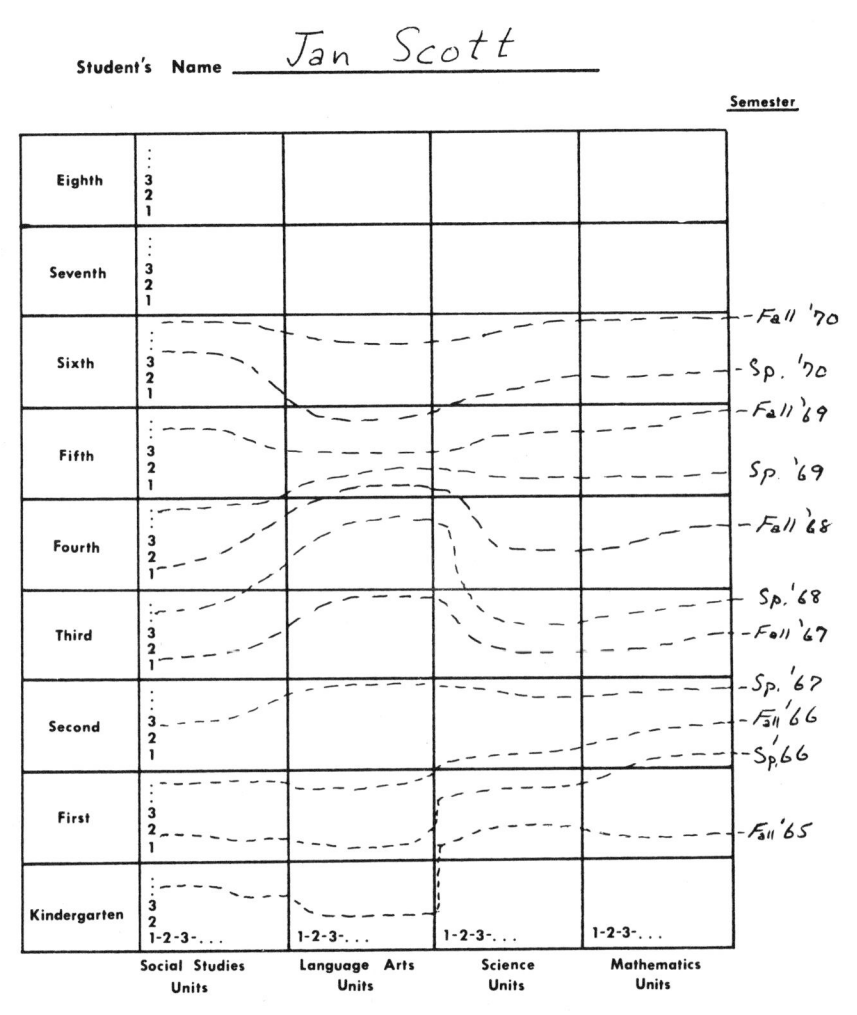

Student's Name Jan Scott

Subject Matter Sequences

Figure 131 — Continuous Progress Scale — Achievement Profiles

The use of an achievement profile would indicate to teachers, students, and parents, where the student is and where the major emphasis in time and instruction should be placed. If the student is progressing fairly evenly in all subject matter areas and approximately with his own age group, then the student and his teachers would be free to go into any type of enrichment learning that the student would like and the teachers feel the student might be interested in. On the other hand, if there are valleys in the student's achievement profile which indicate that the student is not up to where he should be in certain areas, then more time and teaching effort should be concentrated on the specified learning objectives in those areas.

Of course, the profiles as indicated in Figure 131 only go from kindergarten to eighth grade, but this could easily be expanded up to twelfth grade and would then of course include different subject matter areas with the common expectations of those areas. This type of a profile could also be expanded up to include undergraduate college instruction and should probably also be expanded in a downward direction to include preschool learning activities. Because of the wide variation in students entering kindergarten, it would be of great value to have an achievement profile which would cover the common expectations of all students entering school, and then preschool activities would be especially designed for students who in their normal home environment are not able to keep up with what is considered normal child development. Young children who, in their homes, are progressing normally, would not necessarily need some kind of academic preschool. Entrance into the regular, formal school situation (kindergarten or first grade), would be determined by the students' preschool achievement profile being at the prerequisite beginning points for formal instruction, rather than the fact that the student is 4, 5, or 6 years old. In this way, students who may achieve prerequisite entry levels at ages of 3 or 4, will start at that age, whereas other students who have not achieved the prerequisite entry levels for formal education at the kindergarten or first-grade level by the time they are 5 or 6 years old, will have been identified earlier as not progressing normally towards these goals, and will have been attending some kind of academic, preschool activity, which is specifically designed to prepare the student to start the formal school at the kindergarten or first-grade level. It is very possible that some students just may not be ready to start until they are six or seven or eight years old. At least when they do start, they will be at an equal level with other students with whom they may be learning, and their progress through the school will be determined by their achievement, rather than the typical situation in which some students start kindergarten or first grade two or three years behind their classmates and get progressively further and further behind as they go through school, until such time as they either drop out of school or are failed out of school.

Obviously, when using the achievement profiles as a grading system, some students will take longer to go through school than other students, which should be considered a normal situation because not all students are the same. At least under this approach, once the student does complete high school instruction, everyone will know that he or she has learned certain specific things, and that the high school diploma refers to minimum content learned, rather than to attendance in an elementary or secondary school for twelve or more years, regardless of learning.

The establishment of national, regional, state, and local minimums for achievement would also bring about a real equality of education for all. Previously, *equal education* has been interpreted as the student being placed in an equal school building with equally trained teachers as other students have or bussing the students from one school to a more equal school. Since the bussing is not accompanied by necessary changes in the academic program to eliminate previously developed cumulative ignorance, then putting different types of students in the same environment does not assure *equal education. Equal Education* should be measured in terms of learning, so that equal education means that learners from different groups have at least learned the same amount as a minimum, and this minimum should be sufficiently high, so that the students will not be penalized in any future attempts to further his own education in whatever direction the learner wants to go. In guaranteeing *equal education* as measured by learning, it can be easily seen that for students who are suffering from cumulative ignorance, increased amounts of money are going to have to be spent in a variety of ways in order to help these learners learn what they are going to have to learn, in order to participate in our society. This does not mean that students without cumulative ignorance will have less money spent on them; this would be up to the local school district to decide one way or the other, but state and federal funds would be utilized to make sure that every student, regardless of where he lived and what school he attended, would be involved in a teaching-learning situation in which one way or the other at least 90 percent or more of the students would learn the national, regional, state, and local minimums of achievement.

Although the achievement profiles are a useful type of individual achievement record and useful for reporting achievement to parents and students, when a teacher has a lot of students, it may be more convenient for teachers to use charts to record student progress. The names of the students can be written down the left hand side and the numbers of the SO's across the top. This chart can be kept in the chalk-rail of a classroom or can be posted on the wall of a teacher's office. At any time, anyone can see where a student is. It can be useful in a parent-teacher conference to indicate a child's progress in comparison with other students without the negative aspects of curve grading. It can also be used by the teacher to see at a glance which students are on the same objective and which students need the most help.

NOTE: In a situation where students progress at their own pace, some students tend to procrastinate. In order to decrease this problem, at the end of each unit on the chart, put a column entitled *Predicted completion date* in which based on the student's rate of progress at that point, the teacher predicts the completion of the course. Where a student is very slow, the prediction at the end of the first unit may indicate that the student won't finish the course for several years. I have found this column to be a useful motivator particularly when a student who is procrastinating also wants to graduate or be promoted.

c. THE ABI ALTERNATIVE

The ideal grading system (achievement profiles) will be very practical *AFTER* teachers have agreed upon the minimum common core SO's of all their courses. Once teachers have even identified the minimum common core SO's in one or more (but not all) courses, it would be possible to use a sort of check list in which the SO's are listed on some form and as the student achieves a SO, it is checked off. The problem becomes one of what to do during the transition stage. I and many other teachers at all levels of education have found the ABI system to be functional. Since most parents, teachers and students are very familiar with the traditional letter grade system (A, B, C, D, F), using at least two of the traditional letters (the A and B) helps in communicating the goals of the Learning Systems Approach. The use of an "I" (incomplete) instead of the letters C, D and F helps to eliminate the negativeness of the traditional approach to grading. Some teachers have not been able to accept my criteria for differentiation between an A and a B, so they prefer to use only an A and an I. My preference for the A, B, I over A, I grading is that I, like many teachers, am not confident that everything we can measure is equal to all we want. Writing SO's is a learned skill and at the present time not many teachers are so good at it that they are willing to say with confidence that a given list of SO's represents all that should be learned in a given unit or course. For most teachers, they would feel better saying, *This list of required SO's represents what should be learned to the best of my ability to specify.* This statement implies that as the teacher's ability to specify SO's improves, the list of required SO's may also change. In other words, there are probably some unspecified objectives in most or all courses which should be learned but as yet have not been identified and remain for the time being as a GO or part of a GO not because they can't be measured but because the teachers haven't developed their skills sufficiently to specify and measure them.

I define the letter grade of "B" as equal to 100 percent of all the required measurable SO's, the letter grade of "I" is given for any achievement level less than 100 percent. The letter grade of "A" is reserved for above and beyond the required SO's of the unit or course. There is a temptation among traditional teachers to use A, B, I where the "B" is 90 percent achievement and "A" is the 100 percent achievement. This means that those students getting a "B" would miss 10 percent of the required SO's and would possibly suffer from cumulative ignorance. If the "B" was given for 100 percent of the required SO's, and the "A" was given for a certain number of extra SO's, then the question becomes one of if the extra SO's are important enough to give a student an "A" for learning them why shouldn't the extra SO's be required of all students? If the extra SO's are not important enough to require all students to learn them, then they are probably not important enough to give a student an "A" for learning them. Based on this reasoning, the "A" grade should not be given for learning more of the same things the "B" grade is given for. Since the required SO's are indirect cognitive and sensory objectives, then the "A" grade could be concerned with the affective domain. However, since students don't really have direct control over the development or change in their attitudes and values (only on how they exhibit them), it isn't fair to grade students on their emotional tendencies or on their acting ability (putting on the external appearance of the desired attitudes and values). Therefore, I have found it useful to use the "A" grade as representative of a specific number of hours[7] spent helping other students in the same course learn the required SO's. The value of this use of the "A" grade is that in going back over the SO's and helping other students learn them, the students learn them *better* (not measurable). Every teacher I have talked to agrees that when you teach a unit or course, you learn it *better* (still not measurable). Even though the *better* is not measurable in cognitive and sensory learning, as the student learns the SO's *better*, the student's attitudes towards the SO's are positively increased and this change and direction can be measured by semantic differentials or other similar attitudinal measuring instruments. Since most or all teachers would like their students to learn the cognitive and sensory objectives *better* and to develop increased positive attitudes towards the course, its utility or application, and/or towards the program or career preparation that the course is a part of, this use of the "A" grade becomes very useful for all concerned. Remember, in measuring affective domain objectives, the evaluation has to be based on compar-

---

[7] There is no magic number of hours, but a specified number is necessary so the students know when they have achieved the "A". I have used 20 hours for a three credit semester course and 16 hours for three credit quarter course. Other teachers using this approach have used numbers from 10 hours to 25 hours. Generally, most students who try for an "A" on this basis put in more hours than the required number for the "A".

ing a posttest of the attitudes at the end of the course with a pretest of the same attitudes at the start of the course. The "A" cannot be given on the basis of certain changes in attitudes as the students will put on external signs to indicate the desired changes to get the "A" even though they actually don't feel that way. In the process of demanded or requiring an attitude change for the "A" grade, you may actually develop internally the opposite of what you want — an increased negative reaction.

In using the A, B, I concept, be sure that you as the teacher are the one to select who a student tutors and also demand that measurable learning takes place during the tutoring sessions. Because some students may not be able to learn from other students or have learning problems that the students can solve, it is useful to have a guideline such that if the students are working together for over an hour and learning isn't taking place, both the student and his or her tutor should come to the teacher for help. Maybe the student has a problem that only the teacher can solve. If that is the case, the tutor could be assigned to another student needing help or could work with the teacher in trying to solve the learning problem.

Every student in a class should have a chance to try for the "A". Even the last student in a class to achieve the "B" or 100 percent of the SO's can work with the next class and still get an "A". In addition to the benefits for the learners, this approach also allows a teacher to significantly increase the individualization of instruction by using all the students who want the "A" as tutors. A more general benefit to society is that in the process of working with and helping others, the student becomes more humane and concerned about his or her fellow-persons.

Under the present curve grading approach where the majority of students learn "C" worth or less, educators are forcing the students to accept mediocrity which decreases a person's desire for excellence which in turn decreases some of the students' potential humanness. With the majority receiving "C's" or less, there is actually peer group pressure not be exceed mediocrity. By demanding excellence, the student's desire for excellence can be increased, peer group pressure for excellence can be increased and a person's humanness and self-confidence can be increased.

Because many teachers have and were taught and graded under the old system where the different grade levels were associated with intelligence, some teachers will find it difficult to accept that with extra time and different methods and materials that 90 percent or more of the students can learn 100 percent of the required SO's. For these teachers, in order to convince themselves, they might want to try using only A, B, C, D and I for one semester or quarter, A, B, C and I for the next semester or quarter, A, B and I for the next semester or quarter (where the "A" and "B" have the traditional relationship), and then the A, B and I where the "B" represents 100 percent achievement of the required SO's.

There is a temptation on the part of some administrators and registrars to change an "I" to an "F" after a certain length of time. This is not acceptable. It would be like saying to a patient in a hospital, *I'll give you one year to get well. If you aren't well in that time, I'll kill you!* On the other hand, after an "I" grade is left unchanged for a certain period of time, it is reasonable to ask the student to reestablish that he or she is still intellectually or sensorially at the same place on the check list of required SO's as he or she was when he or she previously stopped trying to complete the course. Any SO's which were previously learned but since have been forgotten, should be relearned before completing the course.

Students should have the privilege of leaving the "I" on their record indefinitely. It should indicate that the student started the course and got part way through the course and decided that the course was not something he or she needed or wanted to finish. If desired, a rule could be made that after a certain length of time, i.e., four or five years, all "I's" are dropped from the student's record. If the student wants to take one of these courses again, the student would have to start from the beginning but could test out of the parts the student already knows.

A few students like being professional students and may try to take advantage of this approach and take "I's" in all courses and never finish any courses. To save society from sponsoring this type of student, it should be reasonable to set a maximum number of "I's" a student can have. After a student reaches this maximum number of "I's", the student and/or the student's parents would be required to pay an increasing percentage of the costs of the student's instruction as the student increases the number of incompleted courses until the student and/or the parents are paying the complete cost of the instruction. In contrast, students who are able to complete more courses in the same time period than the average student might be able to pay proportionately less in situations where students have to pay fees and tuition. This condition usually indicates that the students are able to learn with less help from their teachers than the average student.

A different view of school financing could look on the costs, fees, or tuition as a student's rental of faculty and facilities for a period of time. Students who learn faster would not only get through sooner but at lower cost unless the student elected to take additional SO's, units, and courses. Students who take longer than average to learn would still get through, but it would take longer and cost the student, parents, or society more.

d. STUDENT ERRORS

Under the traditional approach to testing in education, student errors are considered the fault of the student and are considered a negative concept because of its relationship with levels of intelligence. Under the traditional view of mental capacity which is viewed as a limiting factor, the lower the score on a test, the lower the student's mental capacity or level of intelligence. As mentioned earlier, the traditional approach utilizes negative evaluation in that the results of the evaluation are used to label the student and nothing is done about any non-learning identified in the test (student errors) because if the score indicates mental capacity then it is assumed that there is no use trying to teach the student what he or she is incapable of learning.

In sharp contrast, under the Behavioral Learning Systems Approach to testing in designed instruction, student errors are considered no one's fault except possibly the instructional materials if the test was given after the student used the materials. Most important is the fact that student errors are viewed as a positive concept under the systems approach because the errors indicate the direction of subsequent instructional activities. Under the systems approach, mental capacity is considered an ability rather than a limiting factor and as an ability, capacity can be increased. Therefore, whenever students make mistakes, the teacher in performing the new role as an Instructioneer, looks on student errors as guidelines or a road map towards increasing the students mental abilities (capacity). It is assumed that the student can learn whatever was missed if given time, if any relevant cumulative ignorance is eliminated, and if the teacher is willing to vary the method and materials of instruction to fit the student's needs for learning (which does not mean that the SO's are changed).

> NOTE: As pointed out in Chapter VI, Volume II, students who have experienced successful learning events in the home, community, or school, may be better at picking out or identifying the best learning methods and sometimes even the best learning resources for themselves than the teacher who doesn't know the students. However, being novices in whatever courses or subjects the students are taking, they do not know best what SO's they should learn. Once the required learning has been identified by the teacher the students are relatively free to pick the method and the resources needed in order to learn the SO's.

Admittedly, there are times in which students make mistakes on purpose, but these occasions are rare and should not be mistaken as representing most or all student errors. For example, some students in taking a placement test may purposely make enough mistakes to get in a lower level course in which the student knows he or she can achieve a grade of "A" relatively easy. Some other students who know that they are further advanced than some of their friends may purposely make mistakes in order to be more like their friends. Some students when given a stupid question like *Who is buried in Grant's tomb?* may answer it wrong on purpose because they feel a stupid question deserves a stupid answer. Another situation when a student might make an error on purpose is when in answering a multiple-choice question, the student knows the answer the teacher wants, but the student disagrees with the teacher's choice and picks another choice that he or she believes to be the correct choice knowing that it will be scored as incorrect. A final example illustrates a student error which I inevitably did wrong on purpose as a student. This is the situation in which the test item usually starts out with *In your opinion* . . . and the teacher will give a certain number of points for the correct *opinion*. Actually, no matter what the student's opinion is, it is correct as the student's opinion. The student's opinion may be invalid according to certain rules of logic, but it is still the student's opinion. Generally, it is rather obvious to most students that the recognized correct answer to the opinion question is usually the teacher's opinion. As a student, even if I actually agreed with the teacher's opinion, I would generally state an opinion which would be in conflict with the teacher's opinion because it led to good arguments. However, these instances of intentional student errors are rare and in the vast majority of student errors, the student either honestly thinks he or she is right, is guessing he or she might be right, or just doesn't know the answer. In any of these latter instances, the student errors represent opportunities for teaching not something wrong with the student. Whatever it is a student already knows there isn't much a teacher can do about it except change it if necessary; but, whatever it is a student doesn't know, a teacher can help the student learn it!

5. STUDENTS' RIGHTS IN THE EVALUATION PROCESS

Traditionally, students don't have many rights in the evaluation process and frequently suffer or benefit from the process at the whim or fancy of their teachers. The same conditions used to prevail at many schools (and still does at some) as far as the evaluation of teachers were concerned. During the past several decades and particularly during the 1960's, while there was a shortage of teachers, teachers' organizations demanded certain rights and were able to get most of them through negotiations. In a publication of the National School Public Relations Association, *Evaluating Teachers For Professional Growth,* they listed 10 points which have been repeatedly emphasized by teachers' organizations as being the teachers' basic rights in evaluation situations. In looking at the instructional situation as a humane environment, it should be acceptable by teachers and all educators that students also should have some basic rights in evaluation situations. Therefore, in considering students and teachers as partners in the instructional process, I would like to present a parallel list of students' rights based on the basic rights of teachers as identified by their own organizations.

1. *The purpose of teacher evaluation must be clearly understood to be improvement of instruction, not for formal, legalistic purposes of firing, termination of tenure, salary, and promotion.*

> 1. The purpose of student evaluation must be clearly understood to be for the improvement of instruction, not for the traditional purposes of obtaining grades (particularly failure), defending suspensions, punishment, selecting or eliminating certain students from continuing on to higher levels of instruction, placement of students in groupings with designed cumulative ignorance (multiple-tracking), and/or to cause embarrassment by publicly listing scores and/or grades with the accompanying implied limits of intelligence.

2. *Evaluation, then, must go hand in hand with a comprehensive plan for career development and improving total teacher performance, including, for example, inservice training, a staff of helping teachers (teacher counselors), and teacher aids.*

> 2. Evaluation, then, must go hand in hand with a comprehensive plan for achieving the specified goals for instruction as identified by society, parents, teachers, and students themselves, including, for example, developmental (remedial) services to eliminate prior cumulative ignorance, a variety of instructional methods and resources, and time to learn all of the goals.

3. *Evaluation must not be done by just one person, but by a team, including at least one peer skilled in the teacher's specialty.*

> 3. Evaluation of the student must not be controlled wholly by one teacher, it should be open to review by others including at least one peer similar to the student (see the next unit on the Instructional Grievance Committee).

4. *Evaluation should be open and without subterfuge. For example, the time, place, and conditions of any visitations should be agreed upon in advance by teacher and evaluator.*

> 4. Evaluation of the student should be open and without subterfuge. For example, the time, place, and conditions of any testing should be agreed upon in advance by the student and teacher (no pop-quizzes).

5. *Criteria for evaluation and the traits to be judged should be agreed to and clearly understood by all parties before the process begins.*

5. The criteria for evaluation of the student and the SO's to be learned and tested should be agreed to and clearly understood by all parties (students, teachers, administrators, school boards, parents, etc.) before the process begins (at the beginning of each course and/or unit.)

6. *Those who do the evaluating should be trained for the job, and must themselves be evaluated regularly.*

6. Those (teachers) who do the evaluating of the students should be trained for the job,[8] and must themselves (the teachers) be evaluated regularly.

7. *Evaluation should be an ongoing, long-term process, that takes note of a teacher's over-all performance and of progress between periods of evaluation — not a one-shot, stand-or-fall rating.*

7. Evaluation of the students should be an ongoing, long-term process, that takes note of a student's over-all performance (achievement profile card) and of progress between periods of evaluation[9] — not a one-shot, stand-or-fall rating.

8. *Opportunity must be provided for the teacher to see the evaluators' report and to consult with them before their report goes into his permanent file, and to write a reply to their report, if he wishes,*

---

[8] At the present time only about half of elementary and secondary school teachers and less than 10 percent of higher education faculty have been trained in testing. Since the traditional courses on testing and measurement are filled with the teaching of malpractices, these courses are practically useless. As a result, very few teachers at the present time are properly trained to evaluate the students in their classes.

---

[9] This is in reference to the use of preentry tests at the beginning of instruction which measure the student's level of prerequisite knowledge and skills, pretests at the beginning and during instruction which measure the student's level of knowledge and skills which would be learned in the instructional unit or course (SO's), and posttests at the end of instruction to determine the need for subsequent instruction. For example, a student who is presently in sixth grade but is actually operating at two or three grade levels below where he or she should be, would be taught at that level to eliminate cumulative ignorance and would be evaluated on his or her progress from that point. This would be in contrast to the traditional approach which would ignore individual differences and teach all students as if they were at the same level and evaluate their progress from the beginning of the course as presented by the teacher regardless of where the students actually were at the beginning of the course. This comparison illustrates the difference between a teacher who teaches students (systems) and a teacher who teaches course content (traditional).

that will be attached to it in his file. Every district should have procedures whereby a teacher may request to have material he or she considers obsolete or irrelevant removed from his or her file.

> 8. Opportunity must be provided for the student and/or parents to see the teachers' reports and to consult with them before their reports go into the students permanent file, and to write a reply to their report, if the student and/or parents wish to, that will be attached to it in the students' file. Every school district, college and university should have procedures whereby a student and/or parents may request to have material the student and/or parents consider obsolete or irrelevant removed from the student's file.

9. *Above all, evaluation must take place in a constructive and nonthreatening atmosphere. The teacher must feel that improvement of his performance is a cooperative effort involving him, his evaluators, and others on the school staff. No matter how well designed — in the abstract — an evaluation program may seem, if it is perceived by teachers as negative or punitive, it will not improve teaching, but will lower teacher effectiveness because of teacher fears and lowered morale.*

> 9. Above all, evaluation of the students must take place in a constructive and nonthreatening atmosphere. The student must feel that improvement of his or her achievement is a cooperative effort involving the student, the teacher, instructional specialists, parents, and even qualified members of the community. No matter how well designed — in the abstract — an evaluation program may seem, if it is perceived by the student as negative or punitive, it may not improve the student's achievement, but will lower the student's effectiveness because of fears and lowered morale.

10. *Finally, if teachers are to be evaluated, then all other educational personnel should be evaluated too, up to the highest levels of administration.*

> 10. Finally, if students are to be evaluated, then all other instructional personnel (including teachers) should be evaluated too, up to the highest levels of administration (including state and national offices of instruction).

> a. INSTRUCTIONAL GRIEVANCE COMMITTEE
>
> In line with parallel rights, I believe that students have the right to have an Instructional Grievance Committee just as teachers have

their grievance committees. Students need to have some form of recourse in the face of unfair teaching practices. Yes, a student could file suit in a court of law, citing an educational malpractice; however, it would take too long and the injustice would have already had its negative effects on the student. It is assumed that a student can go over the teacher's head to a department head, a principal, a dean, a superintendent, a president, etc.; however, administrators are more or less pledged to support the teacher, so students really don't have recourse. They are virtually at the mercy of their teachers. If instruction and education are really as important in a students' life as we all say, then it is far too important to leave its fortunes and misfortunes in the hands of one person, the teacher, without a safeguard.

The Instructional Grievance Committee should be made up of one or more teachers, one or more students (peer group), one or more administrators, and one or more persons from the community. The Committee should not be involved in opinion arguments, i.e., the teacher doesn't like me, I don't like the teacher, etc. Their major emphasis should concern instructional problems. For example, if a student is doing passing work or better right up to the end of the course and all of the sudden the student is failed or given a grade much lower than expected. The student should go to the teacher first and ask for an explanation. If the student isn't satisfied, the student should be able to request a hearing in front of the Instructional Grievance Committee. If the teacher refuses to cooperate with the Committee or their decision to give the student a more reasonable grade, the Committee should have the power to change the students grade or to at least attach a rebuttal report to the teacher's grade report. If a student is given a grade of less than 100 percent, and the student wishes to learn whatever he or she missed in order to raise the grade to 100 percent or to get an "A", and the teacher refuses to let the student know what it is that the student didn't learn and/or refuses to let the student have the additional time in order to learn what the student hadn't learned yet, the student should be able to have a hearing in front of the Committee. If the teacher refuses to cooperate with the decision of the Committee to identify what the student missed and let the student learn it or to raise the grade to an "A" or the number to 100 percent, the Committee should have the power to raise the student's grade.

If it makes sense for teachers to have a Grievance Committee, it should also seem sensible for students to have an Instructional Grievance Committee. As it is in the case of the teachers' committee, the very existence of the Instructional Grievance Committee and the fact that students have recourse, should have a marked effect on the behavior of teachers in the evaluation situation.

C. EVALUATION OF TEACHERS

Under the traditional approach to education as it was practiced decades ago and still is in some schools, students and teachers were considered to be individually different. However, these differences were considered to be primarily genetic in nature and as such nothing much could be done to affect these differences. Those students and teachers who were at the high end of the *normal curve* were given "A's" and merit raises respectively. Those students and teachers who were at the low end of the *normal curve* were failed and fired respectively! This period in education was associated with a high degree of authoritarianism in which each level in the pyramid of educational positions had practically absolute control over the people in lower levels of the pyramid. Descriptions of what students were supposed to learn and of what teachers were supposed to do were very general. Evaluation was primarily subjective in nature and as such, those students and teachers who appeared to be in the high end of the *normal curve* were often there more because of personal feelings and relationships with people in higher levels of the pyramid than because they were *genetically* superior. As a result of entropic drift and not specifically knowing what the results of the educational process should be (the SO's), the emphasis was on the process itself including the teacher and the learning environment.

Sort of a second stage resulted from the efforts of educators trying to make the educational process more measurable and defensible. The emphasis in this stage was on the accreditation of schools based on certain process criteria and on the evaluation of the teachers' performance in the process. During this stage and in most schools today, various check lists were developed for use by administrators in the evaluation of teachers. The items on the check lists were similar to GO's in that they were not directly measurable and as such were subjectively interpreted by whoever did the evaluating. The use of any check list assumes that there is one best way for a teacher to perform and in case the criteria on the check list were too general to be measurable, the model against which most teachers were evaluated would be the self-image of the person doing the evaluating, i.e., *How would I look if I was teaching this course?* This method of consciously or sub-consciously evaluating the teachers in comparison to the imagined performance of the administrator or evaluator also assumes that there is one best way (the administrator's way). In either case, to assume that there is one best way to teach ignores the existence of individual differences among students. When this method of evaluation was combined with the traditional renumeration system, teachers who were perceived as being *good* (most like the person doing the evaluating) received the promotions and merit pay, if any was given. Similar to the first stage, individual differences in teachers were considered to be mostly genetic and as such nothing much could be done about negative evaluations except to fire the teacher or to just not renew the teacher's contract.

In a third stage, there were four trends that converged to affect the evaluation of teachers. There was a growing movement to specify student learning objectives and to individualize instruction which was in conflict with the traditional use of GO's and class oriented education. A parallel movement showed a growth in measurable items for evaluation of teacher behavior. Simon and Boyer (1970) listed over 2,400 categories across 79 different observational systems for evaluation of both teacher and student behaviors during the educational process. In conflict with this growing movement which tended to emphasize the individual differences among teachers, the union movement which was also growing, was emphasizing via their negotiations that teachers should be treated essentially as being all the same, i.e., same teaching load, same size classes, same hours, and the same pay. The only differences recognized by most of the unions were differences in seniority and degrees.

During this last stage, the concept of accountability entered the evaluation process. As the costs of education increased, more and more administrators, school boards, parents, legislators, and other noneducators became concerned about the lack of a comparable increase in the results of the educational process. Because the teachers and students are so closely related in the educational process, teachers' organizations who were against teacher accountability and any evaluation system which would identify the individual differences of teachers also had to be against any evaluation system of students which would tend to show that teachers are different in their ability to produce student learning. As a result, the growing trend of accountability and individualism is being met with a growing trend to avoid any evaluation, a *do your own thing* approach (so the results can't be traced to anyone), and a type of socialism which is not so much the traditional political version but is primarily anti-individualism. It is almost *normal* in education to preach one thing and practice another, i.e., talking of individual differences in students but keeping them in classes and treating them as all the same. The problem with the present conflict is that most teachers today are really convinced of the individual differences among students and to varying degrees try to recognize these differences; however, simultaneously the teacher organizations are saying and trying to practice that teachers are the same. This internal conflict or dissidence detracts from a teacher's effectiveness in the educational or instructional process.

If learning is the real purpose of instruction, then that should be the measure of a teacher's effectiveness. The lists of *good* teaching behaviors are useless by themselves when unrelated to the real purpose of instruction. If a teacher is having trouble bringing about certain learning in certain students, then these lists of teaching behaviors may be useful in reference to solving the problem of non-achievement if it is a teaching problem. As more and more students learn on their own or with other students, the criteria on the check lists for evaluating teachers from the traditional point-of-view as a presenter of course content become obsolete and inappropriate. Given the same SO's and matched classes of students and the criterion that 90 percent or more of the students have to achieve 100 percent of the SO's, two or more teachers could and probably would achieve the criterion in a variety of ways which would reflect the ways that each individual teacher teaches best rather than some assumed *good* teaching behaviors that all teachers are supposed to emulate. The same would hold true within the classes also, the students in achieving 100 percent of the SO's would do this in a variety of ways which would reflect the ways that each individual student learns best rather than some assumed *good* learning behavior that all students are supposed to emulate.

NOTE: All of the research concerned with a particular method, a list of teaching behaviors, techniques, etc. (which are man-made) are in the category of *educational* research and as such should be considered as a *non-science*. Research concerned with what methods, teaching behaviors, techniques, etc., are necessary to bring about specified learning (a natural phenomenon) in a specific group of students are in the category of *instructional* research and as such should be considered as a *science*.

According to the USOE report of the Education Profession 1971-72, *Part I — The Need For Teachers in Our Schools and Colleges*, one of the greatest needs is for quality in teachers. Quality in this report is defined as:

— Positive attitudes toward students;

— Orientation to individual student needs or interests rather than subject matter;

— Flexibility in approach, willingness to experiment, openness to change; and

— Sensitivity to other cultures

These characteristics are an integral part of the Instructioneer role, but are only a part of the traditional presenting role by chance. Notice that these are affective domain characteristics and as such, they can not be developed directly by demand, they can only be created indirectly. Present training in most teacher training institutions and present teacher evaluation in most schools do not facilitate the development of these needed characteristics.

1. THE TRADITIONAL TEACHERS' ROLE AND EVALUATION

Although a teacher's perception of his or her role very much affect what the teacher does, in evaluation situations, the perception of the teacher's role as viewed by the evaluator becomes very important as a factor affecting what a teacher does due to the principle of evaluation under which a person tends to do those things which the evaluator uses as criteria for evaluation.

The evaluation of elementary and secondary school teachers is usually based on the teacher's ability to complete activities that are usually thought to occur during the particular course or grade level, such as complete the presentation of the textbook, present certain demonstrations, etc. In addition, the elementary and secondary classroom teachers are evaluated on the basis of their degrees, the number of credits they have taken beyond the degree they presently hold, number of years teaching, whether or not they are involved in creative or innovative *teaching* activities which bring positive public relations, and whether or not the teacher maintains a teaching-learning environment which does not result in an excess of student or parent complaints.

This tendency to do what others want us to do develops a type of chain reaction which is rather resistant to change, unless the entire sequence of events is changed. The teachers will want to do those things that the superintendents and/or principals use to evaluate them. The superintendents and/or principals will want to have their teachers do the things that will be in accordance with the ways or criteria that the school board is going to use to evaluate them. In turn, the school board is going to encourage the performance of activities which are in accordance with what the voting public is going to use to evaluate the school board. Under the traditional hierarchy or pyramid of authority, the administrators and board members who are furthest away from the educational process affect what is done in the classroom via the evaluation process. Since many parents, administrators, and school board members are concerned about discipline in the classroom and tend to evaluate teachers on their ability to maintain discipline, many teachers, in turn, list the learning of how to maintain class discipline as a critical teaching skill.

Teachers in higher education are initially evaluated on the basis of their academic degrees. But once the faculty member has obtained a position, then subsequent evaluations are based primarily on the number of their publications (books, journal articles, etc.), their involvement on committees, conferences, etc., and the degree to which the faculty member develops a local, state, or national reputation, which is usually measured by the number of requests for this person to do outside consulting with other groups. A factor of growing importance in the evaluation of higher education faculty is their ability to write successful proposals which bring money to the school. This factor is usually referred to as *grantsmanship*. Of interest in this game of *grantsmanship*, is the fact that the person who is very successful in writing grants is not successful because he or she has identified a problem in the teaching-learning situation or in society and then applied for a grant to research this problem. Almost the exact opposite is what actually happens. The successful person in *grantsmanship* finds out what the government or a foundation is giving money for and then their objective is to develop that particular *problem*. Because of this type of evaluation, there are staff members at almost every college or university whose objective is to get money, not to solve problems.

The relationship of the subject matter which the faculty member teaches with respect to the national goals and interests and also the degree of shortage of faculty in that particular subject matter area also very definitely affect the evaluation or value of a faculty member.

Since higher education faculty are evaluated on a basis of their ability to publish and since the easiest way to generate publications is through research, there is a strong tendency on the part of higher education faculty to not only want to be involved in reserach, but to demand the opportunity to be involved in some kind of research. Of course, in these efforts to publish and to do research that results in publications, there is little room left over to teach students. The *publish or perish* concept in higher education is another example of entropic drift where the means became the ends. Publishing new materials was thought to be a means of or an indication of being up to date on the latest events, trends, etc., in a person's field of study. However, since what is published is rarely evaluated as to its value as a contribution to a field of study, entropic drift occurred and quantity became the objective instead of quality. The availability of graduate students who can take over some of the teaching tasks, assist in developing research, and in many cases even doing the major portion of the writing of the materials to be published, offers a very definite incentive in the hiring of new faculty. In fact, at conferences involving higher education faculty, faculty who can say they don't teach any undergraduate classes are looked up to as having *arrived* at a successful level of teaching in higher education.

As a result of the fact that *quantity* of publications is the criterion for evaluation rather than *quality* of the publications, most teachers do not particularly look forward to reading their professional journals and books because of the necessity to search through the *quantity* in order to find something (hopefully) of *quality*. Similar to the *publish or perish* concept, faculty are also evaluated in part on whether or not they have presented any papers at regional or national conferences. In fact, some colleges and universities will only support an educator's trip to a professional conference if the educator is making a presentation of a paper during the conference. As a result of this, conferences are filled with educators who are making presentations in order that they could come to the conference and be evaluated positively back on their campus, not necessarily to make presentations of content that are relevant to the theme or needs of the conference participants. This makes most conferences similar to the professional journals in that there is a lot of *chaff* that has to be sifted through before finding the good *grains* of wisdom.

As a result of the present evaluation practices in higher education, the more capable faculty tend to gravitate away from teaching into areas of research which will result in publishable material. It is important to remember that institutions of higher education are supported by the public primarily on the basis of student learning, and as a secondary function to do research that may improve society as a whole. When we start evaluating and paying teachers on the basis of their ability to facilitate student learning, the better teachers may once again come back to working with students. Those who are involved in research may be concerned with research that improves student learning and not necessarily research that will give them a publishable article.[10]

In changing over to individualized instruction, there will be fewer and fewer classes where individual differences among students are ignored. As a result, teachers who are accustomed to the presenting role may want to resist the change because under the systems approach, there aren't any classes of students who are all at the same place in their learning such that a teacher could make presentations to them. The use of *Scholarship* sessions could be a useful substitute which would not only satisfy a teacher's need to make presentations but could also serve as a measure of *scholarship* and might well be as good as or a better measure than publishing or presenting papers at some conference.

---

[10] In my experience of working with faculty on the improvement of instruction, a teaching innovation that helps more students learn more is always worth one or more publishable articles that are of great interest to their colleagues. The key thought to remember is that when the primary motivation is to help more students learn more, a side benefit of finding successful solutions to learning problems will be one or more publishable articles that will be of interest to the researcher's colleagues. When the primary motivation is to publish something (or anything), the affects on student learning are minimum, if any at all, and the published article is of minimum interest, if any at all, to the researcher's colleagues.

Scholarship sessions are scheduled whenever a teacher, administrator, student, or even a lay person in the community has something they think is interesting to present to other students, teachers, administrators, and people from the community. There are no GO's or SO's that have to be written by the presenter. There is no required attendance, no grades, tests, or evaluation of the participants. There is no specific length of time that the sessions have to last. There function is purely a scholarly interaction between people interested in enlightenment. In such a free environment, if the presentation is uninteresting, a rehash of available information, or so complex that no one understands it, people may not even come to it or if they come they may leave early. Consequently, the scholarship aspect of a faculty member can be at least partially evaluated by how many scholarship sessions did he or she put on?, how many people attended and who were they (students, teachers, lay people from the community)?, how long did the session last?, and how long did the people stay?

In community colleges and junior colleges, the evaluation of faculty tends to follow the same criteria used to evaluate elementary and secondary school faculty, but with more emphasis on the academic degrees obtained by the faculty member. Depending on the particular community college or junior college, the faculty members may be evaluated to varying degrees on the same basis described previously for evaluating most faculty in higher education.

A very strong factor in the evaluation of a faculty member in higher education are the opinions of his or her peer group. These opinions often determine whether or not a faculty member gets promoted. Therefore, there is an ever-present social pressure not to upset your colleagues if you are trying to get promoted. If the majority of the faculty are traditional educators, then this pressure is exerted against faculty who may want to improve the teaching-learning situation by doing something anti-traditional. It is very common for teachers to get very excited about improving instruction such that more learners are learning more, but then the pressure from their colleagues slowly but surely either forces them to drop the innovations or it may be sufficient pressure to force the teacher to resign or to stop the renewal of their contract (if not a tenured teacher). To varying degrees, these pressures are also exerted on teachers at the secondary level and even at the elementary level of education.

Notice that among the various criteria identified in evaluating teachers at all levels of education, nothing has been said about the teachers' ability to help students learn. Because faculty are not required to specify learning objectives in their courses and the relationship between course objectives and test items on tests has never been established as an important relationship, the only evaluation of faculty in reference to the teaching-learning situation in higher education is on the ability of the faculty member to stay within certain limits in giving grades to their students. In some cases, these limits are specifically set down and communicated formally to the faculty member, and in other cases, these limits are communicated rather informally to the faculty member. On almost any college or university campus in the country, the new faculty member rather quickly finds out the percentage of "A's", "B's", "C's", "D's", and "F's" he or she can give without being suspected of being too easy or too hard. It is important to point out that it is not necessarily considered a positive point of evaluation if the faculty member stays within these assigned percentages for grading, but if he or she deviates significantly from the norms of the school, then the faculty member may be negatively evaluated. Of particular interest here, and critical for students, is the belief among many faculty in higher education, that the higher the percentage of failures, the higher the standards of a particular course or school. Since a faculty member is capable of failing any percentage of students he desires by designing the tests accordingly, standards set by tests that fail a high percentage of students are arbitrary and false. Faculty members of schools that assign the majority of their students "A's" and "B's" in their courses are considered by many members in higher education as having low standards. If these "A" and "B" grades are not defensible on the basis of learners' learning specified objectives of their courses, then it is my opinion also that the faculty member or school has low standards. But these are low standards because there is little, if any, correlation between the grades, learning and what happens in the classrooms, not because of the percentage of failures or nonfailures. On the other hand, faculty members of schools that assign the majority of their students "D's" and "F's" in their courses are considered by many members in higher education as having high standards. If these "D" and "F" grades are not defensible on the basis of the learners' not learning specified objectives of their course, then it is my opinion that the faculty member or school does not have high standards. If a teacher cannot identify what it is the students did not learn, but still gives out low grades, it is rather obvious that the teacher is artibrarily creating an image of high standards. If in fact, the teacher can defend the low grades on the basis of most of the students not learning what they are supposed to learn, then it is very likely that this teacher probably cannot teach, and an evaluation should be made accordingly. Although a variety of criteria may be used to evaluate teachers, at the present time, it is not normal in education to evaluate a teacher on the basis of whether or not learning is taking place in the teacher's classroom.

In business and industry, standards usually have some sort of relationship with quality, and as such, standards in education should have a relationship with quality of learning taking place in a particular course or school. As anyone knows who has been in college, the number of credits for a course are determined by the number of hours a week the class meets, and has little, if any, relationship with the amount of work that is involved in the course. Almost all college and university students have had the experience of taking a three-credit course that should have had 12 credits because of the amount of work involved, and they have also probably had a five-credit course that should have been given only one credit at the most because of the absence of any learning activity. As a result, the fact that someone has had so many credits worth of college courses does not guarantee anything in reference to learning. All it means is that a student has sat in a classroom in front of a teacher for so many hours. Just as we are not able to guarantee what a high school diploma means in reference to learning, all that can be said about a bachelor's degree is that a student has spent 2,000 hours in a classroom in front of a teacher. A master's degree represents 500 hours more and a doctorate represents another 500 hours plus a dissertation. In view of the fact that diplomas and degrees are awarded on the basis of time rather than learning, they actually become endurance awards, rather than awards for academic achievement. This evaluation of credits on the basis of time rather than learning very seriously affects the concept referred to as *teaching load*. In junior and community colleges, most teachers carry a 15 to 18 credit load, which means that they actually meet with students in a classroom 15 to 18 hours a week on the average. In four year colleges, the teaching load varies from 12 to 15 credits and in universities the teaching load varies from 9 to 12 credits. Since there is no part in the evaluation of faculty that concerns what students learn in a course, there are extreme variations from course to course and teacher to teacher. At one extreme, you may have the teacher who wants to put in just the minimum number of hours per week in and out of the classroom. In order to minimize the number of hours outside the classroom, this type of teacher assigns a minimum amount of work for students to do which would necessitate any outside involvement of the faculty member. At the other extreme, there is the faculty member who may be putting in the same number of classroom hours but is very concerned about the need to publish, is very concerned that students learn what is in the course, and also believes that the quantity of learning activity is related to quality. This type of teacher usually assigns a great deal of outside work, which in turn generally results in a great deal of outside work for the teacher.

It is important to point out that since credit hours taught is the criterion used to evaluate *teaching load*, there is little, if any, difference noted between the teacher who might be teaching 12 credits (four classes of three credits each) in which there is an average of 15 students in each class and the teacher who has the same teaching load of 12 credits, but has an average of 80-500 in each class. Because the number of students taught by an individual teacher in higher education is generally not a consideration, it becomes obvious that the emphasis in teacher evaluation as it relates to classroom behavior concerns the *presentation* of the course content rather than on helping each individual student learn whatever it is they are supposed to learn.

Although there is some credit given for creative *teaching* in higher education, this aspect of the teaching-learning situation is not quite as important as it is in elementary and secondary education. Presently, at all levels of education, *creative teaching* is usually defined as creative ways of presenting content, **regardless of learning.** If students happen to learn more because of the innovative effort, this is usually a bonus. *Creative teaching* should be defined as creative ways of helping learners learn more of the objectives of a given course.

In spite of all the problems, there are many teachers at all levels of education who try very hard to improve the teaching-learning situation by making it more effective and more efficient to the best of their ability. Since the criteria for evaluation of teachers used by deans, departmental chairman, superintendents, supervisors, or principals, does not include learning, then the concept of student learning has to take second place, whereas it should be first; therefore, the teachers who do take time to try to improve learning in their classrooms may be evaluated negatively.

a. STUDENT EVALUATION OF TEACHERS

At the present time, student evaluations of teachers is not much better than a popularity poll. In examining many forms used by students in evaluating their teachers, it is obvious that the students are being asked to evaluate teachers on criteria which the students are not qualified to evaluate and which have very little to do with the main purpose of teaching — STUDENT LEARNING. For example, a common question is:

Were the course objectives specific and clearly stated?

If experienced teachers have trouble spelling out specific objectives for their courses, how is the student supposed to know whether or not the objectives were *specific and clearly stated?* Have the students had training in how to critique whether or not objectives are SO's or GO's? Student evaluation forms also include questions which are similar to those used by traditional administrators in their evaluation of teachers and they are just as irrelevant, i.e.,

Was the teacher neatly and appropriately groomed?

This question is just as bad as when teachers evaluate students on the length of hair, etc. If it could be proved that a sloppy and/or inappropriately groomed teacher can not teach and a sloppy and/or inappropriately groomed student can not learn, then maybe these questions might be relevant. At the moment, it is the question itself and others like it that are inappropriate for evaluating both teachers and students. Most of the questions can only be answered in terms of student opinion in absence of the factual evaluative criteria which could be learned in a training program. As such, the evaluations are subjective and are influenced by the emotions of the moment. For example, a common question is

Was the teacher's course well organized?

Since the students have not been trained to critique the organizational ability of their teachers, the answers to the above question are subjectively affected by the relationship between the student's perceived grade in the course and the student's received grade. If the student received a grade lower than he or she expected, the teacher's course was obviously disorganized (according to the student). If the student received a grade higher than he or she expected, the teacher's course was just as obviously well organized (according to the student).

The foregoing does not mean that all of the questions on the evaluation forms are inappropriate, there are some very good questions that students are very qualified to answer and the answers should be useful for the teachers in trying to solve learning problems, i.e.,

— Were you given a list of objectives to be learned at the beginning of the course?

— Did the teacher appear to teach these objectives? If not, cite one or more examples where you think the teacher did not teach one or more of the objectives.

— Did you learn the objectives of this course? If not, which objectives didn't you learn?

— Did the tests and/or evaluation of the course appear to match the stated course objectives? If not, cite one or more examples where you think the evaluation did not match the stated objectives and/or where the stated objectives were not evaluated.

— Were you given opportunities to learn from your errors by correcting mistakes in the tests, essays, etc.? If not, cite instances in which the opportunity was not given.

— When you had trouble learning, did the teacher offer and give individual help? If not, cite instances of learning problems you had where no help was available.

— Were you given resources and time to learn which were appropriate to your abilities? If not, cite one or more examples where you were expected to learn in the same way and/or in the same time as other students in spite of your non-learning.

— When the question of relevance or usefulness came up with respect to the objectives of the course, was the teacher able to, point out the relevance or usefulness of the objective? If not, cite instances where course objectives were questioned and the teacher was unable to answer the questions.

2. TEACHERS AS INDIVIDUALS

In addition to recognizing individual differences among students, the recognition of individual differences among teachers is way overdue in our instructional systems. No one who has ever attended a school would ever say that all teachers are exactly alike, or even very similar. There are a great number of differences among teachers. Some teachers at all levels of instruction are extremely dedicated to their work and put in many, many hours to help students achieve what they think the students are supposed to achieve. Some teachers in elementary and secondary levels look on their jobs as an 8:00 to 3:00 job, five days a week, nine months a year, and resent any intrusion on their personal time. At the college and university level, there are some teachers who also put in only the minimum time necessary to collect their paychecks. In fact, many deans, superintendents, and departmental chairmen have told me that one of their hardest tasks every year is the assignment of some teachers (who have tenure) to teaching situations where these teachers will do the least damage to students!

There are also teachers in education who didn't even want to be teachers in the first place. Because of the arbitrary failing levels established in many departments of our colleges and universities, many students end up in teaching who have failed out of their original major interest area and have had to take their second, third, or fourth occupational choice. It is very possible that some of these teachers would be better off not working directly with students and could concentrate their energies in the development of instructional materials following the guidelines and results of the teachers who are working with students. In addition, teachers who do not like to work with students could be involved with instructional research in which the contact with a given group of students would be at a minimum.

Admittedly, the vast majority of teachers want to be *good* teachers, but their image of what is *good* varies considerably from teacher to teacher, in addition to the differences among teachers as to their ability to teach. One teacher's version of *good* could be interpreted as being able to end up with a normal curve of results. Another teacher's version of *good* could be interpreted as having a positively skewed curve of results such that there are more "A's" and "B's" than in the average class. Another teacher's version of *good* could be interpreted as having a negatively skewed curve of results such that there are more "D's" and "F's" than in the average class. Of interest, is the fact that all three teachers could behave in the same manner in the classroom according to the traditional check lists. Only their testing and grading behaviors are different and these wouldn't be detected by the traditional check lists. At the same time, three other teachers could view the normal curve of results as being *good*, yet their behaviors in the classroom could vary considerably. These variations in *goodness* are possible because there is little commonality between classes except the role of the teacher, the size of the classes, the time schedule, and possibly the general topics or content to be covered. Under the traditional approach, it is not necessary to have any relationship between what the course is supposed to teach (GO's), what is actually taught, what is actually learned, and what is tested.

It is important to point out that in a situation in which we have not specified exactly what it is the students are supposed to learn, the difference between the good and poor teacher is of greater significance to the learner than the difference between the good and poor teacher under a Learning Systems Approach. In a teaching-learning situation where the objectives have not been specified and learning occurs by chance, the presence of a good teacher who has a broad background and a wide variety of learning experiences increases the chances for learning to occur. If the good teacher is teaching good students who also have broad backgrounds and a variety of learning experiences, then a great deal of learning can take place even if by chance. This would be like radios with good receiving equipment picking up signals from a broadcasting station with strong transmitting signals. If the good teacher with a broad background and a variety of learning experiences is teaching poor students who have weak backgrounds and limited learning experiences, there will still be a fair amount of learning taking place by chance although not as much as when the good teachers are with good students. This would be like radios with poor receiving equipment picking up signals from a broadcasting station with strong transmitting signals. If a poor teacher with a weak background and limited learning experiences is teaching good students, the learning results could be almost as good as the last situation, but not as good as the first situation. A significant difference, however, is that in the second situation, the level of learning is more a result of having a good teacher, whereas in the third situation, the level of learning is more a result of having good students. The third situation would be like radios with good receiving equipment picking up signals from a broadcasting station with weak transmitting signals. But when the poor teacher who has a weak background and limited learning experiences is teaching poor students who also have weak backgrounds and limited learning experiences, very little learning can take place by chance. This would be like radios with poor receiving equipment trying to pick up signals from a broadcasting station with weak transmitting signals.

Under the Learning Systems Approach where learning objectives have been specified, the efforts of the teacher to teach by design will be much more successful than under the chance learning situation regardless of whether the learners have a strong background or a weak background. Under the traditional approach, *goodness* of the teacher or student is determined by the breadth and depth of experiences which will facilitate chance learning, and *poorness* of either the teacher or student decreases chances for learning. Under the Learning Systems Approach, *goodness* is determined by the teacher's ability to diagnose the learning problem and to prescribe a solution that will help the students learn, and *poorness* of the teacher only affects how many students the teacher can handle and *poorness* of the student only affects how long it will take the student to learn or the choice of materials from which the student will learn. In using the same broadcasting-receiving analogy, the systems approach would be like sending out specific cassettes to the individual receivers to be used when appropriate and as long as necessary to fit the individual needs rather than have the reception of the message dependent upon the quality of transmitting and receiving equipment.

Although there are situations where the students are separated into more homogeneous groups, probably the most common situation is where the students in any one class are very heterogeneous. Since the classes are similar in composition, then the greatest variable affecting differences in achievement between classes is the teacher. However, it is important to point out that any differences may not be observable because there is little commonality in what is taught and tested. Even the use of standardized tests won't bring out the differences because the standardized tests are not necessarily related to what is happening in any classroom, it is considered wrong for teachers to teach what is on the test (effectively or otherwise), and the results of the tests are already part of the design of the tests regardless of what teachers do or don't do.

Under the present approach to teaching, teaching is considered an art and when students get a master or good teacher they should consider themselves lucky because master and good teachers are too often the exceptions rather than the rule in educational institutions. (How many master teachers have you had as a student?) Also, under the present approach to teaching, the individual differences among teachers are reflected in variations of achievement by their students such that students who have poor teachers or teachers with poor attitudes don't learn very much and will eventually suffer from cumulative ignorance. Consider Figure 132 in which five classrooms each have a different type of teacher but all classrooms have the same number of students. The different levels of teachers is based on the sole criteria of

Master Teacher	Good Teacher	Fair Teacher	Poor Teacher	? Teacher
30 Students	30 Students	30 Students	30 Students	30 Students

Figure 132 — Different Teachers — Same Number of Students

being able to facilitate learning, i.e., given the same type of students, the same subject, the same amount of time, and the same learning environment, the master teacher will be able to help more students learn more than the good teacher. In a situation like this, which is very common at all levels of instruction, the students' education may depend more on which classroom he or she is assigned to rather than on whether or not he or she is a good student. With reference to the differences among teachers in their ability to facilitate learning, not only does this not affect the number of students assigned to them, but these differences do not necessarily affect how much they are paid. As mentioned previously, the criteria used for increasing teachers' salaries are usually based on the number of years the teachers are with the school system, how many summer school courses they have taken, how much they have published, what their degrees are, etc. Whether or not teachers are able to help students learn is generally not taken into consideration. Under the present approach to paying teachers, we pay teachers to be in front of a classroom of a certain number of students and present the content of the course regardless of the learning that does or does not take place.

Consider the present traditional situation where teachers with different ability levels as to how well they can facilitate learning are all given the same number of students and from time to time the better teachers are promoted into administrative positions (away from students) in contrast with the Behavioral Learning Systems Approach where a teacher would be given a student and class load appropriate to their ability. Good teachers would teach more students and/or possibly more courses while the poorer teacher would teach fewer students and/or possibly fewer courses. The critical criteria would be that for both teachers, 90 percent or more of their students would have to learn 100 percent of the required SO's. Their remuneration would be proportionate to their ability to teach (as measured in terms of student learning). Since abilities are in part nature and in part nurture, poorer teachers could improve their abilities to be as good as the good teacher if they wanted too. (Money and other types of remuneration are generally quite motivating.) Given that there is a *master* teacher who can be identified, some traditional educators would say let's observe what he or she does and teach it to other teachers as the model behavior. The problem is that since each person is different, the behaviors that are effective for one personality may not be very effective for another personality and the reactions of students to the same behavior exhibited by two different personality types may vary considerably. Therefore, copying the specific performance of the master teacher or any other mode of teaching behavior cannot be equally successful because of the individual differences in teachers.

One of the sad aspects of the present situation is that there are teachers at the low end of the effectiveness continuum and they are affecting students negatively and they have been for decades. Although even tenured teachers can be dismissed, it would be a rare event if a teacher was dropped or identified for retraining because he or she was not effective.

According to the New York Times, out of a citywide teaching staff of over 55,000 in New York City, only 170 regular teachers and only 82 substitute teachers were marked as *unsatisfactory* over a five year period. Applying the normal curve concept, out of 55,000 teachers, there might be about 1,800 master teachers; about 7,000 good teachers, about 37,000 fair teachers; about 7,000 poor teachers; and about 1,800 questionable or unsatisfactory teachers!

3. THE TEACHERS' ROLE AND EVALUATION UNDER THE BEHAVIORAL LEARNING SYSTEMS APPROACH

In addition to recognizing individual differences between teachers, we also have to change the teachers' role from that of a *presenter of course content* to that of a *manager* or a *diagnostician and prescriber* of appropriate learning experiences. As pointed out and discussed in detail in Chapter V in Volume I, the teachers' role has to change. Learning has to become a primary purpose of instructional institutions. Once the teacher makes the change, he or she will find that the new role is much more important and much more professional than the traditional role. The teacher will have more freedom than he or she has ever had. In the past where the emphasis was on learning by chance, the new role of the teacher as an *Instructioneer* puts the emphasis on learning by design. Instead of ignoring individual differences among students and blaming non-achievement on genetics as is the case in traditional education, the *Instructioneer* looks on non-achievement as a learning problem to be solved and recognizes individual differences among students as to the materials and methods necessary to solve the learning problems. Instead of a situation in which there is almost a chance relationship between the non-measurable course objectives, what teachers teach, and what is tested; the *Instructioneer* is concerned about maintaining a high correlation level between the measurable course objectives, the instructional materials used by the students, and any evaluation instruments. In order to achieve a situation in which students learn by design, the *Instructioneer* has to learn about identifying GO's and SO's, selecting appropriate instructional materials, developing evaluation instruments which match the SO's, and how to solve learning problems. No longer is it possible to teach without having any training as is the case for most teachers in higher education.

a. PRE-SERVICE TRAINING FOR TEACHERS

One of the main reasons why non-education faculty in higher education rejected the need for any training in traditional teaching is that they couldn't see any differences between the teaching behaviors of the faculty in the departments or schools of education and the other faculty in the other departments in the college or university.

On most college and university campuses throughout our country, the schools or departments of education represent the most traditional and conservative group of faculty on the campus. These schools or departments of education should be rampant with innovations in teaching and learning and unrecognizable as being copies of other schools and departments on campus. As specialists in teaching and learning, schools and departments of education should be able to establish minimum learning standards wherein 90 percent or more of their education majors learn 100 percent or more of the objectives of every education course regardless of the time or learning modes necessary to achieve this minimum level. This assumes that the teachers of these courses know or can define specific measurable objectives for each of these courses. If the non-graded concept is good enough for elementary and secondary schools, why isn't it good enough for the teacher training institutions? Isn't it time to put the verbal lectures on educational innovation into practice — not in the campus laboratory school or only in the audio-visual courses — but throughout the instruction curriculum? The methodology and technology is available today to create teachers who are REAL teaching-learning specialists.

From the point of view of our society in reference to the relative importance of education faculty vs. other faculty, the comparison would be highly in favor of the education faculty. Besides being directly responsible for the teaching and learning of a significant percentage of the almost ten million college and university students (those who are majoring in education), education faculty are indirectly responsible for the teaching and learning of almost 60 million students in elementary and secondary schools. The results of the education faculty's effectiveness or ineffectiveness has affected, is affecting, or will affect every person born and raised in our country. What the teachers in our elementary and secondary schools do or do not do to their students will to a great degree affect the success of college or university students in all subject matter areas, and even more basic, what they do or do not do to their students may affect whether or not the students will even go on to a college or university. Since these teachers in the elementary and secondary schools are products of the education faculty, it is difficult to imagine a more important and critical role in our modern society than that of a *teacher of teachers-to-be* such as the education faculty of our colleges and universities.

On almost every college and university campus throughout our country, the faculty in the schools and departments of education are considered by the faculty in other colleges, schools, and departments as being somewhat lower in *professional quality.* Although the majority of education faculty are aware of this negative attitude, there are a few education faculty members who have never been exposed to situations in which this attitude becomes apparent. As viewed by education faculty who are aware of this attitude: some feel that this attitude held by the *non-education* faculty is a result of a psychological defense mechanism developed from guilt feelings about their role as a teacher without ever having any formal courses or training in *how to teach;* some feel that there may be a basis in fact for this attitude and tend to avoid meeting or mixing with faculty from the other subject areas; but the majority of education faculty who are aware of the existence of this attitude try to ignore it.

If the role of education faculty in our modern society is really that important, what is the reason for the existence of this negative attitude? Theoretically, education faculty should be considered specialists in the teaching-learning situation and as such, faculty members in other subject matter areas who identify learning problems should be able to get help from the *teaching-learning expert.* Let us assume that this should happen on a campus and a faculty member who has identified a learning problem goes to the School of Education for help. After inquiring at the main office, he is directed to see a particular professor who happens to be teaching a class at the moment but will be out of class in about 15 minutes. Instead of waiting in the office, the faculty member decides to go up to the professor's classroom thinking that while he is waiting maybe he can pick up some good teaching ideas by observing the *teaching-learning expert* in action. After watching the education professor in action for about ten minutes, the disappointed faculty member leaves thinking to himself, *After 15 or more years as a teaching-learning specialist, this education professor doesn't teach any different than I do and I have never had one formal course on how to teach. Of what value can all those education courses be? Besides, he did not even practice what he was preaching.*

If the majority of college and university faculty learn how to teach as well by chance as the education faculty do by years of undergraduate and graduate education courses, then maybe the output of our schools should be of no surprise to society. Only 75 percent of our entering first grade students graduate from high school and the average graduate takes with him or her only nine years or less of cumulative education. Only 25 percent of our entering first grade students are able to graduate from a college or university. Are these students also learning more by chance and in spite of the educators rather than because of the educators? It is possible to take *The Big Gamble* out of education and have learning happen by design rather than by chance. In an age of mass education at all levels, we can not continue to consider *teaching* as an art with master and good teachers a rare experience in the educational life of our students. *Teaching* can be a science in which the majority of teachers are good teachers and are capable of getting 90 percent or more of their students to achieve 100 percent of the instructional objectives of their courses. Instruction faculty can and should be setting an example for all teachers to follow.

If training to be an *Instructioneer* can really change what teachers do such that they are more effective and efficient in helping students learn, then all teachers at all levels of instruction should be required to take this training (including all faculty in higher education). Of critical importance, at least all of the teachers in higher education who are responsible for teaching students who plan to be teachers should be required to take this training such that *teachers can then teach as they were taught and as they were taught to teach.*

In pre-service training, there are two key points to keep in mind: first, the product is the objective and the process necessary to achieve the product is a variable; second, if student learning is the primary purpose of instructional institutions, then the primary evaluation of any student studying to become a teacher should be on the student's ability to facilitate learning in other students.

Traditionally, due to entropic drift, the process of education (teaching) and the teacher who controls the process are and have been the primary emphasis in the educational event. In the new role as an *Instructioneer*, the product of instruction (learning) and the students whose needs control the instructional event are the primary emphasis in the instructional event. Sad to say, the vast majority of schools and departments of education in our teacher training institutions are still concentrating on the obsolete role of the teacher as a *presenter of course content*. Ironically, many of these schools and departments of education are using modern means to teach the obsolete role. For example, an increasing number of these schools and departments of education are installing the latest in television equipment to be used to record the micro-teaching (the teacher as a presenter) of mini-lessons. The evaluation of the experience is on how well the student performed as a teacher (presenter). Rarely is the evaluation of the experience based on how much the students (being taught by the student-teacher) learned during the experience. Even rarer, if at all, is the student-teacher expected to work with the students until 90 percent or more of the group has learned 100 percent of the SO's of the mini-lesson.

Sweeping the teacher training world is the concept of *Competency Based Teacher Education* (CBTE) or *Performance Based Teacher Education* (PBTE). Both of these names refer to the same thing which is an individualized, continuous progress approach towards the development of a teacher who is a presenter of course content in the traditional sense. The emphasis is on students learning specific measurable teaching behaviors similar to what are found on the check lists used to evaluate teachers. As mentioned earlier, the use of check lists or the specification of teaching behaviors assumes that there is a single best model for teaching which denies individual differences in teachers. The point to remember in trying to get all teachers-to-be to perform in an identical manner (behavior) is that there is little, if any, evidence to show that students learned or failed to learn because a teacher used or didn't use a particular gesture, did or didn't turn his back to the students while writing on the chalkboard, or most of the other points used to evaluate a presentation. The use of modern instructional methods and technology to teach an obsolete role is ultimately self-defeating.

A very difficult point to remember is that in almost every instructional unit developed along the lines of a Behavioral Learning Systems Approach (in all subject matter areas and at all levels of instruction), the SO's refer directly to the behaviors of the students who are learning the unit EXCEPT in those courses where the students are learning to facilitate learning in other students. In recognizing that the methods and techniques which work for one teacher may not be as effective for another teacher, the SO's of teacher training instructional units refer directly to the achievement levels of the students being taught by the student-teacher and only indirectly to the actual behaviors of the student-teacher.

Instead of teaching student-teachers on an individual basis how to teach classes of students, we should be teaching student-teachers on an individual basis how to teach other students on an individual basis. Instead of teaching student-teachers on an individual basis by design on how to teach by chance (curve grading), we should be teaching student-teachers on an individual basis by design on how to teach by design (90 percent or more learn 100 percent of required SO's). Instead of teaching student-teachers on an individual basis via a system which recognizes individual differences in learning on how to teach in a classroom which ignores individual differences, we should be teaching student-teachers on an individual basis via a system which recognizes individual differences in learning on how to teach in a situation which also recognizes individual differences. Although the achievement levels of education majors in education courses may have increased due to CBTE or PBTE, the same achievement levels of the students the student-teachers are teaching probably hasn't changed much (curve of grades). Hence, the value of CBTE or PBTE can be challenged.

Depending on a person's point-of-view, it would be possible to look on CBTE or PBTE as a systems approach if the competencies refer to the role of the teacher as an Instructioneer, i.e., being able to solve student learning problems, to raise the achievement levels of students being taught by the CBTE student-teacher such that 90 percent or more learn 100 percent of the required SO's of courses, to be flexible in setting up the learning environment such that it reflects students' learning needs, etc. However, if any of the competencies refer to the traditional role of a teacher's presenting behavior, then CBTE cannot be considered as a systems approach.

Teachers of professional Instructioneer courses have to practice what they preach and make the emphasis on the student-teachers ability to facilitate learning in others such that 90 percent or more of the students learn 100 percent of the required SO's of an instructional unit. Teachers of professional Instructioneer courses have to be in the forefront of establishing minimum common core SO's in their courses. This may mean that some courses will be condensed or eliminated because too often education courses are established because practicing teachers need more credits in order to make more money rather than because there is something important to learn. The teachers of professional Instructioneer courses should be in the forefront of any movement to eliminate the traditional educational malpractices found at all levels of education. They should also be in the forefront of a movement to require all teachers at all levels of instruction (including the other faculty in higher education) to learn how to teach and test by design and how to facilitate student learning such that 90 percent or more of the students learn 100 percent of the required SO's of the instructional units. For students who plan to teach a particular subject matter area (English, mathematics, biology, etc.), there should be a special course in that subject matter area for teachers. It is not enough to know the content as other students might be required to do. Teachers-to-be need to know potential and known learning problems and possible solutions in their subject matter area if they are going to help students solve their learning problems.

Over the years, I have asked over 200,000 teachers who attended my seminars as to how many were evaluated during their practice teaching experience on the basis of the level of achievement of the students they were teaching. The responses of the teachers at these seminars varied from zero to a high of five percent. As with teachers who are already teaching, student-teachers are generally evaluated on the basis of their performance as a presenter of course content, as a manager of the classroom, and as a specialist in developing interaction between students and teacher (Interaction Analysis) regardless of whether or not the desired teacher behaviors facilitated student learning.

In order to develop student teachers who are concerned about learning, their teachers have to indicate their concern about learning by making the primary criterion for evaluation of student teachers their ability to facilitate student learning. The following guidelines for one or more successful practice teaching experiences may be helpful in developing student-teachers into Instructioneers:

1. It is customary for students in courses where they have to develop a curriculum unit of some kind to select a subject matter area and unit which they know well in order that the preparation time is minimized. Since the student already knows the topic well, no matter what method is used, the student will be reasonably able to teach it, and help some or most of the students learn the SO's of the unit. This is particularly true for students who are already teachers and are taking the course for extra credit or for an advanced degree. If the teacher (as a student) selects his or her best curriculum topic as a unit to develop, any differences in student learning because of the unique method being used will be difficult to identify. As a result, the value of the exercise is minimal and the students (particularly teachers who are students) develop a negative attitude towards the course because they didn't learn anything useful. The critical guideline is to have the student-teacher identify an instructional unit that is a problem for students, i.e., even the better students score consistently lower in this unit than in other units. This can be done by having the student

teacher work with a teacher (preferably one who is teaching what the student plans to teach) and identify a unit that the teacher has found to be a problem unit for students to learn. Teachers who are taking the course as students should identify a problem unit in one of their own courses. Data should be submitted as proof that the unit is a problem unit, i.e., grades or scores of students who have previously had the unit.

2. The student-teacher should identify the GO's and SO's to be learned in the unit and the GO's and SO's representing what the students should know before starting the unit (prerequisite knowledge and skills). The content of the GO's and SO's should be approved by the teacher of the course containing the problem unit. The form of the GO's and SO's should be checked and approved by the teacher of the course the student-teachers are taking. It is critical that the SO's are really specific and measurable.

3. The student-teacher should then make up the evaluation instruments such that the evaluation items match the SO's. A pre-entry test to identify any potential cumulative ignorance problems and a pretest and/or posttest to identify any student-learning problems while going through the unit and to verify achievement. The student-teacher should submit the evaluation instruments to the teacher of the preservice course to make sure the items or criteria for evaluation match the SO's, i.e., their shouldn't be any so-called *objective* type test items (multiple-choice, true-false, and matching) as these rarely match SO's.

4. Then the student-teacher should utilize whatever techniques, methods, and/or materials that he or she thinks will work in facilitating student learning (the lesson plan). This step should be prefaced with the use of the evaluation instruments to find out where the students really are in reference to the GO's and SO's of the unit and should be followed up with the use of the evaluation instruments again to find out how effective the student-teacher's instructional design was in achieving the SO's of the unit. The results of both uses of the evaluation instruments should be submitted to the teacher of the pre-service course as an aid in evaluating the student-teacher's instructional design.

5. The student-teacher should then submit a revised lesson plan designed to facilitate the learning of whatever SO's were missed by the students during step four. This plan should be tried out and followed up with another evaluation to identify which SO's

have now been successfully achieved and which SO's and which students still needed further help. This data should be checked by the teacher of the pre-service course.

6. Step five is repeated by the student-teacher as often as necessary until 90 percent or more of the students learn 100 percent of the SO's of the instructional unit.

7. Once step five is achieved, and if necessary, step six, the student-teacher should prepare a report reviewing the instructional process he or she designed. The function of this step is to see if the number of times that step five was repeated can be reduced by making the original lesson plan and revised lesson plans more effective and still achieve the goal of 90 percent or more of the students achieving 100 percent of the SO's of the unit.

It has been my experience that the cooperating teachers in whose courses the student-teachers are working will want duplicate copies of all materials used by the student-teacher because the process solved a learning problem for the teacher which makes the teacher look better. These cooperating teachers are usually eager to have more student-teachers to help them solve more learning problems. In addition to developing positive attitudes in the cooperating teachers, this process develops positive attitudes in the student-teachers because they were successful in solving learning problems and they found that they could affect the learning of students.

Of unique interest is the situation in which most special education teachers are generally taught most of the role of the Instructioneer, however, the teachers who teach students how to be special education teachers don't always practice what they are preaching and once the special education teacher gets into a school, he or she is usually evaluated on the same basis as the other teachers. Both of these factors detract from the teacher's actual performance of the Instructioneer role and encourage the performance of the more traditional role of the teacher. Given that special education teachers do try to carry out the role of an Instructioneer, it is too bad in our schools that only those students who are in serious trouble academically, the educationally and mentally retarded, get the teacher who is concerned about student learning on an individual basis. Too bad that all teachers aren't special education teachers so all students could have an Instructioneer for a teacher. However, one of the problems in the special education teacher training and in the special education classrooms is that since these teachers work with students with poor academic records, the teachers-to-be are taught not to expect too much. As such, in accordance with the self-fulfilling prophecy, many of the special education students do not achieve as fast or as much as they might be able to. Another problem is when a student has learned successfully in special education classes where the teacher is concerned about individual progress and then goes back into the traditional classroom where the teacher is concerned about the class, the subject matter, and his or her performance as a presenter of course content. Generally, when the special education student goes back into the traditional classroom, it is considered by others as a positive promotion (socially and educationally); however, in terms of the individual who is learning, it is actually a negative promotion (individually and instructionally).

b. TEACHERS ROLE AND EVALUATION

Probably the most influential factor affecting the teacher's role is the evaluation process which in turn is affected or determined by the perception of the teacher's role as held by the person (the principal or department head) who does the evaluating. The perception of the teacher's role held by the evaluator is in turn affected by how he or she is evaluated (higher level administrators). The chain of influence as affected by evaluation goes all the way to the top including school boards, taxpayers, regents, state and national education offices and legislative bodies.

The second most influential factor affecting the teachers role is how the teacher views his or her own role as a teacher. The teacher's perception of his or her role as a teacher may be in conflict with or support the evaluator's perception of the teacher's role, or the two perceptions could be sufficiently unrelated that a teacher could perform both without either one affecting the other. Joseph Axelrod in a Jossey-Bass publication, *Facilitating Faculty Development,* suggests six different traditional roles (the parenthetical comments are mine):

1. The teacher as a *midwife* helping students give birth to ideas (none of which are specified, so help has to be random and any ideas which are born are a result of chance);

2. The teacher as a *horticulturist* sowing seeds of wisdom which may fall on fertile or barren ground (nothing is done to improve on the seeds or to fertilize the soil for better reception);

3. The teacher as a *God* making clods into disciples and if they resist, fail them (no "A's" given in these classes because only *God,* the teacher, is perfect);

4. The teacher as a *craftsman* who is primarily concerned with rote learning (which is better than random or no learning);

5. The teacher as a *lecturer* who is primarily concerned with putting on a good performance with good content (this is the

presenting role associated with most traditional perceptions of the teacher's role); and

6. The teacher as an *artist* who places an emphasis on inquiry (with no SO's and no directions, this is sort of a combined *do your own thing* approach where the teacher's path and the students' paths may or may not coincide or even cross).

In these traditional roles, if there is a content or subject emphasis, the students have to adjust to the subject. If the teacher is in the spotlight, the students have to adjust to the teacher. In either case, due to entropic drift, the underlying function of education as perceived by these roles is to provide a place for teachers to *do their thing* and to provide some students for the teachers to *do their thing* to! In addition to these traditional roles, another role is appearing on the educational scene and that is the teacher as a *laborer*. As teacher organizations become stronger and since the primary negotiating issues are teacher hours and money, there are teachers who look on their job primarily in terms of the time they have to put in (the shortest possible) and the money they make (the most possible). What they do during the day while they are with students isn't really that important. Their own leisure time is even more important than their activities as a teacher.

The Instructioneer role emphasizes the teacher as a *professional* where the primary function of the teacher is to facilitate learning in students for the benefit of the students and society. How they go about achieving this goal, the time they want to put in and the amount of money they want to earn, is up to the teachers and should be part of their academic freedom. As a professional instructioneer, the teacher should be accountable for the following:

1. Identify at least the minimum common core SO's of whatever subject or course he or she is teaching (ideally as a cooperative program with other teachers who are teaching the same subject or course);

2. To communicate these minimum common core SO's to the students and/or parents of the students;

3. To use assessment instruments which match the SO's;

4. To use positive evaluation such that the assessment results are considered as a diagnosis to be followed by a treatment based on the diagnosis;

5. Non-achievement is looked on as a student learning problem which the teacher should try to solve;

6. Don't let cumulative ignorance develop such that it limits the student's success in subsequent courses and particularly if the cumulative ignorance limits the career choices of the student;
7. To recommend students to other learning problem specialists when the teacher is unable to solve the problem and facilitate learning; and
8. In career programs, to let students know the probabilities of actually obtaining the various jobs the program is training them for.

Possibly an indication of the correctness of the Instructioneer role is the fact that despite which traditional role a teacher may perform in the classroom during scheduled class times, almost every teacher performs the Instructioneer role before and after classes in the classroom and in the hallways of the school. During class time in a traditional classroom, if a student makes a mistake on a test, it is considered a genetic problem, the student is graded or scored down, and nothing is done to alleviate the student's learning problem (negative evaluation). However, if the student should make the same mistake in answer to the same question during a conversation with the teacher before or after class on an individual basis, most teachers (if they have the time) will try to help the student solve his or her learning problem. The teacher will try a variety of methods or pathways to solve the problem. The possibility that the student can't learn it or that the teacher can't teach it is not considered until many attempts to solve the problem have been tried (in contrast to the typical traditional classroom behavior of trying one or at the most two pathways to learning and if the student doesn't make it, non-achievement is blamed on genetics). I have never met a teacher who graded or scored students down for making mistakes during informal conversations before or after classes. Therefore, one could say that the primary function of this three volume set is to just get teachers to take the role they are already practicing before or after classes in the classroom or hallways and bring it into the regularly scheduled classes!

In evaluating a teacher's success in the Instructioneer role and also to identify any problems the teacher may have in order to help the teacher be more successful, there are three things that the evaluator needs for every course a teacher may teach. If a teacher specializes in a single course which is taught to different groups of students, then there would only be one set of these three items. If a teacher is teaching different courses, there should be a set of the three items for each course. These sets of items should be available to the evaluator. It is not necessary to even visit the teachers classroom to evaluate what is happening as far as student learning is concerned. The three items are:

1. A list of the GO's and related required SO's of the course and if there are skills and knowledge which are necessary as prerequisites, a list of these SO's. For those teachers who do not have these lists yet, they should provide whatever course objectives that are available.

2. Ideally, two evaluation instruments should be available, one used to evaluate achievement of the prerequisites SO's (preentry test) and another to evaluate the achievement of the required SO's of the course (pretest and/or posttest). Practically, a copy of all evaluation instruments which are used in the course, i.e., all paper and pencil tests; lists of criteria used to evaluate essays and term papers, projects, and performances; placement examinations; unit, midterm, and final examinations; pop quizzes; etc.

3. Ideally, the evaluator should have the raw score results on an item by item basis of the two evaluation instruments which have been given at the beginning of the course and again just before the evaluator begins to evaluate the teacher. For those teachers who do not have these two evaluation instruments, the evaluator should have the raw score results of whatever evaluation efforts the teacher has made of the students. Letter grades or adjusted number scores should not be accepted because they can be manipulated too easily and as such, are generally meaningless in reference to the actual levels of student learning.

With these three items in hand, the evaluator can set them out on a desk and go through the following process:

1. Compare whatever course objectives that are available with whatever evaluation materials that are available. Assuming that whatever it is that a teacher wants students to learn should also be what the teacher evaluates, the first step is to identify the correlation between the objectives and the evaluation instruments.

    a. Check for noun correlation. Any nouns specified in the objectives should be in one or more test items or evaluation criteria, i.e., if a fact (a person's name, a place, a date, an event, etc.) is mentioned in an objective, there should be one or more test items concerned with the fact; if a process (analysis, solve, synthesize, etc.) is mentioned in an objective, there should be multiple test items or evaluation criteria concerned with the process; etc.

    b. Check for verb (behavioral) correlation. Any verbs specified in the course objectives should also be found in one or more test items or evaluation criteria and should be associated with the same noun.

Essentially what is being checked in these two steps is to see if what the students were supposed to learn is what was being evaluated. Since it has never been stated as a requirement in most school districts, colleges, and universities that what you want students to learn is what should be evaluated, it will almost be a normal situation to find in most classrooms that there is a low correlation between the course objectives and the course evaluations. The problem to take note of is that the further away the evaluation is from the objectives, the more useless and meaningless are the raw score results. A common indicator of a correlation problem is when a teacher uses any so-called *objective* type test items (multiple-choice, true-false, and matching items). Rarely do any of these items match or have a high correlation with desired course objectives. When the teacher evaluator identifies a situation where what is being evaluated by the teacher does not match what the teacher says the students are supposed to learn in the course (objectives), then the evaluator is well within the functions of his or her role to call the teacher in and tell the teacher essentially, *I am not trying to tell you what to teach or what to test as that is your role; however, I think you should be consistent and either test what you want your students to learn (change the tests to match the objectives) or change what you say you want the students to learn to match what you are evaluating (change the objectives to match the tests).* Until the objectives and the evaluation instruments match, the results of the instructional process can not be evaluated.

    At this point, many of those teachers who do not have a good correlation between their course objectives and their evaluation instruments will not be able to make the appropriate changes without help. It is the obligation of the evaluator to provide in-service training for the teacher to help them correct the problem.

    When the evaluator finds there is a high correlation between the course objectives and the evaluation instruments, then he or she should go on to the next step.

    2. Look at the raw score results. Test items or criteria for evaluation which were missed by relatively few students are indications of individual differences among students and learning problems which probably should be solved on an individual basis. Test items or criteria for evaluation which were missed by a relatively large group of students are indications of design problems in the methods and/or materials used to teach those

objectives and can probably be solved on a small group basis using alternate methods and/or materials. The difference between the preentry tests and the course pretests given at the beginning of the course and the same tests given just before the evaluation of the teacher indicates the achievement of the students which the teacher was able to facilitate within the time frame.

In a class where the students are considerably behind in their prerequisite knowledge and skills, the students may achieve a great amount and yet, not even start on the course they were registered to study. The teacher (as a teacher of students rather than of a course) has to take the students where they are and take them as far as possible. In another class where the students already know most of the course, the students may not have achieved as much, and yet, 90 percent or more of them may have completed 100 percent of the course objectives. In measuring the amount of student learning a teacher can facilitate, it is not enough to only know where the students are at the end of an instructional unit or course, it is critical to know where the students were at the beginning of the unit or course. In evaluating the teacher, it is important to know how much student learning the teacher is able to facilitate in how many students and it is also important to evaluate what the teacher is doing about non-achievement. Is the teacher planning and/or carrying out individual and small group meetings to solve student learning problems? If yes, is the teacher having success in solving the problems? If the teacher is not doing anything about non-achievement or is not having much success in solving student learning problems even if the teacher is trying, this may indicate a need for in-service sessions aimed at helping the teacher learn how to solve student learning problems. The evaluator may send the teacher to the Instructional Crisis Squad for emergency help in solving critical learning problems (many students involved in the same problems).

NOTE: No teacher should be fired or their contract not renewed as a result of this evaluation. If anything, the teacher who is having a lot of teaching problems (can't seem to facilitate much learning) should be given an "I" for incomplete. If teachers are supposed to use positive evaluation with their students and solve their learning problems rather than grade them down or fail them, then those who evaluate teachers should also use positive evaluation and solve their teaching problems rather than just criticize them or fire them. After all, very few, if any, teachers at the present time have been or are being taught how to be Instructioneers by their teacher training institutions or graduate studies departments and very few, if any, teachers were specifically hired because they were able to facilitate learning in students!

If a teacher who has been identified as needing help refuses to accept help or to take any in-service training and also refuses to try to improve student learning levels by solving student learning problems, then the teacher should be taken out of the classroom and placed in a non-pay status until the necessary effort is put forth. If no effort is made over a set period of time, the teacher should be dropped as a liability.

(1) HIRING PRACTICES

At the present time, few teachers at any level of education are hired on the basis of whether or not they can facilitate student learning. It is assumed that they can teach (in the traditional style). If an administrator wants to hold the teachers accountable for student learning, one of the first steps is to start making this a criteria for hiring. Since teacher training institutions and graduate departments do not specifically teach their students to perform the Instructioneer role, this step will force the teacher training institutions and graduate departments to make some changes and start teaching their students how to facilitate student learning up to the desired quality level of 90 percent or more of the students learning 100 percent of the required SO's of a course.

Under a condition of a shortage of teachers, an administrator may have to take what teachers he or she can get and depend on an in-service training or the Instructional Crisis Squad to help improve the teachers' abilities to facilitate student learning. Under a condition of a surplus of teachers, it shouldn't be too hard to set up parallel teaching situations similar to the practice teaching experience described on pages 977-9 wherein the teachers competing for a job have an opportunity to identify and solve a learning problem concept or unit. Given other criteria are equal, the applicant that should be hired is the one that can bring about greater increases in student learning than other applicants working for the same amount of time, with the same learning problem, and with similar students.

The use of standardized National Teacher Examinations to identify good teachers is an administrative malpractice as the test is probably culturally biased, is irrelevant to the knowledge and skills needed to be an Instructioneer, and in being standardized, the results are programmed into the test. The use of the results of this test in hiring is similar to a teaching situation where students are promoted on the basis of test results and yet the teacher's tests do not match the teacher's course objectives which makes the results meaningless as a basis for promotion.

Many teacher training institutions have used and are using video tape to record and evaluate student teachers as to their ability to be presenters of course content, managers of the classrooms (discipline), and to interact with students (regardless of whether or not the students being taught by the student-teachers have learned anything). Some institutions are offering video tapes of actual student-teacher performances to prospective employers. These might be acceptable, if the video tapes were accompanied by a list of the SO's being learned by the students in the video taped unit and the raw score results of a test given at the beginning and end of the video taped unit so the prospective employer can estimate the amount of learning the student-teacher was able to facilitate.

c. IN-SERVICE TRAINING AND THE INSTRUCTIONAL CRISIS SQUAD

Most in-service sessions for teachers are put on for two reasons: it makes the administrator look like he or she is trying to help improve whatever is happening in the school and/or the administrator has a feeling that the teachers need some help in one or more general areas. In-service training generally has a negative reputation. Because most in-service sessions are not based on specific needs of teachers and are not individualized such that teachers who need them, attend the sessions, and those who don't need them are excused. Teachers for years have been accustomed to expect little, if any, useful information to come out of in-service sessions. The fact that most teachers still keep attending these sessions, knowing that these sessions will probably be a waste of time, points out their motivation and determination to be good teachers.

Under the traditional teacher's role and the traditional methods of evaluating teachers, what happens in the classroom (except for the days the teacher is being observed and evaluated) is up to the teacher. Dr. James, Dean of the Stanford School of Education, is quoted as saying, *when teachers get out of their meetings and close the door to their classrooms, things go on pretty much as they have for decades in most schools.* Unless the teacher evaluation procedures and the teacher's role are changed, the best methods, techniques, and/or resources can be made to fail in the privacy of the classroom.

Given that a school district, college, or university wants their teachers to change their roles to that of an Instructioneer and the administrators are willing to evaluate the teachers accordingly, then in-service sessions should only be scheduled when a need is identified. There should be SO's written for the sessions based on the teachers needs and evaluation instruments set up to evaluate achievement. Based on the results of the tests, only those teachers who need the training should attend. The administrators should treat the learning of the in-service SO's just as they want the teachers to treat their students and the learning of their course SO's. There should also be a follow-up evaluation to identify achievement and any needs for further in-service training. The same or better quality standards should be expected of the teachers, 90 percent or more — hopefully 100 percent — of the teachers should learn 100 percent of the SO's of the in-service unit.

Although most administrators will admit that most brand new teachers (fresh out of college or university) need in-service help before they can become an effective teacher in the classroom, they typically hire the same college or university teachers who were ineffective during pre-service training to put on ineffective in-service sessions. (Possibly, if the college or university teachers were more effective, they would lose a lot of consulting business!)

Regional and national conventions which are supposed to achieve some in-service type responsibilities have the same problems as most in-service sessions. The primary objective is to have a convention not to affect the people who might attend the convention. Convention themes should be based on identified needs of the group involved and there should be follow-up activities to evaluate the success of the convention and to design necessary subsequent conferences to complete the achievement of the convention SO's.

If a teacher has been identified as needing help to facilitate student learning, it may be necessary to use the Instructional Crisis Squad because by the time other teachers with similar problems can be identified and an in-service session arranged, too many students in the teacher's class will have lost a lot of learning time. The Instructional Crisis Squad is an action group that can help the teacher solve student learning problems sort of *on the run* (while the class is going on). The membership of the Instructional Crisis Squad might include most or all of the following:

— One or more teachers who might be thought of as master Instructioneers in that they have successfully performed the Instructioneer role in facilitating student learning by solving their learning problems. Ideally, one or more of these teachers would be in the same subject area as the teacher needing help.

— A librarian and an audio-visual specialist who are acquainted with the selection and preparation of individualized learning materials. This could be one person who is trained in both areas or it could be two separate people.

— A guidance and/or counseling staff member or someone trained in psychology.

— A principal, department head, or other administrator who is an instructional leader, has had experience solving other teachers' problems, and has the authority to get things done.

- One or more students who have proven their ability to tutor other students in the subject matter area involved in the instructional problems.
- One or more curriculum specialists in the subject matter area involved in the instructional problems.

A point to remember in the composition of the Instructional Crisis Squad, is that the members of the Squad may change depending upon the subject matter specialty of the teacher needing help. The basic core of the Squad would be relatively constant and would include the administrator, the librarian, the audio-visual specialist, and the guidance and counseling staff member.

d. CLASS SIZE

Throughout the country teachers in elementary and secondary education, and even in higher education, are requesting and/or demanding smaller classes and lighter teaching loads (number of hours in classroom each week). These requests are generally based on the assumption that by having smaller classes or by decreasing the teacher's teaching load, this will improve the quality of education. To my knowledge, there has not been a single request for smaller classes or lighter teaching loads in which the teacher has specifically identified what it was the students were not learning because of the size of the class and/or because of the teacher's teaching load. I have also never heard of a teacher who having identified what wasn't being learned due to class size and teaching load, was willing to guarantee that if given the smaller class and/or the lighter teaching load, that the students would learn whatever it was they were missing.

Of interest, the concept of 25 students to one teacher can be traced back to the Talmud Baba Bathea which contains this instruction

> *One teacher is to have twenty-five pupils; if they be fifty, then two teachers must be appointed; if they be forty, the teacher has to have an assistant.*

The talmudic doctrine was set in an age where most learning took place orally. The idea of students learning on their own from books, films, television, etc. wasn't considered. Yet, with all the materials available for independent study, the primary traditional role of the teacher is an oral one in which the teacher is still the presenter of the major part of the course.

At almost every seminar I have conducted, one or more teachers have asked me what size class I thought was right for teachers and students. Realizing that teachers are as different in their abilities as any other group of people, it would be false to claim that any one class size is right for all teachers IF one is also considering student learning. If student learning and cost are not to be considered, then the ideal class would be the smallest possible (one). However, the taxpayers and society can't afford such a situation. There is very little, if any, research that shows increased learning occurring when class size is reduced. Since traditional education ignores differences in teachers, it would be easy to prove that smaller classes improves learning by putting a more effective teacher in the smaller class and a less effective teacher in the larger class. If you wanted to prove the opposite (larger classes are better), you could put the more effective teacher in the larger class and the less effective teacher in the smaller class.

As long as a teacher is teaching in the traditional role as a presenter of course content, class size is almost irrelevant. Characteristics of this role can be readily identified. If in a given school there were five classrooms with 40 students in each classroom (total of 200 students) and the class size was reduced to 25 students in each classroom, this would necessitate three more teachers and three more classrooms and would increase the cost of the education of the 200 students by 60 percent. Would this reduction in class size affect *quality* of instruction? Probably not if the improvement in the *quality* of instruction refers to students receiving better grades. Because most teachers use some form of curve grading and curve grading, as discussed in Chapter VI, (Volume II) is based on percentages, then no matter how you split up the 200 students, collectively the same percentages of "A's", "B's", "C's", "D's", and "F's" will be given. This would be particularly true for teachers who looked on their major role in the classroom as one who is supposed to present information to the students. As long as teachers are primarily concerned with presenting information then what the teacher does in the classroom wouldn't be any different for 20, 40, 100 or 500. Until the teacher changes his or her role in the classroom, reducing class size may do nothing except increase the costs of education.

Another characteristic of the *presenter of course content* role is the need for preparation time to prepare presentations. This involves a needless waste of human talent to reinvent curriculum wheels as if no one has ever taught the teacher's course before. Just think of it, almost 100,000 teachers teaching each of the subjects offered in elementary school, about 50,000 teachers teaching each of the subjects in secondary school, and from 6,000 to 10,000 teachers teaching each of most of the subjects in undergraduate education. Not only do the presenters resist accepting what others have done, but from year to year they even resist using their own work of the year before. There has just got to be some communality in the same course from teacher to teacher and from year to year. However, as many people in the educational television field realize, if a teacher has developed a series of videotape recordings presenting the major content of a course and then that teacher leaves, the teacher that comes in to teach the course will utilize the videotapes for possibly one semester or at most a year and then, on the basis of remarks such as *The material is obsolete, It is presented from the wrong point of view*, etc., the videotaped materials will be discontinued. The major problem is not the obsolescence of the material, the problem is that it is not the new teacher's face on the videotape or their voice on the audiotapes.

Other characteristics of the presenter role which makes class size irrelevant are:

— the use of *teacher* aids to aid the teacher to have more time to present rather than *learner* aids to help students learn more;

— the use of class-oriented audio-visual aids such as the overhead projector, the 16mm film projector, etc.;

— the treatment is given first and any evaluation is given second because in that way the teacher doesn't really know about student differences and can ignore them and give all of the students the same treatment;

— the design of education will not only ignore differences in students, but will also ignore differences in teachers (same class size, same teaching load, same pay, etc.);

— given the emphasis on the teacher, there is no need for SO's as these would tend to place an emphasis on the students;

— if there are any SO's, the correlation with any evaluation instruments will be low in order to maintain a curve's worth of achievement (if the SO's and tests matched, the students might learn too much and ruin the curve);

— in observing the classroom, there will be a lack of students learning on their own and most of the class time will be spent as a class (all students doing the same thing at the same time);

— reluctance or inability to specify what an "A" and "B" (or other top grades) stand for; and/or

— most grades or scores indicate achievement levels of less than 80-90 percent ("C's", "D's", "F's", etc.).

The contemporary role of the pseudo-humanist where the teacher is the companion of the students and operates under the philosophy of *Who am I to tell the students what to learn?* is another situation in which class size is irrelevant. After all, if the students are doing their *own thing*, what difference does it make if there are 20, 50, or 100 students in the class. Other characteristics of this type of situation which makes class size irrelevant are:

— the students set their own SO's;

— there are no grades, tests, or evaluation; and/or

— all students get the top grades and the teacher can't defend the grades in terms of learning.

If teachers wanted to individualize instruction such that each learner progressed at his own pace starting from wherever the student was intellectually but also wanted to keep the role as a presenter of course content, then the size of the class could seriously affect learning because the teacher would have to have time to present the course content to each individual student whenever the student is ready. Obviously, to have teachers repeating their presentations for each student in their classes would be a poor use of the teachers expertise when a book, tape recorder, or television could probably make the presentations almost as effectively as the teacher. If the teachers in trying to individualize instruction and to develop the independent learner were willing to let students learn on their own, the size of the class is only limited by the teachers ability to manage an effective and efficient instructional situation such that 90 percent or more of the students learned 100 percent or more of the course objectives. It is not necessary to have the human teacher present the course content, but it may be necessary to have a human teacher available to sit down with the student and solve a student's individual learning problem.

Of course, in many states the accrediting commissions establish the size of a class, so it is very difficult to change it. If it was possible to eliminate the standards concerning the number of students in a classroom or that a teacher can teach, then it might very well be possible to pay teachers up to several times their present income without actually costing the taxpayer an extra penny. Since the school districts, colleges, and universities design their budgets on the basis of so many dollars per student, then it seems very appropriate to pay teachers on the basis of so many dollars per student.

Just because one teacher is teaching more students than another teacher doesn't necessarily mean that the first teacher would have to have a bigger classroom. Learning, if directed, can take place by design away from the teacher, out of the classroom, and if appropriate even out of the school. In a recent year, almost five million students were learning by correspondence home study courses — away from teachers — out of classrooms — and yet the teachers of these home study courses were teaching hundreds of students!! In contrast with correspondence courses in which students study and learn when they are ready to learn, school buildings and classroom schedules are designed for the convenience of teachers to meet with students and at a time when the teachers are ready to teach which may not fit the time when students are ready to learn. This does not mean that correspondence instruction is necessarily better than the in-school instruction, but even with all of the same problems (lack of specified objectives, inadequate testing, misuse of testing, etc.) that the in-school instruction has, the correspondence teachers do not perform the role of presenting course content and students do learn away from teachers and out of schools which proves it can be done. By combining some of the best concepts of correspondence instruction with the best concepts of in-school instruction, class size (students in the classroom) could be reduced by letting some of the students learn on their own. It is tragic to see teachers and administrators at an impasse during negotiations over class size (a difference of two or three students) when any teacher with a class of over 20 students can effectively reduce his or her class by at least five or more students just by letting those students who want to and can learn independently, to learn on their own.

Under the traditional approach to education, the costs of education on a per student basis are the lowest in elementary school and increase as the educational level increases up to the greatest cost per student at the graduate level. Since the major factor in the cost of education is teacher salaries, it should be noted that teacher salaries are generally the lowest at the elementary level and increase up to teachers of graduate students who are generally being paid the most. There are two factors which are in conflict with these increasing costs from elementary to graduate level. First of all, since instruction builds and cumulative ignorance is the greatest problem affecting student learning at all levels of instruction, it would seem that the lowest levels are really the most important because as a foundation, all subsequent learning is dependent upon it. If the lower levels are really that critical, more money should be spent on the students at the lower levels. A second factor is that as students progress through the system, they should be learning how to learn on their own and as such, the teachers should be able to handle more students and at a lower average cost per student.

Keeping in mind that the two greatest factors affecting class size are: the teacher's ability to facilitate student learning such that 90 percent or more of the students learn 100 percent of the required SO's, and the students' ability to learn on their own, then if any classes are reduced, it should occur at the lowest levels of instruction. By inverting the costs per student such that the greatest costs per student are at the elementary level and the lowest costs at the graduate level, the elementary teacher would be able to earn a salary in line with their importance to the system. If the elementary teachers are not successful in helping students learn critical foundation SO's, the learner's potential for eventual success is severely limited and subsequent teachers will have more learning problems to solve. On the other hand, if the elementary teachers are successful, not only will the learner's potential be almost unlimited and subsequent teachers met with fewer learning problems, if the learners are assigned to an ineffective teacher at some later date, they may be able to learn in spite of the teacher which indirectly would make the teacher appear better than he or she really is. Although the costs per student would decrease as the level of instruction increases, the higher level teachers would be able to earn as much or more because they could handle more students (minimum or no cumulative ignorance to interfere with learning — hence, fewer problems and an increasing number of students able to learn independently).

Consider the following analogy. In the early 1930's, telephone operators went on strike because they were being replaced by dial telephone equipment. Any telephone company representative will tell you that today if we were to go back to the old system of picking up the telephone and talking personally with the operator and having her connect you directly to whomever you were calling, there are not enough women in the United States, if all of them were telephone operators, to handle the traffic. If you were to divide the number of telephone operators we presently have into the number of telephone subscribers, you would find that the number of telephone subscribers per operator is much greater than it was in the early '30's, but actually in a given day the telephone operators may work with a fewer number of subscribers than they did during a given day back in the 1930's. To carry this analogy into education would suggest that by taking advantage of the fact that many students can learn on an independent basis, particularly when utilizing systems-designed materials and under the right type of planning, the teachers actually could manage the education of more students but actually be meeting on a day-to-day basis with less students than they are presently.

e. TEACHING LOAD

Under the traditional approach to education, teaching load is generally defined in terms of the number of hours a teacher has to meet with students. As a general rule, elementary teachers spend more hours in contact with students than subsequent levels of teachers. Graduate teachers spend the least amount of time with students. Since teacher salaries usually increase from elementary to graduate levels and the teaching load decreases from elementary to graduate levels, this has a double effect on the increasing costs of education per student. The American Association of University Professors (AAUP) is now recommending a teaching load of nine hours per week in colleges and six hours per week in universities. Graduate faculty in many colleges and universities are already only teaching six hours per week and in some schools they are asking this to be reduced to three hours per week. Undergraduate faculty at the university level generally only teach 9-12 hours or credits per week. Four year college faculty teach 12-15 hours or credits per week and community college faculty teach 12-18 hours or credits per week. It is a normal human behavior to try to get by with the least amount of effort necessary to maintain a given position, but within another decade, if the present trends continue, many colleges and universities may have full time faculty who are essentially *artists-in-residence* without any teaching responsibilities at all.

As a result of these variations in teaching load and the tendency for humans to do the least work necessary for the highest remuneration, there is a tendency among higher education faculty towards (seeking behaviors):

— to work at the university graduate level;
— to originate and/or to offer courses which will have small enrollment, enough to keep the course going, but not enough to keep the faculty member overly busy (this privilege is usually only available to faculty who teach upper division classes);
— to design the student learning experiences such that faculty work is minimized; and
— to use tests that can be corrected and graded by machine.

Remember that class size and teaching load are generally considered as separate concepts except in elementary schools where teachers are teaching in a self-contained classroom and class size is frequently interpreted as teaching load. Being separate concepts, it is possible in higher education for one teacher to be teaching four three-credit courses with minimum enrollment of 12 students per class for a total student load of 48 students and another teacher (usually a new teacher) who is teaching the same load of four three-credit courses, but there are 50 or more students in each class or even 100 or more students in each class for a student load of four or more times that of the other teacher. Another point to remember is that teaching load is generally not affected by the number of different courses a teacher teaches except at some secondary schools. In other words, a teacher who teaches four different courses is considered to have the same load as a teacher who teaches four classes of the same course. Because teaching load is not generally affected by the number of students or whether or not the students are learning, it should be apparent that the teaching load concept is based on the traditional role of the teacher as a presenter of course content which in turn makes class size irrelevant. In some secondary schools where there is a difference in the teaching load between a teacher who teaches multiple courses and a teacher who teaches multiple classes of the same course, the difference is based on the fact that the teacher who is teaching the multiple courses needs more time to prepare their *presentations*. Ironically, the elementary teacher who teaches the most hours also generally teaches the most different courses.

A common student problem resulting from the definition of teaching load and class size limitations is that frequently students can't get a class they need or want because there aren't enough students wanting the course to offer it, there are too many students wanting the course and there isn't enough space, and/or the course is only offered at certain times. As a result, many students take courses they neither need nor want in order to be carrying a full load and/or to graduate at the right time, and their motivation to learn is decreased accordingly. In California and in several other states, there is a movement to charge students extra fees when they take excess courses. In most cases, the taking of extra courses is more a result of faculty teaching load and class size limitations than it is a student problem. Another common problem usually found in small schools is the limited course offerings because the faculty are operating under the same teaching load and class size limitations as found in the larger schools.

Although the one-room school is being phased out of modern education, I like to refer to it as a model in reference to some aspects of the best concepts in the Behavioral Learning Systems Approach to instruction. The problems with the one-room school is that the teachers frequently had the least amount of training (which when thinking of the traditional teacher training is not necessarily a bad thing) and eight years of an ineffective teacher is terrible for the students. However, eight years of an effective teacher could be great. In some of the older one-room schools, it wasn't uncommon to have students progress at their own pace and change grades in the middle of the year. The one-room teacher taught up to ten grades and an average of five subjects for each grade. The teacher rarely presented anything to the whole class (all grades). The emphasis was on getting the students to learn on their own in order that the teacher would have more time with other students. In talking to teachers about individualizing instruction, one of the most common remarks is on how impossible it would be to have two or more levels of learning in the same classroom. One-room schools have up to ten levels going on at the same time. As far as class size limitations, I've never heard of a one-room school teacher who said to the one student in fourth grade, *Sorry, we can't offer fourth grade this year because there aren't enough students!* I have also never heard of a one-room school teacher who said *There are too many fifth grade students to fit in the fifth grade row, some of you just can't go on to fifth grade because there aren't enough seats.*

Under the Behavioral Learning Systems Approach, teaching load is primarily considered in terms of the number of students who the teacher can help achieve 100 percent of the required SO's in some average amount of time. In an effort to downgrade the need for effectiveness and efficiency in education, Stephen Bailey of the American Council on Education quotes a story about the response of a president of a university to a rural member of the state legislature when the legislator was shocked to hear that the university faculty only taught nine hours per week. The president's comment was, *Sir, you are famous for your stud bulls. Would you judge their value by the number of hours a week they worked?* Supposedly the legislator was chagrined and nevermore questioned the faculty teaching load. What the legislator could have said is that his famous stud bulls are famous because of their ribbons which have been won as a result of the bulls themselves; however, their value is determined by the number of cows they can inseminate successfully (resulting in calves) and the bulls' effect on the *goodness* of the calves resulting from the interaction. Similarly, the legislator might have liked to see faculty evaluated not only on the basis of their degrees and ribbons, but on the number of students they can interact with and mentally inseminate successfully with measurable learning which will improve the *goodness* of the students. No matter how many ribbons a stud bull has, or how much fertilizer the bull can spread around, unless the bull can produce measurable results in others, he is practically useless regardless of how many hours he puts in trying!

f. THE SLATE CRITERIA FOR REMUNERATION

The salaries of most elementary and secondary teachers are presently based on schedules which have little, if any, relationship to student learning (the primary purpose of education) and also ignore any individual differences among teachers as to their ability (natural and nutured) to facilitate student learning. Most salary schedules are primarily based on the academic degrees achieved by the teacher and length of service (seniority). An increasing number of school districts also have different levels of teachers on their salary schedules, i.e., department heads, team leaders, differentiated staffing positions, etc. The salaries of higher education faculty are generally based on their academic position; lecturer, instructor, assistant professor, associate professor, and professor; however, the salary schedules are affected by a teachers academic degrees and his or her organizational position: department head, project director, etc. One of the major factors affecting salaries in higher education is a teacher's beginning salary. This varies considerably depending upon who the teacher is. As a result, one of the easiest ways to get a bigger than average salary increase for a good teacher is to change schools. Whereas the school a teacher is working for may only offer a 5-10 percent increase in salary in a given year, if the teacher is well known in his or her field, the teacher may be able to quit and go to another school for a 20-50 percent increase in salary. Although the teacher salaries in higher education are not as scheduled as they are in elementary and secondary education, increases in salary are generally as uniform (usually on a percentage basis) and are just as unrelated to student learning (the primary purpose of education) and individual teacher differences as to their abilities to facilitate student learning.

According to NEA Research Report 1970 — R12, *Salary Schedules for Teachers 1970-71*, the average teachers' salary rose 65 percent between school years 1957-58 and 1966-67 and 31 percent between school years 1966-67 and 1970-71. Since teachers' salaries are the major part of any school budget, any changes in salaries directly and almost proportionately affect the school budget. During these same time periods, there has been a decrease in class size and a decrease in the teachers' teaching load. Supposedly, the increased salaries and decreased class size and teaching load were granted on the basis of increased *quality* of education. This supposed increase in *quality* has not been identified and can not even be inferred from any measures of student learning presently being used. As such, the existence of this increased *quality* can be challenged. In fact, students who are in the *front line* of the teaching-learning event rarely, if at all, notice any differences in the classroom as a result of increased teacher salaries, decreased class size, and/or decreased teaching load. Whereas in most labor unions, increases in remuneration for the laborer is at least in part balanced by greater efficiency and/or effectiveness in the production processes in an effort to try to maintain or increase productivity;[11] in education, the increases in remuneration and benefits for the teacher (smaller classes, lighter teaching loads, etc.) are not accompanied with increased efficiency and/or effectiveness. The result is a reduction in productivity such that the actual costs per student actually increase much more than the apparent increase indicated by increasing the teachers' salaries. Philip Combs in his book, *The World Educational Crisis: A Systems Analysis* (1968), stated that

---

[11] In contrast to the decreasing productivity of teachers, the productivity of American workers actually increased during 1974. In a situation where earnings are increasing and there are no changes in the production process, productivity decreases. In order to maintain productivity levels in a situation where earnings are increasing, it is necessary to make matching effectiveness and efficiency adjustments in the production process. For productivity to increase at the same time that earnings are increasing, it is necessary to make greater than just matching adjustments in the effectiveness and efficiency of the production process. In the case of teachers, each of the three factors (increased earnings, decreased class size, and decreased teaching load) cause productivity to decrease.

An economist would infer from this that education is *a rising cost industry* — that its input costs (at constant prices) for each similar unit of output follow an upward trend line over the years. If this is the case, as it seems to be, the implications are serious and far-reaching. It means, in effect, that each year, ad infinitum, an educational system needs more finances simply to accomplish the same results as in the previous year. If it wants to do more, and to do it better, it will need a still larger budgetary increase — all this apart from keeping up with inflation . . . Meanwhile, if the productivity of teachers is not rising apace with teachers salaries — and there is little reason to believe that it is — costs per student will keep rising. This expectation is reinforced by a recent pioneering — if controversial — study in the United Kingdom, which concludes that education's productivity in England has actually been declining. Its author makes no claim to infallibility or to the universal applicability of the findings. But there is good cause to suspect that if similar studies were made elsewhere, they might reach similar conclusions.

In response to statements such as these which involve words such as efficiency, effectiveness, and productivity, it is not uncommon for some pseudo-humanists to claim that the efficiency cultists are trying to dehumanize the teaching-learning situation by making it like a factory. On the contrary, many of the teacher organizations are trying to impose a labor type factory environment on what should be a professional situation. The salary schedules are mechanistic and do not reflect the human differences of the teachers nor of their students. The imposition of a set number of working hours regardless of the effects on the learners and learning is more factory like than a situation where student learning rather than teacher earning is the emphasis. Any evaluation system which recognizes individual human differences among students and teachers has got to be more humane and less factory-like than a system in which these human differences are ignored.

When one examines the critical role that the teacher plays in the future lives of all of their students, and also how important the teacher's role is in the development of our country, it is rather easy to come to the conclusion that teachers are underpaid. On the other hand, if one was to compare the educational needs of our country, and then look at the actual output of our schools, it is possible to come to the conclusion that some teachers are being overpaid in reference to the efficiency and effectiveness of the teaching-learning situation which they have designed.[12]

---

[12] Readers are requested not to quote the first comment concerning the teachers being underpaid or the second comment concerning teachers being overpaid, in such a way that one or the other is left out. If either of these comments are to be quoted, they should be quoted together and in context.

In working with parents, I am convinced that if parents knew they were getting increased quality or productivity (quantity), they would approve increased salaries. As a minimum, teachers should at least show concern by eliminating some or all of the traditional negative malpractices. Many teachers say that they can't make these changes, but if they are able to demand more money for less productivity and get it, then teachers should be able to demand the elimination of the malpractices. I can't imagine any parents, taxpayers, and/or school boards rejecting increased identifiable quality in student learning.

In most school systems, the only way a teacher can receive compensation above and beyond the mechanistic salary schedules is to be promoted out of the classroom and into an administrative position. The sad part of this arrangement is that in order to be promoted, the teacher generally has to be fairly *good* in the classroom which does not mean the teacher will be a good administrator and could suggest that the teacher's replacement in the classroom is not as *good* as the teacher who was promoted. The result could be that the *goodness* in both the administrative position and the teaching position is decreased.

The most obvious alternative to recognize differences in *quality* of teaching ability is the use of merit pay.

In the past many educational institutions have tried *merit pay* as an incentive for teachers. Although many colleges and universities have merit pay options for rewarding outstanding faculty, there are not many elementary or secondary school districts that offer merit pay. Because most *merit pay* increases are based on vague and ambiguous criteria and generally end up being given to *friends* of the supervisor, principals, superintendents, department chairmen, deans, or presidents, the concept of *merit pay* results in negative reactions from most educators. The SLATE criteria for remuneration are a form of *merit pay*, but the increases in pay are based on specific, measurable criteria which are not as affected by subjective evaluation as are the traditional merit pay plans.

(1) COST PER STUDENT AND TEACHER SALARIES: CAUSE OR EFFECT?

Under the traditional approach in most educational institutions all the costs of educating students are added up and then divided by the number of students to arrive at the cost per student. As teachers get salary increases, the cost of educating students increases. As a result, changes in teacher salaries are the cause for subsequent changes in the costs for educating students. However, many state and federal financial supports or contributions are based on the number of students in attendance at the schools or in the attendance or percentage of attendance of certain special groups in the schools.

The major teacher organizations are trying to equalize teacher salaries throughout the individual states via statewide collective bargaining and eventually there will be efforts to equalize teacher salaries on a national basis via national collective bargaining. To a degree there are efforts to equalize salaries on a national basis already in that as one teacher group hears about what another group is earning, they want to have at least the same or better salaries.

In a parallel movement and probably to achieve the same ends, teacher groups and parent groups are pushing for an equalization of costs per student wherein many districts whose costs per student are below average would receive more money from the state. Supposedly, the extra money available for those school districts whose costs per student are above average would be used to upgrade the lower than average districts (which would then allow the teachers in these districts to obtain higher salaries). The redistribution of monies would be handled by the state and in some future date by the federal government.

There are several major problems with the traditional approach and the present trend of school financing. First of all, as with the whole traditional school environment, the primary emphasis is on the teachers and what the teachers earn rather than on students and what students learn. Secondly, as with many other aspects of the traditional school environment, entropic drift has occurred such that instead of the costs per student being the emphasis, most of the arguments on school finance concern the means or where the money comes from rather than on the end product or what the money will be used for. Taxpayers and legislators have observed several cycles of the increases in teacher salaries which were supposedly based on accompanying increases in the *quality* of student learning. Since the increased *quality* in student learning hasn't occurred and teacher organizations tend to resist accountability efforts to identify any changes in the *quality*, taxpayers, parents, school administrators, and legislators are beginning to interpret the rhetoric on increasing the *quality* of student learning for what it really is: increasing teacher salaries and benefits and decreasing the teachers' responsibilities and productivity which in turn more than proportionately increases the costs of education. Because of the teacher emphasis rather than the student emphasis, the students, administrators, parents, and taxpayers in those districts who are already paying above average on a per student basis are afraid that the equalization of costs per students will not only lower the amount of money spent in their district per student, but will result in a decrease in measurable *quality* of education in their district.

Under the Behavioral Learning Systems Approach, the emphasis has to be on the student and student learning. In reference to teacher earnings, any changes in the costs per students' learning should be the causes for resulting effects or changes in the teachers' earnings which is a reverse of the traditional situation. There should also be state and national efforts to equalize the students' achievement of state and national minimum common core SO's and the costs necessary to bring this about. Whereas the present efforts to equalize the costs per student on a statewide and national level are frequently seen as endangering the local autonomy of school districts, if the areas of responsibility and accountability are identified and separated, the desires of the community can be encouraged rather than threatened.

The national funding of any instructional efforts should be concerned primarily with the identification, specification, and student achievement of the national minimum common core SO's of all courses which are offered nationwide from preschool to graduate levels. There should be a basic cost per student that our federal government would be willing to pay to make sure that at least 90 percent or more of the students nationwide would learn 100 percent of the national minimum common core SO's. This basic cost per student would then be affected by the criteria discussed later on in this unit.

The state funding of any instructional efforts should be concerned primarily with the identification, specification, and student achievement of the state minimum common core SO's of all courses which are offered statewide and are above and beyond the national minimums. This allows for and encourages freedom and differences in what is offered and learned by students in each of the states without affecting the national minimums. There should be a basic cost per student that each state government would be willing to pay to make sure that at least 90 percent or more of the students statewide would learn 100 percent of the state minimum common core SO's. This basic cost per student would then be affected by the criteria discussed later in this unit.

The school district funding of any instructional efforts should be concerned primarily with the identification, specification, and student achievement of the school district minimum common core SO's of all courses which are offered districtwide and are above and beyond national and state minimums. In large school districts, which include multiple community groups, there should be procedures by which individual community groups in cooperation with the teachers in the school or schools located within each community, could develop any additional minimum common core SO's for one or more or all of the courses offered in the community. These procedures would encourage and allow for local differences in what is offered and learned by students in different school districts and even in the different communities within large school districts. There should be a basic cost per student that each school district would be willing to pay to make sure that at least 90 percent or more of the students in any one course would learn 100 percent of the district minimum common core SO's. This basic cost per student would be affected by the criteria discussed later in this unit.

In addition to the basic costs per student contributed by the national and state governments and the school district, a certain percentage of these funds from all three sources should be available to encourage individual differences in what teachers themselves may want to require of the students in their courses and to encourage individual differences in what each student may want to learn above and beyond what is required. Funds from this supplementary support could also be used to encourage the scholarship functions whereby individual students, teachers, and even people from the immediate community can present and discuss topics of their own choosing to whatever groups of students, teachers, and people from the community who care to attend.

In establishing these average basic costs per student contributed by national, state, and school district agencies, it should be remembered that these are in reference to any given level of instruction, i.e., preschool, elementary, secondary, undergraduate, and graduate. Since the foundation of instruction is so critical, the vertical levels of costs per student should reflect the importance of the level. At the elementary level, not only are the students learning the basic skills and knowledge critical for success in subsequent schooling, they are also developing the attitudes and values that will keep them in school and will affect their entire life and the future and direction of our society and country. Therefore, in contrast to the traditions of education where the lowest cost per student is at the elementary level and increasing up to the highest cost per student at the graduate level, I would suggest an inversion of the traditional scale such that our largest investment per student is at the elementary level and then decreasing to the lowest cost per student at the graduate level.

NOTE: This would not mean that the elementary teachers would necessarily earn more than graduate teachers as the elementary teachers would probably teach fewer students. By the time students get into secondary schools, colleges, and universities, their lack of cumulative ignorance which impedes student and teacher progress, their ability to learn independently, and their positive self-images (developed from prior years of success) would allow teachers at higher levels to manage the instruction for greater numbers of students than the elementary teachers could manage and without that much more effort. If teacher earnings were based on student-oriented factors then the higher level teachers could earn more than the teachers at the lower levels provided their productivity in accordance with the criteria discussed in this unit was high enough.

Given that very few of the teachers who are presently teaching were actually taught how to teach (as measured in terms of student learning) and that very few teachers were hired because they could facilitate student learning, there will be a tremendous need for inservice training during the transition stage from the traditional approach to teacher earnings to the systems or SLATE approach to teacher earnings. During this transition stage, no teacher should be paid less than they are presently receiving even through their productivity is relatively low. If after inservice training and having help from the Instructional Crisis Squad, a teacher is still not able to be effective and efficient enough to earn his or her present salary in accordance with the SLATE criteria, then it may be appropriate to discuss with the teacher a reduction in salary, a change in position, or termination. Under no circumstances should students be made to suffer the development of cumulative ignorance as a result of non-achievement in any course because some teacher isn't able to do his or her job.

Also, during the transition stage, the SLATE criteria will refer to the average student the teacher is teaching in any one course. At a later time, the SLATE criteria can refer to each individual student.

As new teachers who have been trained to facilitate student learning as an instructioneer come into an instructional institution, they should be able to be effective and efficient enough to earn a good beginning professional income in accordance with the SLATE criteria.

The SLATE criteria for remuneration are:

a. The fundamentality of the course,

b. the heterogeneity of the courses taught;

c. the length of time teaching a course;

d. the average IQ score of the students taught;

e. the number of students taught;

f. the average entering level of students taught;

g. increases in what is taught and learned;

h. the average time needed for achievement; and

i. the average cost needed for achievement.

In order for any of these criteria to be applied (to be eligible for merit pay), at least 90 percent or more of all the students a teacher is teaching should be achieving 100 percent of the required SO's (national, state, and local minimum common core SO's). Any changes in accordance with the SLATE criteria can only be credited if there is no loss in the minimum quality of 90 percent of the students learning 100 percent of the required SO's. Criteria a, b, and g yield only additive merit credits whereas the rest of the criteria yield both additive and subtractive merit credits. Additive merit credits are given when the change in the average student is in a direction where greater teaching skills are needed. Subtractive merit credits are given when the change in the average student is in a direction where fewer teaching skills are needed. In arriving at a teacher's earnings, the additive merit credits are added together and the subtractive merit credits are added together and subtracted from the total sum of additive merit credits. Any variations in the weight of the merit credits of each criteria and the actual dollar value of the resultant merit credits would have to be negotiated at the local level or possibly at the state level.

(a) *The Fundamentality of the Courses Taught*

This criteria is an extension of the criteria built into the basic cost per student wherein the elementary or preschool student cost is highest and the graduate student cost would be the lowest. This decreasing scale can be defended on the basis of the fundamentality of the courses, i.e., if a student doesn't learn to read, write, and/or do basic mathematical operations, subsequent teachers have to work harder to help the student learn. In the process of going through school, almost every student will start a sequence of courses in which the first course is basic and can affect both student and teacher success in subsequent courses. Any teacher who is teaching a basic course should be given additive merit credits in accordance with the number of students in the basic course who achieve 100 percent of the required SO's. Instead of only giving additive merit credits to the basic course, a decreasing scale of additive merit credits could be assigned to a sequence of courses such that the successful teaching of the first course gets the most additive merit credits and the successful teaching of the last course in the sequence warrants no additive merit credits.

(b) *The Heterogeneity of the Courses Taught*

At the present time, some educational institutions either pay a teacher extra because they teach multiple courses or they give the teacher a lighter teaching load because the teacher supposedly needs more time to prepare their presentations for the different courses. Under the Systems Approach, a teacher who is teaching different subjects and/or courses should be given additive merit credits because the teacher is solving a greater variety of student learning problems and has to be knowledgeable in more areas. The base line for determining additive merit credits would be the teacher who teaches only one course to all of his or her students in one or more classes or individually. The increasing levels of heterogeniety can be determined from the following sub-criteria:

— the number of different courses in the same subject matter areas

— the number of different subject matter areas

(c) The Length of Time Teaching a Course

It is traditional to pay a teacher more the longer the teacher serves with a particular educational institution regardless of whether or not the teacher was able to facilitate learning. I could understand rewarding a teacher for a year of service during which the teacher consistently was able to maintain a quality level such that 90 percent or more of his or her students learned 100 percent of all the required SO's. However, if a teacher was not able to maintain this quality level and other teachers or the Instructional Crisis Squad had to take over some of the teacher's students so that the students didn't suffer because of the teacher's inadequacies, then I believe it would be difficult to defend giving this teacher any extra money for a doubtful year of service.

This criteria is not actually connected with the length of a teacher's service, yet it concerns how long a teacher has been teaching a particular course. The guideline for this criterion is that the longer a teacher is teaching a course, the easier it should be to maintain the high quality level of the Systems Approach. A teacher who is assigned to a course for the first time will have a more difficult time to reach and maintain the quality level of 90 percent or more of the students achieving 100 percent of the required SO's. Therefore, a teacher who is teaching a course for the first time and can maintain the high systems quality level should receive additive merit credits. This could be based on a decreasing scale of additive merit credits such that the most credits are given the first year the teacher teaches a course and then a decreasing number awarded each year for the next two or three years. These merit credits are only given if the quality level is maintained each year.

(d) The Average IQ Score of the Students Taught

The use of this criteria might seem in conflict with my earlier statements against such tests. My objection to the IQ tests is that the results are interpreted as indicating the mental limits of students when in fact there is no known limit of intelligence. The utility of most IQ tests is that they typically reflect the students' verbal ability. As such, students with average and higher IQ scores are generally able to learn from available verbal materials and have a high potential for independent learning with these materials (hence a teacher could teach more students easier). Students having below average IQ scores doesn't mean that they can't learn, but it does mean that their present verbal ability is low enough to indicate the students will have trouble learning from available verbal materials. In order to maintain high quality levels, the teacher of below average IQ students will have to utilize a greater variety of learning resources and experiences which are non-verbal and/or the teacher may have to nurture the students verbal ability in addition to the required SO's to the point where the students are able to utilize available verbal materials. Therefore, starting from the base line of an average IQ score of 100, the lower the IQ average of a teacher's students, the more work the teacher would have to do to maintain 90 percent or more of the students achieving 100 percent of the required SO's, and the more additive merit credits the teacher should acquire. Conversely, the higher the average IQ score of a teacher's students, the easier it will be for the teacher to maintain 90 percent or more of the students learning 100 percent of the required SO's, and the more subtractive merit credits the teacher would acquire. If the average IQ score of a teacher's students was 100, then the teacher would not acquire either additive or subtractive merit credits.

In reference to verbal ability, it is important in solving student learning problems to remember that low verbal ability scores as indicated by most IQ tests can be a result of two factors or a combination of the two factors. The most common factor concerns the obvious fact that the student has trouble reading, probably has a low vocabulary level, and other problems associated with low verbal ability. This factor can be reduced or eliminated by teaching the elementary school SO's dealing with reading and vocabulary or by using learning materials which are appropriate (low verbal) for the skills and knowledge levels of the students. The second factor concerns the students ability in the language of instruction. A student who may be proficient in a language other than the language of instruction (usually English in the United States) may score low on an IQ test because the student doesn't know English very well. This factor can be reduced or eliminated by teaching the student the necessary facility with English or if possible, use materials written in the language the student is familiar with. The most difficult problem to solve in this area is when a student has both a verbal ability problem and a language problem. In order to reduce or eliminate this double problem, the teacher has to nurture both the students' verbal ability and the students' language ability. The combined problem can be identified by using IQ tests in English and in the language the student uses. If the student scores low in both, chances are the student has the combined verbal and language problem. In such a case, the teacher should get double additive merit credits inversely proportionate to the scores on the two IQ tests.

Some teachers may not feel qualified to teach verbal ability or to teach English as a second language. In that case, the teacher might try to locate or develop instructional materials at the lower verbal or non-verbal levels or in the language the student uses. If this isn't possible, the teacher may refer the student to a specialist in teaching verbal ability and/or English as a second language.

NOTE: Remember that the intelligence level of any student at any point in time is a combination of nature and nurture. Nothing can be done about the natural contribution, but lots can be done about nurturing the intellect of the student. As such, intelligence as a human ability is capable of being increased. Intelligence is not a static characteristic which might be attributed to a machine.

There might be a tendency for the better teachers to purposely seek out the poorer students in order to earn more money which would be fine. This might suggest that the poorer teachers might be left teaching the highest IQ students. This would not necessarily be the case; since most high IQ students are capable of a great deal of learning on their own, a very good teacher could work with a very large number of high IQ students. If the poorest teacher did end up working with the highest IQ group, this would be a way of putting the teacher into a situation where possibly the least amount of damage can be done to our society by the incompetency of the teacher because the majority of the higher IQ students would learn in spite of the teacher.

(e) *The Number of Students Taught*

This criteria is in reference to the total number of students a teacher teaches whether it be just the 30 students a teacher has all day in a self-contained classroom or the 100-200 or more students a teacher might teach during a day or week of multiple classes. An obvious increase in productivity occurs when a teacher teaches more students. To be eligible for additive merit credits, the increase in number of students has to be accompanied with no loss in quality, 90 percent or more of the total group of students have to learn 100 percent of the required SO's.

The base line for determining additional students would be the average number of students normally assigned to a teacher at the teacher's particular level of instruction and/or in the teacher's subject matter area. In small school districts, colleges, and universities, it may be necessary to include a number of other schools in order to arrive at a valid average number of students for a particular instructional level and/or in a specific subject matter area. These base line averages should be determined before using the SLATE criteria. Because some teachers normally teach large numbers of students (particularly at freshman college level) and other teachers normally teach smaller numbers of students, changes in numbers of students is on a percentage basis. For example, a teacher that normally has 30 students is able to handle three more students with no loss in learning for all 33 students. This situation would indicate a 10 percent increase which in turn represents a certain number of additive merit credits. Another teacher may normally teach 150 students (five classes of 30 students each) and is able to add 15 more students with no loss in learning quality for the 165 students. This situation also indicates a 10 percent increase and the same additive merit credits as the last example.

The rationale supporting this criteria is that as a general rule, the fewer students a teacher works with, the more the teacher will get to know the students' learning styles and the easier it should be to solve the students' learning problems. Conversely, the more students a teacher teaches, the less a teacher will get to know the individual students and their learning styles and the more difficult it will be to solve the students' learning problems. As such, in reference to the base line averages, a teacher who teaches more students and maintains the quality level would get additive merit credits. Conversely, a teacher who teaches fewer students than the average would get subtractive merit credits.

(f) The Average Entering Level of Students Taught

In reference to the desired and necessary prerequisite skills and knowledge, the lower the average achievement level of the students at the beginning of instruction, the more additive merit credits the teacher should get provided that not only did 90 percent or more of the students learn 100 percent of the prerequisite SO's (eliminating cumulative ignorance), but they also went on to achieve 100 percent of the required SO's of the course. It is possible under conditions where courses overlap that entering students will already have achieved all of the prerequisite SO's and even some of the required SO's of a course. Under this condition, the teacher's work would generally be easier. Therefore, the higher the average entering level of a teacher's students, the more subtractive merit credits the teacher would acquire.

This criteria would only be relevant during the transition stage from the traditional approach to education to the Behavioral Learning Systems Approach to instruction. Once the systems concepts are part of the instructional event, few, if any, students would start a course with any cumulative ignorance as they wouldn't be allowed to leave prerequisite courses without achieving 100 percent of the required SO's of the courses. Also, since students will be able to start and stop courses at any time and the lists of required SO's of courses are openly available, the overlap from one course to another course will also disappear.

(g) Increases in What is Taught and Learned

This criteria concerns the adding of more SO's which would have to be justified as being important and approved by two or more of the teacher's colleagues in the same subject matter as being good objectives. The additional objectives would be credited towards increased earnings on a percentage basis because in some subjects it is easier to specify objectives than in other subjects. For example, a teacher who is teaching 200 objectives in mathematics and adds 20 more objectives would be credited with a 10 percent ($\frac{20}{200}$) unit towards this criteria for increased earnings. Another teacher who is teaching 20 objectives in music and adds two more objectives would also be credited with a 10 percent ($\frac{2}{20}$) unit towards this criteria for increased earnings.

NOTE: There might be a tendency for some faculty to generate lots of SO's of little value in order to earn more money; however, since the SO's have to be approved by the teachers' colleagues and are also publically available to students, parents, and other visiting teachers, I have confidence that teachers under such open conditions might actually tend to make the SO's of higher value and probably difficult to achieve. As a check and balance against SO's that might be made difficult in order to impress a teacher's colleagues, remember that in order for the teacher to get additive merit credits for the extra SO's, 90 percent or more of the teacher's students in the course have to achieve 100 percent of the extra SO's.

The base line for determining additional SO's would be the required minimum common core SO's of a particular course (national, state, and/or local) as identified by the teachers who teach the course using the method described on pages 527-40 of Volume II. If there are less than three teachers teaching a particular course in a school district, college, or university, then teachers in other schools should be involved in the identification of the minimum common core SO's.

(h) The Average Time Needed for Achievement

This criteria concerns the amount of time needed by the average student to achieve 100 percent of the required SO's of a course. Since very few teachers have classes of students in which 90 percent or more of the students achieve 100 percent of the required SO's of the courses, the base line for determining merit credits has to be established after the systems concepts have been put into effect. Once the average time for completion of the required SO's has been established, then teachers who are able to help students learn faster such that the average time is reduced should be given additive merit credits. Teachers whose students take longer than the average time would be given subtractive merit credits. Since the amount of average time needed to complete different courses may vary considerably, the increases or decreases in time should be figured on a percentage basis in determining additive or subtractive merit credits.

(i) *The Average Cost Needed for Achievement*

This criteria concerns the average cost of instructing students such that 90 percent or more of the students achieve 100 percent of the required SO's of the courses. As with the last criteria, since very few teachers have classes of students in which 90 percent or more achieve 100 percent of the required SO's, the base line for determining merit credits has to be established after the systems concepts have been put into effect. Once the average cost for achievement of the required SO's has been established, then teachers who are able to help students achieve the required SO's at less cost then average should be given additive merit credits. Teachers whose students cost more to achieve 100 percent of the required SO's of their courses would be given subtractive merit credits. Since the average cost needed to complete different courses may vary widely, the increases or decreases in costs should be figured on a percentage basis in determining additive or subtractive merit credits.

(2) AN EXAMPLE AND OTHER COMMENTS

Based on the use of the SLATE criteria for remuneration, the teachers who are earning the greatest remuneration are those who have the greatest productivity in facilitating student learning by being able to solve students' learning problems effectively and efficiently. Teachers who are earning the least amount of remuneration are teachers whose productivity in facilitating student learning is low because they haven't been able to solve students' learning problems very effectively or efficiently.

The most effective and efficient teachers are ones that can minimize their personal involvement in repetitive learning problems thereby releasing themselves to maximize their personal involvement in unique individual learning problems. As sort of a rule of thumb, any learning problem that takes over ten minutes to solve and over five students during a month have the same problem, the teacher should take time to package it or ask a curriculum unit to prepare it for the teacher. The effective and efficient teacher is also able to identify where the learner is in reference to what the student is supposed to learn and will start the student from there eliminating any prior cumulative ignorance. This practice will not only help students learn faster and easier, but it is success oriented and will build up the students self-image and his or her impression of the instructional event. This teacher will also be adept at locating materials and methods for learning that will fit or be close to the materials and methods each student can learn best from.

Under the SLATE remuneration plan, teachers who are able to successfully teach more students than some other teachers can also earn more money without necessarily affecting the overall instructional cost per student (see Figures 133 and 134). In comparing the two methods of paying teachers, Figure 133 represents a traditional approach wherein there is a *normal* curve of ability in both teachers and students. Assuming that $400 of the cost of a student's education is directly attributable to the costs of having a teacher and that there are some differences in teacher salaries, Figure 133 also represents a traditional salary schedule wherein the differences in teacher salaries has little, if any, relationship to the teacher's ability to facilitate student learning.

SCHOOL A (traditional approach — teacher cost $400 per student)							
Type of Teacher	Students per Teacher	No. of Teachers	Total No. of Students	Average No. of "A" & "B" Students	Average No. of "C", "D" and "F" Students	Average Salary per Teacher	Total Salary per Group
Master	30	3	90	24	66	$13,500	$40,000
Good	30	6	180	48	132	12,750	76,500
Fair	30	12	360	96	264	12,000	144,000
Poor	30	6	180	48	132	11,250	67,500
?	30	3	90	24	66	10,500	31,500
Totals		30	900	240	660		$360,000

Figure 133 — Traditional Remuneration Schedule for Teachers and Students

School A (Figure 133) which is using the traditional approach, assigns each teacher 30 students, regardless of the teacher's teaching ability. If there is a *normal* curve of teaching ability and nothing is done to identify the below average teachers nor to specifically help them improve their ability to teach, then 270 students, almost a third of the students, are exposed to the poor or questionable teachers. Under the traditional use of curve grading, approximately 240 of the students would receive "A's" and "B's" while about 660 students would receive "C's", "D's", and "F's". If there is any relationship between the teacher's ability and what students learn, then even the "A's" and "B's" given by the poor and questionable teachers (72 students) can be challenged as to their relationship to high quality achievement. In addition, because there is no identified common core learning among teachers of the same course in traditional education nor is it usual to have any SO's in any of the courses, even the students with high levels of achievement in the classes of the better teachers may be of doubtful value and utility.

1012

Figure 134 represents a school in which individual differences among teachers are recognized and encouraged particularly when these differences help some teachers facilitate more students to learn more. Although there are at least eight criteria which could be used to reflect these differences in additive and subtractive merit credits, only the criteria of more students is reflected in Figure 134 as an example of what could occur when using the SLATE criteria for remuneration.

\multicolumn{8}{	c	}{SCHOOL B (Learning Systems Approach — teacher cost $400 per student)}
Type of Teacher	Students per Teacher	No. of Teachers	Total No. of Students	Average No. of "A" & "B" Students	Average No. of Incomplete	Average Salary per Teacher	Total Salary per Group
Master	80	3	240	216	24	$32,000	$ 96,000
Good	60	6	360	324	36	24,000	144,000
Fair	30	10	300	270	30	12,000	120,000
Totals		19	900	810	90		$360,000

Figure 134 — SLATE Remuneration Schedule for Teachers and Students

School B which is using the Learning Systems Approach assigns each teacher as many students as they can successfully teach (90 percent or more of the students have to achieve "A" or "B" (100 percent of the course). Because the teachers are evaluated on the basis of how many students they can help achieve the goals of the course, it is possible for master and good teachers to earn considerably more than the fair teacher at no extra cost to the taxpayer (both School A and School B spend $360,000 in salaries for the 900 students at $400 per student.) Whereas in School A almost a third of the students had poor or questionable teachers, in School B all of the students had a master teacher, a good teacher, or at least a fair teacher. Under the Learning Systems Approach in School B, the master teachers and good teachers are paid salaries that are appropriate to their ability and are much closer to the business and industry equivalent for this kind of capable professional individual. The most important benefit is that in School A only 240 students are achieving the goals (unspecified) of the course ("A" or "B"), whereas in School B 810 students or 90 percent of the students are achieving the goals (specified) of the course ("A" or "B"). Under the Learning Systems Approach, it may be necessary for the teacher to have the part-time assistance of a learner's aid, additional tape recorders, film projectors, etc., in order to successfully manage the instruction of large numbers of students. Therefore, it may be necessary to budget a part of the teacher's increase in salary to pay for this additional equipment, i.e., instead of the teacher earning $32,000, the teacher may receive $27,000, and the balance budgeted for equipment. This still allows for a doubling of the teacher's salary.

NOTE: Although these tables may seem more appropriate for elementary or secondary classes, similar tables could be prepared to reflect higher education.

There will be objections by some educators and some teacher organizations to the use of some or more of these criteria. The educators who would be most concerned about the use of these criteria are those that are doubtful about their ability to help students learn. The teacher organizations which would object to the use of these criteria are apt to be ones that want to ignore individual differences in both teacher and student and emphasize sameness or socialistic concepts. These organizations see the teacher as a laborer rather than as a professional and over a period of time, the maintenance of the organization and the increase in power of the organization and its leaders becomes more important than students, student learning, and sometimes even more important than the teachers as individual members. Besides the potential objection of some teachers and some teacher organizations, it is difficult to imagine others who would object against students learning more and teachers earning more without causing increased taxes.

g. TEACHER SURPLUS OR A SHORTAGE OF STUDENTS AND LEARNING?

In the traditional approach to education with its emphasis on teachers and teaching, it should be expected that during the sixties one of the problems of education should be identified as a shortage of teachers and in the seventies one of the problems of education is a surplus of teachers. Suggested solutions to these problems usually emphasize doing something for teachers. In the sixties, the salaries of teachers and the teaching environments were improved to attract more teachers and to keep those who may change to other career fields. Now that there are more teachers, similar solutions seem to suggest that by *improving* the teaching environment (smaller classes and lighter teaching loads) more teachers could be hired (increasing the costs) and of course the salaries should be increased for all teachers even though productivity has been decreased. Note that although improvements in learning are implied, rarely are any increases in learning specified and even rarer would these increases be guaranteed in return for increased costs. In the face of a surplus of teachers, a criticism of the SLATE criteria and particularly the table in Figure 134 will be the fact that fewer teachers will be used creating a greater surplus. During the sixties, some questionable teachers were hired to fill a space in front of a classroom. In a situation where tenure protects teachers from administrators but it doesn't protect students from teachers, a lot of the questionable teachers were able to stay in education.[13] As mentioned earlier, every administrator's hardest task each year is the placement of certain teachers where they will do the least damage to students. As the systems concepts and accountability are integrated into a school, these teachers will be identified (not to fire them, but to help them). If these teachers refuse to improve their ability to teach and resist working with the Instructional Crisis Squad, then it would be better for all concerned if they quit or were removed from teaching. The point to keep in mind is that it may take fewer teachers to accomplish the present instructional task at higher levels of achievement; however, there are other areas of instruction which need teachers. Instead of identifying the problem as a shortage or surplus of teachers, we should identify the problems in terms of the learning needs and desires of our society.

First of all, not only is education the only profession that fails its clients by design (curve grading), but it is also the only profession that cuts its own financial throat by design. Since many aspects of school budgets are affected by the number of students in attendance, to purposely reduce the number of students by suspending them, flunking them out, or just not accepting them actually reduces the amount of money available to pay teachers. In a school district in Canada, the teachers were negotiating for a package of teacher benefits which would cost the school district about $500,000. They were told by the school board that the money for their requests was not available. It just happened that in this particular high school district about 400 students had been failed or dropped the year before. The province's contribution to this school district for those 400 students (if they were still in school) would have been about $500,000! By being more effective and efficient in helping students learn and be successful in schools these teachers could have had the benefits they wanted.

Instead of pushing out over a million drop-outs each year from our secondary schools and over half a million students from our colleges and universities, we should be teaching them and solving their learning problems.

> NOTE: An increasing request of teacher organizations is the right to eliminate students from their classes and from school. Various writers in education want to eliminate compulsory attendance laws. Both of these suggestions reduce the number of students and the

---

[13] Tenure in teaching should be conditional on the basis that the teacher will maintain certain minimum levels of teaching ability as measured in terms of students achieving required SO's. Tenure should also not be used to protect teachers who are trying to brainwash their students such that the students are against our country, the community, parents, and any form of authority.

money available for teacher salaries. As pointed out on pages 43-4, Volume I, only 71 percent of our entering first-grade students are presently completing high school, whereas thousands of educators have indicated that they believed that at least 95 percent should be completing high school. If we were able to reduce the dropouts such that 95 percent did remain in school, this would necessitate a 20 percent increase in high school teachers just to take care of the students who would be staying in school. In addition, if we had as many students going on to two years of college as the thousands of educators have indicated such that 75 percent of our entering first-grade students would be completing two years of post high school training or education in contrast to the present 27 percent, this would necessitate about 175 percent increase in post high school training and education faculty. If our colleges and universities were able to graduate 55 percent of our entering first-grade students instead of the present 18 percent, this would necessitate approximately a 200 percent increase in junior and senior college level faculty.

Even under the traditional approach, the keeping in school and teaching of drop-outs could employ 50,000 more teachers. In giving these students more success, we will probably reduce vandalism, juevenile delinquency, and adult crime which would make more tax monies available for the needs of the instructional environment. A common retort to this suggestion is that not everybody needs more education. Surveys which result in showing a certain percentage of workers are over-educated assume that these people will never be promoted into positions in which they will need whatever education they have and may even need more. If it can be assumed that formal education or instruction helps the students to live and function in our society, then it would be difficult to think of too much learning.

NOTE: A study by the University of Texas for the U.S. Office of Education found that one out of five adults lack the basic skills and knowledge necessary to live and function effectively and efficiently in our society. This means that over 23 million American adults are in need of further education.

As the need for preschool is identified in more and more areas, more teachers will be needed. Where are we going to get the teachers to teach this additional year or years of preschool education? They are going to have to come out of the normal supply of teachers which usually teach the regular grades in our schools. If present trends continue, there will be an additional 5 million children, 3 to 5 years old, enrolled in public or voluntary programs by 1975. As more and more people change jobs during their lifetime, more teachers will be needed in career areas. As people have more leisure time due to shorter work hours, there will be an increased need for teachers in adult instructional activities. As more areas are identified as being necessary for effective participation in our society, more teachers will be needed. Some of these areas have already been identified (page 630 in Volume II), i.e., how to raise children, how to get along with your fellow men and women, how to enjoy your leisure time activities, etc. As more and more people have success in schools, more people will retain positive attitudes towards schools and will be more apt to want more instruction.

Some teachers are not in teaching because they want to be teachers but because they either couldn't get into their primary preferred career because there were no openings or they were failed or discouraged from continuing in their preferred career studies because of low grades, low achievement levels, and/or cumulative ignorance due to ineffective teaching situations. Under the systems approach, more students will be able to be successful in their preferred career areas and will not have to accept their second, third, or fourth career choices.

As teaching becomes more professional and there really is relevant training necessary to become an Instructioneer, there will be fewer part time teachers who will be qualified to teach and hence more full time teachers will be needed. Also, since under the Systems Approach a teacher can teach multiple levels of a course or multiple courses simultaneously, more courses can be offered which in turn will attract more students and necessitate more teachers.

Typically, requests for more money are to build more buildings, to pay teachers more money, and to initiate special programs. In reference to increasing the school facilities, notice that the basic assumption is that students have to learn in a classroom and in front of a teacher. This is not the case at all if the students know what they are supposed to learn. Many adults as students have learned more out of the classroom than in the classroom. Once this basic assumption can be eliminated, we may very easily find that many of our high schools and colleges can handle two and three times as many students with the same facilities, but at any one time, there may be less students in the buildings than are using the facilities presently. However, the increase in students could also increase the need for teachers even though there is no increase in physical facilities. Money which would normally be used to provide more traditional facilities, could be used to hire more teachers.

A conference of the National Association of State Universities and Land Grant Colleges held in May, 1970, revealed that over 50,000 qualified students were turned away by universities in the fall of 1969 because of a lack of space and they predicted that more than 87,000 qualified students would be turned away in the fall of 1970. University of California President, Charles J. Hitch, stated in a message to the University regents, *We cannot continue to take more and more students every year and crowd them into existing buildings.* Notice the assumption implied by this statement — *students can't attend the university and learn unless they are in a building!* By allowing students to learn on their own away from schools, the same physical space can accomodate more students and more teachers.

Given the ineffective and inefficient traditional educational system and the decreased productivity of teachers, the costs of education are such that many students don't attend school. By making the schools more effective and efficient, it should be possible to reduce the student charges for instruction (tuition, fees, etc.) which might encourage more students to go to school and create a need for more teachers.

4. PROFESSIONALISM VS. UNIONISM

Teaching has been considered a profession for a long time; however, as pointed out on pages 7-20, Volume I, teaching in traditional education is more of an art than it is a profession. This is primarily because there are three basic characteristics of a profession: there should be a specialized knowledge and skills; there should be high standards of achievement; and the prime purpose should be public service. Since most teachers in higher education have not had any of this specialized training and they still teach essentially the same as teachers who have had the training, it can be concluded that having the training doesn't effectively change what a teacher does and hence the training is ineffectual and irrelevant and does not actually represent a *specialized knowledge.* Curve grading wherein half of the students have to be below average and the majority of students learn less than 75 percent of most courses, refutes the criteria for high standards of achievement. The emphasis on teachers and teaching rather than on students and learning changes the emphasis from an outward public service orientation towards an inward selfism.

The trend towards selfism in contrast to public service is evidenced by the use of teacher strikes to gain measurable benefits for teachers with only implied non-measurable benefits for students and a resistance towards accountability for student learning. Teacher strikes started with one in 1965 and increased to a high of 181 during the 1969-70 school year. In the beginning as in most union movements, there was a definite need as most teachers were underpaid in relation to their training (even if inadequate) and in relation to their importance in our society. However, once established, the use of strikes to gain personal benefits for teachers becomes like a drug in that the benefits are such to make one a little heady, i.e., increasingly more money for increasingly less work. Once the problems which brought about the need for the strikes has been eliminated or considerably reduced, the organization should be also eliminated or reduced in activity. However, with the emphasis on self and due to entropic drift, the union which started out serving the teachers ends up being served by the teachers. Instead of serving school administrators, the teachers end up serving union administrators.

Depending upon the developments brought about by this growing militancy among educators, it is possible that these strikes could be the beginning of the end of public education. This will be brought about by an impasse between the educators who want to have their demands fulfilled and the administrators or boards of education who would like to fulfill the demands but are unable to because of the taxpayer resistance. The problem with the taxpayers is that they have been involved in a process called *selective perception*, which essentially means that they see, listen and read only what they want to, not what is necessarily presented to them. This means that when the militant educators are demanding certain educational reforms because the teaching-learning situation is so terrible, the taxpayers only hear *the teaching-learning situation is terrible.* As a consequence, across our entire country the taxpayers are becoming more and more aware of the fact that there are problems in our schools and they are beginning to wonder what has happened to all of the money that has been spent in education. Consequently the impasse can be described in this way: the educators are saying essentially, *Give education more money and we will do a better job*, while the taxpayers are saying, *Do a better job and we'll give education more money.* During the past decade, most taxpayers said, *Okay, we'll give you more money to improve the educational environment.* After several increases in teacher benefits without any increases in student benefits, the taxpayers are becoming more reluctant. The first sign of the *beginning of the end of public education* will be when the impasse between the taxpayers and educators results in a school district or college being closed for an entire semester or quarter. The taxpaying public will not stand idly by and let their children go without an education, and neither will industry. During the past several decades, business and industry has been spending more and more money in education and training. In a recent year, business and industry were estimated to have spent in excess of $12 billion in education and training activities, and what with the development of the large educational corporations, business and industry will be ready to step in and offer to the taxpaying public a guaranteed education (90 percent or more of the learners will learn 100 percent of the required curriculum objectives). It is also very possible that business and industry will be able to offer this guaranteed education at costs significantly below what the taxpayer is now paying for public education. Consider for a moment the potential savings in a situation where in every elementary school, junior high school and high school throughout our country, in excess of 100,000 teachers in almost every subject-matter area are trying to re-invent the curriculum *wheel* in their subject-matter area as if for the first time. In higher education there is the same problem except there is only a matter of 10,000 to 20,000 teachers trying to re-invent the curriculum *wheel* as if for the first time. It is ironic that in our country, with approximately 150,000 teachers teaching first grade, and during the past several decades close to 1 million teachers have been teaching first grade, we do not know specifically, measurably and observably what students should know before they start first grade and what they should know when they finish first grade. By emphasizing the professional aspects of teaching it should not be necessary to turn instruction over to business and industry and it should be possible to gain most of whatever an individual teacher wants by increasing his or her productivity and services to the public.

a. AFFECTIVE LEARNING AS AFFECTED BY THE TEACHING ENVIRONMENT

Professionalism with its emphasis on public service concentrates on helping students be successful in their chosen careers and as a member of his or her community and of our society. On achieving these ends, the professional teacher has to recognize individual differences among students and cope with them not as negative characteristics, but as positive clues in finding solutions to student learning problems. In showing that the professional teacher cares about students, student learning, the community, and the nation, the students of professional teachers also learn to care about others. The professional's *other* orientation sets an example for the students in learning to get along with others.

In contrast, unionism promotes selfism and that the group desires can be gained at the expense of others through various devices including violence if necessary. Since most negotiations are based on the assumption that teachers are all the same, the recognition of individual differences in students is de-emphasized by example. Students hear and see striking teachers in their reactions to other non-striking teachers, administrators, and taxpayers. The negative statements and actions which the students observe do not contribute to their happiness in a society which they hear condemned. It is not unusual for teachers who have either been on strike or are in the middle of difficult negotiations to *lean on* non-striking teachers and children of parents who are actively against the striking teachers. In fact, techniques of *leaning* or pressure tactics are taught to teachers during union meetings. Oddly enough, although some teachers resist efforts to establish any commonality in learning which might benefit students and cite academic freedom, they accept regional and national commonality in learning how to pressure for their desires. Can you imagine professional doctors who in wanting to charge higher fees apply pressure or *lean on* their patients by making them sicker or killing them or professional lawyers who *lean on* their clients for higher fees by losing their cases? In some school districts where teachers are concerned about their own personal safety and they condemn student violence, during teacher strikes, the non-striking teachers are threatened by their striking colleagues in full view of the students. It shouldn't be too much of a surprise that student violence and riots followed the rise of teacher militancy.

Teachers are in a unique position to affect the attitudes, values, and beliefs of students particularly because the students emotional tendencies are just beginning to take shape. In trying to help students *clarify* their own values, the teachers can easily indoctrinate the students with their set of values. As teachers accept the values of their unions, they tend to pass on these values to their students. As more and more teachers state that they want to develop, change, and/or *explore* the attitudes, values, and beliefs of their students, the more important it becomes to specify affective learning objectives involved in these situations and the more important it becomes for an administrator to know the attitudes, values, and beliefs of the teachers, the community, and the students. Students will tend to have the attitudes, values and beliefs of their parents unless acted upon by some outside force. If the outside force is the community, the conflict in attitudes, values, and beliefs is usually observable in the environment of the community. If the parents don't like it, they can move. If the outside force consists of one or more teachers in a school, the conflict in attitudes, values, and beliefs is very difficult to observe because the conflict is more subtle and is hidden in the privacy of the classroom in which students are exposed to the attitudes, values, and beliefs of teachers for almost two to three times as many hours each day as they are exposed to their own parents. Because the changes in attitudes, values, and beliefs is subtle and hidden, parents don't realize that these changes have occurred until something happens resulting in a conflict between parent and child — both claiming the other *doesn't understand and is wrong.* In a sense, teachers who take it on themselves to change the attitudes, values, and beliefs of their students to be in conflict with their parents, may be liable for alienation of affection.

Centuries ago, a philosopher, in recognizing the emotional impressionability of students, said, *Give me your children until they are seven and I will rule the world!* As the unionism movement increases among teachers and professionalism decreases, there is a remote but possible situation in which a few people at the top of the teacher's union will be able to indirectly control the direction of our country by creating certain attitudes, values, and beliefs in the teachers who are members who in turn will create these attitudes, values, and beliefs in our young people.

Although parents may be rather passive about the learning or non-learning of cognitive and sensory domain objectives, many parents can become very active when their children start learning from teachers attitudes and values which are in conflict with those held by the parents or when the students aren't learning those attitudes and values held by the parents and community. Not only should teachers be careful about choosing textbooks which espouse conflicting emotional tendencies, but they should be careful not to teach attitudes, values, and/or beliefs which are in conflict with those of the parents or the local community.

During the past decade, there have been many teacher-community conflicts over certain books. The teachers typically push academic freedom and openness to other ideas and the parents are resisting the teaching of attitudes, values, and beliefs which are in conflict with theirs. The problem in most of these teacher-community conflicts is related to entropic drift in that since the teachers haven't identified any SO's to be learned from the materials to be used, the materials themselves have become the objectives. Since there are no SO's, the community is left up to its own imagination as to what the possible SO's might be. Where these books contain certain literary techniques which students should learn and the teachers claim that these techniques aren't available in other literary works, then the learning of the techniques has very limited utility and probably shouldn't be taught and learned. If there are other books which contain the techniques and the community objects to one of the books, then the teachers could use any one of the other books. However, if the not so hidden objective is to change the students' attitudes and values in the direction of the teachers and against their parents and the communities, then I think the teacher(s) are in an area they don't belong in. As a minimal condition, sort of a *honesty in packaging and labeling* (consumer protection), courses in which teachers intend to teach subversion of national, state, local, and/or parental authority should be labeled as such. Some educators become overly impressed by the power they have in affecting student opinions and feel they have the right and obligation to change society via subverting the minds of children and alienating them from their parents. Because children cannot control the development of emotional tendencies, particularly when they only get the teacher's side, parents and administrators should monitor very carefully the learning and teaching of affective objectives. In fighting the authority of administrators over their working environment, some teachers consciously or unconsciously teach their students to rebel against authority. William Miller, a deputy superintendent in the Wayne county Intermediate School District in Detroit, Michigan, wrote in the December, 1974, issue of the *Phi Delta Kappan* that whereas traditional education was to perpetuate society, schools and educators should become change agents and change society into the type of society that teachers want *characterized by humaneness and a redistribution of power!* I don't think communities want or expect teachers to change society. After all, as long as teachers have trouble teaching reading, writing, and arithmetic, they might be just as ineffective in teaching social change and create more problems than they solve.

> NOTE: Remember, very few teachers in elementary and secondary schools have been taught *how to teach by design* by teachers in the teacher-training institutions who also *taught by design — objectives.* Also, very few teachers in higher education have been taught *how to teach by design* because all that is necessary to teach in higher education is to have advanced degrees (masters or a doctorate) in the general subject area that the teacher is supposed to teach. It is not considered important in higher education that the teachers know anything about how to teach or about how to test for the achievement of what they are trying to teach.

I can partially agree with teachers who resist being held accountable for the learning of objectives that they weren't involved in setting, but then if teachers won't specify the objectives they want students to learn in their courses, then in this decade of accountability, someone else will probably specify the objectives for them. If teachers are getting paid as professionals, then the teachers should accept the professional responsibility and put their reputation on the line and commit themselves as to what is important to learn and what is not so important to learn. Teachers who are not afraid of being held accountable should welcome the use of specific objectives because it makes the whole concept of teacher evaluation much more objective and open minded. It brings real academic freedom to the classroom. As long as a teacher can prove that learning is taking place, the teacher should have freedom to do what they want and to come and go as they please.

As the concept of accountability based on specified objectives looms ever larger on the horizon of teacher evaluation, many teachers in trying to escape the inevitable try to avoid it by either trying to discredit the whole concept of specifying objectives or to claim that the really important things happening in the teaching-learning situation are the things you can't measure and in particular the things which you can't measure that fall into the affective domain (attitudes, values, and beliefs). Of course the hope for many of these teachers who are trying to avoid accountability is that it will be much harder to specify and measure affective domain objectives. As such, it may become a standard part of teacher evaluation to evaluate key attitudes, values, and beliefs on a pretest and posttest basis, not so much to check on how much the teacher was able to develop desired attitudes, values, and beliefs, but as sort of a fuse or protection against serious subversion of desired attitudes, values, and beliefs.

Assuming that a teacher wants to develop attitudes, values, and beliefs which are more or less in agreement with the desires of the students' parents, the community, and our society, to not be successful in developing or increasing these affective objectives or actually develop negative attitudes, values, and beliefs by mistake, would be considered as ineffective. However, if a teacher's personal objective was to develop attitudes, values, and beliefs which are in conflict with those desired by the students' parents, community and our society, then the observed ineffectiveness could actually be very effective subversive teaching.

NOTE: With respect to the evaluative terms *positive* and *negative* as used in the affective domain, these are not absolute evaluative terms. The positiveness and negativeness of an attitude, value, or belief is always in reference to those attitudes, values, and beliefs which are considered desirable by the students' parents, the community, and our society. It should be obvious that a certain attitude which might be considered as positive in one society could be considered negative in another society. In the same way, a value which might be considered positive in one community might be considered a negative value in another community. A belief held by one student's parents and thought of as a positive belief, could very easily be considered a negative belief by another student's parents.

Although students develop many of their attitudes, values, and beliefs while in school, they also come into a classroom with a set of emotional tendencies: some of which are new, weak, and subject to change or solidification and some of which are already entrenched, strong, and very resistant to change. If the students come into contact with teachers who have conflicting belief systems, problems can occur. O. J. Harvey, University of California, suggests that there are four belief systems:

1. A belief in concrete things and a positive closed mindedness;
2. A belief in concrete things and a negative closed mindedness (usually strongly anti establishment);
3. A belief system which is between the concrete and abstract systems and is also between closed and open mindedness (both positive and negative); and
4. A belief in abstract things and open minded.

I would like to suggest a slight change in these four systems and make it into five categories and place them on a continuum. (Figure 135).

SYSTEM 1—	SYSTEM 3 —	SYSTEM 4 —	SYSTEM 3 —	SYSTEM 2
Closed Concrete Positive	Positive	Open Abstract	Negative	Closed Concrete Negative

Figure 135 — A Continuum of Harvey's Belief Systems

Harvey reports that in his research, teachers who have belief systems No. 4 (open-minded and belief in abstract things) are able to bring about greater achievement in students and are more resourceful and innovative.

NOTE: In being open minded, System 4 teachers are probably more willing to solve student learning problems via alternate pathways and as such are really acting the role of an Instructioneer — hence greater student achievement.

Harvey stated that in his research sample, he found only seven percent of the teachers were System 4 teachers and that there were no System 2 teachers. He also found that most administrators were System 1 people. In reference to teacher evaluation, since teachers tend to do those things that reflect what administrators are going to evaluate them on, if the mental model of teaching in the mind of the administrator is himself or herself (System 1), then most teachers at the time of evaluation would tend to act like System 1 teachers because that is looked on by the administrators as *good teaching behaviors.* Since the traditional educational system tends to hire, retain, and promote teachers who are like the administrators, then a majority of System 1 teachers would most likely be found in a school system. Although Harvey didn't find any System 2 teachers, they are close enough in their teaching behaviors to System 1 that the System 2 teachers would be considered System 1 teachers. The anti-establishment and anti-authority attitudes of the System 2 teachers would probably not be identified during the hiring or evaluation procedures. The negative attitudes, values, and beliefs would probably only come out in the privacy of the classroom where the teacher can inculcate the students with their negativeness.

Under accountability concepts where learning becomes the goal of instruction, the System 4 teachers will look good, the System 1 and 2 teachers will not be as successful and will tend to blame the lack of achievement on genetics rather than on their lack of flexibility and resourcefulness in solving student learning problems.

In reference to the interactions of these belief systems as held by students and teachers, young students whose belief systems are just forming and who are accustomed to parental authority might react in the following ways:

1. students who are Systems 1, 2, or 3 may feel more comfortable with teachers who are Systems 1 or 2 and with programmed instructional materials;
2. students who are System 4 (probably brought up in a permissive environment) would probably be unhappy or dislike teachers who are Systems 1 or 2, but with their open mindedness, these students might still be able to learn particularly if they had a choice of learning pathways in the learning of SO's;
3. students who are Systems 4 would feel at home with a teacher who is also a System 4;
4. students who are Systems 1, 2, or 3 would probably feel insecure and a need for more direction if with a Systems 4 teacher.

Because very young students' emotional tendencies are not strongly developed, they will tend to get along with most teachers and may tend to become whatever systems type their teachers are. However, as the students get older, their belief systems become clearer and stronger.

1. Systems 1 students would probably react negatively to a Systems 2 teacher;
2. Systems 2 students would probably react negatively to a Systems 1 teacher;
3. Systems 1 and 2 students might tend to run over and take advantage of a Systems 4 teacher; and
4. Systems 4 students would probably feel uncomfortable with a Systems 1 or 2 teacher but would probably accept the teacher as part of the *school game.*

Since people tend to learn what they do, the best way to develop teachers who are Systems 4 is to have them solve student learning problems. As they learn that different pathways for learning the same SO's may be the best pathways for different students, the teachers may become more open minded. As the teachers have success in their endeavors, they may become more positive towards their role and society. As the students observe their teachers becoming more open minded and they see that different pathways for learning are best for different students, they may tend to also become more open minded. As the students have success, the image of themselves and society may become more positive.

b. PROFESSIONAL RESPONSIBILITIES

Almost every teenager is familiar with the following parent response to the teenager's request for something viewed as a privilege by the parent, *If you want the privileges of an adult, you also have to accept the responsibilities of an adult!* This can also be said of the teaching *profession*. During negotiations and particularly in statements given to the public media, teacher organizations frequently state that they are *professionals* and as such, they should be given the privileges of professionals, i.e., freedom in decision making, relatively high income, etc. As pointed out in Chapter I, Volume I, traditional education does not represent a profession because it is not based on the three basic characteristics of a profession: specialized knowledge necessary to teach (most higher education faculty have not had any training in teaching, setting objectives, nor in testing); high standards of achievement and conduct (a normal curve's worth of achievement is not only acceptable but the goal of traditional education and includes designed non-achievement and failure); and the prime purpose of public service (an ineffective and inefficient traditional education does some things which are not in the best interests of the public, i.e., pushing out students and causing them to be a liability for society, damaging the self-image of millions of students through designed failure, indirectly affecting negatively the emotional tendencies of millions of students (punishing students with learning experiences, alienating their loyalties, etc.).

In becoming a profession that is critical for the success and self-fulfillment of the individuals in our society, teachers at all levels of instruction have to learn *the specialized knowledge* of being an Instructioneer who teaches and facilitates learning by design; to institute high standards of achievement and conduct such that 90 percent or more of our students learn 100 percent of the required SO's of their courses (through the recognition of individual differences in students and teachers); and to remember that in performing *a public service*, the welfare and future of our society and our students is more important than anything else.

As a guideline, I have written *The Socratic Oath* for teachers (see footnote 14).

In the process of acquiring these professional characteristics, professional teachers and professional teacher organizations should make every effort to eliminate from their own and other teachers' practices those practices that are in conflict with the best interests of our students and our society and professionally can be termed *professional*

---

[14] Copies of *The Socratic Oath* are available on parchment paper ready for framing (8½"x11") for $1.00 from SLATE Services, P.O. Box 8796, Fountain Valley, California 92708.

THE SOCRATIC OATH

You do solemnly swear, each person by whatever he holds most sacred, that you will be loyal to the profession of teaching and just and generous to its members; that you will lead your lives and practice your art in uprightness and honor; that into whatsoever educational institution you shall enter, it shall be for the good of the learner to the utmost of your power, you will set yourself up as an example to your students by constant efforts to keep abreast of the changes in your field of study, adding what is new and dropping what is obsolete; that you will endeavor to determine the knowledge level of new students and adjust the course to their needs and, if appropriate, remedial studies for some and advanced placement for others; that you will exercise your art in such a manner that every student in your classes regardless of race, creed, or economic status will progress positively through the content of your course; that you will exhaust all available methods, media, and instructional materials if necessary in order to help the student learn all of the objectives of your course; that within your power you will not allow any student in your classes to proceed to subsequent courses without achieving all of the prerequisite behaviors available in your course and necessary for a successful progress in the subsequent courses. These things do you swear. And if you will be true to this, your oath, may prosperity and good repute be ever yours; the opposite if you shall prove yourselves forsworn.

Copyright 1966 - Donald K. Stewart - all rights reserved

malpractices! It is very important for teachers as professional Instructioneers that they be the ones to eliminate these malpractices on their own rather than waiting until an informed and concerned public (students, parents, taxpayers, legislators, etc.) force professionalism on teachers via malpractice suits, student and parent boycotts, and legislation! These malpractices were listed and described in my book, *Educational Malpractices: The Big Gamble in Our Schools,* and are included here for the reader's convenience. In addition to the 41 listed in my book, two others should be added.

42. When a teacher or administrator suspends a student from ongoing classes without making arrangements for a continuation of learning via alternative instructional services, it is a design for the development of cumulative ignorance and potential failure and as such, is not in the best interests of the student and our society.

43. When a teacher directly or indirectly designs learning experiences which develop in students attitudes, values, and beliefs which are in conflict with those held by the student's parents, and the majority of people in the community and nation and

cause the students to be alienated from their families, the community, and the nation. This alienation causes emotional pain and other problems for the students, their parents, and society and as such, is not in the best interest of the students nor of our society.

The original 41 are as follows:

Malpractices Against Students at all Levels of Education

1. When a teacher requires a student to learn from certain materials, particularly textbooks, knowing that the student is not able to learn from these materials because the student reads at a level which is below the actual reading level of the textbook, i.e., students in tenth grade who read at fifth or sixth-grade level are given materials to learn from which are written at the tenth-grade or higher reading level; college freshmen who read at eighth or ninth-grade level are given college textbooks to learn from which are written at the professorial level, etc. When the student shows that he or she can't learn from the materials in these situations, the student is failed or graded down.

2. When schools, school districts, colleges, and universities enroll students from the so-called *disadvantaged* group in regular classes, knowing that these students have sufficient cumulative ignorance that they cannot learn in the regular classes and are destined for failure.

3. When a teacher allows a student to leave a course or grade level knowing that the student has not achieved the knowledge and understandings, skills, etc., which are necessary to enable the student to succeed in a subsequent course, i.e., a student receiving "C", "D", or "F" in a course which is a prerequisite for a subsequent course. This would apply to even the "A" and "B" students if the teacher used curve grading and the achievement of the "A" students was below 100 percent of the objectives or test items of the course.

4. When teachers design or school districts, colleges or universities require their teachers to design a teacher-learning situation in which a certain number or percentage of the students have to fail, regardless of the level of learning.

5. When students who are taking a course over for a second time because of a low grade are required to take the entire course over again, instead of the 20, 30, 40 percent or more that they did not learn when they took the course the first time.

6. When a teacher purposely misleads the student as to what he or she is to study, or is vague and ambiguous about the learning

requirements of the course, while the tests for the course are made up of test items requiring achievement of specific learning objectives.

7. When a teacher or administrator disciplines a student who is caught with a copy of a test (without answers) before it is given. (It is presently considered wrong for a student to find out what he or she is supposed to learn).

8. When a teacher fails a student for not answering test items which the student's classmates who answered the test items correctly at the time of the test will forget and not be able to answer correctly at a later date (three months, six months, a year, etc.) The student who fails at the end of a course keeps the failure for a lifetime, while many of his classmates, who in a short time may forget the same things, continue to carry throughout life the grades that they received.

9. When a teacher starts a course at the beginning of a textbook, knowing that some of the students already know part of the course, and other students are lacking the necessary prerequisites to even start the course.

10. When teachers teach students certain facts, how to deal with facts, how to interpolate certain facts, how to diagnose situations based on certain facts, etc.; then they test the students' knowledge with multiple-choice test items, which test the students' ability to discriminate between answers, which may or may not be an important behavior, and it may not test the behaviors of dealing with facts, interpolating facts, diagnosing situations, etc. In other words, when teachers teach students certain things during the course, but test the students' achievement of something else which was not taught or learned during the course. A similar situation is when teachers use charts, graphs, visuals, films, slides, tape recordings, phonograph records, demonstrations, etc., in their teaching, and then turn around and test with words only.

11. When a teacher marks a students' answer to a test item wrong in a situation where the test item is actually asking for the student's opinion. If the test item asks for the student's opinion, whatever the opinion is, it cannot be wrong on the test. The teacher may disagree with the student's opinion, but it is still not wrong. If the teacher wanted the student to answer a test item with the teacher's or someone else's opinion, the test item should be stated in that way.

12. When teachers ignore the results of tests which indicates the student's learning needs (test items which are answered wrong) and direct the student to go on to a subsequent unit, knowing that the student didn't learn everything he was supposed to learn in the previous unit.

13. When a teacher makes up tests and evaluates students' progress based on these tests, while at the same time the teacher has not had any special training on the critical skill of testing for the achievement of course objectives. (Very few teachers at any level of education have had this training.)

14. When teachers, school districts, colleges, or universities require students to pass or learn the requirements of a course by a certain date, which assumes all students can learn at the same rate. If the objectives of the course are important and relevant to the students, what is the difference if they learn them two days later, a week later, a month later, or two months later, or if an individual student takes the final exam two, three, or four times in order to indicate achievement of the course objectives. (If certain objectives are important enough to grade a student down for not learning them, then they should also be important enough to see to it that each student learns them).

15. When school districts, colleges, or universities automatically change an *Incomplete* grade to an "F" after a certain length of time. Does the necessary learning in order to complete a course all of a sudden become useless, or is it too late for a student to learn after a certain date?

16. When teachers, school districts, colleges, universities, and even state departments of education use the same textbooks and/or other learning experiences for all students in a given course, knowing that because of individual differences among students in how they learn will result in differences in achievement. In order to have equal opportunity for achievement, unequal students need unequal materials, textbooks, etc.

17. When teachers do not bring about quality control in the teaching-learning situation by having at least 90 percent or more of the students achieve 100 percent or more of the course objectives ("A" and "B" students).

18. When a teacher fails or gives a student a lower grade for not learning something that the teacher is not able to specify exactly what it is that the student did not learn.

19. When a teacher designs a course and/or tests in order to have *high standards* as indicated by more than ten percent of the students failing. (To fail any student is a malpractice, but some teachers in higher education fail as high as 70 percent or more of a class for the sake of *high standards.*)

20. When a teacher gives up trying to help a student learn important objectives without having tried many alternate pathways to

achieve the desired learning (if a child is sick, and one method of treatment doesn't work, how many different methods or treatments should the doctor try before he gives up?)

21. When a teacher gives a student an "A", "B", "C", "D", or a so-called *soft 'D'* instead of an "F" to get rid of the student or to be a *nice teacher* knowing that the student has not achieved the level that the grade is supposed to represent and that the student hasn't learned sufficiently to be successful in subsequent courses.

22. When a teacher has a student perform certain activities which have no specified learning goals, particularly if this takes the student away from other activities which do have measurable learning goals or objectives. (This is a particularly serious problem in elementary school where the students spend many hours in a variety of activities without any specific learning objectives and at the same time many students are learning only "C", "D", or "F" worth of those activities that do have measurable learning objectives.

23. When a teacher requires students to attend a class in which the teacher has no specific learning objectives (if the teacher doesn't know what he or she wants the students to learn, how can the teacher tell which way to go to get there, and how will he or she know when the students have arrived there?)

24. When a teacher limits the number of students receiving "A" or some other symbol indicating highest achievement, by establishing barriers to maximum achievement, particularly in situations where the teacher is unable to specify exactly and measurably what "A" achievement stands for. If we can specify maximum learning or "A", then every student should have the opportunity to achieve an "A". If a total class achieves maximum learning, then the total class should receive "A".

25. When a teacher's subjective evaluations are the basis for determining part or all of a student's progress through a course and the results of the evaluation of the student's achievement varies from teacher to teacher such that the grade or result of the evaluation is more of an indication of which teacher is doing the evaluation than of what the student actually achieved. (It is very common for the same essay to receive different grades from different teachers, which indicates a lack of specified grading criteria. This is very critical when two or more teachers are teaching different sections of the same course.)

26. When a teacher designs a teaching-learning situation such that students are not informed as to how they are going to be evaluated until it is too late for the student to prepare adequately for the

evaluation. This type of situation creates varying degrees of anxiety which may result in various forms of cheating or in extreme cases, attempted suicide.

27. When a teacher tells a class of students at the beginning of a course that a certain proportion (sometimes as high as one-third, one-half or more) will fail in the course, even before the teacher has had an opportunity to test the students in order to find out whether they were prepared for or not prepared for the course, and then to design a teaching-learning situation that is so difficult, ineffective, and inefficient so as to live up to the prediction of failures made at the beginning of the course.

28. When a teacher, department, school, school district, college, or university requires students to take standardized tests which are camouflaged as achievement tests but in fact are not based on the achievement of specific measurable objectives and their primary purpose is to spread students out over some type of curve(s). This is a particularly serious malpractice when the results of these disguised tests are used to place students in certain courses or levels of instruction.

Malpractices Against Students in Elementary and Secondary Schools

29. When a teacher uses a learning activity as a form of punishment which very quickly convinces the student that this particular learning activity is always punishment. This occurs particularly in elementary school where students are punished by having to write certain phrases or sentences many times, to write extra essays, assigned extra problems to solve; or in physical education classes where erring students are made to run around the gym or field and/or to perform certain exercises as punishment.

30. When a teacher who is teaching in a multiple-track or varied ability group situation compromises on the objectives of the course in order that all groups will spend the same amount of time in learning (semester, year, etc.) knowing that the students in the lower tracks or groups will not learn enough to be successful in subsequent courses unless the objectives for the subsequent courses are also compromised.

31. When teachers and school districts practice *social promotion* in which a student who fails one year is automatically passed on at the end of the next year, regardless of whether or not the student learned anything the second year. This practice places the student in a learning situation in which the high degree of cumulative ignorance prohibits or significantly reduces the capability of the student to learn.

Malpractices Against Students
In Higher Education

32. When the teachers who are responsible for the effectiveness and efficiency of the teaching-learning situation have little, if any, formalized training in not only the problem of testing, but in how to teach and are given a minimum, if any, guidelines as to the objectives of the course. This is particularly in reference to the use of graduate students as teachers and also to teachers who are teaching for the first time. It is a very serious problem because it puts into jeopardy the future education, occupation, and potential earnings of the students who are in the teaching-learning situation.

33. When teachers in teacher-training institutions indoctrinate students who are planning to be teachers into utilizing a variety of educational malpractices through teaching, demonstration, and requiring the students to perform these malpractices in order to get credit or a grade in a course of a learning experience. This malpractice also applies to other professional schools in which the students are required to perform in a certain manner to get a grade or credit in the school, but that same performance if done by a professional out in the field would be considered a malpractice.

34. When teacher-training institutions, school districts, and state departments of education require students to take a certain number of education courses, knowing that the majority of these courses as presently being offered are of little, if any, practical value to students planning to be teachers.

35. When school districts and state departments of education require teachers in elementary and secondary education to take additional courses in some college or university in order to receive increases in salary, knowing that the majority of these courses as presently being offered are of little, if any, practical value to the practicing teacher.

36. When national professional organizations such as medical, dental, nursing, real estate, etc. require the aspiring professional to take standardized national examinations which utilize a high percentage of verbal multiple-choice questions, knowing that the critical decision-making behaviors of the professional are primarily based on what they see and what they hear, not on what they read, and that in the real world, the alternate choices in the decision making process are developed by the professional in his own mind rather than being developed by someone else using designed trickery and presented to him on a piece of paper. (This malpractice forces most of the professional schools to test their students' achievement of critical professional behaviors with irrelevant and unreal multiple-choice questions rather than testing directly for the achievement of the real critical behavior.)

Malpractices Which Indirectly Affect Students At All Levels Of Education

37. When diplomas, degrees, teaching certificates, etc., are awarded on the basis of time and courses taken rather than on the basis of learning. If educational institutions are established to facilitate learning, diplomas, degrees, etc., should be awarded on the basis of achievement of specified learning.

38. When teachers are evaluated on the basis of degrees, length of time teaching, quantity of published materials, extra credits taken, etc., rather than on the basis of how many students they can teach all of the objectives of their courses. School budgets are based on so many dollars per student. Why not pay teachers for how much learning they facilitate!

39. When *academic freedom* is defined as the teacher's freedom to do anything he or she wants to in the classroom, regardless of whether or not students learn and of whether or not the teacher's *freedom* includes taking *freedom* away from the students.

40. When state and regional accrediting associations give official accreditation to a school at any level because the school has the right number of books in their library, minimum number of square feet per student, certain number of teachers with specified degrees, certain physical facilities, etc., and yet necessary learning is not taking place within the school, because of existing malpractices or negligence. Also, to withhold accreditation from a school because it does not have the correct number of books per student, square feet per student, number of students per teacher, etc., when the school is able to produce measurable learning in their students which is greater than the neighboring accredited schools.

41. When school districts, colleges, universitites, state departments of education, and the U.S. Office of Education continue to maintain and support existing malpractices which actually interfere and inhibit learning while at the same time ignore and resist the development of minimum standards of *learning* (not maximum). This should take place in every subject at every grade level in all schools under their jurisdiction, so that no student is penalized for not learning what he needs to know in order to participate in our society, just because he was in a certain class under a certain teacher, or in a certain school in a certain city in a certain state. (Just as we have local minimum health standards so as not to endanger human lives, we need minimum educational standards so as not to endanger the future potential of our students.)

•••

c. PART-TIME AND SUBSTITUTE TEACHERS

A significant if not major part of adult education and evening courses are taught by part-time teachers who have had little, if any, training for their position. It would be obvious in hospitals and medical clinics that they shouldn't use untrained people in professional positions just because there was a need for a part-time professional or a need for a professional at a time when other full-time professionals would rather be home. It should also be obvious that every part-time teacher should have the necessary specialized training and supervision such that neither the students nor society suffer because of the part time teachers' incompetance and/or lack of training. It is not enough that part-time or full-time teachers have had academic and/or practical experience in the subject matter areas they are teaching, they need to know how to help students learn. Therefore, everything said in reference to the evaluation of full-time teachers is applicable to the evaluation of part-time teachers.

In most school districts, substitute teachers have to be certified in the same manner as the regular faculty. However, in their role as substitute teachers, they are primarily expected to keep the students in their classes busy and out of mischief. It is usually not expected that students will learn very much. This should not be surprising in a situation where even the regular teachers are not specifically sure what the students should be learning.

Under a systems approach, at least the part-time teacher will be teaching the same minimum common core SO's to their students that the full-time teachers are helping their students learn. When the SO's of a course are known and a record of each students progress is kept, a substitute teacher will be able to step in any classroom and facilitate student learning by helping students progress from wherever they are.

d. PROFESSIONALISM vs. UNIONISM: A COMPARISON

In comparing unionism to professionalism, it is important to point out that the traditional educators view of professionalism was like that of an artist in which the emphasis is on man-created things and the demands for academic freedom isolated educators from one another. In being isolated, there were no shared goals and no sense of belonging to a professional group. As such, it was fairly easy for school boards and administrators to keep dictatorial control over teachers. The National Education Association (NEA) as a traditional professional organization found it difficult to be effective in solving teachers' problems in an environment where teachers wanted to be independent and isolated from one another.

With the advent of unionism wherein all teachers in the group were paid the same and worked the same hours in similar environments, the union provided a unifying force and gave teachers a sense of belonging and through collective action they gained a sense of power over those who used to have power over them. It is not surprising that NEA has become more of a labor union than a professional organization.

Under the Systems Approach, professionalism is viewed as a science in which the emphasis is on learning — a natural phenomenon. With identified minimum common core SO's, teachers will have a commonality in teaching and learning problems around which to gather. It should be possible for a professional organization to serve the teachers and their students without resorting to the collective bargaining model of the labor union.

There are many different models which could be followed. The traditional model is a hierachical model in which those above control those below. This model is generally associated with government, the military, and business. Many teacher and student groups prefer the shared authority model but there are actually two different versions of this model. Under one version, decisions in all maters are shared regardless of whether or not the matter is related to ones expertise and position. Because it is possible for a majority to be in positions other than those related to a particular problem, decisions can be made that are ineffective and not based on anything but a subjective opinion. Because everyone is involved in every decision, the use of this version of the shared authority model can be very time-consuming. The other version of this model is where the shared authority is represented by a sharing of decision making such that each group makes decisions about the problems the group is concerned with. This is the professional model described in the transposition of controlling influences wherein teachers collectively and individually make the decisions in teaching and learning problems, administrators make decisions in reference to helping teachers help students learn, business types make business decisions. As a professional model, everyone works together to improve their common goal — student learning.

The collective bargaining model is sort of a model of *war* in which a variety of violent activities are condoned and even encouraged. The basic assumption is that there are sides which are in conflict. Since teachers are frequently examples which students follow, the violence, blackmail, and *gang* type pressure tactics of traditional unionism are out of place in what should be a professional humane environment.

Professionalism	Unionism
1. Emphasizes doing for others in an outward form of humanism.	1. Emphasizes what a group can do for themselves, an inward form of selfism.

NOTE: Our country's success has been built on the humanistic thesis of doing for others. Many of our country's present problems are a result of selfism in which each group wants their benefits at the expense of others, i.e., spiraling inflation.

Professionalism	Unionism
2. Success is in terms of all groups cooperatively helping all students learn what they need and want to know.	2. Success is in terms of fighting and outwitting other groups (administrators, school boards, legislators, parents, and taxpayers) regardless of effects on students.
3. Benefits are gained by being more effective, efficient, and increasing productivity.	3. Benefits are gained by being less effective, efficient, and decreasing productivity.
4. Teachers are recognized as individuals in reference to their ability to help students learn which in turn is reflected in terms of their teaching load and remuneration.	4. Teachers are treated as if they are all the same in reference to their ability to teach as reflected in their teaching load and remuneration.
5. Teaching load defined in terms of students which enlarges course offerings due to multiple course and/or multiple level classes, i.e., similar to the one-room school.	5. Teaching load defined in terms of classes which limits course offerings due to minimum and maximum enrollment and class size.
6. Teacher activities demonstrate capitalism and democracy.	6. Teacher activities demonstrate socialism and autocracy.
7. Responsible for actions to students, parents, taxpayers and society.	7. Responsible for actions to self and organization.
8. Better teachers tend to teach more courses and more students.	8. Better teachers tend to teach fewer courses and fewer students.

Professionalism	Unionism
9. Student differences recognized by differences in learning pathways needed to learn all of the required SO's and by differences in learning above what is required.	9. Student differences recognized by differences in what was not achieved as a result of ignoring student differences in learning.
10. Emphasis is on maximizing student learning at the expense of all concerned.	10. Emphasis is on minimizing teacher involvement at the expense of all concerned.
11. The primary commonality concerns an orthodoxy of learning.	11. The primary commonality concerns an orthodoxy of the teaching-learning environment (all the same for teachers and students.)
12. Welcomes accountability criteria dealing with learning as it proves that the professional is a professional.	12. Resists accountability criteria dealing with learning which may prove that some teachers are ineffective and/or that ignoring individual differences in teachers and students is detrimental to students.
13. Working in and striving for a teaching-learning environment which recognizes individual differences among teachers and students tends to create a teacher who is open-minded not only in the teacher's work but also in the teacher's social life out of school.	13. Working in and striving for a teaching-learning environment which ignores individual differences among teachers and students tends to create a teacher who is closed-minded not only in the teacher's work but also in the teacher's social life out of school.
14. Application of the factory model is inappropriate because although the product of student learning may be similar as a minimum (minimum common core SO's), the process varies with the teachers and students involved.	14. Application of the factory model is inappropriate because although the process is the same for teachers and students, the product of student learning varies with the teachers and students involved.

Professionalism	Unionism
15. Application of the humanist model is appropriate because individual differences in students and teachers is recognized and the welfare of students and society is of primary concern.	15. Application of the humanist model is inappropriate because individual differences in students and teachers is ignored and the welfare of the teachers is at the expense of the welfare of students and society.

e. ADDITIONAL BENEFITS OF ACCOUNTABILITY AND PROFESSIONALISM

As a result of increased professionalism on the part of teachers and accountability in terms of facilitating student learning, there are some general benefits and some unique benefits which will accrue. Of particular importance are the benefits realized by the students. More students will get individualized attention when necessary. More students will find success in learning. Cumulative ignorance will be reduced which will reduce learning problems for students and teaching problems for teachers. By giving students success in schools which are socially approved institutions, students may have less need to seek success in activities which are not socially approved, i.e., vandalism, juvenile delinquency, youth gangs, etc. The elimination of failure will also reduce the *failure syndrome* which pushes students into non-approved activities. There should also be a dramatic improvement in the instructional environment and in the instructional results in urban ghetto schools. By eliminating the malpractices and instituting professionalism, students will learn that we care about them and their future. As a result, there should be a reduction in the so-called generation gap and an increase in the understanding of others. A unique benefit will be a reduction in selfism in students while at the same time emphasizing and facilitating individual differences among students.

As some teachers fear, increased accountability and professionalism will facilitate the identification of weak or poor teachers. Contrary to the belief of many teachers, the teachers who are identified as being not very effective or efficient will not be fired. They will be offered help to improve their ability to teach and their confidence in their ability to teach (as measured in terms of student learning). Yes, if the poor teachers refuse to accept help and refuse to improve their efforts to facilitate student learning, then they may be released from teaching duties which will be a benefit for the students who might have had one or more of the poor teachers and might actually benefit the poor teachers themselves by removing them from a non-success oriented environment.

Under a situation where classes have to be equal in size, registration procedures force students to take courses from teachers who may not only be ineffective but are also unaware of their ineffectiveness. As some teachers reach the goal of getting 90 percent or more of their students to learn 100 percent of the required SO's of their courses, it may be possible to have open registration such that as many students as a teacher can handle can enroll in his or her courses. If the teacher can maintain the high quality level of achievement even with the additional students, then the teacher should earn more money in accordance with the increase in students. Under these conditions, the poor teacher may find out that few, if any, students want to take courses from him or her and hopefully the teacher will be motivated to try to improve on his or her ability to facilitate student learning.

For teachers, the increased emphasis on accountability for student learning and the decreased emphasis on the traditional criteria used to evaluate teacher performance will bring about an increase in their freedom as professionals. When student learning is the most important product of our schools and student differences can be recognized, the teachers will be free to use whatever materials and/or methods they find successful in bringing about the desired learning. A particular technique, method, or resource which is selected for use would probably reflect the individual characteristics of the teacher and the student whereas the SO's being learned would probably reflect the combined expertise of many teachers.

When student learning becomes the controlling influence, not only will students have open exit and open entry to a course (can start and complete a course at anytime), but teachers will have much more flexibility in their time schedules. As long as a teacher can prove via accountability that his or her students are learning as much or more than they would under average or traditional conditions, the teacher should be relatively free in controlling their own time schedule. Whereas most teacher contracts are for nine or ten months, under increased accountability and professionalism, it would be possible for teacher contracts to be in terms of facilitating student learning rather than time. As such, if a teacher can prove that all of his or her students have learned all of the required SO's of the teacher's courses, then the teacher will have fulfilled his or her teaching contract for that school year. If the teacher is effective and efficient enough to get all of his or her students to achieve all of the required SO's before the usual end of the year, the teacher should be free to leave early. As a result, the teacher has more time off which could be very motivating to a lot of teachers and at no cost to the taxpayers. Letting teachers off early when they have completed their contracts will probably be as difficult for tradition-oriented administrators as it is for tradition-oriented teachers in letting students go early when they have completed the learning of all the required SO's. In comparing the traditional situation versus the Behavioral Learning Systems Approach, everyone involved benefits by making the change. More students learn more of what they should learn. Increased success in schools should decrease student problems in other areas. Teachers get more time off and society gets more for their financial investment.

D. EVALUATION OF ADMINISTRATORS

As with teachers and students the evaluation procedures used to evaluate administrators are strongly influenced by the perceived role of the administrator and the hidden principle of evaluation. The traditional view of the administrators role is that of a manager of the physical facilities and personnel of the schools. Frequently administrators are ex-teachers who have been promoted because they were good teachers (managed the classroom or department well) and/or because they took administrative courses in order to make more money as an administrator. Similar to the situation with teachers in higher education, administrators in higher education generally haven't had specialized training in educational administration.

Administrators in elementary and secondary education are traditionally evaluated on a slightly different basis than the administrators in higher education. The evaluation of elementary and secondary administrators is essentially divided into two parts. The first part concerns the negative aspects of administrative tasks. School boards and supervisory administrators expect the administrators under them to maintain essentially the status quo of the school environment; they shouldn't have too much student trouble or parent trouble and should be able to keep their faculty from being the recipients of any negative gossip or controversy which would tend to develop a negative image for the school building or school district. In addition, the school administrator should be able to live within his budget. As far as the potential positive types of evaluation go, if an administrator is able to somehow afford in his budget some of the *mod* fashions in education which will contribute to the development of a positive image of the school, this is considered to be very good. If the administrator is able to somehow satisfy all of the different factions of the school board and community groups in reference to what should be included in the curriculum and what should not be included in the curriculum, this is considered good. Only during the last few years, since the existence of the Elementary and Secondary Education Act, have administrators been partially evaluated on the basis of how much money they are able to bring into the school via grants from the state, U.S. Office of Education, and possibly from outside foundations. As far as learning is concerned, at the elementary and secondary level, administrators are not evaluated in any way on the basis of how much actual learning takes place in their schools. However, some administrators are partially evaluated on the basis of their students' performance on standardized tests in comparison with students in other schools and other districts. Since standardized tests are not based on any known list of objectives, the results of standardized tests have little relationship to the actual levels of achievement occurring in the schools. Because this lack of relationship is not generally known, most educators and non-educators assume there is a strong relationship between the results of standardized tests and the actual learning taking place in the schools. As such, if the students score much lower than the students of some other corresponding district or school on some national standardized test, the administrator will probably have to answer for this problem or be replaced. On the other hand, if the students have average or above average scores, the evaluation of the administrator is unaffected. Since the evaluation of administrators is not generally positively enhanced by good test results but is affected negatively by bad test results, it is rather natural that administrators should resist efforts at any kind of national evaluation. If the national evaluation was based on important learning objectives that all students should attain, then administrators should welcome evaluation of this kind in order to identify the learning problems in the system, but as pointed out earlier, the major emphasis of standardized tests is to fit students on a curve of some kind, rather than to truly identify what is critically important.

Administrators in higher education at the lower levels are still, in part, traditionally evaluated on the basis of the publish or perish dictum, and almost all administrators in higher education are traditionally evaluated on the basis of how many projects (generally measured in dollars) that are granted to the department from outside funding agencies. This is particularly true when it comes to deans, and of course, as is widely known, the presidents of colleges and universities have become, in many ways, directors of fund-raising campaigns, rather than actually administering the affairs of the educational institutions. In some ways, the lower level administrators in higher education are also evaluated on the number of faculty members in the department, and the number of students who are taking courses offered by their particular department or division. This tends to promote departmental empire building. In reference to any evaluation of administrators on the basis of learning which might take place in higher education, there are two very strong contributing factors. The first factor is the concept of academic freedom in higher education, which assumes that the faculty member knows what he is doing in the classroom and it is nobody else's business what occurs there. The second factor is the maintenance of the *status quo.* This again refers back to the idea in higher education that if you have a normal curve of grades, then things look good, and if you really want to have high quality, there should be a higher percentage of "D's" and "F's". At the present time, there is a growing tendency away from this point of view and in a growing number of schools they want to indicate that things are better than usual, so they give a higher percentage of "A's" and "B's". The point to remember is that the assignment of the actual letter grades depend on the philosophy, policy, and/or the eccentricities of the faculty member when they start assigning letter grades, rather than having any direct relationship to what the individual student has or hasn't learned in reference to the course content.

The traditional evaluation of administrators in junior colleges and community colleges is a mixture of some of the aspects of the evaluation procedures for elementary and secondary schools and also some of the aspects of the evaluation of administrators in higher education. But here again, it is unusual for an administrator to be evaluated on any measurable quantity or quality of learning that takes place under his supervision.

Whereas there has been a lot of effort put forth in trying to quantify the evaluation of a teacher's performance in the traditional education environment, the criteria used for evaluation of administrators are still fairly subjective. The following sample statements are typical of those found on most lists of criteria used by higher level administrators, school boards, regents, etc. in the evaluation of lower level administrators.

1. The principal's ability to carry with him in his decisions the parents of his students and the good wishes of the local community.
2. The extent of the involvement of staff in future oriented decision-making.
3. The extent to which the school organization has built into itself creative forces for continued survival.
4. The principal's provision of a visible kind of commitment, through dynamic leadership, when introducing creative change into the school.
5. The provision for feedback in upgrading the effectiveness of administrative decisions.
6. The provision for a free-flowing communication network so that a creative open atmosphere may prevail in the school.
7. The development of a school climate in which diverse people with highly individual skills can function as a team.

8. The principal's projection of a feeling for justice which evokes the confidence of teachers in him.

In addition to being evaluated by higher level administrators, administrators are evaluated by the teachers over whom they administrate. As in the case of students evaluating teachers, the process of having teachers evaluate their administrators is very similar to a popularity contest. The criteria used are very subjective and depend very much on the interpersonnel conflicts and agreements between the teachers and administrator and on the degree of conflict and agreement between their professional beliefs and philosophies of education. As in the case in the traditional evaluations of students and teachers, the evaluation of administrators is designed as a negative instrument in that the results are not diagnostic such that the administrator can do more of those behaviors which resulted in positive opinions and do less of those opinions which resulted in negative opinions. For example, the following questions are samples from questionnaires given to teachers for the evaluation of their administrators (using a four point scale).

1. Do you feel he treats you fairly?   3   2   1   0
2. Do you feel he is honest with you?   3   2   1   0
3. Do you feel he exhibits administrative leadership expected of his office?   3   2   1   0
4. Do you feel he exhibits intellectual stimulation that should bexpected of his office?   3   2   1   0
5. Do you feel that he is responsive to the needs of students?   3   2   1   0
6. Do you feel that he is responsive to the need of the faculty?   3   2   1   0

For the sake of statistics, these subjective reactions are converted into a number which is then treated as objective data. To make these questions of any value, each question should be accompanied by a second statement, *cite one or more situations which support your opinion and include constructive suggestions for improving the administrators behavior in areas where you might have a negative opinion.*

In an attempt to decrease the high degree of subjectivity and to improve on the effectiveness and efficiency of the operation of the school, some school districts, colleges, and universities are embracing the concept referred to as SMBO (School Management by Objectives). The concept has been borrowed from business, industry, and the military. Generally in education, the concept is applied from the top down such that top administrators set up their objectives and try to reach them before lower level administrators set and try to reach their objectives. At a later time, teachers are expected to set their teaching objectives and to reach them during a period of time. As a rule, teachers and administrators set their objectives for the performance of their role in conference with the person above them in the traditional school hierarchy. Although the SMBO concept and the Behavioral Learning Systems Approach have similar foundations and some common terminology, there are some very important differences.

1. Under SMBO, each person has their own objectives which they personally try to achieve.

    Under BLSA (Behavioral Learning System's Approach), the students have the objectives and all other personnel are directed towards helping the students achieve their objectives.

2. Under SMBO, student learning objectives, if any, are the last to be identified because they are at the bottom of the hierarchy.

    Under BLSA, student learning objectives are set first because they are at the top of the hierarchy and the actions and objectives of teachers and administrators are dependent upon what students need to learn.

3. Under SMBO, as under the traditional approach, there isn't any designed cooperation of commonality of SO's among teachers who are teaching the same course nor among administrators who have essentially the same type of job. Each person reinvents his or her SO's as if no one else has or is performing the same role.

    Under BLSA, the design includes the cooperative identification of SO's which are commonly used by teachers who are teaching the same course and administrators who have essentially the same type job.

4. Under SMBO, the primary emphasis is on increased effectiveness and efficiency of the operation of the school.

    Under BLSA, the primary emphasis is on increased effectiveness and efficiency of student learning.

NOTE: Given the present ineffectiveness of schools wherein over half of the students learn "C" worth or less of their courses, the institution of SMBO without changing learning effectiveness will result in the school becoming very effective and efficient (in the operation of the schools) at being ineffective and inefficient (in facilitating student learning)!

1. THE ADMINISTRATORS ROLE AND EVALUATION UNDER BLSA

Under the BLSA, administrators are divided into two different basic roles. Those administrators who are concerned with the provision of physical facilities which make up the teaching-learning environment should be trained in business and administrative tasks similar to hospital administrators. Their role is to help teachers facilitate student learning by providing the environment necessary to bring about the required and desired student learning. Whereas at the present time, most of the educational environment is provided as a result of teacher and administrative decisions with little, if any, reference to the learning or non-learning of SO's, under BLSA, the instructional environment is set up and changed only in reference to the students' learning of SO's. Stated another way, in the traditional educational environment, teachers and administrators frequently accept ideas and/or purchase materials which are solutions to problems which have not been identified and may or may not exist. In the BLSA instructional environment, teachers will identify the problems first and then try to locate or develop the solutions to the problems. The instructional business administrator's answer to all requests for changes or additions to the learning environment will be the question, *What is it that the students are not learning now that they will learn as a result of the requested change or addition and how will this expected increase in learning be evaluated?* This administrative role will be evaluated in terms of the effectiveness and efficiency of the school operation as it facilitates or inhibits student learning.

During the past decade many conferences of administrators, particularly principals, have been devoted to the identification of their role in education. The consensus seems to be that the preferred role would be that of an *Instructional Leader*. However, in the traditional educational situation where student learning has not been specifically identified, it is very difficult to be a leader when you don't know where you are going. As such, most of the discussions about the leadership role of the administrators (principals) is mostly rhetoric and does not result in much action. Under BLSA, where required and desired student learning has been identified and the emphasis is on facilitating student learning, the administrator can really become an Instructional Leader. The word *leader* should not be defined in terms of one who controls and makes all of the important decisions. The Instructional *Leader* under the BLSA is one who leads in the demonstration of effective and efficient instructional practices, an indirect leadership role. The primary evaluation of the administrator under BLSA concerns how much the administrator helped teachers facilitate student learning. In accomplishing this role and its professional responsibility, the instructional administrator would be involved with most or all of the following tasks. The smaller the school district, college, or university, the more of these tasks that would be performed by a single instructional administrator. Conversely, the larger the school district, college, or university, the more that these tasks would be divided up among various levels or specialties of instructional administrators.

a. Assist teachers who are teaching the same courses to identify the minimum common core SO's of those courses.

b. Assist in the development of relevant SO's be helping teachers identify citizens in the community who can contribute in the setting of required SO's in those courses which are directly related to *real world* activities.

c. Assist teachers in the identification of common teaching-learning problems.

d. Assist teachers in the identification of solutions to common teaching-learning problems.

e. Help disseminate successful learning problem solutions to other teachers.

f. Assist or conduct the process concerned with the hiring of new teachers such that the teachers with the best ability to facilitate student learning are the ones hired to teach.

g. Assist new teachers and part-time teachers by providing them with the lists of required SO's for the courses the teachers will be teaching and providing them with the materials presently being used to facilitate student learning of the required SO's.

h. Assist substitute teachers to maintain a continuous learning environment with a minimum decrease in the students rate of learning due to the absence of their regular teacher.

i. Assist teachers in the identification and solution of an individual teacher's teaching problems and student learning problems.

j. Assist in verifying teacher accountability and student learning.

k. Assist teachers in the improvement of their instructional abilities via the Instructional Crisis Squad and/or in-service training sessions which are designed to solve identified instructional problems.

l. Assist students in their quest for a fair and successful instructional environment via the student's Instructional Grievance Committee.

m. Assist in verifying and monitoring the development of attitudes, values, and beliefs which are consistent with those of the community.

n. Assist teachers in their requests for necessary materials and equipment via the business administrator by helping them defend the need for such materials and equipment [obviously, those materials and equipment which will be the most beneficial (facilitate learning) for the most students in the most courses should have priority over less critical materials and equipment.]

o. Assist and/or operate an evaluation and research department which helps teachers in their evaluation of students and is concerned with the improvement in the effectiveness and efficiency in learning those minimum common core SO's which are identified as being agreed upon and required by the local teachers, but are not part of those minimum common core SO's which are identified as being agreed upon and required by the teachers throughout the state or nation.

p. Act as a communication link between the school boards or regents and the teachers by helping the members of the school boards or regents to understand what is happening in the schools and what the needs of the teachers and students are and to help teachers understand the desires and needs of the community, state, and nation as expressed via the school board or regents.

Because of the different levels of administrators found in most school districts and in all colleges and universities, it is important to point out once again the difference between the traditional educational approach and the BLSA. Under the traditional approach, the pyramid of levels of administrators indicates the direction of authority. From the top which is usually a single administrator (superintendent, director, or president) decisions are handed down through each level to the bottom of the administrative pyramid which usually consists of a number of people (principals, department heads, team leaders, etc.). Since the direction of authority is from the top down and the recipients of the benefits of these decisions (the students) are at the very bottom, it should not be unusual that the distance between the decision-maker and those affected by the decisions results in some decisions which are not only irrelevant to the teaching-learning environment but may actually interfere with student learning.

Under the BLSA, the pyramid of controlling influences is inverted such that the primary function for the schools, student learning, is at the top of the pyramid. The emphasis in the inverted pyramid is on how each level is concerned with helping the level above to help the level above it, etc., until at the top the teachers are helping students learn. Each level of administrators is concerned with helping the teachers or administrators perform their role in the improvement of instruction (student learning). Succinctly, traditional education is concerned with authority whereas BLSA is concerned with cooperative support.

2. COUNSELING AND GUIDANCE STAFF: A NEW ROLE AND EVALUATION

Although counselors and guidance staff members are not administrators under the traditional viewpoint because they do not have authority over teachers or other administrators, counselors and guidance staff members fit into the administrative category under the BLSA because they are in a unique position to give help and support to teachers.

In the traditional educational situation where few, if any, SO's have been identified, it is difficult for the counseling and guidance staff to help teachers and students with specific learning problems. In addition, the training of most counseling and guidance staff emphasizes that student abilities to learn are determined by genetics and as such are static and can't be changed (a critical premise to accept if one is going to accept IQ tests as being valid in the measurement of intelligence). Given this type of training, counseling and guidance staff typically ignore the problems which students have that are created by the school enviroment, i.e., failure, suspension, cumulative ignorance, etc. Any attention given to problems caused by the school environment center around helping the student accept his or her situation and to cope with failure and discouragement since it is assumed that nothing can be done about the student's intelligence. There is also the belief that any affect that the environment might have on the student's learning abilities is mostly limited to the environment external to the school's environment (family, community, peer groups, etc.). As such, most counseling and guidance discussions center around events in the external environment.

As a result of the lack of direct involvement in the teaching-learning environment, counseling and guidance staff are considered to be in the periphery of the environment and as such are the first to be reduced or eliminated when the funds are short.

Under the BLSA, where SO's have been identified, the counseling and guidance staff could work with students and teachers in finding the solutions to difficult learning problems. In the BLSA, it is assumed that there is no such thing as mental limits and that mental abilities can be nurtured to equal or surpass natures contribution to intelligence. As such, IQ tests are considered not to be a valid measure of a static characteristic, but a measure of certain abilities at a particular point in time and subject to change at any time. Where most administrators work primarily on a cooperative basis with all of the people they are supposed to help and support, counseling and guidance staff could work with individual teachers and individual students. Given that the counselors can do little to change the external environment, they have had to be content with helping the student cope with the environment as it is. However, the counselors in being a part of the school environment, can change that environment and as such, can help the student not only cope with school conditions but to help the student change the situation so as to minimize any aversive effects of the school environment.

The most immediate action that counseling and guidance staff can take at all levels of education with the most beneficial and noticeable results is to identify after each grading period and particularly at the end of semesters or quarters all of the students who have received a failing grade. At the present time, many teachers may not be able to individualize instruction, but the counseling and guidance staff can. By meeting with the teachers, the counseling and guidance staff could help the teachers identify what it was that the students didn't learn that led to the student's failure. Assuming that the teachers are able to identify whatever the students didn't learn, then the counseling and guidance staff should set up small group or individual sessions with the goal of helping the students learn what they missed (as an absolute minimum, they should learn enough to get a passing grade). Not only will this benefit the students (giving them success instead of failure), but it will benefit the community (more successful students and fewer potential recipients of welfare and unemployment). Given that in most schools their financing is affected by the number of students enrolled and attending, the process suggested above will save students from dropping out and from being pushed out and as a result will maintain funds which would have been lost. For example, in colleges and universities where they are worried about a decreasing enrollment, if instead of failing 25 percent or more of the freshman class as is the *custom* (curve grading), the faculty and the counseling and guidance staff would solve the students' learning problems, there would be more students staying in school and more money to operate the schools. Using this approach, the counseling and guidance staff can not only document their humanitarian value to the students, but they can document in dollars the value of their services in helping more students have success and stay in school.

Another aspect of the new role for counseling and guidance staff members would be to serve on the Instructional Crisis Squad and help teachers solve learning problems and to serve on the Instructional Grievance Committee and help students receive a fair deal. For example, in the process of asking teachers what it was that a student or students didn't learn, if a teacher indicates that he or she doesn't know what it was the students didn't learn or admits that the grade was purely subjective, then the Counseling and Guidance staff member should suggest that the grade be changed or the matter should be taken to the Instructional Grievance Committee.

In a similar fashion, Counseling and Guidance staff members could and should be very much involved in identifying and eliminating the educational malpractices in their schools.

As specialists in solving student learning problems, Counseling and Guidance staff members would probably be involved in the evaluation and research division of the school district, college, or university. In this role, they would help teachers evaluate achievement of SO's and would help do necessary learning research dealing with the minimum common core SO's of courses that have been agreed upon by the teachers in the school district, college, or university but have not been agreed upon on a statewide or national basis.

E. EVALUATION OF LOCAL SCHOOL BOARDS, REGENTS, ETC.

As indicated earlier, the primary function of the school board, board of regents, or other similar groups is as a communication link between the public and the educators. A secondary function is a monitoring role. Given that teachers have not identified what specifically should be learned in the schools, entropic drift occurred and the process of schooling became more important than the results of schooling and the monitoring role became a controlling role in which the educators served the board rather than the board serving the educators and the public. For a long time, the boards power was sufficient to do whatever they wanted. The increasing power of teacher organizations and the increasing concern of legislative bodies over the problems, the ineffectiveness, and the increasing costs of education has decreased the absolute power of the boards over their schools.

When the school boards or members of boards of regents are elected by taxpayers, then the evaluation of the board may take many forms but essentially the evaluation form is filled with negative aspects. In other words, there are very few *plus* things that a school board can do that would be looked on favorably, unless in some kind of a comparative situation among several school districts, one school district is shown to be superior. If the better district is given some small measure of praise, the majority of the praise will go to the teachers and administrators. In the school district which was shown to be inferior, the taxpayers may get upset with the administrators and with the teachers, but the only real action that they have been able to take in the past, is to use their voting right to eliminate one or more of the school board members. Generally, the board is evaluated on the basis of did or didn't they raise taxes, were they able to maintain a school district that didn't get involved in any great controversy, and here again, the school board members will try to please all factions of the taxpayers if possible, in reference to how the students dress, what courses they take, etc. Since the school board member is really the only one the taxpaying public can have recourse to as far as action against that person, the school board members often suffer for educational practices they have no control over, mainly because they do not have any training in education and are not able to evaluate the teaching-learning situation in the classroom. Of course, there are some school boards that will attempt to solve problems that arise in the educational institutions, regardless of whether or not they know anything about the teaching-learning situation. Of interest, is the extent to which school boards will go in cases involving discipline in the schools with reference to hair styles, clothing styles, sex education, etc., but in actual efforts to demand quality education (as measured by more students learning more), the efforts become quite minimal. This misdirection of effort can easily be predicted because the schools that the school board members went to when they were young were as equally inefficient and ineffective as the schools today and what was *good enough* for them is supposed to be *good enough* for the students today. Even at the school board conventions and conferences, many of the speakers are faculty from schools of education who in many ways will reinforce the maintenance of the status quo.

The evaluation of regents or trustees (usually found in institutions of higher education) who are appointed to these positions for varying terms is quite similar to the evaluation of school board members, except that the taxpaying public or other financial supporters for the institution do not have direct access to indicate their evaluation by voting against the member of the board of regents or trustees. In the case of higher education, the members of the boards or regents and trustees generally serve at the pleasure of some higher body, i.e., governor, legislature, etc. As in elementary and secondary education, boards of regents and trustees are not normally evaluated in any way whatsoever on the basis of learning that is or is not taking place in the institutions over which they administrate. An exception might be in the case of comparative, standardized testing or national or regional surveys on course offerings, faculty degrees, publications, etc., which may show a given school in a particularly bad light.

Under the Behavioral Learning Systems Approach (BLSA) where the required and desired results of education (SO's) have been identified, the school boards and regents can go back to their original functions.

In communicating to the teachers and the administrators, the board should have identified what the desired goals of the community are and in cooperation with teachers translate these goals into SO's. In communicating to the public, the board should be able to describe the success the school is having in facilitating student learning of the minimum common core SO's, particularly those desired by the local community. Another aspect of the communication function of the boards is to communicate the financial needs of the school to the appropriate agency or group and to defend the needs in terms of learning. Although the state departments of education and the state boards are concerned with facilitating communication and cooperation among the local school districts, colleges, and universities, the local boards can also initiate cooperative efforts by communicating their needs and problems to other schools, the state office, or the U.S. office of education.

As the process of instruction gets more complex and the size of the school district, college, or university increases, the secondary function of the boards may well become the more critical function. The monitoring role should be concerned with at least the following areas:

1. to be sure that the overall emphasis of all concerned is on student learning and that schools are there for students not for educators;
2. to be sure that all concerned work together cooperatively and supportively to increase the effectiveness and efficiency of the instructional environment;
3. to be sure that the priorities in financing are such that funds for solving learning problems in the learning of required SO's gets precedence over other areas;
4. to be sure that the minimum common core SO's are achieved and if not, that something is being done about it;
5. to be sure that existing educational malpractices are eliminated;
6. to be sure that attitudes, values and beliefs that are in conflict with those desired by the parents, community, state, and nation are not being developed by design by teachers who are against our present form of society;

NOTE: If students on their own develop attitudes, values, and/or beliefs which are in conflict with those desired by parents, community, state, and nation, this should be acceptable in a free country such as ours. However, if a teacher purposely develops negative emotional tendencies in students knowing that the resulting conflicts between students and parents or students and the community will be destructive for the students and society, then the teacher is guilty of professional malpractice. The critical point to remember is that students have not been trained to resist undesirable indoctrination and are not able to control the internal development of these negative emotional tendencies. A trained teacher can relatively easily subvert the minds of young students in the privacy of the classroom. Even adults in the military have to be trained to resist brainwashing and they are not always successful in resisting the development of undesirable attitudes, values, and/or beliefs.

7. in reference to the affective domain, if one of our goals is to develop students who are concerned about others in contrast to selfism, then the board might want to be sure that there are multiple opportunities for students to help others, i.e., student tutoring, summer or year long programs in which students work at helping others here in our own communities, etc. (Vista Corps or Peace Corps type activities).

F. EVALUATION OF STATE BOARDS AND OFFICES OF INSTRUCTION

In the fifty states of the United States, the state boards of education vary all the way from some that are almost completely ineffective to some that are extremely effective, as far as trying to aid in carrying out the traditional programs of the school districts and colleges in the state. In general, the only way the local taxpayer evaluates these state boards of education is on the basis of whether the local school district received its share of money from the state under various existing programs administered by or through the state department of education. Because of the long history of local autonomy in the school districts, very few states have had to worry about any kind of state-wide comparison with other states in reference to the quality of education students receive within the states. Teachers, school administrators and school boards quite often evaluate state departments of education informally, but of course they are not in a position to affect the state department of education, so their opinions do not have too much of an effect. On the other hand, the state department of education is in a position to control certain financing that may go to a given school district. As a result, there is a temptation that even if the local school district does not like what the state department is doing, they won't say anything. Most state departments try to get involved in efforts which will help the schools in their states develop a quality curriculum by having available a number of supervisors in various curriculum areas. Since many of the consultants to the state department are from teacher-training institutions within the state, the emphasis of most of the state departments of education through their supervisors is mainly on the presentation of the curriculum and not necessarily on the learning which the curriculum is supposed to facilitate. (This, of course, is the emphasis in most teacher training institutions.)

In many states, the state departments of education are involved in selecting textbooks to be used by the schools within the state. Of interest is the fact that although all educators talk about individual differences in students, the actions of the state departments of education indicate that they are assuming that all students are the same. For example, the students are all required to be in front of a teacher generally 180 days a year; they also require the students to learn from the same textbook or from one of three, four, or five textbooks, which denies the existence of individual differences and points out that what is important is that every student has the same treatment and not necessarily the same learning. Also, many state departments of education are involved in the accreditation of school districts within their state, and in some cases influence the accreditation of colleges within the state.

The state department of education's accrediting procedures follow very much the same line as that of the regional and national accrediting associations in that they accredit schools which have fulfilled certain requirements. These requirements vary from state to state, but generally concern such things as: how many square feet of window space per student, how many books in the library per student, how many students in a teacher's class, what degrees do the teachers have, what are the subjects that are offered, does the school present a healthy environment, etc. To my knowledge, there is no place on the accrediting forms of any state department of education, regional or national association in which they ask, *Are the students learning?* or *How much are the students learning?* This is because we don't evaluate or accredit schools on the basis of learning.

There are some schools which do not fulfill all of the requirements of the accrediting agencies, but in which learning is taking place by design. On the other hand, there are schools which have been accredited and do fulfill all of the requirements of the accrediting agencies, but most learning is taking a place by chance. If the accrediting team does indicate a concern for learning, generally this is indicated by an examination of the grades to find out whether or not the grades fit some kind of curve. In fact, at a college in which many of the teachers were starting to use some of the concepts which I recommended in order to help more learners learn, the regional accrediting team criticized one department because they weren't giving enough "D's" and "F's" (designed failure). In reference to this, it might be possible for a school to lose its accreditation (or not get accredited in the first place) because too many students are learning.

Since teacher-training institutions are indirectly responsible for the learning or lack of learning of millions of students the accreditation of teacher-training institutions should be an extremely critical procedure. But here again, these schools are not accredited as a teacher-training institution on the basis of their ability to train teachers-to-be on how to help their future students learn. They are accredited on the same type of basis as any other school in higher education. This is supported by the fact that a very small percentage of teacher-training institutions require that their students be evaluated in practice-teaching on the basis of whether or not the students they were teaching learned anything. The major emphasis and evaluation is on presentation of content, not on learning.

To a degree, the state departments of education are evaluated by the legislative groups and indirectly by the taxpayers. Generally, they are left pretty much on their own, and as long as they maintain a status quo and don't get the taxpayer too upset and are able to live within the budget that they get, then there are no real problems.

1. THE ROLE AND EVALUATION OF STATE OFFICES OF INSTRUCTION UNDER THE BEHAVIORAL LEARNING SYSTEMS APPROACH

In the role as a facilitator of learning whose emphasis is on the support of local school districts, colleges, and universities in their efforts to facilitate learning, the primary concern at the state level should be on those minimum common core SO's which have been identified and agreed upon by the teachers throughout the state but not throughout the nation. Initial efforts should be directed towards identifying statewide minimum common core SO's. Once these have been identified, state funding can be directed towards the learning of those SO's and towards the identification and solutions of learning problems associated with these SO's. Any accountability legislation at the state level should be concerned with the learning of the statewide minimum common core SO's.

Because of the high levels of intrastate mobility of students, the state has to accept the responsibility of identifying the commonalities in courses with the same title that are taught in schools throughout the state. Again, it may be important to point out that the direction is not to make all courses the same (maximum) but to identify what is in common as a minimum.

The state department of instruction should also set up a research division that is concerned with any needed research in identifying solutions to learning problems associated with the statewide minimum common core SO's.

One of the important functions of the state office of instruction would be the facilitation of cooperation and sharing among the various local school districts, colleges, and universities of SO's and solutions to learning problems that they may have in common.

Since an increasing share of the instructional dollar iscoming from the state, the state office of instruction is in a good position to encourage the change over in the schools from the traditional operation with its emphasis on teaching to the BLSA with its emphasis on student learning by tying funding to the achievement of the statewide minimum common core SO's rather than the present criteria of attendance regardless of learning.

G. EVALUATION OF THE U. S. OFFICE OF INSTRUCTION

The U.S. Office of Education, which has grown considerably in the past decade, particularly in reference to the amount of money that is channeled through this agency, is evaluated by Federal legislators and indirectly by educators throughout the country. But since the educators, school districts, colleges, universities, school boards, and state departments of education are not in a position to affect the U.S. Office of Education, they generally try to do whatever they can to please the U.S. Office of Education. The U.S. Office of Education may in turn give grants to educators, school districts, etc. which will help them to be evaluated in a positive form in their respective situations. The U.S. Office of Education is in a very good position to affect learning throughout the country and at all levels of education; however, since they are not evaluated on the basis of the amount of learning that they facilitate nationally, the majority of projects granted funds under the U.S. Office of Education are not in turn evaluated on the basis of any measurable improvement of learning and hence the effect of USOE efforts on learning are minimal. Most USOE projects are evaluated on a variety of criteria (not including learning). Consequently, billions of dollars are being spent in programs and projects in which no one really knows exactly and measurably how much, if any, additional learning has taken place. Since the largest single source of funds for education is the U.S. Office of Education, proposals for grants are developed and designed by educators and others on the basis of which projects or programs will be most likely funded, rather than on the basis of some educator identifying a learning problem in his school and trying to solve this problem through the help of local, state, or Federal funds. Consequently, specialists in grants are people who know the kinds of projects the U.S. Office of Education wants and the wording in the proposals that will encourage acceptance rather than being specialists in identifying instructional problems in their respective institutions. Because of this lack of emphasis on learning, the most important criteria in evaluating research in education is the design of the research and the strength of the statistic used to evaluate the research. Whether or not an acceptable level of learning took place or if there was a measurable improvement in learning, is not really considered important. As proof of this, an examination of a wide variety of educational research indicates on the posttest scores that the students still only learned approximately half of whatever it was the tests were testing. This should indicate right away that regardless of the statistic used, the instructional materials and methods were quite ineffective. Although the success of programs such as Upward Bound and other remedial oriented programs around the country which are funded by the U.S. Office of Education should be a credit to the activities of the U.S. Office of Education, they actually emphasize the ineffectiveness of our present system of education. Why should the taxpayers have to pay twice for what should have been done correctly the first time? Even more important, why should students be forced to go through the same things a second or third time taking more time out of the students' lives than is necessary? In addition, the initial attempts to learn which were met with failure most likely seriously and negatively affected the students self-images and attitudes towards the rest of society.

Instead of being the leading influence on changes in education, the U.S. Office of Education has become a strong force in the maintenance of the status quo, with all its inefficiency and ineffectiveness. This is probably because most of the personnel have been educated along traditional lines. If the readers of proposals are traditional educators and particularly if they are faculty in schools of education, only those proposals that are in line with traditional emphases will be positively evaluated. Hence, maintaining the status quo of ineffectiveness and inefficiency is what is rewarded. Ironically, the maintenance of the status quo in education results in the need for greater expenditure of funds in welfare, unemployment, and retraining programs such as Job Corps., Manpower Development, etc. If instruction at all levels of education is to play such an important part in the lives of our young people, then the instructional system from the students and teachers in the smallest school up to and including the United States Office of Education should be held *accountable* for the learning that is or is not taking place and for the spending of educational dollars in such a way that will maximize learning in the most effective and efficient ways.

1. *THE ROLE AND EVALUATION OF THE U. S. OFFICE OF INSTRUCTION UNDER THE BEHAVIORAL LEARNING SYSTEMS APPROACH*

In the role as a facilitator of learning whose emphasis is on the support of state and local school districts, colleges, and universities in their efforts to facilitate learning, the primary concern at the national level should be on those minimum common core SO's which have been identified and agreed upon by teachers throughout the nation. Since this has not been done as yet, the initial efforts of the U.S. Office of Instruction should be directed towards identifying the national minimum common core SO's. Once these have been identified, federal funding can be directed towards the learning of these SO's and towards the identification and solution of learning problems associated with these SO's. Any accountability legislation at the national level or national assessment should be concerned with the learning of the national minimum common core SO's. Instead of proposals being funded on the basis of someone's area of interest with little if any transference to other schools and other situations, proposals for federal funding should only be granted if they deal with an identified learning problem in the learning of national minimum common core SO's. In that way, the results of the project will have national implications.

Because of the high levels of interstate mobility of students, the U.S. Office of Instruction has to accept the responsibility of identifying the commonalities in courses with the same title that are taught in schools throughout the nation. As with the state emphasis, the goal is to identify what is in common as a minimum to be learned not as a maximum to be learned.

The U.S. Office of Education (hopefully the U.S. Office of Designed Instruction) already has the National Institute of Education (NIE) which is supposed to be the research arm of the U.S. Office of Education. Given that most teachers have not identified what they want students to learn, that minimum common core SO's have not been identified, and that entropic drift has shifted the emphasis from the results of education to the process of education, the present efforts of NIE are relatively ineffectual. It is not surprising that NIE is having trouble with the Congress in regard to its funding and purpose. There is a great need for the identification of national minimum common core SO's and research towards the successful achievement of these SO's by all students. As a result, there will probably be an emphasis on the part of the new U.S. Office of Instruction on basic or foundation courses because the SO's in these courses are more apt to be identified as minimum common core SO's.

One of the important functions of the new U.S. Office of Instruction would be on the facilitation of cooperation and sharing among the fifty states of identified SO's and the solutions to learning problems that they may have in common.

Since an increasing share of the instructional dollar is coming from the national level, the new U.S. Office of Instruction would be in a good position to encourage the change over in the state offices of instruction and in the schools from the traditional operation with its emphasis on teaching to the BLSA with its emphasis on student learning by tying federal funds to the achievement of national minimum common core SO's rather than on the present criteria of the attendance in schools of certain groups of students regardless of their levels of learning achievement.

CHAPTER IX

INSTRUCTIONAL RESEARCH: A NEW ROLE

General and Specific Objectives

GO — To understand why most traditional educational research is irrelevant, impractical, and of little value in reference to classroom instruction.

- SO — State the difference between a science and a non-science as identified in this chapter and give two or more examples of each (defend your examples in terms of the definitions of a science and a non-science or art form).

- SO — State why the agricultural and psychological models for research are not appropriate for instructional research.

- SO — Differentiate between the types of problems traditionally researched in education versus the type of *learning problem* described in this chapter as to their appropriateness for instructional research.

- SO — Locate and describe two or more research studies which are examples of the traditional types of problems usually researched. (Point out where the emphasis is on man-made phenomenon rather than on learning.)

- SO — List the three categories of traditional research and give an example of each and state at least one of the potential problems with each category which can make the value of the research questionable.

- SO — Describe at least three ways in which the tests used in research can bias the results of the research such that the results are invalid.

- SO — Given a situation where an external *normed* test is used to evaluate achievement, describe the four options available to the teacher.

GO — To understand and appreciate the value and role of research in a Behavioral Learning Systems Approach to Instruction.

> SO — Describe the three modes of research and make a statement which defends why one of the modes is more appropriate for designed instruction than the other two.
>
> SO — Define the six characterisitcs of designed instruction as stated in this chapter.
>
> SO — List the three factors used to evaluate the design of an instructional environment and how each factor is derived.
>
> SO — Given the data from at least two research reports, determine the values for the three factors.[1]
>
> SO — Given a journal containing three or more reports of educational research, critique each report from the point of view of the six criteria listed on pages 1099-1100.
>
> SO — Describe the priorities for instructional research at the national, state, and local levels (include the two most important tasks for each group and a delineation of the areas of responsibility).

---

[1] If these SO's are part of a course, the teacher should be sure to select research reports for this SO so that they have all the information necessary to determine the three factors.

Because of the length of this chapter and as an aid to the reader, I am including that part of the Table of Contents that covers this Chapter.

Chapter IX — Instructional Research: A New Role 1061
A. Science vs. Non-Science or Why Educational Research has Failed! 1064
   1. The Identification of Research Problems 1068
   2. The Ignoring of Individual Differences 1069
   3. Media and Method Research 1071
   4. Tests: The Critical Hidden Variable (GIGO) 1075
      a. Correlation Problems in Constructing Evaluation Instruments 1076
      b. The Use of Subjective "Objective" Type Test Items .. 1078
      c. Percentage of Test Items Correct Not Necessarily Equal to Percentage of Objectives Achieved 1079
      d. The Invalidity of Standardized (Normed) Tests 1083
B. The Role of Instructional Research in the Behavioral Learning Systems Approach to Instruction 1090
   1. Modes of Research 1093
      a. Theories of Instruction and Instructional Research .. 1095
   2. Instructional Design Evaluation: A New Tool for Research 1096
      a. Evaluating Examples of Educational Research 1101
C. Priorities for Instructional Research 1108
   1. The National Institute of Education: Traditional Research Hidden Under System's Concepts and Terminology 1111
      a. The Actual Direction of NIE Research and Subsequent Reductions in Funding 1118
   2. The Need for Regional, State, and Local Institutes for Instructional Research 1120
D. Teaching, Research, and the Role of the Teacher 1121

INSTRUCTIONAL RESEARCH: A NEW ROLE

Educational Researcher: *I have good news and I have bad news. First the good news. Due to the National Institute of Education and other U.S. Office of Education funding sources, funds for research are on the increase and hundreds of projects are spending millions of dollars. Now for the bad news. We're researching in the wrong direction!*

According to a General Accounting Office (GAO) report to Congress,

More than $200 million in educational research has produced little evidence of significant impact in classrooms.
Washington Monitor, *Education USA,* Dec. 17, 1973

Almost everyone agrees that basic research in education has not produced many results that excite admiration. Years ago, when the first Encyclopedia of Educational Research appeared, Isaac Kandel (1950) recorded his doubts of the extent to which the mountain of material reviewed there would lead to improvement in educational practice. More recently Tom Lamke (1955) wrote,

If the research in the previous three years in medicine, agriculture, physics, and chemistry were to be wiped out, our life would be changed materially, but if research in the area of teacher personnel in the same three years were to vanish, educators and education would continue much as usual.
(Robert Ebel, *Phi Delta Kappan,* October, 1967, 81-84)

... we usually find that problems in education that are investigated turn out to be either trivial, or they bear little relevance to classroom practice. ... The researchers keep refining their procedures, largely but not exclusively statistical procedures, seemingly unaware of where the crucial problems lie. An elaborate research methodology has evolved around the investigation of inconsequential events.
(J. Myrar Atkin, Journal of Research in Science Teaching, 1967-68, No. 5, 338-45.)

A. SCIENCE vs. NON-SCIENCE OR WHY EDUCATIONAL RESEARCH HAS FAILED!

If learning is supposed to be the most important product of our schools, then instructional research should be concerned with increasing learning for more students. However, a very critical factor inhibits this type of research. As long as teachers are not able to specify what it is that their students are supposed to be learning, it is impossible to carry on any research to increase or even affect the unknown learning. As a result of not having any SO's (specific objectives) for the students to learn, two other factors have developed to further inhibit the carrying on of relevant and effective research. First, entropic drift affected the teacher's role in the classroom. Whereas the teacher's role should be to help students learn, when teachers don't know what it is that students should be learning, the process of teaching becomes more important than the results of teaching (student learning). In a similar fashion, educational research has concentrated on the process of education rather than on the results of education and on the process of the research (procedures) rather than on the results of research. As a result, educational research became a non-science because of its emphasis on man-made phenomenon (teaching methods, teaching media, various environments, etc.) Similarly, the emphasis on teaching rather than on learning made the traditional teacher's role an art form rather than a science.

Under the Behavioral Learning Systems Approach to instruction where the desired and required SO's have been specified, the teacher's role as an Instructioneer is concerned with facilitating measurable learning. Since the emphasis is on learning and *learning* is a natural phenomenon the teacher's role as an instructioneer can be a science rather than an art form. Similarly, instructional research can also become a science if the emphasis is on learning rather than on man-made phenomenon.

There are two research models which are generally followed in most educational research: the agricultural model and the pyschological model. Probably the most influential in traditional educational research is the agricultural model because the analytical procedures in traditional educational research were originally borrowed from agricultural research in which significant gains in crop production and livestock growth meant meaningful increases in farm income. It must be remembered that the original crop yields and growth rates with which the experimental results are going to be compared, are already considered maximum under existing conditions. If the normal yield of an average acre of oats was three bushels and some agricultural researcher was able to increase this to four bushels per acre, this would be of value because three bushels per acre was considered maximum. If it was possible to get three bushels of oats per acre and a researcher in an experiment got only one bushel per acre in the control acreage and two bushels per acre in the experimental acreage, his results would not be very valuable because other farm researchers would be more concerned with why he didn't even get a normal yield in either the control or experimental acreages. In traditional education where most teachers don't know specifically what the students should be learning in their classes and there is little in common between classes having the same course title (taught by different teachers), it is impossible to identify whether or not research results were greater than or less than normal learning levels. As a result and due to entropic drift, the primary emphasis has been placed on the statistical procedures. Using the proper statistics has become more important than whether or not significant differences were identified. The more power that the statistical instrument being used in the research has, the better the research from a traditional point of view (regardless of the utility of the research).

There are two major differences between the objects of agricultural research and the objects of instructional research.

— No one knows the *absolute maximums* in crop production per acre nor the *absolute maximums* in rate of livestock growth. If an educator has specified the objectives for his course or has his tests made out, then the educator does know the *absolute maximum* learning possible — 100 percent of the objectives or test items.

NOTE: Once we have arrived at the point where the minimum common core SO's have been identified (national, state, and local) and 90 percent of these SO's, then the direction of instructional research will more closely follow the agricultural model. We will be trying to find out ways to accomplish the same task faster and/or cheaper with no loss in learning.

— In crop and livestock production research, the primary goal is to use gentic control in breeding such that there is a minimum of differences between individual plants or animals and a maximum of yield for a minimum investment in the production environment. In designing instruction for humans, it would be unethical and considered immoral to impose genetic controls on breeding and individual differences among students are encouraged. Therefore, the primary goal has to be on manipulating the environment rather than students.

Educational research that indicates pretest scores of 20 percent to 60 percent or higher and posttest scores of 40 percent to 80 percent may be able to show significant gains in learning (depending upon the size of the sample), but the most important data are being overlooked. Pretest scores of 20 percent to 60 percent or higher indicate that the learners already know a considerable amount of the content of the teaching-learning situation and will probably be bored with the method of teaching, no matter what it is. Posttest scores of 40 percent to 80 percent indicate that whatever the teaching-learning situation is, it was ineffective. When working with human learners, pretest scores should be as close to zero as possible and posttest scores should be as close to 100 percent as possible. Significant differences in *learning gains* based on pretests and posttests of a single learning pathway are not relevant to the situation. If we really believe that learners are unique individuals with many differences, then it should be obvious that to find one pathway that will work for all students is impossible. Secondly, to achieve statistical significance in *learning gains* in which the pretest is above 20 to 30 percent and the posttest is only 15 to 40 percent higher but still less than 80 percent, then the fact of statistical significance is not nearly as important as the two questions, why were the students forced to be bored by going through materials that they already knew (20 to 60 percent pretest scores) and why didn't the materials teach what they were supposed to teach (40 to 80 percent posttest scores). Significant differences in learning achievement between two or more learning pathways where the learning levels attained are in the range of maximum learning (90-100 percent of objectives) may be of interest for increased effectiveness if other variables of the pathways are equal (cost, time, convenience, etc.). However, this would be typical of traditional research wherein as a non-science, the objects of the research were the methods or learning pathways which are man-made and the impossible goal is to find one pathway that will work for all students.

Traditional and contemporary educational research has used *learning* as a dependent variable, *methodology* as an independent variable, and *time* as a constant. If *learning* is as important as we claim, then our goals should be to maximize *learning* first (effectiveness) and then try to achieve the same levels of learning but at lower costs, shorter time, etc. (efficiency). Research that is carried out under a Behavioral Learning Systems Approach should consider *learning* (100 percent of the required SO's) as a constant and *time* as a dependent variable. Since no one method, resource, or environment will be effective for all students or even for very many students (remember, traditionally only a few students ever learn 100 percent), *methodology* will not only be a dependent variable, but it will represent multiple pathways made up of whatever methods, resources, and environments that are necessary to help students achieve 100 percent of the required SO's.

If our major emphasis in educational institutions is *learning*, then our research goals should be to minimize pretest scores and to maximize posttest scores, instead of trying to find significant differences. Through the Behavioral Learning Systems Approach, remember that pretest scores indicate (1) are students really ready to start the instructional unit (do they have the prerequisite behaviors) and (2) how much of the course do the students already know? Posttest scores would indicate the effectiveness of the materials used in the teaching-learning situation and student errors indicate need for change in whatever the approach that was previously used.

The psychological model applied to instructional research is even more inappropriate than the agricultural model as far as helping more students learn more. The purpose in psychological research is to study the nature of man which makes it a science but the emphasis is on the treatment and how it affects man in contrast to the purpose in instructional research where the desired affect (learning) should be defined and the emphasis should be on finding the right combination of treatments which will bring about the desired affect. The psychological research design and tests are aimed at forcing the appearance of individual differences in any resultant scores by giving the same treatment to people who are different; whereas in instructional research, the design and tests should be aimed at helping all students to achieve the desired or required SO's by giving different treatments to people who are different. Given a situation in which a certain behavior (SO) or set of behaviors (SO's) are associated with a certain mental and/or emotional condition (GO), psychological research is directed towards explaining how a given mental and/or emotional condition was developed (already in existence) whereas instructional research would be directed towards the actual process needed to develop the given mental and/or emotional condition. To a degree, psychiatric research, and instructional research are similar in that a variety of treatments may be used to bring about certain mental and/or emotional conditions (GO's) as inferred from observable behaviors (SO's). In both psychiatric and instructional research, the best treatment or treatments are the ones that work. The major difference between psychiatric and instructional research is that psychiatric research deals primarily in trying to develop normal behavior and associated mental and/or emotional conditions where none existed before. As a general statement, psychological and psychiatric research is more concerned with learning and changes in the affective domain whereas instructional research should be more concerned with learning and changes in the cognitive and sensory domains.

1. THE IDENTIFICATION OF RESEARCH PROBLEMS

In identifying a problem to research, the traditional educational researcher generally depends on his or her own interest areas, the interest areas of his or her superiors (this assures positive evaluation by the superior), and/or the interest areas of people associated with various funding agencies (this approach assures funds to do research and the more funds obtained, the more positive the evaluation of the researcher by his or her superiors). Given that the *problem* is identified via areas of interest, it is possible to research a *problem* that really isn't a problem at all. As a result, it is easy to end up doing research in trivia. Because other people may not be as interested in a particular area as the researcher, the research may have little utility.

Relevant research with widespread application can only occur when the problem being researched has been identified as an actual problem and there are a lot of people who have identified the same problem. In an educational situation where it is not known what should be learned, it is difficult to identify any learning problems to research. As such, most educational research centers around teaching or *presenting the course content* problems rather than learning problems. In an instructional situation where there are SO's, but non-learning is expected and not viewed as a problem, teaching problems still remain as the research emphasis. In an instructional situation where there are SO's and non-learning is considered a problem, but there are no minimum common core SO's which have been agreed upon by teachers over a wide area, the research could deal with real learning problems but the results would only be useful to those teachers who might want their students to learn the same SO's. In an instructional situation where there are identified minimum common core SO's which have been agreed upon by teachers throughout a large area and non-learning is considered a learning problem, research could deal with actual problems and the more students in the area that have the same learning problem, the more important the research, and the greater the application of the results.

Given that few teachers have specified the learning objectives for their courses, it should not be surprising that the problems being researched in education are not very important. Also, given that commonality in SO's among courses with common titles is more dependent on chance than on design, it should not be surprising that most educational research has limited application.

In order for instructional research to become as important and useful as it could and should be, there is going to have to be a concentrated effort on the part of all concerned with the instructional environment to first, identify the important SO's in all courses, and second, to identify the minimum common core SO's for all courses at the local, state, and national levels. The funds for identifying the local minimum common core SO's should come from local sources. Similarly, funds for identifying the state and national minimum common core SO's should come from state and national sources. Once the different levels of minimum common core SO's has been identified, national funds can be used to research the learning of national minimum common core SO's which have been identified as learning problems in most of the states. State funds should be used to research the learning of state minimum common core SO's which have been identified as learning problems. Local funds should be used to research the learning of local minimum common core SO's which have been identified as learning problems.

2. THE IGNORING OF INDIVIDUAL DIFFERENCES

Traditional educational research continues to try to find one pathway for all students even though educators have been talking about individual differences for decades and it is an accepted fact that students learn at different rates, learn best via different methods, have different interest areas, are motivated for different reasons, come to the learning event with different levels of learning skills (controlled more by environment than by nature), and have varying degrees of cumulative ignorance. It might seem logical to someone not in education who recognizes that individual differences exist that if a single pathway was used for learning by different students that different levels of achievement should be an expected result because the one pathway was probably not the best pathway for each student. It would also seem logical to that person that if subsequently other learning pathways were used that were more appropriate to the individual learners, that most or all of the students could achieve all of whatever was supposed to be learned. However, in traditional educational research and even in traditional education, the concept of mental *limits* as revealed by IQ scores has been borrowed from psychology and relieves the educator from having to try more than one pathway (no matter how inappropriate) because whatever the achievement levels are, the traditional educator believes that they are more affected by genetics than be environment. That's why most traditional educators are not disturbed when a Spanish speaking student is given an IQ test in English and the low score places the student in a mentally retarded class. With the advent of bilingual education, many traditional teachers are being surprised when they realize that when Spanish speaking students are given instructional materials in Spanish they are able to learn as well as other English speaking students in spite of the fact that the Spanish speaking students scored low in an IQ test written in English.

There is no such thing as a limit to learning, so differences in achievement are caused more by ignoring the individual differences among students than by any genetic differences. The results of any research that ignores individual differences is affected by the failure to recognize that these differences exist and consequently the research is irrelevant and useless in real world situations where these individual differences do exist.

Recognizing that individual differences do affect learning and research results, it is possible for a researcher to design his or her research in such a way that almost any desired results can be obtained. For example, if a researcher wanted to prove that a particular method wasn't very effective, the researcher could pick a topic and a population of students who lacked sufficient entry behaviors to learn successfully in the topic regardless of the method used. If a researcher wants a particular method to look good, then the researcher could pick a topic that is of high interest value to the population of students from which the sample will be drawn. Where there are high levels of interest, the achievement levels will tend to be high regardless of the method used. If a researcher wanted to prove that programmed instructional materials (linear type) were not very good and that the branching type programmed material was better, the researcher would pick a topic and a population of students such that most of the students would know some of the objectives covered by the unit. The sample of students using the linear program would have to go through material they already knew and would become bored which would affect their achievement. The sample of students using the branching program would be able to skip over the material they already knew which would tend to maintain interest and achievement. The same research results could probably be achieved by selecting a population of students who tend to be anti-authoritarian and/or open minded. Any sample of these students would probably feel negative about a linear type programmed material because they would resist having to follow a single pathway.

Given that different students learn best in different ways using different cognitive styles, then any method of instruction that is similar to the cognitive learning style of the majority of the students in a sample will look as if it is superior to another method which may be in conflict with the cognitive learning style of the students.

The point to remember is that when educational research ignores individual differences among the students used in the research, these same differences affect the results of the research anyway and make the research of limited value in classrooms where other students also have individual differences.

3. MEDIA AND METHOD RESEARCH

Educational research involving some type of media and/or some particular teaching method are good examples of non-science research because they are man-made and are not natural phenomenon. This type of research generally falls into three categories:

a. Old versus Old: which is typified by the comparison of two established methods or media, which have been used by a number of teachers at various locations.

b. Old versus New: this approach is typified by the comparison of some new idea or relatively new idea with an existing method or medium that is being used or has been used much more extensively.

c. New versus New: this approach is typified by the comparison of two new media or approaches, neither of which has been used very much.

The first approach, Old versus Old, has formed the basis for thousands of dollars of experimental research, such as one reading method against another reading method, an off-the-shelf television program versus face-to-face teacher in the classroom, an off-the-shelf programmed instructional unit versus television or face-to-face classroom experience, etc. Although thousands of dollars have been spent in this kind of research and are still being spent in this type of research, there are some critical questions that should be raised, and have been raised by other educators. Let's assume that we are comparing one teaching method (TM_1) against another teaching method (TM_2). After the students in

	GROUP A TM_1	GROUP B TM_2
Situation 1-2	$Test_1$	$Test_2$
Situation 1-1	$Test_1$	$Test_1$
Situation 2-2	$Test_2$	$Test_2$

Figure 136 — Evaluating Old vs. Old Research

Group A have been exposed to teaching method 1 and the students in Group B have been exposed to teaching method 2, which test do we use? If we use the test that was designed to test the objectives of TM_1, with Group A and we use the test that was designed to test the objectives of TM_2 for Group B, the question immediately arises, what if the two tests are testing different objectives (situation 1-2). How can we then use the statistical data resulting from this research if two different tests are used? It should be obvious that the same test should be used for both groups. Look at situation 1-1. If we use the test that was designed to teach the objectives of TM_1 for both Group A and Group B, which group is going to learn the most (assuming there is a high correlation between the test for TM_1 and what is taught under TM_1). Unless TM_1 and TM_2 are exactly the same, which they are not likely to be since they are both off-the-shelf or have been used for some time, it should be obvious that Group A (TM_1) will turn out as superior. How about if we use the test which was designed to test what was taught in TM_2? In situation 2-2, where the test for TM_2 is given to both groups, it should be obvious that the results from using the test for TM_2 (assuming a high correlation between the test for testing the TM_2 and the content of TM_2) would indicate that Group B (TM_2) is superior. As a result, the use of Old versus Old in comparative media or method research does not seem to be a very practical approach because of the high possibility that the instructional materials used with the different media or methods contain different objectives (although using the same topic) and consequently the tests will favor the instructional materials and the media or methods that the test was originally designed for. In some instances, there has been an attempt to mix the two tests. Here, it depends upon the percentage of the test items that favor one method over another as to which group (media or method) is identified as being superior. As such, Old vs. Old type research is generally biased and of little value.

In reference to the second approach to media or method research, Old versus New, the effort has been to try to make the two situations equivalent. For example, in television research, in order to make the two situations equivalent, the television camera transmitted exactly what went on in the classroom which normally was a teacher talking. Not surpirsingly, research indicates no significant differences between the two approaches. In trying to compare face-to-face instruction — (the old method) which is not usually based on specific objectives versus programmed instruction (the new method) which is based on specific objectives, the list of objectives that were used to write up the program are typically given to the instructor. As should be expected, the results generally indicate no significant differences. However, it is necessary to point out that in the conclusion of such research, where the statement is made that *there is no difference between programmed instruction and fact-to-face instruction*, it is necessary to add to the statement, *there is no difference between programmed instruction and face-to-face instruction when the instructor has a list of objectives in his or her hands.* Since very few instructors lecture to their classes with a list of specific objectives in their hands, this type of research has limited application. Here again, in the second approach to research, the tests that are used and the degree to which the tests really measure what was taught under the old method or the new method, quite often determines the superior method and not necessarily what the students actually learned. Hundreds of thousands of dollars have been spent in this type of research to find out that there is no significant difference between televised instruction and face-to-face instruction, or programmed instruction and face-to-face instruction.

The traditional teacher or administrator will use these results as an excuse not to utilize televised instruction, programmed instruction or other new media and methods because there are no differences in the amount of learning. Under the Behavioral Learning Systems point of view, research results indicating no significant differences become very important. If the students can learn just as easily from a recorded or printed medium as they can with a live teacher, then the teacher can be *replaced* into a more effective role (Instructioneer) in the teaching-learning situation, rather than the traditional role of just presenting course content. After all, if almost anything can present the content of a course without measurably affecting learning, why not let something else do that job. The teacher's role as an Instructioneer is much more critical to student learning and can only be performed by a human being.

The third approach to media or method research is the New vs. New and is currently popular with the U.S. Office of Education in their attempt to find out what each method or medium can do best in the teaching-learning situation. Thousands of dollars are being spent in comparative media or method research in order to identify what types of learning experiences are best taught by what kinds of media or methods. Because the effort is to try to find a specific type of learning that is unique for a specific type of media or method, most of the materials used in the New versus New research are developed from scratch. To illustrate some of the problems in this type of research, let me use two examples (see Fig. 137). In the first experiment, we'll compare audio tape and slides versus audio tape only. After Groups A and B have gone through their materials, the students are given a verbal test, testing only those concepts and objectives that are available in the audio portion of either approach. It is rather obvious that the results

	GROUP A	GROUP B
First Experiment	Audio tape and slides	Audio tape
Second Experiment	Single concept films with sound	Laboratory practice

Figure 137 — New vs. New Research

are going to end up indicating no significant differences, unless the visuals and the slides contained conflicting objectives, in which case the students would have to split up their attention and you might be able to prove that the audio tape-slides resulted in less learning. On the other hand, if the test that was used tested some visual objectives that were available on the slides, but not available on the audio tape, it would be very simple to prove that the audio tape-slides were superior to the audio tape only. In the second experiment, we are going to compare a single-concept film laboratory experiment versus the actual practice by the learner in the laboratory. If the students are tested with a paper and pencil test, which may or may not include visual testing, the chances are very good that you will end up with no significant differences between the two situations, and in fact, if some paper and pencil activity was involved in the viewing of the single-concept films, it would not be too difficult to prove that the students using the single-concept films were able to learn more. On the other hand, if the test used was a performance test in the lab and depending on the complexity of the laboratory experiment, it might be quite easy to prove that Group B is the superior group.

Actually, if a researcher is given his or her choice of one or more of the following four factors, it is possible to arrive at almost any result desired.

    a. **The Sample of Students.** Because individual differences among students are generally ignored, these differences can be utilized to bias the research results and no one will challenge it as long as good statistical procedures are followed.

    b. **The Topic of the Instructional Materials.** Because students interest levels are different with different subject matter areas, it is possible to select an instructional unit and a student sample such that their interaction will bias the research results in whatever direction the researcher wants.

    c. **The Competitive Media or Method Used.** Because certain media and/or methods are better suited to certain content learning experiences and/or to certain student learning styles, it is possible to bias the research results in particular directions.

    d. **The Tests Used to Obtain Data.** This is the most critical factor and is also the factor which can be manipulated the easiest in trying to obtain certain results.

Because of this potential for creating a bias in the research, the results have very limited application and utility.

4. TESTS: THE CRITICAL HIDDEN VARIABLE (GIGO)

The term "GIGO" was coined by data processing people in working with computers. Sometimes people are tempted to accept any data coming out of a computer without being concerned about the validity of the data that went into the computer. If the data put out by the computer is obviously faulty, there is a tendency to blame the computer. In defense of the computer, data processing specialists use the acronym "GIGO" which stands for *garbage in-garbage out!* If the data going into the computer is not valid, then the data coming out of the computer is also not valid. The use of very expensive and complex computers cannot change the validity of the data.

In a similar manner, in educational research, if the data to be manipulated by various statistical instruments is invalid, no matter how powerful the statistical instruments are nor how expensive and complex the computer used to carry out the necessary computations, the results are still invliad. Over the past decades, probably because the emphasis in traditional education is on the educational process rather than on the results of education, the major emphasis in educational research has been on the procedures and process of the research and particularly on the statistical instruments used rather than on the results of the research.

There are a variety of labels given to different tests, but for my purposes, labels are not as important as how the test was constructed and what is it used for. Most tests used in the educational process are self-made tests that are developed, constructed, and/or written by the teacher in the privacy of his or her own office or classroom. As I pointed out in Chapter VI, Volume II, few teachers are qualified to make tests because they have not had any training in this critical skill. Those who have had courses on traditional educational measurement are in even a worse situation because they have now been trained on how to manipulate data and/or test items to get whatever results they desire regardless of the actual learning levels of the students taking the test. These same problems are carried over into educational research although there is probably a much greater use of ready made tests in research than is used in the classroom. Supposedly, ready made tests have already been verified as being valid in terms of traditional validity whereas self-made tests are supposed to be verified in reference to its validity, reliability, etc. before being used in research.

a. CORRELATION PROBLEMS IN CONSTRUCTING EVALUATION INSTRUMENTS

The most critical problem in the development of evaluation instruments, whether used in the classroom or in educational research, is the correlation between the objectives of the learning event and the evaluation instrument. Technically, the only valid evaluation instrument is one that exactly matches the SO's of the instructional event. The further away the evaluation items are from the SO's of the instructional event, the greater the degree of GIGO and the more useless the research results. Since in traditional education it is unusual for teachers to have any SO's (specific objectives), the correlation between the evaluation items and unknown objectives is doubtful and at best is not much better than chance. Therefore, most traditional tests are constructed to give results that match the traditional view of what can be expected from a sample of students. The expectation is that the range of learning abilities in an average classroom will approximate a normal curve. As such, tests are designed to give a normal curve of results regardless of actual achievement levels. Tests constructed in accordance with these intentions are referred to as *normed* tests or as *standardized* tests. Since, at the present time, there are no agreed upon lists of *standardized* objectives, *all* normed or standardized tests have correlation problems, GIGO problems, and are of little value to educators.

In recognition of the faulty data generated by *normed* or standardized tests, some educators and researchers claim to be using *criterion* tests. Ostensibly these tests are supposed to be designed such that the evaluation items match the objectives. However, since few educators and educational researchers have had training and experience in developing SO's, correlation problems still exist even when *criterion* tests are used. For example, the National Assessment of Educational Progress (NAEP) uses what they refer to as *criterion* tests; but the evaluation items are not based on lists of SO's. The NAEP evaluation items are based on general objectives (GO's). As such, the correlation should be better than when there are no objectives at all, but since GO's do not specify what should be learned, there is still considerable latitude in the selection of the evaluation items. Consequently, the NAEP staff decided to use three categories of evaluation items: items that 90 percent of the students in the sample could get right, items that 50 percent of the students in the sample could get correct; and items that only 10 percent of the students in the sample could get correct. Because of the traditions in educational research, traditional educators see nothing wrong with selecting evaluation items that bias the results of the national assessment. It continues to amaze me however that it is considered acceptable by traditional educators to select test items because they will give certain results and then they are upset by the predetermined results. For example, if a test item is selected in the national assessment because it is expected that only 10 percent of the students in the sample will get it correct and then after the assessment it is discovered that only 11-15 percent of the students can get the item correct, no one should be surprised or upset about the low level of achievement because the test item did what it was designed to do! The problem is that although traditional educators know that these test items are selected because they reliably result in some level less than 100 percent, when they look at the results, it is somehow assumed that the students should have achieved 100 percent.

In checking research, if in the procedures it states that the test used was a normed or standardized test, you can almost automatically assume that the research is useless and invalid as far as actual achievement levels are concerned. If in the procedures it states that a criterion test was used, you have to check further. If the criterion test is based on GO's, the test is also practically useless because the results of using the test were probably designed into the test regardless of the actual achievement levels of the students in the sample. If the criterion test was developed from SO's, one would think that the test should be good. This is not necessarily the case. More often than not, the objectives that are called SO's are not actually specific and measurable. As a general rule, the more specific and measurable the objectives are (specificity is a continuum), the greater the chances are that the evaluation items have a high correlation with the objectives. Even when the objectives are specific and measurable, it is not unusual for the evaluation items not to match the SO's. Traditionally in education, it has not been thought necessary that what a teacher teaches should be the same as what the teacher tests for. In fact, it is traditionally considered bad ethics for a teacher to teach students whatever it is the teacher is going to test them on (Don't teach to the test!) After all, if a teacher taught students what was on the test, they might all learn it and deserve "A's" and then no one could be failed and the average would be an "A" or 100 percent rather than a "C" or about 70 percent achievement. Teachers actually have to be taught how to trick students and manipulate test items in order to get test results that fit the *normal curve!*

Therefore, the only way that the correlation level between the objectives and the evaluation items can be ascertained is to actually see and compare the list of objectives and the list of test items. In checking educational research, it is an extremely rare event that a list of the instructional objectives of the unit used in the research is available for inspection. Although not as rare an event as having a list of the SO's, it is still rare that a copy of the evaluation instrument is included in a report on the research. Stop and think of all the educational research you may have read. How often was a copy of the evaluation instrument included in the report? Probably not very often. Given that the list of SO's for the instructional unit used in the research is not available nor is a copy of the evaluation instrument, the value of the research can be doubted and discounted as probably being useless.

b. THE USE OF SUBJECTIVE *OBJECTIVE* TYPE TEST ITEMS

I have looked at thousands of specific objectives during the past fifteen years and it is extremely rare to find a specific objective that can be tested on a matching basis by any of the so-called objective type test items (multiple-choice, true-false, and matching). As a result, almost any test containing these types of test items can be assumed to have less than 100 percent correlation with any listed or non-listed SO's. Of the many negative aspects of objective type test items that make them unsuitable for use in an honest instructional system, the most critical is the concept of *detractors*. This concept concerns the use of words, phrases, and/or choices (in multiple choice items) which are put into the test item to either detract the student from getting the right answer or to detract the student from selecting any of the wrong answers. The use of *detractors* is partially based on the concept of selective perception in which a person sees what he or she wants to see and hears what he or she wants to hear. We do not always see and hear what is actually there. This is why students don't study very much for objective type examinations. If a student knows the content too well, he or she will fall for the detractors and make mistakes. The best way to study for an objective type examination is to study casually throughout the course and then cram just before the test and pay attention to names, dates, and other trivia. Although these test items are referred to as objective type test items, they are only objective from the point of view of scoring or grading. A professional test item writer can take almost any multiple choice item and by keeping the stem and the correct choice constant, he or she can vary the detractors and wrong choices in such ways as to get almost any percentage of students to answer the item correctly (from almost zero to almost 100%). This fact reveals that the writing of the so-called objective type test item is very subjective. and what makes it worse is that the subjectivity is hidden and in most cases the degree of subjectivity is unknown. In looking at the distribution of scores resulting from a so-called objective type test, remember that the distribution is more affected by the person or persons who made up the test than by what the population taking the test knows about what is supposedly being tested by the test. In other words, the author or authors of objective type tests knowingly or unknowingly have already built into the test the distribution of scores before the students even take the examination. In fact, when the results of an objective type test fit the previously specified distribution (such as a *normal* curve), it is called a valid test.

In checking educational research reports, if in the procedures it states that the so-called *objective* type test items were used in the test from which the data was derived (particularly if the items are multiple-choice items), there is little value in reading the rest of the report. The test items most likely do not match the SO's (if there are any specified) and the results of the data have been biased by the writer of the items regardless of the actual achievement levels of the students. Educational research results which are based on data from objective type test items are examples of GIGO and are practically useless.

c. PERCENTAGE OF TEST ITEMS CORRECT NOT NECESSARILY EQUAL TO PERCENTAGE OF OBJECTIVES ACHIEVED

Given the traditional situation where there are generally no objectives, the above statement translates into *the percentage of test items correct is not necessarily equal to the percentage of different test items correct.* In other words, there could be four types of test items on a test and different quantities of each type on the same test (see Figure 138). In designing the test, the same four test item types could be included but the percentage of each type could vary and could affect the results in the form of a total score. For example, if type I test item

	TEST ITEM TYPE	NO. OF ITEMS
	I	15
	II	10
	III	5
	IV	2
Totals	4 types	32 types

Figure 138 — Test Item Type vs. No. of Items

was found to be easy and type III was found to be difficult, and a researcher wanted the students to score high, the researcher would use more type I items and fewer type III items. If the researcher wanted the students to score low, the researcher would use more type III items and fewer type I items. All four types of test items would be in both tests yet the results would be considerably different without really changing the level of the student's achievement of the four types of test items.

In reference to specific objectives and matching test items, it is important to remember that there are two basic types of objectives: rote memory or factual objectives and process or thinking objectives. As far as rote memory objectives are concerned, there is only one test item that will test for the achievement of a rote memory objective. Therefore, the percentage of test items correct is equal to the percentage of rote memory objectives achieved. In reference to process objectives, if there is only one test item for each process objective, then the percentage of test items correct is equal to the percentage of process objectives achieved. However, seldom will a concerned educator accept achievement or non-achievement of a process objective on the basis of a student's performance on one test item. As such, most tests of the learning of process objectives include two or more test items which are testing the same objective. Consequently, the percentage of test items correct is not equal to the percentage of process objectives achieved (except where there is an equal number of test items used to test for the achievement of each process objectives). Given that a student might understand and has achieved a process objective, it might be possible for the student to make a computational or some other error in one problem out of five (80 percent of test items correct) but a teacher might consider that the student has achieved 100 percent of the SO.

In Figure 139, the criteria for evaluation is 80 percent of the test items. Where this criteria is applied to a test which is testing for the achievement of multiple process objectives (five in this case), it is possible

SO's	Total No. of Test Items	80% of Test Items	A 20% of SO's	B 40% of SO's	C 60% of SO's	D 80% of SO's	E 100% of SO's
I	25	20	25	19	17	10	20
II	20	16	15	15	13	20	16
III	15	12	10	11	15	15	12
IV	10	8	7	10	10	10	8
V	5	4	3	5	5	5	4
	75	60	60	60	60	60	60

Figure 139 — 80 Percent of Test Items Does Not Necessarily Mean 80 Percent of SO's

to have a wide variation in the achievement of the objectives. To be sure that the students were not just lucky in answering one test item for each SO, the teacher in this example made up 25 test items to test the first SO, 20 test items to test the second SO, 15 test items to test the third SO, 10 test items to test the fourth SO, and five test items to test the fifth SO (see Figure 139). If there are 75 test items in a test which is being used to test for the achievement of five SO's and the criteria for successful achievement is 80 percent, this would allow a student to miss any 15 items. Depending on which 15 test items are missed, it would be possible to have 20 percent, 40 percent, 60 percent, 80 percent, or 100 percent achievement of the SO's and still stay within the specified criteria for evaluation of the *test items*. In applying the 80 percent criteria to each of the five SO's, the student would have to achieve at least 20 out of the 25 test items for SO I, at least 16 out of the 20 test items for SO II, at least 12 out of the 15 test items for SO III, at least eight out of the 10 test items for SO IV, and at least four out of the five test items for SO V.

In Column "A", the 15 test items that were missed were spread through SO's II, III, IV, and V such that the student was able to achieve the 80 percent criterion only one SO or 20 percent of the SO's.

In column "B", the 15 test items that were missed were spread through SO's I, II, and III such that the student was able to achieve the 80 percent criterion in only two SO's or 40 percent of the SO's.

In column "C", the 15 test items that were missed were spread through SO's I and II such that the student was able to achieve the 80 percent criterion in only three SO's or 60 percent of the SO's.

In column "D", the 15 test items that were missed were only in SO I such that the student was able to achieve the 80 percent criterion in only four SO's or 80 percent of the SO's.

In Column "E", the 15 test items that were missed were spread through all five SO's such that the student was able to achieve the 80 percent criterion in all five SO's or 100 percent of the SO's.

In Figure 140, the criteria for evaluation is 80 percent of the SO's. Where this criteria is applied to multiple process SO's being tested simultaneously, it is possible to have a wide variation in the number of

		80% of	80 Percent of SO's Achieved				
SO's	No. of Items	Test Items	SO-I Missed	SO-II Missed	SO-III Missed	SO-IV Missed	SO-V Missed
I	25	20	0-19	20-25	20-25	20-25	20-25
II	20	16	16-20	0-15	16-20	16-20	16-20
III	15	12	12-15	12-15	0-11	12-15	12-15
IV	10	8	8-10	8-10	8-10	0-7	8-10
V	5	4	4-5	4-5	4-5	4-5	0-3
	75	60	40-69 53%-92%	44-70 59%-93%	48-71 64%-95%	52-72 69%-96%	56-73 75%-97%

Figure 140 — 80 Percent of SO's Does Not Necessarily Mean 80 Percent of Test Items

test items correct. In the example used in Figure 140, 80 percent achievement of the five SO's means that one of the SO's can be missed. Depending upon which SO is missed, 80 percent achievement of the SO's could be met while at the same time achieving from 53-92 percent of the test items if SO-I is missed, achieving from 59-93 percent of the test items if SO-II is missed, achieving from 64-95 percent of the test items if SO-III is missed, achieving from 69-96 percent of the test items if SO-IV is missed, and achieving from 75-97 percent of the test items is SO-V is missed.

In the traditional educational setting where specific objectives are not usually identified and test items testing the same behavior are not grouped or identified as being essentially the same and scores on the tests are usually cumulative scores covering the whole test, the problems indicated in Figures 139 and 140 still exist but are usually hidden and any negative results are ultimately blamed on genetics, home environment, etc. rather than on a lack of the testmaker's knowledge about the relationship between objectives and test items. For example, in a class of 30 students being taught in a traditional manner, there will be about 20 students who will get "C" grades. If the "C" grade represents a score of about 70 percent of the test, the 30 percent that each of the 20 students missed is assumed to be the same. However, it would be a rare event if all 20 students missed exactly the same test items. A more likely result would be that all of the items that were missed by the 20 students collectively would be the total test. In other words, each test item would probably be missed by one or more students. (Remember, under the traditional approach, a test item that most or all of the students know is considered a bad item because it doesn't discriminate and is usually dropped — even if it is important!) In actuality, the 30 percent that each of the 20 students missed is different from the 30 percent that any one of the other students missed. Among the 20 students, there are probably one or more students whose 30 percent missed is like column "E" in Figure 139 in which there is little, if any, cumulative ignorance developed. Among the same 20 students, there are probably one or more students whose 30 percent missed is similar to columns "A", "B", "C", and "D" in Figure 139. Consequently, in not recognizing the relationship between objectives and test items, even though their scores might be the same, the amount of cumulative ignorance that each student takes with him or her could vary from practically nothing to involving the non-learning of over a majority of the course objectives. This particular point challenges the validity of almost every letter grade given in the traditional educational setting and of almost all educational research in which the data to be statistically manipulated comes from tests.

d. THE INVALIDITY OF STANDARDIZED (NORMED) TESTS

Because few educators are actually involved in the preparation of standardized tests and even those that are or have been involved probably didn't actually realize what they were doing, it is important to review how standardized tests are developed particularly since a lot of educational research data comes from the use of standardized (normed) tests. (This topic is covered in more detail in Chapter VI, Volume II). The actual development of standardized tests generally consists of three steps: the development or collection of potential test items; the elimination of items which do not discriminate very well; and the validation of the remaining test items such that the results of using these items on a random group (sample) of students will fit some kind of predetermined curve. For example, see Figure 141, Column A represents the first step of developing or collecting a thousand possible test items. These items could be intended to test students' achievement of a specific course or a sequence of courses or, over a period of time, the students' achievement of a total curriculum. Column B represents the second step in which the thousand test items are tried out on representative samples

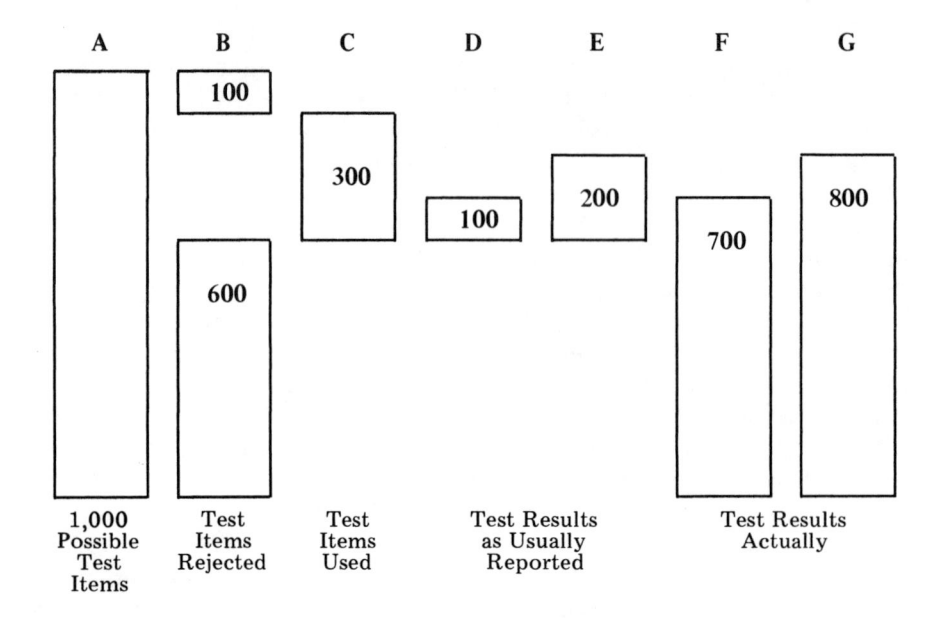

```
    A       B        C        D        E        F        G
           100
                    300
                            100      200             800
                                              700
           600
  1,000   Test     Test   Test Results      Test Results
 Possible Items    Items  as Usually         Actually
   Test   Rejected Used   Reported
   Items
```

Figure 141 — Development of Standardized Tests and the Interpretation of the Results

of students. In professional testing circles, test items that approximately 65% or more of the population taking the test answer correctly are considered not very good items because they don't *discriminate*. At the other extreme, test items that approximately 35% or less of the population taking the test answer correctly are also considered to be not very good items because they don't *discriminate*. The best test items in professional testing circles are ones in which from 35% to 65% of the population taking the test answer them correctly. These test items are considered good *discriminators*, and when used with a normally distributed group of students (according to ability) then the results of the test should approximate a normal probability curve (bell curve). By including more of the items that most students can answer correctly, the resulting curve will have a positive skew to it (the hump in the curve will shift towards the high end and make most of the students taking the test look good). By including more of the items that most students can't answer correctly, the resulting curve will have a negative skew to it (the hump in the curve will shift towards the low end and make most of the students taking the test look bad).

During the process of the second step in the example illustrated in Figure 141 (assuming a normal curve of results is desired), it is discovered that all or most of the students can answer about 600 of the items correctly, and that very few, if any, students can answer another 100 of the items. Consequently, these two groups of items are eliminated from the potential standardized test because they do not discriminate between students. Column C represents the remaining 300 test items which are now refined such that the results of using these items on any sample of students fits the desired curve. This refinement is accomplished by changes in the wording in the test items such that a few more students will get it wrong or a few more students will get it correct. The very process of refining the test items in order to get a certain percentage of students who can answer them correctly is proof that the items are very subjective. In reference to Columns A, B, and C, consider the following three questions:

> Column A — Remembering that the primary criterion for selection of items was that they discriminate and a secondary criterion that the test items are easy to grade or score, what if very few of the test items represent important learning objectives?

> Column B — Remembering that the criterion for elimination of the test items is based on the fact that too many students can answer the item, or not very many students can answer the item, what if those items which were eliminated represent critical learning objectives?

> Column C — Remembering that the remaining items to be used in the test are selected because of their ability to discriminate, what if these items are able to discriminate better than the items which were eliminated because the items concern trivia or irrelevant content, which about 50 percent of the students won't bother to try to learn?

Columns D and E indicate possible test results when this hypothetical standardized test is used with two students, two classes, two schools, two different school districts, etc. In Column D, the student or students who took this test averaged only 100 test items answered correctly. In Column E the student or students who took this test had an average of 200 correct test items. Usually, the results of the use of this standardized test would be reported in such a way that the student or students represented in Column E have learned twice as much as the student or students represented in Column D, which has been the case in many instances in our country. Results of standardized tests have been used as the basis for millions of dollars in changes in curriculum materials and even in some instances the firing of superintendents, principals, teachers, or even the replacement of some school board members. The results of the comparison of the two students, two schools, etc., as represented by Columns D and E are a mirage. Remember, the test items which are used are those which emphasize discrimination between students, so the test results exaggerate the differences. The student or school represented by Column E is not twice as good or 100 percent better than the student or school represented by Column D. How about the 600 items in Column B which were eliminated because most or all of the students knew those items? A more realistic comparison of the two students or schools would be Columns F and G, which now only represent a 14 percent difference, rather than a 100 percent difference. In some standardized tests, the original population of test items could consist of thousands of items. As long as the makers of the test can eliminate the non-discriminating test items in order to magnify the differences, it would be possible for an apparent 100% difference in test scores to actually be only a few percent difference if the total original population of test items were used. With reference to Column A in Table I, most testing companies would try to insist that most or all of the original group of 1000 test items are important. If that was true, then it is very possible that some of the items eliminated in Column B actually were important. Representatives of testing companies that prepare standardized tests insist that not many important items are eliminated. In other words, out of the original 1000 test items, the remaining 300 which are used in the final test are the best discriminators and also the most important. If this was truly the situation, then the student who only got 100 test items right on the test should be taught the remaining 200 items and the student who got 200 test items right should be taught the remaining 100 items in order that they both can learn *all 300 of the professed important items.* In actuality, the students wouldn't be taught the items they missed because that would ruin the curve and invalidate the test. That's why standardized tests are hidden from teachers and students. If these tests actually tested for the achievement of identified important learning objectives, then teachers could teach the students what was on the tests and a good result would be when all students achieve 100 percent of what professional educators and test makers believe to be important.

If it is reasonable to assume or to expect that test items important enough to use in tests, to use for assigning labels (slow learner, mentally retarded, high achiever, etc.), and to influence the spending of thousands and perhaps millions of educational dollars should be highly correlated with important objectives, then notice that although there are standardized achievement tests used at almost all levels of traditional education and for professional certification, there are no comparable lists of standardized objectives. Therefore, the results of the use of traditional standardized tests are meaningless and of little value in education.

Because of the arbitrary concept of validity, a whole mythology has been built up by the standardized testing companies and spread throughout the traditional education scene that it is bad to *teach to the test*. Consider for a moment — if a test really tests what it is that you want students to learn, what is wrong with teaching students what you want them to learn. On the other hand, if the test doesn't really test what you want the students to learn, then it would be wrong to teach what you don't want them to learn (the test) but it would also be wrong to use the test since it doesn't test for the achievement of important things.

In professional careers in which the key to practice the profession is dependent on passing standardized objective type examinations, unique and potentially tragic results can occur to the aspiring professional and the professional's future clients. The test items in the standardized tests rarely correlate very highly with the desired real world behavior. Consider the following:

- Doctors — has any doctor performed heart surgery and after opening the chest cavity found a multiple-choice item written on the faulty heart?

- Dentists — has any dentist drilled out a cavity and found a multiple-choice item written in the bottom of the hole?

- Nurses — has any nurse ever found a multiple-choice item written on the face of a patient?

- Cosmetologists — has any beautician ever found a multiple-choice item written on the scalp of a client?

- Pilots — has any pilot ever found a multiple-choice item suddenly appearing on the windshield when a flight problem occurs?

The learned behavior of answering multiple choice items is useless as the items never appear in the same form again in the professional world. The defense used by many national organizations is that they are testing for minimum safety standards for the professional and his or her client. In the case of nursing, there are approximately 900 points in the Board tests. If asked, the State and National Boards will claim that all 900 points are important. *NOTICE:* nurses are allowed to practice even though they only have to achieve a score of about 350 points out of the 900 points. How dare the nursing associations allow these nurses to go out and practice knowing that they only know approximately a random one-third of the so-called minimum safety standards. If the tests really tested for minimum safety standards, a nurse achieving 898 points should have to learn the other missing two points. Of course, it would then be appropriate to let the nursing schools and the students know what they should know in order to be safe. But if they were allowed to see the tests, the nursing schools might teach the minimum safety standards by design and all nurses might be successful —*What a tragic happening?* Of course, the saving grace of the situation is that almost all of the objective type test items are irrelevant so not knowing them doesn't really hurt. What could cause trouble is that since the tests don't really test what is important for the professional to know, then no one really knows if the professionals are actually qualified to deal professionally with their clients.

In a situation where the outside tests which are used to evaluate achievement don't correlate very well with the desired objectives and are also irrelevant, the professional schools are met with four options.

1. Teach and test in preparation for the outside tests and overlook teaching and testing what is important for the professional to know and do. In this case, most or all students would pass the tests but would not be able to perform adequately as a professional.

2. Teach and test what is important for the professional to know and do and overlook the teaching and testing of the students on how to cope with the standardized tests. In this case, the students might make great professionals, but most of them would never get a chance to practice because they wouldn't be able to pass the standardized tests.

3. The third option, is the one most professional schools choose. In this option, they teach what they think the students need to know and do as professionals, but test in a fashion that trains the students to prepare for the standardized tests. The problems with this option is that the schools still have not tested the students' achievement of what is important for the professional to know and do and in testing in a fashion similar to the standardized tests, they are testing for the achievement of something they haven't taught and hence is unfair!

4. The fourth option is the one I recommend for use in all professional schools until something is done to increase the correlation between important professional objectives and the standardized tests. This option is more time consuming and expensive, but it is the only safe alternative for the aspiring professional and his or her future clients. Under this option, the schools would teach and test for the achievement of important professional objectives and they also would have crash sessions where they would teach and test the students on how to beat the irrelevant objective type standardized examinations.!

The low correlation between certification examinations and critical professional learning objectives during past decades may well be the basis for the increasing number of professional malpractice suits which in turn increase the costs of malpractice insurance. Once professional groups identify the minimum common core SO's needed to be a professional, it may be possible for professionals who can prove they have achieved 100 percent of these minimum common core SO's to be granted a special discount on their malpractice insurance rates. The precedent has already been set as students who have a "B" average or better can get a discount on their automobile insurance.

In view of these problems, consider the latest report on the evaluation of performance contracts released by the office of Economic Opportunity (OEO). The latest results indicate no significant differences in achievement between students in the performance contract and students not in the contract. This should not be very surprising because in the summer of 1970, John O. Wilson, OEO's Assistant Director of Planning, Research and Evaluation, was quoted as saying:

> in order to prevent a repetition of the Texarkana experience (Dorsett was accused of teaching to the test), safeguards will be built into the system and a large enough variety of tests will be used to make it all but IMPOSSIBLE for a company (or a teacher) to TEACH TO THE TEST!

Obviously, the results indicate that OEO's evaluation of performance contracts was successful in using tests which tested for the achievement of things that neither the companies having the contracts nor the teachers not under the performance contracts were able to identify. What the results really indicate is that when teachers (or companies) don't know what the tests are supposed to be testing for, the students probably won't show much achievement of the hidden content. Educators, have known for decades that the easiest way to fail students (discredit a teacher — or companies in this case) is to test the students for achievement of something you know they don't know.

Since very few teachers (and researchers) have identified exactly what it is that students should have been learning in their classes and very few teachers (and researchers) know or have identified what learning objectives the standardized tests are testing for the achievement of, neither the teachers nor researchers are able to identify the correlation, if any, between the classroom learning objectives and the learning objectives implied by the items on the standardized tests. Therefore, research of the type where student learning is the dependent variable and the data is derived from standardized tests should be considered practically worthless and not applicable to the classroom environment. This includes almost all of the research data used by Coleman in his study *Equality of Educational Opportunity* and reused by Jencks in his study *Inequality: A Reassessment of the Effect of*

Family and Schooling in America. It is very easy to prove that schools have minimal effect on student learning when the tests used to measure the level of learning have little correlation with what is being taught and achieved in the schools and the teacher's role emphasizes teaching (the presenting of the content of the course) rather than learning.

B. THE ROLE OF INSTRUCTIONAL RESEARCH IN THE BEHAVIORAL LEARNING SYSTEMS APPROACH TO INSTRUCTION

Four major factors worked together to make most traditional educational research invalid and practically useless: the role of the teacher as a presenter of course content (regardless of student learning); not really knowing what it is that the students should have learned; students' learning abilities have been and are considered to be primarily a result of genetic influences (a normal curve's worth of achievement is normal); and the use of statistical methods which are invalid because of the invalid data. Because of any one or more of these factors, most traditional educational research has ended up with no significant differences among the various methods, media, or instructional materials and, in fact, tended to indicate that even schools and teachers didn't and couldn't make much difference in student learning. In contrast, under the Behavioral Learning Systems Approach to Instruction (BLSA), variations of these same factors could become very important in proving that designed instruction can make a difference in student learning.

In traditional research of the type where the teacher in face-to-face instruction is compared to a variety of other presentation modes, it is assumed that if the competitive mode is as good as or better than the teacher that the teacher will or should be *replaced.* Since most of this type of research ends up with no significant differences, it shouldn't be any wonder that teachers, fearing replacement, are against most modern media and modes of instruction. Under the BLSA, the primary role for the teacher is not to present course content. The teacher's primary role is to identify what should be learned, to diagnose student learning needs, and to prescribe appropriate learning experiences which will facilitate student learning. This new role also includes the identification and solving of student learning problems such that 90 percent or more of the students learn 100 percent of the required SO's. Research in these situations would be of the type where a method, media, or instructional mode is used by itself as the only presenting mode and compared to the same method, media, or instructional mode used as the primary presenting mode plus the teacher who fills in where the primary mode is not successful and/or uses whatever other modes will solve the students learning problems and facilitates learning. Although the comparison of the presentation mode vs. presentation mode plus a teacher is a non-science because it concerns man-made modes, the criteria that the teacher has to work with the students until 90 percent or more of them learn 100 percent of the instructional objectives of the unit helps to keep the research as a science because the emphasis is on producing a certain level of learning (a natural phenomenon). Obviously, because of the higher standard of achievement, the teacher plus the instructional mode should always be significantly better in producing learning than the instructional mode by itself.

In traditional research and traditional education where it is considered normal to not know specifically what students should learn and to have only accidental or chance commonality among similar courses (usually in name only), the emphasis is on the tests and test results and changes in data are more apt to be a result of manipulating the tests and test items than a result of changes in learning or of more effective teaching (remember teachers are not supposed to teach what is to be tested on the test). Given these conditions, it should not be surprising that traditional research is of little value to classroom teachers and any research which might be of value in one classroom is not necessarily of value in other classrooms because of the lack of commonality among classrooms as to what students should be learning. Under the BLSA where the emphasis is on learning, it is critical to not only identify specifically what students are supposed to learn but to identify levels of commonality (national, state, local, etc.) in SO's among courses with similar names. In this way, not only can the results of research on a learning problem be useful to a single classroom, but also to all classrooms that have the same basic commonality of SO's.

In traditional research and in traditional education where individual differences among students are generally ignored, it is assumed that most student differences in achievement are a result of differences in genetics or external (to the school) environmental conditions and it is also assumed that teachers and schools can't make a difference in students' learning. As such, most tests are designed to give a normal curve of results regardless of what students actually know. Since the normal curve is based on *chance*, it shouldn't be surprising that the results of these tests indicate that teachers and schools don't make a difference. Under BLSA, it is assumed that students are all different with respect to how they learn best and it is also assumed that if a teacher varies the learning pathways to fit the students abilities, that most students can learn the required SO's. In addition, it is assumed that student learning abilities are not static, but dynamic and as such, can be changed. Consequently, in the process of solving a learning problem the teacher as an Instructioneer may vary the learning pathway (not the SO's) to fit the learning abilities of the student or could put the student in a special instructional unit which would be designed to increase the student's learning abilities so that the student could learn from available materials or the teacher as an Instructioneer might do a little of both: change the learning environment and change the student's learning abilities. Whereas traditional research keeps reaffirming the *chance* relationship (normal curve) between teachers, the learning environment, and student learning, research under the BLSA will not only show a direct casual relationship between teachers, the learning environment, and student learning, but it will also show that if individual differences in learning abilities (how something is learned not what or how much can be learned) are recognized and responded to, 90 percent or more of our students can learn 100 percent of the required SO's in whatever courses the students take. In addition, the new direction in instructional research will aid in helping the instructional process become more efficient after it has proven that the new instructional process (BLSA) can be very effective.

In the belief that abilities are primarily and to a great extent genetic, research that identifies levels of various abilities at different ages to set norms (like I.Q. tests) is considered to be useful in further identifying students who have abilities which are at levels above or below the *norms*. On the other hand, in the belief that abilities are made up of two parts — nature and nurture — and that the natural or genetic contribution is a *tendency* rather than an actually developed ability, if an ability is not nurtured, then the natural tendency is not given a chance to develop. Since few abilities are actually taught by design, what is being developed and measured are abilities that have developed by chance. As a consequence, the norms which have been established are useful if we want to continue to assume that students will develop their abilities by chance and that little or nothing will be done by design to aid the students in this development.

I don't think that this assumption can be made, so research in identifying different abilities is useful if instruction is then going to be designed to *nurture* the students' abilities. If not, research of this type is useless. Research in the identification of norms under various conditions of *nurturing* the abilities may be useful in identifying various ways and advantages of these ways in *nurturing;* but research in the identification of norms under conditions of chance development has little if any value.

Again, the major effort of instructional research concerning abilities should be to specify a certain level of an ability and research how different students can be instructed to achieve this level. The solving of learning problems is the science of instruction because it is the study of a natural phenomenon (the learning of the ability).

Instead of concentrating efforts on identifying differences in students, research in instructional science should concentrate on the different instructional techniques, media, materials, etc. necessary to eliminate the differences in students' achievement of the minimum common core SO's).

In traditional research, the major emphasis has been on the use of statistical instruments and methods almost regardless of the validity of the data. The development of *normed or standardized* tests and even some of the new pseudo-criterion tests such as the national and state assessment tests are primarily affected by manipulation of the format and design of the test items in order to get desired results rather than reflecting the actual achievement levels of students with reference to a desired list of SO's. The new direction of instructional research as suggested herein places an emphasis on the validity of the data as reflecting actual learning levels of desired SO's. Changes in data should reflect changes in actual learning of students rather than just changes in test item design.

1. MODES OF RESEARCH

As I see it, there are essentially three modes of research which are followed in the study of learning related activities: first, there is research which emphasizes observation of events and activities without trying to control or manipulate what is being observed; second, there is research in which the emphasis is on the controls or manipulations as the independent variables and learning as the dependent variable; and third, there is the new research in which the emphasis is on the results or learning as the independent variable or constant which is produced by various controls or manipulations of the environment as the dependent variables.

The first type of research is typical of a lot of learning theory research in which children and students are observed in the process of learning by chance and then theories are advanced as to how the learning took place within the child or learner. Learning theories based on observations of learning without any controls or design affecting what is being learned or how something is being learned is only of value in situations in which learning takes place primarily by chance. As such, these learning theories are of little value to classroom teachers who should be trying to help students learn by design. Since the arguments and debates among the learning theorists primarily concerns their opinions or theories of what is happening internally in the learners, there is little chance for agreement. Personally, I think that if most of these learning theorists whose theories are primarily based on observations were watching the same group of children through one-way mirrors, they would all claim that what each one was seeing supported his theory (probably affected by selective perception).

The second type of research is typical of almost all educational research in which the emphasis is on the controls, i.e., one method versus another method. Theories are then generated on the basis of how certain controls affect learning or the behavior of the learner. Research in this mode is designed to answer questions of the type, *How well did this treatment do?*, *Is this treatment better than some other treatment?*, etc. Where the emphasis is on the controls or treatments, the research is usually carried out regardless of any relationship to what students should be learning, what the students want to learn, who the students are, and what their learning abilities are. As stated earlier, this type of research is not a science because what is being studied, the treatments, are man made. The *golden pot* at the end of this type of *rainbow* research is that one method, media, etc. which will be best for all learners. Obviously, this type of research ignores individual differences among students in their learning abilities (best ways for learning) and among teachers in their teaching abilities (best ways for teaching). This type of research also assumes a normal curve's worth of *limits* of the learners' abilities and the tests are designed to give results that support the existence of these perceived limits. Learning is treated as a dependent variable and rarely do any of the test items match a list of desired SO's. As such, this type of research is also of little value to the classroom teacher or Instructioneer. In fact, given that a classroom teacher wants or is expected to end up with a normal curve of achievement among a class of students and given that there is a normal curve of abilities to learn represented in the class, the best way to get a normal curve of achievement is to not teach at all. Let learning take place by chance. After all, if the teacher started to *teach*, students who weren't supposed to learn might make it (because of the teacher).

The third type of research is similar to some of the behavior modification research in that a given behavior is desired and the research is aimed at finding out what treatment or series of treatments will bring about the desired behavior. In changing the emphasis from teaching or treatments to *learning*, the emphasis also changes from research on teaching or treatments to research on learning. In this type of research, learning is the constant or independent variable and the dependent variables are time, methods, materials, etc.

In most institutions where research is done, there are two divisions of research: basic research and applied research. Basic research is supposed to be concerned with the development of principles, rules, theories, etc. which are then used as guidelines for the applied research which is supposed to be concerned with finding solutions to practical problems in the real world. However, both basic and applied research have to have a common thread of some kind. Basic research can not be concerned with teaching while applied research is concerned with learning or vice versa because the principles and theories developed in the basic research would be inappropriate for use as guidelines for applied research. Therefore, in order for instructional research to be of value, both the basic and applied research have to deal with increasing or facilitating learning. Basic instructional research could be in terms of general statements regarding the identification of different cognitive, affective, and sensory learning styles and approximate percentages of various student populations (identified by a variety of characteristics) which learn best with what style. Basic research could also be concerned with general statements regarding what instructional environments (methods, materials, and facilities) and what consequences or motivations tend to help learning for what kinds of learners with what kinds of learning styles. Applied research should always be related to the learning of certain SO's and GO's. Obviously, for the applied research to be of value, then the GO's and SO's used in the research should be the same as those used by learners in the classroom and the more learners that need to learn the GO's and SO's, the greater the applicability of the research. As such, most applied research will deal with the learning of identified minimum common core SO's and particularly those that most students are having trouble learning.

a. THEORIES OF INSTRUCTION AND INSTRUCTIONAL RESEARCH

As pointed out in Chapter IV, Volume I, and Chapter VI, Volume II, the main reason that no one has developed a theory of instruction before is that they were looking for one theory which would act as a guideline in all instructional situations. Since learning in the cognitive and sensory domains is brought about differently than learning in the affective domain, no one theory will work. However, two theories of instruction will work. The basic guidelines of both theories are the same but the application of each theory is different in two respects.

The two critical differences between the two theories of instruction is that whereas learning in the cognitive and sensory domains can be accomplished on a direct basis and is individualized in order to get 100 percent achievement, learning in the affective domain can only be accomplished on an indirect basis and is group oriented because it is probably not possible to get 100 percent achievement of affective objectives by all or even most students.

NOTE: For those readers who are interested in a more detailed discussion of the two theories of instruction, see Chapter IV, Volume I. For those readers who are interested in a more detailed discussion of the differences among the three domains of learning, see Chapter VI, Volume II.

Ideally, it would be great if through research we could find out some way of optimizing each of the some 80 different learning variables (identified by Guilford) for each student. The problem is that the various combinations of these variables would result in the need for an almost infinite variety of learning pathways for each SO and related GO. Practically, the medical approach is probably the most effective and efficient way to go. Just as the doctor develops a hierarchy of treatments for each health problem, the Instructioneer should also develop a hierarchy of treatments for each instructional unit. In action, the Instructioneer would use first that treatment which according to experience and/or research seems to work with the most students in learning the GO's and SO's of the unit. In the event of non-achievement, the Instructioneer would then try the next most successful treatment and if that one doesn't work then the Instructioneer would try the next most successful treatment, etc. until the desired learning takes place. As suggested earlier, a given treatment might be different materials, methods, or environments or it could consist of increasing the learner's learning abilities in order to learn from some other common treatment. Just as medical research has found that certain types of treatments will work especially well or not at all for certain types of people, instructional research could provide some general guidelines to the Instructioneer so that instead of using each treatment in the hierarchy of successful treatments, the Instructioneer will be able to skip over some treatments which have been identified as not working for certain kinds of learners or will be able to go directly to some treatments which have been identified as being particularly effective for certain kinds of learners. The major point to keep in mind is that almost all students can learn 100 percent of required SO's if the teachers are willing to take into consideration all of the relevant learning variables for each student.

2. INSTRUCTIONAL DESIGN EVALUATION: A NEW TOOL FOR RESEARCH

Under the traditional approach to education, the design, if any, was to help a group or class of students end up with varying degrees of achievement. Ideally, the achievement levels of the students would match a normal curve. Even the dictionary defines the word *educate* as:

> to develop by fostering to varying degrees the growth or expansion of knowledge, wisdom, desirable qualities of the mind or character, physical health, or general competence especially by a course of formal study.

As mentioned already, given that students are already different, the best way to achieve a variation in achievement is to ignore individual differences and treat all students as if they were the same. However, if a teacher wants to be a professional, the teacher cannot ignore individual differences and has to become concerned about high standards of achievement. As such, designed instruction should be the emphasis of professional teachers rather than *chance* education. In order to have designed instruction, the following conditions have to be met:

    a. the objectives to be learned during the instructional event have to be specified;

    b. the evaluation of the achievement of the objectives has to have a 100 percent correlation with the SO's;

    c. if any learners who are going to take the instructional unit are not prepared to start the instructional event (lack prerequisite knowledge or skills) appropriate supplementary instructional units have to be given to the learners until such time as they are prepared to start the regular unit;

    d. if any learners who are going to take the instructional unit have already learned any part of the instructional unit, they should be allowed to skip over the known parts provided they prove that they already have achieved 100 percent of the SO's in those parts;

    e. any instructional materials used in the instructional event should have been previously tried out on representative samples of learners and have proven their effectiveness in helping learners learn one or more of the SO's of the instructional event; and

    f. the manager, teacher, or Instructioneer of the instructional event upon identifying an instance of non-learning will vary the instructional materials, methods, and/or environment until he or she finds the combination which will enable the learner to achieve 100 percent of the SO's of the instructional event.

For decades in education, the emphasis in educational research has been on trying to find significant differences between the pretest and posttest of one method or between the posttests of two or more different methods. Most critiques of this type of research were based on what the degree of *significance* was and the power and reliability of the statistics used in the research design. Not much attention has been paid to the instructional situation and the test design from which all the data was obtained. Significant differences are almost meaningless if the research data comes from a comparison between a pretest and posttest of the same instructional unit or between a control group who were not instructed at all versus an experimental group who were instructed. It is possible to have significant differences in achievement and the instructional unit could still be ineffective and inefficient.

A more important way to look at research data is to examine the instructional situation from three new points of view: The Boredom Factor, the Instructional Effectiveness Factor, and the Instructional Efficiency Factor. Assuming that the test is designed to test for the achievement of what is covered in the instructional materials, then the higher the pretest scores, the more bored the students will be during the instructional process. Under the concept of individualized instruction, students should start an instructional unit from a point which would minimize any overlap in learning and yet not have any gaps in learning. Therefore, the ideal pretest score should be between zero and 10 percent or an average of five percent. Pretest scores that are higher than this indicates a strong possibility that boredom will contaminate the student's motivation to learn from the instructional materials and in turn also contaminate any research based on the use of the instructional materials. In order to calculate the *Boredom Factor*, divide the pretest score (in terms of percentage) by five (the ideal percentage). For example, in a particular research design, the average pretest score was 18 out of a possible 40. Eighteen is 45 percent of 40 and when 45 is devided by five (45/5) the result is a Boredom Factor of nine which is nine times higher than it should be if boredom is to be minimized. Obviously, a pretest score of 45 percent indicates that almost half of the time the students are involved in the instructional process they are in a non-learning and potentially boring situation.

The second factor is based on the posttest score and concerns the effectiveness of the instructional design. Obviously, if the instructional design is so haphazard that the average learner is only learning "C" (70-85 percent), "D" (60-69 percent), of "F" worth (below 60 percent) of what there is to learn in the instructional unit, then this weakness could very easily contaminate the utility of any data for research. Ideally, a good instructional unit should be effective enough so that students should learn between 90-100 percent of the objectives of the unit with an average of 95 percent. Therefore, the Instructional Effectiveness Factor is the posttest score (in percentage) divided by 95. For example, if in a given research, the average posttest score was 26 out of a possible score of 40 or 65 percent, this would result in an Instructional Effectiveness Factor of 65/95 or .68 which even under normal grading curves is "D" achievement. Consequently, any instructional unit that is so badly designed that the average student only achieves "D" worth of the unit objectives is bound to affect the value of the research data in a negative way. As a general rule, the higher the Instructional Effectiveness Factor, the greater the number of students who are achieving 100 percent of the desired GO's and SO's of the instructional materials and the greater the possibility of the materials being useful as a basic or initial pathway for learning.

NOTE: Remember, instructional materials which may have a high Boredom Factor and a low Instructional Effectiveness Factor for a general student audience could have a low Boredom Factor and a high Instructional Effectiveness Factor for a specific group of low achievers. As such, instructional materials which may be inappropriate as an initial or basic pathway could be useful as an alternate pathway for certain groups of low or non-achieving students.

The third factor is based on the efficiency of the instructional unit and concerns the minimizing of the Boredom Factor and the maximizing of the Instructional Effectiveness Factor. In other words, the ideal instructional unit should have pretest scores between zero and 10 percent and posttest scores between 90 and 100 percent which would result in an average gain of 90 percent (from 5 percent to 95 percent). To determine the Instructional Efficiency Factor, divide the percentage gain of an instructional unit (posttest score minus the pretest score) by 90 percent. For example, in the research cited for the first two factors, where the average posttest score was 26 and the average pretest score was 18, the average gain was 8 or 20 percent (8/40). In this case, the Instructional Efficiency Factor is 20/90 or .22 which is so inefficient, it couldn't help but contaminate the learning situation. The research cited as an example to illustrate the three factors is typical of what should be referred to as GIGO. The data resulting from the use of the instructional unit is so contaminated because the unit was boring, ineffective, and inefficient that the data should be considered *garbage* and consequently, any statistical data resulting from the manipulation of this data is also *garbage*. Oddly enough, this same data resulted in significant differences between the pretest and posttest and as such was published in a professional journal as respectable research.

In examining the results of using tailor-made or ready-made instructional materials or in examining instructional research (and particularly educational research), check the following before making your own conclusions or accepting anyone else's conclusions (particularly if based on *significant differences*).

- If the so-called *objective type* tests were used, you can't make any conclusions nor can you accept any conclusions based on data from these tests.
- Identify the total possible score in the pretest and posttest. If this information is not available, it is not possible to calculate any of the three factors described in this section. Significant differences based on the number of items achieved without

knowing the number of items not achieved makes the significance doubtful.

— If the average pretest score (in percentage) is much over 15 or 20 percent, the resultant boredom will affect the learning situation and any research data based on the learning situation. The Boredom Factor should be less than three or four.

— If the average posttest score (in percentage) is less than 80 percent, the instructional materials are too ineffective to be useful or to result in good research data. The Instructional Effectiveness Factor should be about .90.

— If the average or mean posttest score is close to 50 percent, this may mean that the test was either a *normed* or standardized test or has been designed to be a normative test in which the *best* test items are ones that have been learned or missed by 50 percent of the students taking the test items. As such, the scores and statistics are GIGO because the results have been designed into the test regardless of the actual learning levels of the students.

— Subtract the average pretest score (in percentage) from the average posttest score (in percentage). The difference should be at least 60 percent otherwise the efficiency of the instructional unit will be so low as to affect the value of the data and any conclusions based on the data. The Instructional Efficiency Factor should be about .90.

Under the traditional approach to research, *significant differences can be obtained from data resulting from a boring, ineffective, and inefficient instructional unit.* Under the Learning Systems Approach to instructional research in which the Boredom Factor is minimized and the Instructional Effectiveness and Efficiency Factors are maximized, *there will always* be significant differences between pretest and posttest scores. When comparing the posttest scores of two different methods for significant differences, the value of the significance is still dependent upon whether or not the instructional design of both methods minimized the Boredom Factor and maximized the Instructional Effectiveness and Efficiency Factors.

If LEARNING is the *name of the game* in the instructional process which is supposedly taking place in our schools, then these factors which evaluate the instructional design should be much more important than whether or not there are significant differences (particularly when comparing pretest and posttest scores).

NOTE: Because of the differences between 100 percent of test items and 100 percent of SO's, these three factors should ideally be based on the percentage achievement of SO's rather than on the percentage achievement of test items. In evaluating instructional materials where there are SO's and matching test items, the evaluation can be made on the basis of SO's. In evaluating instructional materials or research where there aren't any SO's, the use of test item data can be used but the results aren't as reliable as it would have been if there were SO's (see pages 1079-83).

a. EVALUATING EXAMPLES OF EDUCATIONAL RESEARCH

Television has a great potential for instruction, but as long as instructional television programs are developed without objectives, this potential might just as well be forgotten. As of 1970, the number of instructional television programs that have been developed according to a systems concept with objectives, testing, etc., could almost be counted on two hands. One such program, *Sesame Street*, has been acclaimed as fantastic, the greatest thing in television, and a model for all instructional television! If other television programs use *Sesame Street* as a model, then instructional television will continue to move into the 20th century in a horse and buggy with both the driver and the horse wearing blinders to keep from seeing what is happening around them. Yes, in comparison with other instructional television, *Sesame Street* is great; but so is the horse and buggy great in comparison to walking! To back up these statements, consider the evidence as presented in the evaluation report of *Sesame Street* prepared by the Educational Testing Service. (The conclusions of the report from the point of view of traditional education were that the series was a *fantastic* success. By looking at the same data from the point of view of a Behavioral Learning Systems Approach the success is pretty empty). According to their own data, the average pretest score of all children in their study was 42 percent which means that the children already knew almost half of what *Sesame Street* was supposed to teach. Obviously this could result in a high level of intellectual boredom for most children even though the series was highly entertaining. If the series was designed so that the children could start from wherever they were intellectually, then the pretest score for each child should be somewhere between zero and 10 percent (of course because of individual differences in what they know, some children would have to see more programs than others). The Boredom Factor should be 1.0 for an ideal instructional situation. With an average pretest score of 42 percent, the Boredom Factor (42/5) for *Sesame Street* is 8.4 or about eight times higher than it should be.

The average posttest score of all the children was 59 percent which means that the series was only successful in teaching 59 percent of what the series should have been able to teach. In most classrooms, a student achieving 59 percent would receive an "F" or at best a "D". Under the current concept in designed instruction, the learners should have learned between 90 and 100 percent of the objectives of the series. Therefore, with an average posttest score of 59 percent, the Instructional Effectiveness Factor (59/95) for *Sesame Street* is about .62.

In looking at the efficiency of the series, an ideal program which minimizes the boredom and starts each learner with a pretest score of from zero to 10 percent and maximizes learning by having the learners learning 90-100 percent of the objectives would result in the average learner gaining 90 percent. The average child in the *Sesame Street* study gained 17 percent. Therefore, the Instructional Efficiency Factor (17/90) is only .19, which is pretty bad.

With a little more analysis of the data it is rather easy to uncover that it took the average child *five hours of viewing Sesame Street to gain the answer to one test item.* As if that isn't bad enough, in isolating the data for the advantaged children in the study, it turns out that they were so bored that it took them an average of *seven hours of viewing Sesame Street* in order to gain enough knowledge to answer one additional test item correctly. *Now that is fantastic!*

Another example concerns some research which was done concerning compressed speech audio tapes which automatically makes the research a non-science because *compressed speech* is a man-made phenomenon. The following statement was taken from the procedures section of the report:

> Two criterion measures were used to assess effectiveness of the compressed and normal presentations: a 20 question multiple choice recall test and a 20 question multiple choice application test. The final 20 recall questions and 20 application questions were combined at random into one test instrument.

First problem is that in using multiple choice questions, the results are affected by the use and selection of the wrong choices. Secondly, since multiple choice questions rarely match SO's, the tests are most likely not criterion measures. Third, since no copy of the test was included in the report, the data should be suspect because self-made tests can be designed to prove anything regardless of the actual achievement levels of the learners. Fourth, the 20 item recall test probably attempts to test for the rate memory of 20 items (SO's) of information; however, it is not possible to predict how many process SO's the 20 item application test was attempting to test because without seeing the actual test, there is no way of knowing how many duplicate items were used to test for the achievement of an unknown number of process SO's (remember that the percentage achievement of process test items probably does not equal the percentage achievement of process SO's).

In a publication entitled *Do Teachers Make A Difference* (OE-58042) published by the U.S. Office of Education, James Guthire reported on some studies concerning the effectiveness of schools. One such study done by Mollenkopf and Melville in 1956 used the results of standardized achievement tests and claimed to find significant correlations between student achievement and the number of special school staff, class size, pupil-teacher ratio, and instructional expenditures per student. Since the standardized tests are not based on any list of standardized SO's and particularly are not based on any list of SO's which the teachers in these schools might have been using and the tests are *normed* tests, the achievement scores are much more representative of chance learning by the students and/or the design criteria of the test makers than the scores might be representative of any designed instructional effort by the school staff.

There is a type of educational research that I refer to as proving that *people who can swim will swim more often than those people who can't swim* in which the results are so obvious that to research the question has to be a waste of time and effort. Back in the mid-sixties, there were several U.S. Office of Education funded research projects which researched the hypothesis *teachers who know about programmed instruction will use more programmed materials than teachers who don't know anything about programmed instruction!* In the publication, *Do Teachers Make A Difference,* Guthrie who mentions a research report by Marion Shaycoft which essentially defended the schools on the basis of the results of researching the hypothesis *students who take a particular subject for three years will know significantly more about the subject than students who haven't taken the subject during that same three years!* Research based on the differences between pretests and posttests in the cognitive domain are practically useless as it would almost be difficult not to get significant differences unless the tests had very little relationship to what was being learned. Similarly, research based on the differences between two groups in the cognitive area where one group was exposed to an instructional unit and the other group (control group) was not exposed to the instructional unit is also practically useless because it would be difficult not to get significant differences as long as the tests related to what was being taught in the instructional unit.

In the same U.S. Office of Education publication, Guthrie also discusses 19 other studies which were all based on the use of standardized tests. Until such time as standardized tests are matched to some standardized lists of SO's which teachers and students are using for teaching and learning, the value and validity of any data and conclusions resulting from the use of standardized tests is doubtful and should not be relied upon for educational nor instructional decision-making.

In another U.S. Office of Education research report by Baker, Schutz, and Sullivan (OEG 7-12-0030-232), a 55 item test was used and the posttest mean scores ranged from 27 to 37, the effectiveness factor ranged from .52 to .71 which makes the instructional units so ineffective as to produce contaminated data. The fact that most of the mean scores tend to be around 50-60 percent suggests that the 55 item test was *normed* such that the results of the tests were built into the tests regardless of actual student achievement.

In a research report to be published in a professional educational journal concerning two different treatments in the presentation of the same material, the following data was generated from the use of two supposedly equal forms of a 100 item objective-type test. Because the items are multiple choice, true-false, and matching, the data is already suspect because biased results are built into the design of the items and because it is highly unlikely that any of the test items will match any of the SO's of the instructional unit.

Traditional Data

	Pretest Mean	Posttest Mean	Gain Mean
Control	37.14	67.03	29.89
Experimental	39.15	69.14	29.89

BLSA — Instructional Design Evaluation

	Boredom Factor	Effectiveness Factor	Efficiency Factor
Control	37.14/5 = 7.43	67.03/95 = .71	29.89/90 = .33
Experimental	39.15/5 = 7.85	69.14/95 = .73	29.89/90 = .33

Figure 142 — Research Data: Traditional vs. BLSA

Given that the test used already had the results built into it and that the test probably didn't match the SO's of the instructional unit, it should not be surprising that there was no difference in the gain of the two treatments. In addition to the problems already pointed out in reference to the test, in assuming that there might be some relationship between the SO's and test items, the pretest scores indicate that there was a high level of potential boredom built into the instructional unit. i.e., the average student knew over seven times what he or she should have known (boredom factors 7.43 and 7.85). Although the design of the statistical analysis may have been good, the design of the instructional unit was at about a "C" level (effectiveness factors of .71 and .73). The efficiency of the instructional unit in comparison to what it should have been was not very good (efficiency factor of both were .33). As a result of the potential boredom, ineffectiveness, and inefficiency of the instructional unit, any data (even if the test was valid) has to be contaminated and not something a teacher who is concerned about increasing student learning would be interested in emulating.

In a large study carried out by the International Association for the Evaluation of Educational Achievement (IEA) in 22 countries, there was a tremendous effort by some 300 experts in reaching agreement on common standards of achievement to be measured (in 15 different languages). Of interest, is that no similar effort was made to develop common standards of what should be taught. Therefore, the data resulting from the extensive survey which purportedly compared achievement levels of students in various countries is misleading in that the scores represented the students achievement of what was on the test. It would be a highly probable situation that the students may very well have learned a lot of other things which were not on the test particularly when there was no identified commonality in So's which teachers tried to teach to their students before the assessment. As a result, what the IEA data really represented was the correlation between what was being taught in the various classrooms and what was being tested on the IEA tests. Of course, given that the tests were most likely influenced by standardized test makers and made use of *easy-to-grade* objective type test items, the results were probably built into the tests (similar to the National Assessment tests here in the U.S.) and rarely matched any of the specified or even implied objectives of the teachers in their classrooms.

In a study at the State University of New York at Geneseo comparing three-year college graduates to four-year college graduates, the data was interpreted as indicating that there wasn't much of a difference between the two groups. Given that no one has identified what four-year college graduates should know or what skills they should have, it shouldn't be any surprise that there isn't much of a difference between three-year and four-year college graduates. If once the minimum common core SO's for college courses are identified and subsequently, what a college degree should stand for besides time spent attending courses, then it may be possible to make a more valid comparison. In addition, since the standardized Graduate Record Examination was used, any resultant data is suspect because of the standardizing procedures and the lack of any identified correlation with what is being taught in college courses.

Lytle and Yonoff reported in the December, 1973, *Phi Delta Kappan,* on the results of a survey they conducted on seventh and eighth grade students who stayed in school during the eight week teachers' strike in Philadelphia during the 1972-73 school year and compared their achievement to a sample of students who stayed out of school during the eight weeks strike. Using standardized Iowa Basic Skills Tests, they found no significant difference in achievement. Their purpose in conducting the survey was to test the question, *What effect does a prolonged, bitter teacher strike have on pupil achievement (cognitive)?* Lytle and Yonoff offered several explanations for the results.

1. Schools have relatively little, if any, effect on student cognitive development (particularly junior high schools).

2. The Iowa tests are not adequate for determining minor achievement differences between groups of urban students.

3. There are qualitative differences in the effectiveness of those teachers who supported the strike as compared to those who did not and they did such a powerful job following the strike that their students caught up with the students who had the eight extra weeks of education.

They also made the following comments:

Of course, the data do not reflect the more subtle effects on students who saw some of their teachers threaten each other, even violate a court order to return to work. In any case, the data do not give much comfort to politicians, journalists, and school administrators who try to create public opposition to teacher strikes on the grounds of harm they do to children.

In view of the contents of this chapter regarding the validity of standardized tests, the more obvious answer to the result of *no significant differences*, is that since the tests have almost a chance relationship to what happens in the classrooms and are not specifically designed to test what is important (there are no standardized lists of SO's used in the Philadelphia schools which are matched to the Iowa tests), it shouldn't be surprising that there were no differences. After all, the same tests which tend to show that schools and teachers don't make a difference in cognitive achievement shouldn't be expected to show a difference between students who stay in school versus those who stay out of school. If there had been a standardized list of minimum common core SO's and matching tests that these teachers had been working from, the resultant data might be much more informative and revealing of what actually happened.

Lytle and Yonoff suggested in their first explanation that schools and particularly junior high schools might have little effect on student cognitive development. In many school districts, the function of junior high schools is sort of like an aircraft *holding pattern* in that the mathematics and reading programs are frequently a summary of what was learned in elementary school and a remedial program for those who didn't achieve what they should have in elementary school. Given this function, it would indicate that differences in group achievement, if any, would probably be harder to identify.

In their comments, Lytle and Yonoff said that the data should not give any comfort to the politicians, journalists, and school administrators who try to create public opposition to teacher strikes on the grounds of harm they do to children. That is one way to look at the data. Another way of looking at the same data is that if teachers can't make any difference in student cognitive achievement, then why should they be given any increases financially (above the increased costs of living) and be allowed to reduce their productivity (smaller classes and lighter teaching loads) or in fact why even have teachers and the accompanying high costs of education?

Of interest, Lytle and Yonoff mentioned the possible negative effects on students in the affective domain by their observing teachers (whom they are supposed to admire and respect) flouting the law and committing acts of violence. Yet, their tests did not include any evaluation of these effects and the *harm* that the politicians, journalists, and school administrators were most likely concerned about were also the negative effects in the affective domain. Quite typically, teacher organizations and most striking teachers in their efforts to avoid accountability for student cognitive development, stress the importance of affective learning. If this is true, then the survey should have included measurements in this important area.

A very common problem in discussions of specifying objectives, accountability, teacher strikes, and negotiations is the switching back and forth between learning in the cognitive domain and learning in the affective domain. In stressing the need for specification of objectives in the cognitive domain, teachers who are against the idea bring up the difficulties in specifying the objectives for love, appreciating a poem, feeling warm in the sun, etc. which are in the affective domain. These same teachers frequently turn around and fail students (with all its negative side effects) for not achieving some cognitive test items (which makes cognitive learning important) and grade students up or down for some affective objective, i.e., attitudes in class, attendance, class participation etc. (which proves that these teachers are, in fact, measuring affective learning). Since cognitive and affective learning are very different in the way they are taught and evaluated and they are both important, it is very important to keep them separated in discussions and debates in order to increase the fidelity of communication and reduce misunderstanding.

> NOTE: The examples of research used in this section should not be interpreted as negative comments on the people doing the research but as negative comments on traditional educational research as it is usually carried out. These studies were picked as being representative of traditional educational research with the problems commonly found in most traditional research.

C. PRIORITIES FOR INSTRUCTIONAL RESEARCH

In setting up priorities for instructional research, it is important to recognize and accept the differences between *education* and *instruction*. Remember that traditional education is based on chance commonality between tests, what is taught, and what is learned and any individual differences among both students and teachers are ignored. The primary emphasis is on teaching with the teachers' role being that of a presenter of course content. The secondary and less important emphasis is on student learning which is assumed to be variable with non-learning accepted as normal. *Problems* to be researched are not really problems in the more commonly held meaning for the word in that a number of teachers have not had a problem in the teaching nor students in the learning of whatever is being researched. Only the researcher has the problem. As such, traditional educational research is relatively unimportant and of little value to the classroom teacher unless the teacher wants to have the same *problem* that the researcher studied.

Instruction has to be designed and there has to be a high correlation between the tests, what is taught, and what students learn. The primary emphasis should be on student learning with the individual differences among students and teachers not only being recognized but playing an important part in bringing about student learning. *Problems* to be researched have to actually be learning problems, i.e., some students are not able to achieve the desired or required SO's in the present learning environment. The closer that the problems being researched are to actual identified problems in student learning, the more useful and the more important the research will be to teachers.

Since it is possible to be both very effective at being inefficient and very efficient at being ineffective, it is necessary to set up general priorities first. If the emphasis is on being efficient, it may be difficult to increase effectiveness. However, if the emphasis is on being effective, it is possible to increase efficiency with minimum affect on effectiveness. Therefore, the primary goal of instruction and instructional research should be to maximize effectiveness in learning such that at least 90 percent or more of the students are learning 100 percent of the required SO's. The secondary goal will be to try to maintain the high levels of achievement and at the same time to try to obtain them quicker and/or at a reduced cost.

In order to increase the effectiveness of designed instruction, the first step would be to eliminate as many of the traditional educational malpractices as possible which would include the elimination of the use of standardized *normed* tests. Secondly, teachers at all levels should try to identify what it is (SO's) that they want their students to learn in their courses or in whatever they are teaching. Then teachers at all levels should try to increase the correlation between what they say they want students to learn, what they teach, what they test, and what students actually learn. For those teachers who have trouble specifying objectives, they might find it easier to use their test items and criteria for evaluation as representing their SO's.

The next major step would be the identification of minimum common core SO's of courses with similar titles. This can be done at several levels at the same time. Teachers in one school who teach the same course could identify their minimum common core SO's while in the same district, teachers in another subject matter area may be identifying the district wide minimum common core SO's for one or more courses. Ideally, the national, state, and local minimum common core SO's should be identified for all courses in which there are two or more teachers teaching the course. The procedures to be followed in identifying the minimum common core SO's are discussed in detail on pages 527-539 (Volume II). The guidelines for instructional problem research are:

    a. that the general problem to be researched is learning;

    b. that the specific problem to be researched is on how to bring about the learning of a SO or set of SO's by a group of students;

    c. that the more students having the same learning problem, the higher the priority of research concerning that problem; and

    d. that the more fundamental the learning problem as far as being a basic requirement in order to learn other things, the higher the priority of research concerning that problem.

As teachers and researchers develop alternate paths to the learning of the minimum common core SO's, they should then develop a hierarchy of learning paths such that the 1st path to be used would work for the most students, the 2nd path would work with the most of those students who couldn't learn from the first pathway, the 3rd path would work with the most of those students who couldn't learn from the second pathway, etc. It should be noted that what may turn out to be the best pathway for students in one area or section of the country may not be the best pathway for students in another area or section of the country. This means that in addition to setting up a general hierarchy of learning paths for most students who are what might be considered average in intellectual skills and in cultural and economic background, researchers and teachers will try to identify a hierarchy of learning paths for students with specific characteristics, intellectual skills, cultural, and/or economic background. Remembering that sometimes it might be easier to teach the student the learning skills necessary to learn from an existing learning pathway than it is to develop a completely new learning pathway, it will be appropriate to develop units which can be used by some students to increase their learning abilities.

Of particular importance should be research dedicated to prove beyond a doubt that learning skills are dynamic and can be nurtured and that they are not static and only affected by genetics. As I mentioned earlier in Chapter V, Volume I, although Jensen of the University of California at Berkeley and Shockley at Stanford are the most vocal among those who believe that intelligence and social background are highly correlated, that intelligence is primarily and almost entirely a function of genetics, and that intelligence has limits above which one can't go, most of the teachers that I have worked with tend to feel this way too. It is a sad situation, but it should be expected. Given that students don't achieve and a teacher fails the students, it is a lot easier on the conscience of the teacher if the teacher can blame the failure on a genetic lack or limit of intelligence rather than on the teacher's lack of effort in trying to solve the students' learning problems. The very serious problem is that as long as teachers believe that there are limits to intelligence, they will not even try to solve the students' learning problems and will assume that the students have reached their intellectual and sensory limits. This is a particularly serious problem with Black, Spanish-American, Indian, and other minority groups.

An interesting result of instituting quality control in learning such that 90 percent or more of the students achieve 100 percent of the minimum common core SO's and no student will be allowed to progress without learning 100 percent of the required SO's, is that learning problems that are usually associated with cumulative ignorance, gaps in learning, or overlaps in units or courses, will be reduced. As a consequence of this reduction, there will probably be a reduction in the need for alternate learning paths.

As a general guideline, research efforts should be directed towards making preschool and kindergarten so effective that 90 percent or more of the students learn 100 percent of the minimum common core SO's, then the same efforts should be directed towards the first grade, then the second grade, etc. on up to and including graduate level instruction. The main reason for this is that as quality control in learning eliminates cumulative ignorance and the need for overlaps among courses, courses will change and some may be eliminated as the application of the BLSA extends upwards through the instructional process. However, because of the seriousness of learning problems at all levels of education, teachers and researchers should not wait for the major revisions resulting from increased effectiveness and efficiency at the lower levels. They should identify minimum common core SO's, identify learning problems, and solve them at all levels of education in preparation for the major revisions to come later.

Once teachers and research have not only proven that 90 percent or more of the students can learn 100 percent of the minimum common core SO's and it has become a common event in most schools, then research should work on improving the efficiency of the process. By developing paths of learning which are more closely parallel to the learning abilities of the students or by developing the learning abilities of the students to match those needed to learn from available materials, the same learning may be produced in a shorter time and probably more economically.

For those who may not think that effectiveness and efficiency in the instructional process are problems, consider the fact that out of 60 million students only five to six million students are learning close to 100 percent of the implied objectives ("A" students). Something has to be done about the learning problems of the other 55 million students. In reference to the efficiency of the process, consider the fact that over $100 billion dollars is being spent on the present traditional process and schools cannot guarantee anything as far as learning is concerned.

1. THE NATIONAL INSTITUTE OF EDUCATION: TRADITIONAL RESEARCH HIDDEN UNDER SYSTEM'S CONCEPTS AND TERMINOLOGY

The National Institute of Education (NIE) was created by the Education Amendments of 1972 which were signed into law on June 23, 1972. President Nixon had this to say about the creation of NIE:

> We must stop pretending that we understand the mystery of the learning process, or that we are significantly applying science and technology to the techniques of teaching when we spend less than one-half of one percent of our educational budget on research, compared with five percent of our health budget and ten percent of defense.

A primary purpose of the Institute is the initiation of a serious, systematic national effort to find ways to make educational opportunity truly equal — the study of what is needed, both inside and outside the school, to ensure that our compensatory education efforts will be successful.

In the planning of NIE, Dr. Harry Silberman, saw the initial structure of NIE as containing four units:

a. a unit to improve education system's practices;
b. a unit to develop research and development resources;
c. a unit for programs to solve major educational problems;
d. a *think tank* to analyze implications of policies.

In addition, the planning unit in the creation of NIE suggested that NIE might show interest in funding

- alternative modes in postsecondary education,
- home-based early education, and
- the improvement of education productivity while maintaining effectiveness levels by various means including technology.

The mandate for NIE is generally stated as *to remedy current shortcomings in educational research and development by fostering and helping finance the growth of an effective national R&D system to lead to the fundamental reform in education.* The legislation creating NIE specifically states that the Institute shall seek to improve education in the United States through:

a. helping to solve or alleviate the problems of and achieve the objectives of American education;
b. advancing the practice of education as an art, science, and profession;
c. strengthening of the scientific and technological foundations of education; and
d. building an effective educational research and development system.

In October, 1972, the Congress confirmed Dr. Thomas Glennon as the first Director of NIE. He stated that the major overall goal was *the development of basic skills in all citizens.* In a letter to the Senate Labor and Public Welfare Committee, Glennon emphasized the need for research findings to be implemented,

What is clear to me is that the NIE cannot be an institution devoted only to fundamental research. It must be deeply concerned with practice. It must find ways that seemingly do not now exist to communicate with practitioners. Of course, it is crucial that it (NIE) have knowledge that is worth communicating.

Glennon felt that NIE had two major responsibilities in achieving its legislative mandate: NIE must produce important knowledge about the educational experience, and NIE must develop an effective system of dissemination so that what is learned can be used. In achieving these responsibilities, Glennon wanted to emphasize:

   a. quality of educational opportunity;
   b. looking into those activities that will help slow down the rate of increase in educational costs while still improving the quality of education;
   c. accountability through the improvement of our ability to measure student and school performance; and
   d. the development through research and regional laboratories of effective curricular materials.

Although the Director of NIE is to have full responsibility for specific program policies and for the management of the Institute, the legislation for NIE also included the creation of an independent advisory council, the National Council on Educational Research, which would establish overall policies for NIE. Once created, the Council stated that their principle emphasis for NIE is on the solution of problems in educational practices and on improved communication between researchers, developers, and practitioners. They felt that the three principle goals were:

   a. the equality of educational opportunity;
   b. the improvement of the quality of education; and
   c. the improvement of knowledge about learning and educational processes.

In analyzing the statements by these people as to the goals and purposes of NIE, the overlapping of statements suggest a possible hierarchy of goals which has not been identified except by implication.

   a. The first goal would seem to be to improve the present educational practices.

In order to achieve this goal, NIE would have to identify those practices which needed to be changed and/or improved such that more students would learn more. It would seem appropriate for NIE to become concerned about eliminating the many educational malpractices found in almost every school while at the same time trying to improve on other practices. Implied in this goal and stated in the legislation which created NIE, is that the practice of education should be advanced as a science and profession. As indicated in the beginning of this Chapter, in order for education to become a science, the major concern has to be *learning* which is a natural phenomenon rather than the educational methods, media, or single path curriculum materials which are manmade phenomenon. In order to advance the profession of teaching (as indicated in Chapter I, Volume I), there has to be a specialized knowledge, high standards of achievement and conduct, and a prime purpose of public service. These three conditions of a profession in traditional education are in desperate need of advancement. Given this primary goal, it would appear that the systems concepts as described in this three volume series is what NIE should be concerned with.

One particular area of educational practice which stands out in all comments concerns:

    b. the improvement of equality of educational opportunity.

There was a time in which formal education was only for the elite. Then came a period in which education was available for all children, but there were great differences among the facilities, the resources, and the teachers in reference to the quality and ability to facilitate learning. The national programs of the sixties were aimed at trying to equalize the educational facilities for all students and in particular for various minority groups. Even with equal facilities, resources and teachers, it became apparent to some educators that in giving an equal learning environment to students who are unequal results in students who are still unequal (particularly in a situation where curve grading is used and somebody has to lose out by getting "D's" or "F's"). In order for compensatory education to work and to fulfill the goals of the American ideal, equal educational opportunity cannot be defined as giving unequal students equal learning environments. What is needed is to define equal educational opportunity in terms of students who are completing high school and/or college with at least a common background of having learned 100 percent of all the minimum common core SO's of their courses. Having had an equal instructional opportunity during formal instruction, the students will have a more equal educational opportunity as they leave formal schooling and go out into the working world. However, in order that students who are unequal to achieve equal instructional opportunity, the learning environments may have to be unequal in reverse, i.e., students with the greatest need also have the more facilitative learning environment.

In a situation where it is normal not to know what should be learned, the tests don't match any existing or implied objectives, most or all of the educational malpractices can be found being practiced, and many students learning in spite of the teachers, it should not be surpirsing that many students don't make it through school or if they do finish school, they have crippling amounts of cumulative ignorance. In order to change the present educational experience, it will be necessary to spell out the SO's for all courses and identify the minimum common core SO's. Then it will be possible to identify non-learning of the required SO's as learning problems to be researched and solved. Only when compensatory education is aimed at solving and correcting identified learning problems will it be able to achieve the intent it was designed to achieve. The third goal would seem to be:

    c. the development of research and development centers and research efforts directed towards bringing about the necessary changes in educational practices in contrast to the past years of traditional educational research which has had little if any effect on education and educational practices.

Very much a part of this third goal are two other goals which should be considered at the same time even though they weren't considered as important as the first three goals:

    d. to solve major educational problems and

    e. to improve productivity while maintaining present effectiveness.

    The major reason for the failure of traditional educational research to affect on-going educational activities is that there weren't any identified learning problems to be solved because few teachers had identified what they wanted students to learn, there was only chance commonality in what was being taught and learned in different schools, and it was considered normal for students not to learn. As a consequence, traditional research concentrated on teaching and the presentation of course content rather than on learning. In addition, most of the tests used in research were invalid because the results were biased by the design of the test and other flaws pointed out earlier in this chapter. The only way that learning problems can be identified and solved is when *what should be learned* is identified. Once many or most teachers have identified their course objectives (SO's), then the minimum common core SO's can be identified. The more teachers involved in the identification of the minimum common core SO's, the more teachers and students that will be able to benefit from the solution to a learning problem associated with these minimum common core SO's. The more students that have trouble learning a minimum common core SO, the more critical it is to find a solution to the problem.

In achieving the fifth goal, it is critical to notice that those commenting on this goal stress the maintenance of present effectiveness levels. This assumes that the present effectiveness levels are satisfactory. They aren't satisfactory! Before trying to increase productivity and efficiency in learning, it is necessary to try to maximize effectiveness in the teaching-learning event. As a minimum, the effectiveness level should enable 90 percent or more of the learners to achieve 100% of the minimum common core SO's in their courses. Therefore, the fifth and sixth goals should be

    e. to increase the effectiveness of the instructional event and then

    f. to improve productivity while maintaining the improved effectiveness.

A lot of research effort will be needed to help teachers identify their course SO's and to identify the minimum common core SO's in courses with the same title. Once this goal has been reached, then research can direct its efforts towards increasing efficiency and productivity in the teaching-learning event. The seventh goal concerns

    g. the dissemination and communication of the results of research to teachers who could benefit from the research.

This goal has been one of the major goals of the U.S. Office of Education for years and particularly during the sixties and up to the present time during which hundreds of millions of dollars have been spent on innovation. The major reason for the lack of success in dissemination of the innovations is that as long as teachers have not identified what it is that students should be learning and there is little, if any, commonality among courses with the same name, there is no need to implement someone else's innovation unless some educator is evaluated by someone else on the basis of whether or not innovations were implemented. Another major problem concerns the traditional role of the educator as a presenter of course content wherein time is a constant and the treatment (teaching innovation, method, media, curriculum, etc.) is the independent variable and learning is left as the dependent variable. As long as variations in learning are considered not only normal but the accepted practice, then why should any teacher change to some other person's innovation. In a sense, when learning is allowed to be a variable, not only is the teacher thinking of teaching as an art form (man-made phenomena), but the teacher is acting like a researcher. The missing role in education is the practitioner who like other professional practitioners lets time and the treatments be the dependent variables and tries to make the major purpose a constant. In education, the major purpose is student learning. When teachers accept their new role as an Instructioneer who tries to maximize learning for all students, then as they identify a learning problem, they will be looking for solutions. If NIE or any other research body have some solutions available for the same problem the teacher has identified, for sure the teacher will use it.

Two similar problems which have made most educational research irrelevant and of little value to teachers concerns the selection of the problems to be researched. Usually, the funding agency sets up some general areas within which the research should be done. These areas are picked because some influential person is interested or concerned about the area or some advisory council has a feeling that the area is important. Since most teachers don't have SO's and common core SO's have not been identified, it would be rare if the area for research emphasis was identified as a specific problem area. In the case of reading, writing, and basic arithmetic, it is fairly easy to see that these areas are problems, but since the SO's have not been identified, it is difficult to set up a research program to solve a problem which has not been specifically identified. One might think that if the research areas are so vague and irrelevant, that educators would complain and refuse to do useless research. However, in education, many educators (particularly administrators) are evaluated on the basis of how much money they are able to get from various funding agencies. If an educator wants to get funds, you do not identify a relevant problem and try to get some money to research it and solve it because chances are that funding agencies won't be interested in your problems and even if they were, tradition-oriented educators who may be the readers of your proposal probably won't be interested. Consequently, the best way to get funds is to find out what the funding agencies and their readers are interested in and make believe you have that problem. Hopefully, some of the money can be siphoned off and used to solve a real problem. If not, at least getting the money is evaluated as a good thing and the salaries, consulting fees, and travel are good. In addition to being evaluated on the amount of grants an educator can secure (regardless of what is done with the money), there is another criteria for evaluation that prompts educators to seek funding. In higher education, most educators are evaluated at least partially on the basis of their *scholarship* which is generally measured by how many books and articles they write, conference papers they present, and consulting they do. Given the ever present *publish or perish* dictum (regardless of quality or relevance), educators try to get funds for some project in order to get material for an article, a conference presentation, or hopefully even a book. Researching any innovation is good even if only to find out that it is ineffective. This creates a problem in that it floods the educational dissemination networks with valueless reports, articles, innovations, etc.

Recently, NIE and Representative Albert Quie of Minnesota have renewed the concept of the *educational extension agent* to be modeled after the agricultural extension agents who were so successful in spreading innovations and indirectly increasing agricultural production. The major problem again is that in agriculture, farmers had common problems and increases in yield are relatively easy to measure. In education, where learning problems have not been identified in specific terms (non-learning of SO's) and there is little, if any, commonality in specific learning problems, solutions to problems (not identified nor shared) will not be so readily accepted and increases in the learning of unknown SO's is difficult to measure. Once teachers specify their course SO's and cooperatively identify the minimum common core SO's and accept the new role as an Instructioneer who wants to maximize learning for all students, then there will be common problems to be solved and common solutions to be shared and increased learning of SO's to be measured.

a. THE ACTUAL DIRECTION OF NIE RESEARCH AND SUBSEQUENT REDUCTIONS IN FUNDING

In spite of all the great goals and suggested directions, NIE has continued on in the traditions of educational research. Because NIE has not encouraged the specification of objectives, they are not able to show any improvement in learning as a result of changes in educational practices. In using the traditional standardized tests to evaluate their effect on education, NIE along with teachers and schools will be shown to be ineffective. Although evaluation has become a critical part of compensatory programs, if no one has actually identified what it is that these students should be specifically learning, then problems in learning the SO's can't be identified and relevant solutions can't be developed.

Not knowing what should be learned in our schools makes it impossible to identify major student learning problems. In lieu of trying to identify problems that need to be solved, NIE has followed the traditional educational approach of developing solutions to problems not yet identified. Obviously, if you don't know what the problem is that the solution is supposed to solve, it is very difficult to evaluate the solution. Among the solutions that NIE has decided to work with regardless of whether or not they have been identified as problems are alternative schools, the voucher plan, and a multitude of curriculum packages developed by the regional laboratories. Notice that none of these solutions are prefaced with *Given your students are having trouble learning the following list of SO's and given they have the following characteristics, this solution may help them learn the SO's.* As long as going to school is measured in terms of time rather than in terms of learning, then most innovations are going to be primarily just different ways of spending that time besides the traditional form of sitting in classes in front of teachers. The present form taken by most alternative schools is based on different educational environments with the goal of keeping the students, the teachers, and the parents happy. As a result, the variations in the quality and the value of alternative schools will be high and the results of having an American education will be more diverse than ever with the average student learning even less of what they need to know to be successful in our society. Given a situation where the minimum common core SO's have been identified and the completion of various levels of instruction carried with it the achievement of these required minimum common core SO's, alternative schools could be very useful in that they could be set up to solve the learning problems encountered by various groups of students who happen to learn best in ways other than the traditional methods. Under this emphasis, students in different alternative schools would still learn the minimum common core SO's. As such, evaluation of the schools as to their effectiveness would be much easier.

The voucher plan has the same problems. The only difference is that the students give their vouchers to the (alternative) school of their choice. Here again, the choice of school is dependent on likes and dislikes of how to spend the time which is supposed to be devoted to educational pursuits. There is little, if any, commonality in SO's to be learned in the different schools. If based on lists of SO's to be learned, the voucher plan which would offer alternate paths to learning might be successful and make a significant impact on education.

In the development and dissemination of a large number of curriculum packages, NIE and the regional laboratories will run into the same problem facing commercial publishers of educational materials. Since there is little agreement as to what should be learned, the market for learning packets of specific lists of SO's is not very large. Until the schools identify common learning and common learning problems, packaged curriculum solutions to problems not yet identified will have minimum impact on education and will present problems in dissemination.

Without really knowing the reasons why NIE has failed to live up to its original goals, the Congress has reduced the funding of NIE and will probably continue to do so until NIE gets out of its traditional educational research *rut* and puts into action the verbal goals they have agreed to achieve. As soon as possible, NIE should do the following:

— set up research to identify the national minimum common core SO's in all courses and at all instructional levels;

— use tests which match the national minimum common core SO's to identify learning problems throughout the country;

— establish priorities in learning problems based on the fundamentality of the SO's which aren't being learned and the number of students having a particular learning problem;

— research and development of solutions to the identified learning problems based on the characteristics of those students who are having the learning problem;

— dissemination of these solutions to the teachers who have students who have the learning problems the solutions were designed to solve;

— as maximum effectiveness is achieved (90 percent or more of all the students in the United States are learning 100 percent of the national minimum common core SO's of their courses), then NIE efforts would be directed towards the increasing of the efficiency and the productivity of schools and teachers; and

— the dissemination of these solutions to teachers and schools throughout the country so as to increase the efficiency and productivity of all schools and all teachers.

2. THE NEED FOR REGIONAL, STATE, AND LOCAL INSTITUTES FOR INSTRUCTIONAL RESEARCH

The more teachers and the more different communities that get involved in the identification of minimum common core SO's, the fewer the number of SO's they will agree on. Conversely, the smaller the area and the number of teachers involved in the process, the more SO's that will be identified as minimum common core. As a result, different areas could have different SO's, different learning problems, and a need for different solutions. This situation lends itself to different levels of responsibility and accountability. NIE could and should be primarily concerned with the nationally agreed upon minimum common core SO's. The regional laboratories could be primarily concerned with the learning of SO's which were agreed upon by the teachers in the region as being minimum common core SO's but were not identified at the national level as being national minimum common core SO's.

At the present time, most states do not have research groups which could be primarily concerned with the learning of SO's which were agreed upon by the teachers in a given state as being minimum common core SO's for the state in addition to those which were agreed upon at the regional or national level as being regional or national minimum common core SO's. However, it might be possible for the regional laboratories to work with the states in their area and perform the research, development, and dissemination functions for the state.

At the local levels (school districts, colleges, and universities), they should also set up research and development departments to be concerned with the learning of SO's which were agreed upon by the teachers in the local instructional unit as being minimum common core SO's in addition to those agreed upon at the state, regional, or national levels as being state, regional, or national minimum common core SO's.

To save duplication of effort, one of the functions of NIE would be to oversee the work of the regional laboratories and where two or more laboratories were working with the same SO's and the same learning problems, NIE should act as a coordinator. In a similar fashion, the regional laboratories would oversee the work of the state research units and coordinate efforts where two or more states were working with the same SO's and the same learning problems. The same function could be performed by the state research unit in relationship to two or more local units who are working on the same SO's and the same learning problems.

D. TEACHING, RESEARCH, AND THE ROLE OF THE TEACHER

For years in higher education there have been discussions among faculty, administrators, regents, legislators, taxpayers, voters, students and their parents over the emphasis given to teaching and to research. The discussions are frequently centered around teaching versus research which seems to assume that research and teaching have very little relationship with one another. At the university level, many graduate faculty work at research which has nothing to do with their teaching activities. As such, funds for that portion of their salaries should really come from some other source than from the instructional budget.

At all levels of higher education, teachers do get involved with research in the same content area as they teach in their classes. As such, the funds to support their salaries usually come out of the instructional budget. Although the primary function of all schools, including higher education, should be to facilitate the learning of their students, the perceived role of the teacher and the evaluation of the teacher strongly affects the kind of research a teacher does and their motivation for doing it. Under the traditional approach to education, the teachers role is seen as a performer whose primary function is to control the content of the course by either presenting it to the students or in directing the students to other sources for the content. Some teachers may turn over the control of the content to the students which is a *cop-out* on the part of the teacher. However, regardless of who has control, the traditional emphasis is still on the content of a course. Evaluation of teachers typically includes an evaluation of their observable *teaching* performance and in higher education, an evaluation of their scholarship is measured by the number and length of publications, papers given at conferences, and consulting activities. The *publish or perish* dictum, the role of the teacher, and natural tendencies set up at least five types of research supposedly related to teaching.

   1.   Doing research to get material to satisfy the *publish or perish dictum*. This is probably the most useless kind of research and because the results can directly affect a teacher's job, it carries greater priority than teaching. Since the quality of the research is rarely considered by those

who are evaluating the teacher, much of this research is of little value to the country, to students, or even to the scholarly community. Professional journals and annual conferences are filled with the results of this type of research which actually deters many teachers from reading their professional journals and from attending the scheduled sessions at conferences. Students of these teachers frequently are involved in generating the material for the teachers research. This is particularly true of graduate students which motivates some faculty to want only graduate students.

2. **Doing research to get out of teaching.** There is a natural tendency for the human being to do the least possible. That is why most teachers want smaller classes and lighter teaching loads (rarely is there an observable increase in learning as a result of decreasing class size and/or the number of classes a teacher teaches). Some graduate faculty in some schools only have to teach three credits or one course as they are busy doing *research*. There are even some graduate faculty that want to be sort of an *artist-in-residence* where they have no teaching responsibilities at all. This type of research may result in a lot of material for the *publish or perish* dictum but given the motivation for the research (to get out of teaching), not much should be expected from these researchers whose salaries increase the costs of education and whose efforts do little to increase the quality or even the quantity of education.

3. **Doing research which may result in material for new courses.** Because the teacher's traditional role is that of a presenter of course content, many teachers get bored presenting the same thing semester after semester, quarter after quarter, or multiple times within a semester or quarter. As a result, teachers are motivated to generate new courses not because there is a student or real-world need for the course, but because the teacher is bored teaching whatever he or she is teaching. In addition, since teachers' teaching load is usually defined in terms of the number of courses taught and rarely on the number of students taught, some teachers are motivated to develop and offer odd-ball courses which will attract enough students to offer the course, but not enough to create a lot of work. Of course, there are some teachers who have identified a need for a course and need time to identify the content of the new course.

4. **Doing research on the general content area of existing courses.** This type of research is similar to the last one in that the motivation is to change the material because the teacher is bored not necessarily because it will benefit the students.

5. **Doing research in general interest areas.**[2] This type of research

---

[2] Research in this category would be very useful in the scholarship function under the BLSA. Since teachers won't have classes of students to present to, many teachers will want to make these scholarship presentations which are scheduled whenever the teacher wants and there is no need to specify objectives; make, give, or score tests; take attendance; worry about time limits; or give any grades.

is a little more difficult to classify as being related to teaching, although like the last two categories, the content of the interest area will find its way into most of the teacher's courses anyway regardless of whether or not it is related to the main topic of the course. Given that some teachers may find the traditional role of teaching as boring because of the repetition of presentations, the opportunity to do research in areas other than the content areas they are teaching is the main reason for staying in education.

The important points to remember in reference to the traditional form of research as supposedly related to teaching is that it is content oriented and concerns the role of the teacher as a presenter of course content. In addition, being content-oriented, the research is a non-science even though the content area is considered to be a science because the emphasis is on the teaching or presenting of the content rather than on the learning of some SO's dealing with the content.

Under the Behavioral Learning Systems Approach (BLSA) to instruction where the emphasis is on learning and on the student, successful teaching can only be accomplished by doing research. In contrast to the traditional approach where the activities of teaching and research are separated, under BLSA, teaching and research are almost inseparable. Although a teacher may use the same course SO's for years, teaching will not be boring because the teacher is not teaching the same SO's, to similar students, the teacher is teaching different students. Since every student is different, the task of the teacher in getting the students to learn 100 percent of the SO's will vary with each student.

In the last section, I outlined the need for research at the national, regional, state, and local levels. Actually, the need for research continues at each level right down to the teacher. For example, although the local research unit is concerned with the minimum common core SO's agreed upon by the local teachers but not by the state, regional, or national teachers, where there are different schools in different parts of the same district, it is possible that the teachers in each school building might have additional minimum common core SO's that they have agreed on but have not been included in the local, state, regional, or national minimums. As such, the teachers involved could cooperatively research any instances of non-learning in order to maximize achievement. The principal of the school in working as an *instructional leader* may coordinate the research and in cooperation with other principals and higher level administrators keep abreast of research being done in other schools so as to minimize overlaps in research work which may have been already done or is in the process of completion at other schools.

In addition, because most teachers will add more SO's to the minimum common core SO's, these teachers must be ready to view the non-learning of these extra SO's as learning problems which they will have to research and solve such that the students can achieve 100 percent of the required SO's of their courses. Here again, the principals should in cooperation with other administrators try to help the teachers in their research and help them to avoid doing research in learning which has already been done at some other school or by some other teacher.

In higher education, the same situation exists except department heads would take on the role of instructional leaders and coordinate some of the research done by teachers. Other administrators would encourage cooperation with other nearby institutions of higher education to minimize overlapping of research. Given that the same course offered at a university, a four year college, and a community college should have minimum common core SO's, there is no reason why the teachers who are teaching the same course couldn't cooperate in research to solve learning problems associated with the learning of the minimum common core SO's of the course. At the moment, it might be tantamount to heresy to suggest that the community college teacher might be able to help his or her university colleagues solve student learning problems, but initially in the changeover from the traditional role of the teacher to the role as an Instructioneer, some community college teachers may have had more experience in designing courses for student learning than their colleagues at the university level.

The important points to remember in reference to research under the BLSA is that it emphasizes learning and the identification and solving of learning problems. Since learning is a natural phenomenon, the research is a science and so is the role of the teacher. In reference to the *publish or perish* dictum, articles resulting from research on common learning problems will be sought after and read rather than avoided.

Given the change in the role of the teacher, the use of the Behavioral Learning Systems Approach to designed instruction, the changes in evaluation of all people in instruction so as to emphasize learning, and changes in the direction and role of research, there is no reason why we can't bring about the necessary major changes in education and as professional Instructioneers make the instructional process a humanizing science which will enable students at all levels of education and from all different genetic backgrounds and environments to achieve all of those wonderful general objectives espoused by educators for years as a defense for the existence of schools but rarely achieved by our students!

CHAPTER X

CHANGING FROM TRADITIONAL (CHANCE) EDUCATION TO DESIGNED INSTRUCTION

General and Specific Objectives

GO — To understand that changes are needed in almost every educational institution (although few schools will make all of the changes suggested in this three volume series, every teacher and school can make at least one or more of the suggested changes).

    SO — Conduct a survey of a faculty and student group using the questions on pages 1131-3. Analyze the resulting data in accordance with the comments on page 1133 and in reference to the concept referred to in each item. Write a report listing each item and whether or not the survey data indicates a need for change. If a change is needed, describe the change in terms of the changes suggested in these three volumes.

    SO — Given a list of the fifteen steps for the BLSA plan for change, describe the activity in each step.

GO — To be acquainted with the many general guidelines for planning change.

    SO — Given a specific group of faculty, identify one or more of the general guidelines which would help them facilitate student learning. Defend the selection of the guideline(s) in terms of faculty need(s) as identified by an analysis of the teaching-learning environment of this specific group of faculty.

    SO — Prepare a plan for change which includes the identification of faculty needs, the design of learning experiences which should solve the problems, alternate paths which reflect identified faculty differences, an evaluation plan which matches the needs, and suggested follow-up activities to increase the teachers success in facilitating student learning.

GO — To develop positive attitudes towards the four basic concepts of the BLSA.

SO — List the four basic concepts.

NOTE: The next two SO's should be done by teachers or students planning to be teachers. Administrators or students planning to be administrators should go through the term project themselves first and then should work with a faculty group or a group of students planning to be teachers as they go through the term project. The role of the administrator should be to help the teachers or students planning to be teachers to solve their problems just as the teachers and teachers-to-be are expected to help their students by solving their learning problems.

SO — All concerned should take a semantic differential attitude test in reference to the four basic concepts before and after doing the term project. (These tests should be anonymously and no one's grades should be affected by these tests).

SO — Given a class of students (to be taught by the teacher or teacher-to-be), identify a unit which is a learning problem (supported by past achievement in this unit), analyze the problem, prepare a primary instructional pathway through the unit, and based on the evaluation of the students after using the primary pathway, prepare alternate instructional pathways such that at least 90 percent or more of the students learn 100 percent of the required SO's. (See page 1140.

GO — To be aware of the problems in many of our educational innovations and the contribution that BLSA can make to help some of these innovations become more effective and efficient.

Because of the length of this chapter and as an aid to the reader, I am including that part of the Table of Contents that covers this Chapter.

	Page No.
Chapter X — Changing From Traditional (Chance) Education to Designed Instruction	1125
A. Bringing About the Change	1131
1. Do You Need to Change	1131
2. System's Plan for Change	1134
3. General Guidelines for Planning Change	1139
4. In-service Training to Bring About Change	1147
5. In-service and Pre-service Training: An Advertisement	1151
a. Publications	1152
b. Using the Series as Textbooks for Pre-service Training	1154
c. Consulting Services	1161
(1) An Example of Contract Seminars — Washington State Community Colleges	1162
(2) Alternate Pathways to Change Available	1169
B. Implications of the System's Concepts as Applied to Education and Educational Innovations	1174
1. Educational Innovations from the System's Point-of-View	1177
a. Bilingual Education	1180
b. Alternative Schools	1181
c. Open Education	1183
d. Value Clarification	1187
e. Early Childhood or Pre-School Education	1188
f. Other Systems Approaches to Instruction	1190
g. Career and Vocational Education	1192
h. Community Colleges	1195
i. Adult Education	1197
j. Irregular Students	1199
k. Racial Integration in Schools	1200
l. Year-round Schools	1203
m. Parochial and Private Schools	1204
C. Questions and Answers About Utilizing the Behavioral Learning Systems Concepts	1205

CHANGING FROM TRADITIONAL (CHANCE) EDUCATION TO DESIGNED INSTRUCTION

> God grant me the serenity to accept
> The things I cannot change,
> The courage to change the things I can
> And the wisdom to know the difference.
>
> — Serenity Prayer

During the past decade and more, there have been numerous publications, articles, and presentations made on the subject of *change*. The major emphasis is usually on the fact that we are living in a world of change and that the rate of change is increasing almost daily. It has been pointed out by many people that students in our schools should be prepared for an everchanging life. Some estimates have been made that the average student in our schools today may change his or her career or vocation four or more times before retiring from our country's work force and that many of the jobs our students will hold aren't even identified at this time. Therefore, it is not enough to just help students learn whatever they need to know now, they have to be taught how to make changes and to learn on their own effectively and efficiently.

In order to facilitate the development of students who will accept change as a way of life and who will be able to adapt to change with a minimum of problems and who will actually be able to benefit from change, it becomes important and almost critical that education as an institution also makes changes and that the people in education demonstrate that they can change. This generally means a de-emphasis on the learning of the facts of today and yesterday and an increased emphasis on the uses of facts, i.e., processes, trends, predictions, etc.

At a conference sponsored by the American Association of School Administrators in the fall of 1972, the participants and speakers discussed the question, *What will schools be like in 1985?* The conference came up with the following list of predictions:

— 25 percent of all high schools will base promotions and graduation on the attainment of measurable skills (abandoning the Carnegie unit system of credits);

— 50 percent of all public schools will be operating on a year-round basis;

- 75 percent of a student's time will be spent in independent or individualized instruction in at least 50 percent of the nation's high schools;
- 33 percent or more of the high school student's learning time will be spent outside of the school;
- 75 percent of the elementary schools will open up to three and four year old students; and
- 30 percent of the schools will have replaced the principal's decision-making role with policy-making bodies of teachers.

In contrast with all these predictions and with the changing life surrounding the schools, most schools have not changed basically from what they were 40-50 years ago. Yes, there have been many innovations which have been introduced, but most of these innovations have not made any lasting impressions on the basic educational process. The major cause for this lack of change is that *teachers tend to teach as they were taught not as they were taught to teach* (if they were taught to teach at all). As mentioned in Chapter VIII, the teachers of teachers-to-be have the most critical role in our society. Therefore, it should be just as critical that teacher training institutions make the change and start training teachers for their new role in designed instruction as the Instructioneer. However, even after the departments of instruction in the teacher training institutions make the change, remember that the teachers-to-be are being taught in other college and university courses by traditional teachers who have not had any training in teaching and before ever entering the teacher training institution, these teachers-to-be have had 12 years or more of traditional education in their elementary and secondary schools. When the new designed-instruction-oriented teacher graduates and goes out to teach in traditional schools, there will be strong peer group pressure from fellow traditional teachers (who have been teaching for years) not to make *waves* which might make them or the school look out-of-date. Is it any wonder why change is so slow. However, if efforts are made at all levels of education to bring about the necessary changes, it can happen. The key guideline is to *change for the sake of increased student learning not just for the sake of change!*

Whereas the major effort and effects of the change to designed instruction will be made by the teachers and will be produced in the students, the initial start generally has to be made by educational administrators because they evaluate the teachers and control the environment within which the teachers work. As is commonly the case, whenever I talk to teachers only, many of them tell me that I am talking to the wrong group. The teachers say that I should be talking to administrators as they would like to do the things suggested in my seminars (similar to this three volume series), but the administrators won't let them change. In contrast, whenever I talk to administrators only, many of them tell me that I am talking to the wrong group as they would like their teachers to do many of the things suggested in my seminars, but they can't find teachers who want to make the changes. The situation sounds like the proverbial problem of the chicken and the egg — which should come first. Although administrators will most likely initiate the changes, groups of teachers, or even groups of students and/or parents can meet with administrators and urge the making of the change to designed instruction. Once the decision has been made to make some changes, it is important that all participants in the process be involved. No matter how good an innovation or change is, an administrator can enforce rules, policies, and procedures which will create an environment within which the change cannot exist regardless of how the teachers and students feel. No matter how good an innovation or change is, a teacher in the privacy of the classroom can perform in such a way that the benefits of the change are nullified or even changed into disadvantages. No matter how good an innovation or change is, students or parent groups can affect the environment such that the innovation or change has to be dropped. Successful and permanent changes have to be a cooperative process in which student learning is increased and the increase is looked on as a positive concept and the teachers and administrators who facilitate the increased learning are rewarded.

There are many reasons why administrators and teachers will make the change. Because I sincerely believe that basically every teacher and administrator wants every student to have success in learning, I think the major reason for changing is because of the fustration which has bothered many educators for years and is the result of the pedagogical conflict between their beliefs in individual differences among students and their actual behavior in the classroom which denies the existence of these individual differences. In addition, many teachers and administrators will change because the concepts make sense and because they want to be more professional in their work. Most new teachers and many of the existing teachers will change because the new role for the teacher is much more humane than the traditional role. Although not all teachers can or even want to be innovators, all teachers can be good imitators. As some teachers change and their colleagues observe their success in helping more students learn more, they will follow. Some teachers will change as a result of being *encouraged* by their administrator. Some teachers may change as a result of a hearing in front of the Instructional Grievance Committee. Some teachers and administrators will change as a result of discussions with parents and/or students about one or more educational malpractices they may be perpetrating on students. Sadly, some teachers and administrators may resist long enough to have to face a malpractice suit and a courtroom experience before accepting the change.

A. BRINGING ABOUT THE CHANGE

There are probably as many different ways to bring about change among faculty and administrators as there are faculty groups. There are some faculty groups who are very traditional and there are some faculty groups which are already practicing most or all of the things suggested in this three volume set, but most faculty groups are probably at various levels in-between the two extremes. In addition to the varied differences among faculty groups, there are almost as many differences among the faculty in any one group (school). The best way to adopt the concepts to these differences is for the administrators and teachers to meet and try to identify how far they want to go as a group and individually and then to identify where they are now. I would be naive to expect any faculty group to accept the total package as described in these three volumes; however, there are at least one or more concepts that any faculty group could accept. As they have success with these concepts, then they can try more until eventually they have made the transition over to designed instruction using the concepts of the Behavioral Learning Systems Approach to Instruction.

1. DO YOU NEED TO CHANGE

Assuming that teachers want all students to learn all of what is important in their courses, the easiest indication of the need for change is to examine the grades being given. If any students are getting less than an "A", 100 percent, or any other mark of excellence and particularly if the majority of students are getting less than the 100 percent mark, then the teachers and students need the system's concepts applied to the teaching-learning event. For a little more evidence, survey the faculty and the students in your school by having them answer the following sets of questions.

Instructors	Students
1. In what percent of your classes do you consider your chief role to be a presenter of information? ____%	1. In what percent of your classes is the instructor's chief role the presenting of information to the class? ____%
2. In what percent of your classes do the students have to guess what you want them to learn in order to pass your tests? ____%	2. In what percent of your classes do you have to guess what you are to learn in order to pass the tests? ____%

Instructors	Students
3. In what percent of your classes do you use curve grading or some other method of grading such that your students get "A's", "B's", "C's", "D's" and "F's"? ___%	3. In what percent of your classes does the teacher use some form of curve grading such that students get "A's", "B's", "C's", "D's", and "F's"? ___%
4. In what percent of your classes do you only let the students see the test items on your tests at the time the tests are given (usually at the end of the learning experience)? ___%	4. In what percent of your classes are the test items on the tests hidden from you until the test is given (usually at the end of the learning experience)? ___%
5. In what percent of your classes do you expect all students to learn the same material in the same amount of time? ___%	5. In what percent of your classes are you expected to learn the same material in the same amount of time as all other students? ___%
6. In what percent of your classes do you present the next lecture even though you know some of the students have not learned all of the prerequisite material of the previous lecture? ___%	6. In what percent of your classes are you expected to listen to a lecture regardless of whether or not you have learned the prerequisite material of the previous lecture? ___%
7. What percent of your students do you assign grades and allow them to leave your classes although they have not learned what you consider important for them to learn? ___%	7. In what percent of your classes are you allowed to leave the class although you have not learned all that the instructor considered important for you to learn? ___%
8. In what percent of your classes does instruction take place by design — students know what they are expected to learn and they are not given credit for the class until they have learned it? ___%	8. In what percent of your classes does the instruction take place by design — you know what you are expected to learn and you are not given credit for the class until you have learned it? ___%
9. What percent of your students know specifically what you consider is important for them to learn? ___%	9. In what percent of your classes have you known specifically what the instructor expected you to learn? ___%

Instructors	Students
10. In what percent of your classes have you informed your students of what you consider important for them to learn by giving them a list of the specific measurable objectives for that course? ___%	10. In what percent of your classes have you been informed of what the instructor considered important for you to learn by receiving a list of the specific measurable objectives for that course? ___%
11. In what percent of your classes do you give the students a pre-test so that they may begin your course at the point indicated by the test (probably different for each student?) ___%	11. In what percent of your classes have you been given a pre-test and were then allowed to begin the course at the point indicated by the test at which you were ready to learn? ___%
12. What percent of the test items used in your courses are on a one-to-one relationship with the specific measurable objectives of your course? ___%	12. In what percent of your classes has there been a one-to-one relationship between the specific measurable objectives of the course and the test items on the tests? ___%
13. In what percent of your classes do you, when a student answers a test item incorrectly, identify his learning problem, diagnose it, prescribe a solution, provide opportunity for additional learning, test to determine if the student has learned it, and continued this process until the student learns the behavior of the test item correctly? ___%	13. In what percent of your classes, when you have missed a test item, does your instructor identify your learning problem, diagnose it, prescribe a solution, provide opportunity for additional learning, test to determine if you have learned it, and continued this process until you did learn the behavior of the test item correctly? ___%

In interpreting the results of the survey, high percentages given as answers by either instructors or students for one or more of questions one through seven indicate traditional problem areas in need of change. Questions eight through thirteen are concerned with basic system concepts. The lower the percentages, the greater the need for change designed to incorporate these system concepts into the instructional process. If there are large differences between the percentages given by the instructors and those given by students for any of the questions, this indicates a need for an analysis of the instructional situation and a potential need for some of the concepts included in the Behavioral Learning Systems Approach towards instruction.

As will be the case in the vast majority of schools at all levels of education, there will probably be an identified need to implement more of the concepts of designed instruction.

2. SYSTEM'S PLAN FOR CHANGE

There are many ways in which one can plan for change. Depending upon the group involved in the change process, a particular method or scheme could succeed with one group and fail with another group. The system's plan for change has proved to be successful if each step has been carried out. To start the planning at the wrong step or to skip over steps, is to invite problems and potentially a lack of success.

Step 1 — Know and understand the present educational and community environment

In every school, these are characteristics which make a particular school unique. Who are the real decision-makers? What are the relationships among students, teachers, administrators, school board or regents, parents, and/or the community? What is the mood of the school and community (progressive, regressive, or static)?

Step 2 — Examine Previous Change Efforts

In every school no matter what the level, someone or group at some previous time has tried to bring about change. What were the proposed changes? Were they implemented? If not, why not? If yes, did the changes bring about the expected benefits? If not, why not? If yes, what procedures or people helped the changes to be successful?

Step 3 — Identification of the Problem(s).

In examining the present educational environment, how many teachers are involved in using how many of the malpractices? How many of the concepts of the BLSA are not being practiced. The key to note in this step is to concentrate on existing problems that are having a negative affect on learning and the lack of procedures or practices which could have a positive affect on learning. Be as specific as possible concerning the learning which can be affected by potential changes. Avoid problems which are based on personal preference and are not related to actual or potential affects on learning, i.e., a particular method or set of materials which have not been proven to facilitate or hinder learning, but a teacher likes it and/or likes someone associated with the method or materials.

Step 4 — Set up a Primary Action Group

It is difficult for one person to bring about change. Locate others who agree that the problems exist and that the changes should be made. If possible, include a few key people whom others will respect. Keep the size of this group around five or under. Try to have the group representative of all concerned in the change.

Step 5 — Obtain Preliminary Approval

As a group, meet with whatever other group(s) or persons who are in a position to affect whether or not the desired changes can be implemented and whether or not the activities necessary for bringing about the change can be carried out. Here is where the key in Step 3 may open a lock. If the problems are closely related to learning, the decision-makers will find it difficult if not impossible to decide against increasing student learning. Be sure to point out that they are not approving of a plan of action at this point. They are only approving of the existence of the problems and the need to plan for changes which will lessen and eliminate the problems thereby increasing learning. Rather than a single group or person, there could be several different groups or persons who are in key positions in the school or in the community. It may be necessary to meet these groups and/or people at separate times.

Step 6 — Dissemination of the Existence of the Problems and the Need for Changes

At this stage, it is important to let as many people as possible know that the problems exist and that there needs to be changes brought about to eliminate the problems. At this point, do not discuss any plan of action yet, just introduce the fact that these problems exist. Again, the key in Step 3 will help. If you publicized a plan of action, people could be against your plan? however, it would be difficult to be against increasing student learning.

Step 7 — Expanding the Ownership of the Problems

This step actually occurs very quickly after Step 6. As soon as you can get *others* to acknowledge the existence of the problems and the need for action, then it is important that the *others* accept and believe that some or all of the problems are just as much theirs as they are anyone else's, i.e., practically every teacher evaluates the majority of their students as being less than "A", 100 percent, etc. which indicates most of the students are not achieving what the teacher wants them to learn.

Step 8 — Definition of Goals for Change

In this step, it is important to involve as many people as possible in the identification of the goals for action so that they will feel that the goals are their goals. Because it is traditional to define goals in terms of the action rather than in terms of the results of the action (frequently the goal of an inservice session is that it was conducted rather than the goals relating to the results of the inservice session). It is very important also that the identified goals will actually solve or at least reduce the problems.

Step 9 — Commitments for Change

In step 5, preliminary approval was given by key people of the existence of the problems and the need to do something about the problems. In this step, it is now important to get commitments from key people for participation in a plan of action, i.e., give necessary time off for inservice sessions, funds for consultants, funds for resources, funds for secretarial time (if necessary), temporary changes in rules or policies to allow for changes which may be in conflict with existing rules and policies, etc.

Step 10 — Developing Alternate Paths to the Goals

Remember that just as one of the BLSA's key concepts is that there should be multiple learning pathways for students, there should also be multiple pathways for the teachers to use to arrive at their goals and solve their problems. As with students, there is no one pathway that will work for every teacher either. This flexibility is important because it demonstrates to the teachers the same flexibility you want them to use with their students. Also, if one pathway is not successful or becomes blocked for one reason or another, it is good to have alternate paths to try. In that way, all the previous planning is not wasted.

Step 11 — Designing the Plan for Change

The plan for change should take into consideration the problems, the goals, the multiple pathways, available finances, and time available to achieve the desired results. At this point, it may be necessary to select one or two pilot problems to work with in which the goals are achievable in a shorter period of time than some of the other problems. It will be a lot easier to make major changes later on if preceded by minor changes which successfully eliminated problems. In setting up a schedule for change, it may be necessary to have a time schedule, but be flexible as far as achieving the goal or change. Just as all students don't learn at the same rate, neither do all teachers make changes successfully at the same rate.

Step 12 — Coordinating the Plan for Change

In this step, it is necessary to make all of the arrangements for materials, resources, people, meeting rooms, etc. which are a part of the plan for change.

Step 13 — Putting the Plan for Change into Action

In the process of putting the plan for change into action, try to obtain internal and external publicity. The internal publicity can be carried out with posters, a school paper, a dinner, a party, etc. External publicity can be obtained through local newspapers, radio and television. This step helps teachers and administrators who aren't quite committed to commit themselves to the change, it helps re-affirm those already committed, and may actually quiet those who might actively be against change because to publically be against increased student learning would not be an appropriate position for any educator to take.

Step 14 — Carrying out the Plan for Change

In some plans for action or for change where only one pathway has been identified, if in the middle of carrying out the plan it is identified that the plan isn't working as planned, the whole plan sort of winds down into defeat which is more noticeable because of the publicity at the beginning. Since there are multiple pathways available to achieve the goals, as one or more are identified as inappropriate, they can be de-emphasized and other pathways giving more emphasis. Depending upon the length of time built into the plan for change (over three months), it may be helpful to set up a special newsletter which would contain items describing the activities and successes of the plan for change. Those teachers who try to change, but for one reason or another aren't very successful, will communicate to other faculty in the lounges, hallways, etc. in an effort to put the blame for their lack of success on the plan for change and/or on the BLSA concepts. To counterbalance this negative publicity, there is a need to spread the news of successes.

NOTE: If part of the plan for change includes the establishment of an Instructional Crisis Squad, then when a teacher starts to have trouble carrying out his or her part in the plan for change, have the Instructional Crisis Squad help the teacher achieve his or her goals or at least help the teacher get back on the track to success. This will not only help the teacher and the teacher's students, but it will avoid the negative *back-room* gossip.

Step 15 — Evaluation and Follow-Up

As with the relationship between specific learning objectives and corresponding test items, the evaluation of a planned change should match any objectives which have been set up. Also, if the objectives have not been quite achieved, then just as has been suggested for non-achievement in learning, set up a revised plan taking into consideration any additional information which was identified while carrying out the initial plan for change which may be helpful in helping the revised plan become successful. Remember, just as no single method or technique or instruction will be successful for all students, no single plan for change may be successful for all faculty (even if several alternatives have been built into the initial plan for change.)

General Comments

An additional form of evaluation which can be used for evaluating in-service sessions or other group activities which are supposed to facilitate change and serves as a good guide for follow-up activities is an open-ended evaluation form which is essentially a lined sheet of paper with the following statement at the top: *As a result of participating in this plan for change (seminar, inservice session, etc.), I intend to do (investigate, initiate, change, write, plan, meet with, etc.) the following:*. Ideally, this form should be prepared in duplicate using carbon paper, NCR paper, or copied in a copy machine so that the teacher can retain a copy for his or her use in carrying out whatever it was the teacher wanted to do. The other copy should be turned into a principal, department head, or whatever the next level of administration is. In line with the new role of the administrator, an examination of these forms will indicate collectively what the teachers would like to do which in turn indicates or suggests how an administrator can facilitate the teachers in achieving what they want. The administrator should then make up a similar form in which the administrator is indicating, *Given these things that the teachers want to do to facilitate student learning, I intend to do the following in order to facilitate the teachers doing what they want to do*. These forms can then be turned into the next level of administration so that person can make up a similar form indicating, *Given these things that the principals (department heads) would like to do to help the teachers help students learn, I intend to do the following to help the principals (department heads) do what they want to do*. This process can and should be repeated all the way up the administrative ladder to the school board members or regents in order to have continuity in goals.

A strategy which can be used that takes advantage of peer group pressure to encourage those who prefer non-action to commit themselves publically to do something is best used between teachers and an administrator and/or between administrators (principals) and a superintendent (or whatever the next level of administrator happens to be). The teachers (or principals) should bring to a meeting their forms indicating what they would like to do to facilitate student learning or in the case of principals, what they would like to do to help teachers help students learn. The leader of the meeting (a principal or department head in the meeting of teachers, a superintendent or dean in a meeting of principals or department heads, etc.) then asks the teachers (or principals, etc.) to tell the rest of the group what he or she plans to do. Initially, this procedure helps to facilitate communication between people involved in change. Those that are planning to do essentially the same or similar things will be identified for later cooperation. Also, what one person wants to do may turn out to be a good suggestion for others who hadn't thought of it. In addition, if the leader of the meeting knows the people he or she is working with, select the order of presentations such that the teacher (or principal, etc.) who will probably plan to do the most speaks first, the teacher (or principal, etc.) who will probably plan to do the next most is next and on down to that teacher (or principal, etc.) who will probably plan to do the least. The leader of the meeting should not tape record this meeting as it will cause inhibitions and decrease the success of the procedure. However, the leader should get either copies of what the teachers (or principals, etc.) say they plan to do, or have a secretary in the meeting who can take fast dictation. With this information and commitments, the leader can then formulate his or her own plans as to how the leader can facilitate the teachers (or principals, etc.) to achieve their goals and follow-up this intitial meeting with periodic checks to see how the teachers (or principals, etc.) are progressing and to see what else can be done to facilitate student learning indirectly via the teachers (or principals, etc.)

3. *GENERAL GUIDELINES FOR PLANNING CHANGE*

The following comments are in no particular order, but are suggested guidelines to keep in mind when planning for change such that directly or indirectly more students learn more (in contrast to most traditional educational plans for change which are generally changes for the sake of change itself).

a. Given a situation in which few if any of the teachers have specific objectives for all of their courses, one would normally think that the first step would be to schedule objective writing workshops and to have the teachers specify their course objectives. This has been done in hundreds of school districts and colleges. Instead of the results showing dramatic increases in learning, the results frequently show little change. The problem is not that specifying objectives is not a good idea, the problem is that after writing all those good SO's, too many teachers go back into the classroom and continue using the same old tests which they used the year before. Remember, students try to learn what is on tests or whatever the evaluation criteria are. If the tests and criteria match the SO's of the course, then the students will learn the SO's. However, if the tests and criteria don't match the SO's, the students will ignore them and keep trying to learn whatever is on the tests. Although many and probably even most teachers do not have SO's for all of the courses they teach, almost every teacher uses tests or evaluates in some way the progress or achievement of their students. If a teacher can accept the fact that SO's and test items or other evaluative criteria should be synonymous with one another, then teachers who have tests or other evaluative criteria actually already have their SO's too. Instead of concentrating on the writing of SO's which may not be used, a workshop should concentrate on converting the teachers' present test items and criteria for evaluation into related SO's. If one of the major guidelines for teachers is that they should start designed instruction wherever the students are, (intellectually) then it should be appropriate to start where teachers are and for most teachers that level is the writing of test items! I have found that teachers can write test items which are specific and measurable better than they can write objectives which are specific and measurable and since the test items and SO's should be synonymous, it shouldn't make any difference which they start with.

b. In selecting a unit or topic for use as a demonstration or pilot unit for the application of the Behavioral Learning Systems Approach, don't select a favorite topic which you or the teacher doing the project know quite well as chances are you or the teacher may already be teaching it well and students are learning it fairly well even if you or the teacher don't have SO's and matching test items. Consequently, any increases in learning will probably be small. For best results, select a unit which is a problem unit in which even the better students are having trouble learning what you or the teacher think they should learn. Most of the problem in the unit is probably because with the traditional emphasis on content rather than on learning, what you really want students to learn hasn't been well defined and identified. By selecting a unit which is a learning problem, you have the best chance of discovering the advantages of using the BLSA and your students will receive benefits from your efforts much faster. (See also page 1159).

NOTE: In all education courses and workshops where the students or participants are supposed to work up a demonstration curriculum unit to demonstrate some method, technique, and/or media, teachers of these courses and workshops should insist that the students or participants identify a unit or concept which they can prove is a learning problem. As a result, they will be much more impressed with whatever emphasis (technique, method, media, etc.) was used because it resulted in changes in learning rather than the usual no significant differences when the students or participants select their favorite topic because they don't want to work too hard.

c. It should be remembered that in changing over to the BLSA, some students and some teachers have become so accustomed to the traditional format, that a change to the new learning environment, even though most students learn more, will be a negative situation. It may be necessary for the sake of some students to simulate a traditional classroom even though the students are using individualized materials. Some students who have become accustomed to the pressure of traditional classrooms in which there were deadlines and someone pushing, may find the new environment too relaxing and will almost stop learning while they are waiting for someone to push them. If this situation bothers both teachers and students, the teacher can set deadlines; however, since learning is more important than time, the teacher has to be willing to give in and allow more time if it is necessary for learning to take place. Personally, rather than set a time limit and then have to give in and change it, I would prefer to demand the quality level of 100 percent achievement and encourage the students to complete their work by giving them estimates of course completion based on present performance. For example, if a student has only completed 10 percent of the course and half of the semester has gone by, I would notify the student that based on his or her performance, it will take at least nine more half semesters or a little over two years to complete the course. Some teachers who are accustomed to giving deadlines may find a more open course to be distressing. However, remember that an important objective to be learned by all students is to be able to pick themselves up and become self-starters.

d. If all of the teachers in any one school decided to accept their test items as SO's and went through the process of identifying the minimum common core SO's in all or most courses, the teachers would be able to set up a continuous progress program within six months using the minimum common core SO's as the ladders of learning upon which the students can progress at their own rate. However not many faculty groups can work together that well and although the possibility still remains, the transition into the new roles will most likely take longer.

e. Encourage the establishment of an Instructional Grievance Committee. Given that almost all teachers want and will defend their right to have grievance procedures, it will be difficult for any teacher to be publically against the students having grievance procedures. The mere existence of the committee will help make teachers more flexible and fair in their relationships with their students and will also help them be more accountable.

f. If an administrator says that a teacher cannot give an "I" (Incomplete) grade because it is not in the accepted grading system and insists on a grade, the teacher can say, *all right, even though the student hasn't completed the course, I'll give a letter grade if you (the administrator) will sign this waiver form.* The waiver form should be similar to the following:

> I, the undersigned administrator, do not want the following named student to complete the learning for course no._____by learning the attached list of specific objectives even though the non-learning of these objectives may cause cumulative ignorance and interfere with the student's learning in subsequent courses. In the event of a malpractice suit brought against the teacher and/or the school, I accept full responsibility for this action.
>
> _____
> (Signature)

If a teacher insists on giving a student a grade of less than 100 percent and an administrator wants the teacher to give the student a grade of "I" and give the student more time to learn, the administrator can ask the teacher to sign a waiver form and then the administrator will accept the giving of the lower grade to the student. The waiver form would say:

> I, the undersigned teacher, do not want the following named student to complete the learning for course no._____by learning the attached list of specific objectives even though the non-learning of these objectives may cause cumulative ignorance and interfere with the students learning in subsequent courses. In the event of a malpractice suit brought against the school, I accept full responsibility for this action.
>
> _____
> (Signature)

If a student hasn't completed a course and the teacher gives the student a grade of "I" (Incomplete) which means that the student will have to stay on in the course until such time that the student learns 100 percent of the required SO's and a parent insists that the student be passed on, the same waiver form can be used.

> I, the undersigned parent, do not want my child to learn the attached list of specific objectives even though the non-learning of these objectives may cause cumulative ignorance and interfere with my childs learning in subsequent courses. In the event that this

action results in conditions which might be termed gounds for a malpractice suit, I accept full responsibility for this action.

(Signature)

The useful aspect of these waiver forms is that no one will ever sign them, but the possibility of their use communicates the seriousness of any action which cuts off learning before the end of a course.

g. In making the switch from the traditional situation in which credit for courses is determined by time to the BLSA where credit for courses are defined in terms of learning, it is important to remember that actually if a student doesn't learn all of whatever learning is included in the definition of a course that the student actually hasn't completed the course and can't be given credit for the course. Whereas traditionally if a student misses too many classes, the student can't get credit for a course (regardless of learning), under the BLSA, if a student doesn't achieve 100 percent of the required SO's, the student can't get credit for a course (regardless of attendance and time). If a student has achieved about two-thirds of the SO's and insists that he or she has the right to learn only "C" worth of a course and should be allowed to get out of the course, then offer to give the student about two-thirds of the credit (67 percent) that is given for the regular course. Be sure to mention that the credit allowed would have to be classified as some other course, i.e., independent reading, because the student didn't actually complete the regular course. Usually in a case like this, the student will learn the rest of the required SO's. It is just that the students have learned in a permissive environment (as is found in most schools and homes) that if one complains enough you can often get by without doing what should have been done.

h. Try to minimize or preferably to eliminate any educational malpractices. If teachers and administrators can only do that, more students will learn more of whatever it is teachers believe to be important as identified by what is on the teachers' tests and what evaluative criteria the teachers use.

i. Try to identify any rules, laws, and/or customs which actually inhibit learning and then try to minimize their enforcement or try to eliminate them, i.e., attendance rules which automatically fail a student after a certain number of absences.

j. Try to encourage teachers to change their role as a teacher from that of the traditional teacher who is concerned about covering the content of the course to that of an *Instructioneer* who is concerned about students learning the required SO's of a course.

k. Try to increase the emphasis on learning by evaluating teachers on the basis of their ability to facilitate student learning, to evaluate administrators on the basis of their ability to help teachers help students learn, and to evaluate students on as objective base as possible (not with the so-called *objective tests* which are actually very subjective in preparation).

l. Since a truly continuous progress approach is not immediately feasible in many schools such that students can start courses at any time and finish them at any time, try to at least minimize cumulative ignorance and communicate to subsequent teachers by forwarding lists of SO's which have not been learned by students and make available to subsequent teachers any resources which may be available to help the students learn the non-achieved SO's, i.e., a third grade teacher could send on a list of non-learned SO's and make available to the 4th grade teacher some third grade materials relating to the non-learned SO's.

m. Try to provide or obtain some release time during the school year for teachers or especially for a coordinator who is working with a number of teachers that are making major changes in the instructional environment and/or going through the process of identifying the minimum common core SO's. Try also to provide or obtain some money for summer work for teachers who have already identified areas of major learning problems and need time and support to make the necessary changes. In either case, the release time or extra monies should be justified on the basis of increased measurable learning.

n. Try to set up an Instructional Crisis Squad who can help teachers on a more individual basis to improve their courses. The members of this unit could include a librarian, an audio-visual specialist, a counseling or guidance person, one or more teachers who have successfully tried the BLSA concepts, and an administrator who has some power to help get things done.

o. Given that no one set of materials will be successful for all students, the ideal instructional environment will offer multiple pathways to the learning of the required SO's. Instead of trying to set up the environment ahead of time in which one buys lots of solutions to problems the students haven't had yet, use whatever materials that are available and only buy or develop new materials when faced with a learning problem that the available materials can't solve.

p. In order to gently nudge reluctant teachers into doing some of the Instructioneer tasks and at the same time start to eliminate some of the malpractices, start out the first year with the least minimum effort which is that all grades of "I" and "F" (or any other grade or symbol which indicates failure) have to be accompanied by a list of what it was that the student didn't learn (SO's, test items, and/or criteria for evaluation). Parents and students should be notified that if the student learns what he or she didn't achieve (as indicated on the list), their grade will be changed accordingly. During the second year, all grades of "I", "F", and "D" or any other grades which indicate similar achievement levels have to be accompanied by a list of what it was that the student didn't learn. During the third year, all grades of "I", "F", "D", and "C" or any other grades which indicate similar achievement levels have to be accompanied by a list of what it was that the student didn't learn. By the third year, there will be a tendency for teachers to give a lot of "A's" and "B's" in order to avoid making up the list of what wasn't learned; therefore, it will also be necessary by this third year to be able to define what "A" or 100 percent and "B" of each course is in terms of SO's, test items, and/or criteria for evaluation. This strategy gives teachers two years to identify the SO's for their courses.

q. Initially, in demanding 100 percent achievement from the students, there may be a tendency for many students to take longer to complete a course than would be the usual time. In order to balance this tendency, minimize any activities which can't be defended in terms of increased measurable learning. This could even include the cancellation of some of the students' scheduled classes (periods) in order to have more time to learn the required SO's. If you or a teacher don't think a class or an activity should be cancelled, ask *What is it specifically that the students won't learn by not attending the class (or by not doing that activity)?* If you or the teacher can't specify the learning that would be missed, then the class or the activity could be cancelled. However, if you or the teacher can come up with a list of SO's that wouldn't be learned, then the classes or activities shouldn't be cancelled.

r. If in scheduling inservice sessions, a teacher says *I can't go because I have classes during that time*, ask the teacher, *What is it specifically that the students won't learn as a result of not being in class?* If the teacher can answer this question with a list of SO's, test items, and/or criteria for evaluation which the students will not learn, then the teacher probably doesn't have to attend the in-service sessions anyway because the teacher may have already learned some or all of the SO's of the inservice sessions.

s. Quite typically when teachers are introduced to some new concepts, there are some teachers who want to go on a trip and visit some other school where the new concepts are being practiced. Unless a teacher has tried out some of the concepts first, the teacher won't know the questions to ask if they did go to visit. In fact, trips should be limited to those teachers who have already indicated their enthusiasm by trying out some of the BLSA concepts. Oddly enough, once teachers get started on the transition from traditional education to designed instruction, some of the best examples of designed instruction in action occur about *20 feet down the hall* from the teacher who wanted to go on a trip.

t.   As a minimum effort, try at least to get teachers to identify what I call *critical objectives*. These are SO's which if not learned will cause cumulative ignorance for subsequent courses. One of the easiest ways to identify the critical objectives is to have teachers talk to teachers of the potential subsequent courses a student might go to and ask the teachers, *What is it that students who start your course need to know in order to have success in your course? Given that some students are having trouble learning your SO's, what is it they should have learned in my course to help them have more success in your course?* These SO's are usually *critical SO's*. Students should be required to achieve 100 percent of these critical SO's.

u.   Since most teachers don't have SO's for their courses, it is difficult to identify the relationship between SO's, test items, and criteria for evaluation. In lieu of not having SO's, it is a useful exercise for teachers to go through their test items and criteria for evaluation and look at them from the point of view that they are SO's which the teacher wants their students to learn. Since many test items are put in tests to facilitate curve grading or to *separate the men from the boys*, a review of the test items and criteria from the point of view of their being SO's and being important will eliminate many test items making it easier for both teachers and students. To aid in this evaluation of existing test items and criteria for evaluation, use the questions of justification (see pages 543-625, Volume II). Also, be sure while examining test items and criteria to separate them into rote memory items and process items. Each rote memory item reflects a matching rote memory SO. Separate the process items such that all items testing for the achievement of the same process are together. Each of these groupings reflect a matching process SO. Although achievement of rote memory SO's can be in terms of the test items or SO's, the achievement of process SO's have to be in terms of the SO's (see pages 1079-83).

v.   Try to get teachers to use preentry tests (prerequisite learning) to find out students' cumulative ignorance early in a course before it creates learning problems. Teachers should also use pretests to find out whether or not any of the students already know part of the course and should be skipped over that part(s) of the course.

w.   Try to get teachers to recognize that students are individually different in the amount they have to learn, their rate of learning, their best mode for learning, their motivation to learn, and that if they are willing to vary the learning environment (not the SO's) to fit the abilities of the student, 90 percent or more of the students can achieve 100 percent of the SO's of their courses.

x.   Try to get teachers to look on students errors as a positive concept rather than a negative concept. Students rarely make mistakes on purpose, so when they do, it is because they don't know whatever it is the teacher is asking them to do. A teacher can't do much about what students already know, but a teacher can do something about a student's non-achievement. Non-achievement points out the existence of one or more learning problems. The teacher's role is to solve the problems such that the students can achieve. *Student errors do not represent something wrong with the student, they represent positive teaching opportunities for the teacher.*

4. IN-SERVICE TRAINING TO BRING ABOUT CHANGE

In talking with administrators in school districts, colleges, and universities, there is one concept that receives almost a unanimous vote as far as importance and need, and that is the concept of in-service training for teachers. On the other hand, if you talk to teachers at the same educational levels, their attitudes toward most in-service training sessions are quite negative because all too often the in-service sessions, particularly for elementary and secondary school teachers are more of the same kind of classes which they had in their educational courses. In talking with teachers who have had education courses in our teacher-training institutions, the majority indicate that over half of the courses they have taken are almost completely useless as far as helping to improve their effectiveness and efficiency in the teaching-learning situation.

NOTE: This does not necessarily mean that half of the courses in education are useless. What it may mean is that those parts of the courses which are relevant for improving the teaching-learning situation are so buried amid irrelevant material that the students can't identify them. Since the primary emphasis of most schools of education is not to maximize learning for all students, the teachers of most of the courses don't take the trouble to identify the relevant material that could help the future teachers be more effective in helping students learn.

An interesting situation occurs in which almost every superintendent or principal that I have talked with over the years has indicated that new teachers who have just finished four or five years of training in a teacher-training institution need in-service training before they can become effective teachers in the classroom. What makes this situation interesting is the fact that generally, the specialists or consultants who are hired to carry out the in-service training are the same college and university faculty who weren't able to accomplish the job in four or five years at the college or university! This may be why some school administrators at all levels of education are going outside of the academic community for consultants from business and industry to help them improve the teaching-learning situation. This does not mean that all in-service sessions conducted by faculty from teacher-training institutions are not of value and that the in-service sessions conducted by consultants from business and industry are all good. Some education faculty put on better in-service sessions than they are able to do in their own college or university environment. There are consultants from business and industry who have just come out of the academic environment and their in-service sessions are very traditional. There are some in-service sessions which could have potential value for the teachers and the students, but the financial, organizational, or attitudinal support which the teacher may need to put into practice the concepts presented in the in-service sessions are often not available from their administrators.

During the past decade, the biggest problem which I have had to overcome in conducting seminars for teachers is the negative attitude which most teachers have towards in-service training sessions. The fact that teachers and administrators keep attending in-service sessions in spite of their negative attitudes towards these sessions, does indicate a very strong positive hope and desire to try to improve the teaching-learning situation. Therefore, any school districts, colleges, and universities which conduct these in-service sessions for their teachers and the teachers who attend these sessions should be commended for their effort, even though the results are usually quite minimal.

The most important factor affecting the achievement of significant results from such sessions is that the overall emphasis of most of the in-service sessions is on the *teacher*. The emphasis concerns what the teacher should be doing in the teaching-learning situation and how they should present content and information to the students. The emphasis should be on the *learner* and how we are going to help the learner achieve the objectives or goals of the courses. A second factor, particularly for elementary and secondary teachers, is that few, if any, of the college and university faculty who taught them in their undergraduate courses, graduate courses, or in-service sessions actually practice what they are preaching. For example, according to most colleges and schools of education, the non-graded school is a good concept. If the concept is really good, why aren't there more than just a few nongraded colleges and schools of education? Most students who are planning to be teachers are being told about the necessity of having specific objectives, yet very few education courses or in-service sessions have specific objectives.

In a growing number of school districts, the teachers are preparing or using specially designed learning packages or instructional units which do have specific objectives listed for each package or unit. This concept is a very big step in the right direction, but the problem is that many of these packages end up by testing the students' achievement with true-false, multiple-choice, and matching test items, because they are easy to grade, and in spite of the fact that the test items are not testing for specific achievement of the specified objectives. The hypocrisy of stating one set of objectives and testing something else should not be surprising because almost all courses in testing teach this hypocritical behavior as being *good* because it results in a nice curve of grades (even though it doesn't measure the achievement of desired objectives.)

The most important factor in developing successful in-service sessions is that they reflect an identified need and that they are designed to satisfy that need. although traditional education is not that concerned about student learning, my experience has been that basically the vast majority of teachers want their students to be successful in learning. If in-service sessions are tied to increasing student learning, their chances for success are better. In addition, the following are some guidelines that I have found to be useful in conducting in-service sessions.

a. If faculty are directly involved in identifying the needs and setting up the in-service session, the rest of the faculty will accept the sessions more readily.

b. If at all possible, it is very good to hold the in-service sessions at a location away from the school environment. Ideally, at some lodge or hotel in a recreation area.

c. In addition to the scheduled sessions during the day which tend to be more formal, it is good to have time during the evening in which the faculty and the consultants or leaders of the in-service sessions can meet informally for discussions. The offering of snacks and particularly *refreshments* will help to bring out more faculty and more discussions.

d. Attendance by faculty should be voluntary. However, administrative encouragement will aid faculty attendance. If administrators demand attendance and make a record of attendance, the action tends to develop an initial negative attitude which affects the success of the in-service session.

e. Frequently, administrators will set up the in-service sessions and then won't attend them. I have found that more change takes place when administrators take time to meet with the teachers in the in-service sessions. What is good enough for the teachers, should be good enough for those who work with and/or supervise the teachers. Attendance by administrators also indicates their approval and support for the concepts being presented.

f. There should be a purpose in having an in-service session besides just the fact that one was held. Given an instructional direction that a school wants to go, the in-service sessions should be based on identified problems whose solutions will facilitate the achievement of the school's goals in the desired direction.

g. Given that an instructional direction exists, then there should be planned evaluation and follow-up activities. Plans for follow-up activities indicates to the participants that something is supposed to happen as a result of the in-service sessions.

h. If convenient, have faculty register to attend so that reminder notices can be sent out, and so that the in-service sessions can be scheduled when those faculty who want to attend are available even if it means scheduling duplicate sessions.

i. If the in-service session deals with course development, be sure to demonstrate both good and bad examples of applications of the concepts presented during the in-service sessions.

j. To avoid statements of the type, *That is a good idea for some other teacher but not very appropriate in my subject matter area*, be sure to give examples of applications in a variety of subjects.

k. If available, involve teachers who are already practicing some of the concepts presented in the in-service sessions.

l. Brainstorm constantly on practical applications of stated principles of developing instructional materials. Faculty members will ultimately come up with the best ideas for development and improvement of instructional materials in their subject fields, but they may need a catalyst.

m. Try to practice in the in-service session whatever concepts the in-service session is supposed to get teachers to do.

n. Build in some form of active-involvement on the part of the participants. The use of active-involvement note-taking forms are very useful in that the format communicates to the participants what is important in the in-service sessions, it facilitates questions at later informal sessions, and unifies what is taken from the sessions.

o. Be ready and able to back up offers of help via the Instructional Crisis Squad or other groups and individuals.

p. Just as there are individual differences among students, there are also individual differences among faculty, so part of the follow-up activities should include small group and individual meetings to accommodate these differences.

q. If at all possible, obtain administrative commitments to reward excellence in teaching (as measured by more students learning more SO's) as this will encourage participation during and after the in-service sessions (assuming that whatever is presented in the in-service sessions can actually help teachers be more effective and efficient in facilitating student learning).

5. IN-SERVICE AND PRE-SERVICE TRAINING: AN ADVERTISEMENT

Although it is very unusual to use the medium of a book for an advertisement and I may be criticized by others for doing it, I believe in this situation that I am justified in doing so. I have been putting on pre-service and in-service sessions dealing with various parts of this three volume set for over 15 years. I wrote my first paper dealing with the System's Concepts in 1961. My motivation for doing this type of work is primarily because I found these concepts to be useful in the teaching-learning process and wanted to share them with other teachers. During the mid-sixties, I became very concerned about those traditional practices which were having negative effects on students. From then on, my primary motivation was to try to eliminate these practices or malpractices (as I called them) so that students wouldn't have to endure them any longer, students would learn more, and teachers could be more professional in their behavior. At that time, I was only meeting with an average of 5,000 teachers per year. In order to increase the number of teachers who would be involved in these important concepts, I stopped teaching in an academic institution and went into full time consulting. Since then, I have met with an average of 25,000 teachers per year at all levels of education. However, the teacher training institutions were graduating about 150,000 new teachers each year who were being trained to utilize most or all of the malpractices about which I was so concerned. That is when I decided to write my first book, *Educational Malpractices: The Big Gamble in Our Schools* which was first published in 1971. My plan and hope was that between my consulting and the book I would be able to communicate to many more teachers. The primary function of the book was to point out the problems with many of the traditional practices and how they were un-professional. Given that teachers at all levels of education claim to be and want to be professionals, it should be expected that not only should they be accorded the privileges of a professional, but they should also want to accept the responsibilities of a professional and the one most important responsibility of a professional is not to commit acts of malpractice or practices which are not in the best interests of their clients (students).

In pointing out what is wrong with the traditional form of education, I felt a responsibility to offer constructive suggestions as to positive practices which could be substituted for those traditional practices which should be eliminated. In order to not take away from the primary function of the book, I only included in this book a 67 page summary of the Behavioral Learning Systems Approach (BLSA) towards instruction.

In discussing the changing role of the teacher from the traditional role as a presenter or transmitter of information to that of an Instructioneer, one of the guidelines that I suggest for teachers in making the change is to minimize the presentation role in order to have more time to meet with small groups of students and/or with individual students. In an attempt to *practice what I preach*, I have put into these three volumes all of what I usually include in my in-service sessions. In a sense, the writing of these three volumes should put me out of business as far as conducting large group in-service sessions is concerned. However, because of individual differences in teachers, some will be able to learn effectively from the books while others may prefer the traditional large group in-service session format.

a. PUBLICATIONS

As an aid in bringing about change, the *Educational Malpractice* book could be used as a text for pre-service training in order to discourage the development of the malpractices by students planning to be teachers and at the same time introduce the basic concepts of the BLSA. This book could also be used as a text for in-service sessions designed to help teachers eliminate these malpractices. This book has also been used effectively with student and parent groups who are also very much concerned about eliminating the malpractices in traditional education. The inclusion of the malpractice dialogues was primarily for the benefit of students and parents to give them a more equal position in their discussions with teachers.

The three volumes of this series, can be used individually or in combination as a basis for either pre-service training or in-service training. Depending upon the needs of specific faculty groups or individuals, various parts of the volumes may be more appropriate than others and may be the emphasis for courses, units, or sessions. Teachers who have already accepted the new role as an Instructioneer may only need Volume II as a guide in developing instructional materials. However, teachers who have not accepted their new role as yet, should really use both Volumes I and II. Volume III is primarily designed for administrators and could be used in pre-service training of students and teachers planning to be administrators and in in-service training of administrators. Teachers should be familiar with the concepts in Volume III so that they can understand what administrators are doing when they attempt to apply some of the concepts suggested in the book. As an aid to the study of these three volumes, I have prepared an Active Involvement Form for each chapter and each book. Contact SLATE Services directly for availability and costs of these forms.

Whereas it is the usual practice of publishers to publish a hard cover edition of a book first and then at a later date to publish a paperback edition if there is a sufficient demand, in an attempt to make these books as economically available as possible, all three books have been published in both cloth cover and paperback editions. Contact SLATE Services directly or through your local book store for copies of one or more of the three volumes.

In addition to these books, I also publish a Newsletter, *DAIRS and Systems for Instruction.* In trying to get teachers to change their role as a presenter of course content and to try to spend more time individualizing instruction, a variety of educational technology has been introduced into the classroom. Although television did take over the presenting role of the teacher, it also is based on the concept of classes of students all progressing at the same pace. During the early 1960's several companies and schools experimented with the concept of dial-access information retrieval systems. These systems allowed the students to dial into a battery of audio tape recorders and/or video tape recorders to retrieve their teacher's presentations or other recorded material at any time and as often as they needed to repeat it. As such, the Dial-Acess Information Retrieval Systems or DAIRS facilitated individualized instruction.

In an effort to increase the use of DAIRS as a way of improving instruction, the DAIRS Newsletter was started in September of 1965. As might be expected, the emphasis was on the technology of DAIRS. During the next three or four years, the number of DAIRS installations in schools went from less than fifty to more than 400. The number of companies installing the equipment went from two or three to over fifteen. Although a few of the schools with a DAIRS installation did try to individualize instruction, most of the schools with a DAIRS continued on as before. As a result, DAIRS became just another form of educational hardware for schools to spend money on in order to be considered *mod.* As the need for educational reform became more and more apparent and the concept of accountability began to rise on the instructional hoizon, it became obvious that the emphasis on hardware in the DAIRS Newsletter was the wrong approach. Starting in 1968, the emphasis on the DAIRS Newsletter changed over to the *improvement in instruction* via the use of the Behavioral Learning System's Approach (BLSA) which may or may not include any hardware. If the use of some technological hardware is a part of the instructional system, it is there because it facilitates learning and has helped solve learning problems not because it is *mod.*

During the past few years, the Newsletter has also changed from one containing comments on up to ten different topics to sort of a single concept Newsletter in which a whole issue is devoted to a single topic. Although the average issue consists of five or six pages, there have been topics which needed twice as much or even more space in order to cover the topic adequately. As a result, these longer Newsletters are considered to be double issues. Normally, the Newsletter is published approximately six times a year, unless there are double issues, in which case, there would only be three Newsletters published during the year. The Newsletter is not published on a predetermined schedule as are most other publications. The Newsletter is published whenever there is something important to say and whenever the writing and publishing can be worked into an already busy schedule. Subscribers to the Newsletter are involved in all aspects and levels of education, designed instruction, and training and live throughout the United States, Canada, and many foreign countries around the world. Contact SLATE Services directly for subscription rates and for a listing and availability of back issues.

In addition to these verbal publications it is my intention to develop a series of filmed presentations which could be used in pre-service and in-service sessions individually or as a series. The content of the films will be taken from the contents of this three volume set and will be primarily filmed lectures with designed involvement via the Active Involvement Forms. Several films will be based on the educational malpractice concept and as such will be particularly useful for student and/or parent groups. These films should be available by the end of 1976 or at least by the fall of 1977. Contact SLATE Services directly for availability and rental information.

b. USING THE SERIES AS TEXTBOOKS FOR PRE-SERVICE TRAINING

As defined in the first volume of this series, instructional materials are differentiated from educational materials in that instructional materials are developed for the purpose of achieving specific objectives and are evaluated on the basis of a test that tests for the achievement of these specific objectives. Therefore, in order for this book to be classified as *instructional* materials, the designs of the pre-service training should include the achievement of specific objectives. The primary objective of any pre-service training or in-service training using this series as textbooks should be to develop highly positive attitudes towards the four basic concepts presented in Volumes I and II.

(1) Concept No. 1 — Role of the Professional Educator

The most important role of the professional educator is to facilitate learning for individual students by diagnosing their learning problems, solving these learning problems, and prescribing appropriate learning experiences, so that students learn. A less important role of the professional educator is to lecture to groups of students.

(2) Concept No. 2 — Learning Ability of Students

It is possible for 90 percent or more of your students to learn 100 percent of whatever you think is important in your course and are able to measure.

(3) Concept No. 3 — Learning Objectives

In order to maximize learning and the effectiveness and efficiency of the teaching-learning situation, the learning objectives of your courses have to be specific and stated in terms of observable and measurable behaviors exhibited by the learner.

(4) Concept No. 4 — Testing

The results of the tests which you give to your students should be diagnostic and be used to determine what is to be taught in the teaching-learning situation. Therefore, testing should be a very critical and integral part of the teaching-learning process, instead of being used primarily as an aid in determining students' grades.

Because these concepts concern attitudes which are in the affective domain, they should be tested before and after the training. I have used the semantic differential for this function and have found it to be very useful. The following chart is a copy of the form that I have used (Figure 143). A separate chart should be used with each concept being evaluated. The key points to remember besides the guideline that the measurement should be based on the difference and the direction of the difference between pretest and posttest, is that testing in the affective domain should be anonymous in order to get more honest answers and that the results primarily evaluate the teacher's design of the course. This particular form of the semantic differential uses five levels of attitude between two extremes of ten pairs of descriptive adjectives. The high and low of each pair have been reversed from the preceding pair in order to avoid someone checking straight down one of the

	Very	Slightly	Neutral	Slightly	Very	
Useless						Useful
Right						Wrong
Skeptical						Believing
Fair						Unfair
Bad						Good
Meaningful						Meaningless
Harmful						Beneficial
Positive						Negative
Reject						Accept
Exciting						Discouraging
	Very	Slightly	Neutral	Slightly	Very	

Figure 143 — Semantic Differential for Evaluating Attitudes

columns without actually considering his or her feelings towards the concept in reference to each adjectival pair. The minimum score would be 10 and would be indicated by check marks at the *very* low end of each adjectival pair. The maximum score would be 50 and would be indicated by check marks at the *very* high end of each adjectival pair. A neutral score would be 30. The score is obtained by counting from the low end of each adjectival pair to the check mark (remembering that the direction of counting reverses with each adjectival pair, i.e., in the first line of Figure 143, the counting starts at the left side over to the check mark; in the second line, the counting starts at the right side over to the check mark; etc.)

In addition to the affective domain objectives, there are cognitive objectives which should be learned. In addition to the SO's I have listed, a teacher may want to make up some more SO's or may want to delete some to more accurately coincide with his or her own personal beliefs and course SO's. Most of the rote memory items are considered important in that they help to change the attitudes of the students or participants. The inclusion of the objectives in the student's textbook is based on the fact that one of the first steps in facilitating learning is to let the students know what they are supposed to learn, which is quite contrary to the traditional approach of hiding from the students what they are supposed to learn and forcing them to guess what they are supposed to study.

A very important part of developing highly positive attitudes is the achievement of the process objective (term project) in which students or participants apply the suggestions made in this series to an actual learning problem which they have identified, analyzed, made up the materials for, tried them out on actual students, revised the materials in accordance with achievement results, and provided additional pathways such that 90 percent or more of their students achieve 100 percent of the learning problem which they have identified. The primary objective of this term project is to have the student or participant involved in the teaching role of *solving learning problems*. Because of the tradition among educators in believing that all or even most of their students can't learn "A" or "B" worth of a course, it is also a very important part of this project that the students or participants stick to the project until such time as 90 percent or more of the students they are working with learn 100 percent of the specific objectives which have been identified for the unit involving the learning problem. Obviously, in order to carry this out, it is absolutely necessary that the students who are in this course and are carrying out a term project have other students available. Since in most cases, the students will not be able to design instructional materials that will maximize learning the first time the students are exposed to the materials, provisions must be made so that students will (1) be able to work with the experimental students until such time as maximum learning takes place, or (2) have time to develop the additional necessary alternate learning paths and then utilize the materials with a subsequent group of experimental students, or (3) if in the student's report concerning the evaluation of the instructional materials they are able to point out clearly enough why they didn't reach maximum learning and the instructor is convinced that if the student was able to make the changes in the instructional materials which the student had suggested that maximum learning will take place, it may not be necessary to wait until a subsequent class is available for experimental tryout of the revised materials.

Most of the students or participants who would be taking courses utilizing this series as textbooks and fulfilling the term project requirement would fit into one of the following categories:

1. Teachers who are presently teaching and are taking evening courses or week-end courses. These teachers should identify a learning problem among their own classes and use their own students as the experimental class.

2. Teachers who are enrolled in a summer course. These teachers could either use students who are enrolled in other summer school courses preferably at the same level that the teachers normally teach or they could wait to complete the project after they are back teaching in the fall and use their own students.

3. Teachers who are on a sabatical or leave of absence. These teachers should be able to corroborate with their colleagues at the school they are on leave of absence from in the identification and solution of the learning problems.

4. Students who are involved in practice teaching and may also be enrolled in the course using this textbook and term project. Arrangements should be made with the cooperating school and teachers, so that the student will be able to use the class of the cooperating teacher as the experimental class and will identify the learning problem and solve it with this class, or subsequent classes, if necessary.

NOTE: In addition to this type of a term project giving the student an excellent experience in maximizing learning in the teaching-learning situation, arrangements of this kind can result in performing an in-service function with the cooperating teachers. Not only would the cooperating teachers end up with instructional materials in their classes which maximized learning, but also they would benefit from observing and working with the students in the identification and solution of learning problems in which 90 percent or more of the learners learn 100 percent or more of the objectives.

5. Graduate students who are planning to teach in higher education and who traditionally have never been asked to take education courses nor usually do any practice teaching. They may still be able to complete a term project as described previously, if arrangements can be made with the colleagues of the instructor of the course, not only in the school or department of instruction, but in other departments and schools of the college or university. Students could be assigned to these teachers and they could still carry out the procedures of identifying a learning problem and solving it. (The above Note also applies to these students and their cooperating teachers.)

Because this role of the teacher as a *solver of learning problems* is so important in the teaching-learning process at all levels, it is hoped that the day will come when all graduate students who are planning to go into college or university instruction will be required to take such a course as described herein, including as a primary objective, the term project. If a course is designed for graduate students, it would be preferable that the graduate students be allowed to work with a faculty member who is teaching a course that the student will be most apt to teach after he graduates.

Among the criteria for evaluation that a teacher may use in evaluating the term project should be the following:

1. Did the student follow the steps of the Learning Systems Approach?
    a. Did the student identify a learning problem by supplying evidence such as excerpts from a teacher's gradebook or an analysis of tests, etc.?
    b. Did the student follow the behavioral analysis as indicated under the Learning Systems Approach by specifying the terminal behaviors of the instructional unit concerned with the problem, the desired entry behvaiors, and the learning objectives of the unit itself, with the corresponding posttests, preentry tests, and pretests?
    c. Did the student try out the tests on the experimental students to identify what was wrong with the present instructional approach. Did the student develop instructional materials that were based on the data and information gained from trying out the tests.

NOTE: In my past experience, approximately 50 percent of the learning problems which have been identified have been solved by just specifying the learning objectives involved and letting the students know what they are supposed to learn. Another 25 percent of the learning problems are solved by the development of test items which have a high correlation with the objectives of the course and with what the teacher is teaching. Therefore, in cases where the specification of the objectives or the development of test items have already solved the learning problem, the following steps may not be necessary.

    d. Did the students try out the instructional materials that were developed, and was the student able to achieve maximum learning (90 percent or more of the learners learning 100 percent of the specified objectives of the learning unit)?
    e. If the new instructional materials did not achieve maximum learning, were the materials revised or alternate paths of learning developed or suggestions made for the revision of materials?
2. Did the students communicate their term project to others?
    a. To the instructor:
       Did the student utilize the approved format for submission of the term project report, as specified by the instructor?
       Did the report fulfill the grammatical and structural standards as specified by the instructor?

b. To other students in the same class through presentations or by furnishing the students with duplicate copies of the term report or by furnishing other students with abstracts of the term report.

c. To the student's cooperating teacher, if any, by giving the teacher a duplicate copy of the report or abstract of the report plus a copy of the instructional materials, tests, and lists of specific objectives.

In order to practice what the course and this book preaches, the teacher who is using this book and the term project in a course should not accept any term project that does not come up to the "A" and "B" level. Any term project, even if it achieves the desired instructional results, that does not reach what the instructor considers an "A" and "B" level, should be returned to the student, with specific identifiable criticisms, so that the student is able to make the appropriate changes and resubmit the project. Traditionally, we condition most undergraduate students to turn in "C" term projects or papers. This is in part due to curve grading, which allowed the instructor to grade term papers without really specifying exactly what the objectives of the term paper or project were. Maximum performance should be demanded of all students, regardless of the length of time or the number of times the student has to upgrade the material.

In order to maximize the student learning involved in this course, there are several suggestions that can be made in reference to the course format. Ideally, it would be consistent with the books if students or participants could start the course at anytime and could finish the course at any time. Because it will probably be several years before *open entry* is feasible, at least the course should be designed to allow for *open exit*. Since most of the material is available in the books, except for additional material that the instructor may wish to include in this course, the course should *not* be set up to meet two, three, four, or five times a week, whether the students need it or not. After the initial sessions and whatever other class meetings are needed to present the additional material the teacher may wish to add to the course, the students should be given a reasonable time to go through the books or those parts of the book(s) which the teacher has decided to include in the course requirements. Students could use the Active Involvement Forms or those parts of the forms which coincide with what the teacher wants the students to learn as a note-taking and learning device and the same forms could be used as a test of the rote memory objectives. Those who can complete this test can now start on their term project. Those who are not able to pass the test at the required levels would then meet with the teacher in small groups or as individuals until such time as they are able to pass the test at the required level. The balance of the course would then be devoted to the instructor meeting with individual or small groups or with the students and their cooperating teachers in whatever efforts that are necessary in order to help the students solve their learning problems in the accomplishment of the term project. As soon as some of the students have completed their term projects to the required level, then classes can be held so that students can make presentations or hand out abstracts and be available for questions from their classmates, etc. The students should be considered as finished with the course whenever he has completed the course requirements, even if this is midway through a traditional term or semester, or if it takes two or three semesters or terms. The completion is measured by the achievement of the course objectives, not by the completion of so many days in a classroom.

c. CONSULTING SERVICES

In my consulting activities, there are primarily two different methods. The first method concerns the contracting with specific school districts, colleges, universities, and other institutions with educational or instructional functions for the performance of specified activities which will aid teachers and administrators in the transition from the traditional approach to the BLSA. The second method concerns the setting up each year of a series of seminars which are held at various locations around the country and are designed to aid teachers and administrators in the transition from the traditional approach to the BLSA. Although both methods have essentially the same goal, the major difference is that whereas in the first method the contract is with a single institution and I am primarily working with the faculty or staff of that institution; in the second method, individuals register for the meetings and pay fees on an individual basis although frequently two or more participants may come from the same institution. The description of these seminars, their locations, and fees are available directly from SLATE Services. The schedule of locations is made up each year early in the fall.

Up until the time that these books were published, my consulting activities wherein I contracted with single institutions consisted of three types of seminars. The first type of seminars were primarily presentation sessions in which I presented varying amounts of what is contained in these three books. These seminars were scheduled to last from one to three days at one time. The presentations were condensed to fit the time available. The typical seminar I conducted was for two days. Attendance at these seminars have ranged from 20 to 5000 teachers at a time. The second type of seminars were typically designed as follow-up sessions after the general presentation seminars. During these seminars,

I worked with small groups and individuals and helped them apply the BLSA to their own courses by looking at any objectives they might have, tests they had been using, and any identified learning problems. The third type of seminars were custom designed to specific needs of a specific faculty group and could concern one or more aspects of the BLSA; design and/or evaluation of curriculum materials, proposals for funding, and/or special programs; the development of a new school, college, or university which will emphasize various aspects of the BLSA; and a variety of other instructional related functions.

(1) AN EXAMPLE OF CONTRACT SEMINARS: WASHINGTON STATE COMMUNITY COLLEGES

As an example of the contract seminars, in the winter and spring of 1970, I had a contract with the state of Washington and I spent 71 days working with the faculty at 21 out of 22 community colleges in the state of Washington. Of approximately 2000 faculty, about 1000 or one-half of them attended the one-day general sessions and the one or two days of follow-up departmental meetings. About 150 faculty were involved in individual sessions. Of particular interest to the readers of this book are some of the results of the project and facts identified during the project. (The rest of this section is taken from a report published in 1970 as an issue of my Newsletter.)

(a) There were at least one or more faculty members somewhere in the state in each subject which is commonly offered at all of the colleges that felt that the *Systems Concept* had *something* valuable to offer to the teaching and learning of that subject.

(b) There were at least one or more faculty members somewhere in the state in each subject which is commonly offered at all of the colleges that felt that the *systems concept* had *nothing* valuable to offer to the teaching and learning of that subject.

Comments: These two statements tend to support a belief among *systems specialists* that the variable concerning whether or not the *Systems Concepts* is valuable depends much more on who the teacher is and what his or her beliefs are rather than on what the subject is. In other words, *all subjects* can utilize the *Systems Concepts if* the teacher believes it will improve the teaching-learning situation.

(c) At about half of the colleges, students were invited, encouraged, and did attend the general sessions with faculty.

Comments: The *Systems Concepts* appear very exciting to students. If large numbers of students are involved, they can be a very strong force in HELPING to bring about change in the traditional instructional patterns of faculty, i.e., when a group of students say to a teacher, *In Prof. Smith's class, we are told what we're supposed to learn in order that more of us can learn. How come in your class you don't let us know what we're supposed to learn? Don't you want us to learn what you think is important (the tests)?* An interesting contrast in *point-of-view* was brought out during the project. Whereas some faculty seemed to think that the *Systems Concepts* consisted of spoon-feeding the students and putting the major responsibility for student learning on the teacher, almost all students felt that the *Systems Concepts* placed the responsibility for learning on the student (the student either learns "A" or "B" worth of the course or they stay in the course with an *Incomplete* until they do learn "A" or "B" worth). The actual major responsibilities for the teacher is to identify what it is that students are supposed to learn and to diagnose and prescribe for any learning problems that the students might encounter in the process of learning.

> (d) A majority of the faculty who stayed through the entire one-day seminar and attended at least one departmental meeting made some *change* in their teaching patterns and/or in their teaching materials. These *changes* ranged all the way from very slight changes involving only a few days of instruction and a few students to a complete re-organization of a course and involving every student in the course. The major emphasis in all *changes* was to help more students learn more of whatever it was the teacher wanted the students to learn.

Comments: Although all of the *changes* were brought about by individual teachers in their own courses, there are several group efforts to coordinate these changes on the basis that having each individual teacher reinvent the *curriculum wheel* on their own is wasted effort.

> (e) The most common *change* made by faculty during the project was to let the students know what they were supposed to learn. Some teachers handed out lists of objectives to the students at the beginning of each unit. Other teachers started the term or instructional unit by giving the students the final examination for the term or unit. Without exception, teachers who let students know ahead of time what they were supposed to learn ended up the term with greater learning by more students than under the traditional approach of *hiding* from the students what they were supposed to learn.

Comments: Any teacher can replicate this result in their own classroom the next time they show a film. Preview the film and write out the questions that students should be able to answer as a result of seeing the film. Then, split the class that will be viewing the film into two groups. Give the list of questions to one of the two groups before they see the film. After showing the film, have both groups answer the questions. So far, in my experience, the group that knows what they are supposed to learn from the film will always learn more than the group that doesn't know what they are supposed to learn from the film.

> (f) The second most common *change* concerned teacher-made tests. Many teachers stopped giving multiple-choice, true-false, and matching test items because they generally have a very low correlation with the learning objectives of the course. In place of the so-called *objective* type test items, most teachers asked students to solve problems, complete statements, and write varying lengths of essay type answers.

Comments: Remember *objective* type test items are called objective only from the standpoint of scoring, i.e., given "c" is the right answer for a multiple-choice item — whether or not the student selected "c" can be objectively scored. The very fact that professional test item writers can take almost any multiple-choice item and by varying the *detractors* in the item can get almost any percentage of students to get the item right or wrong, reveals that the writing of a multiple-choice item is very subjective. In other words, the results of a so-called *objective* test in the form of a distribution of scores is probably more affected by the skill or lack of skill of the person making up the test than by the knowledge of the students taking the test. Even more important is the fact that the multiple-choice format (true-false and matching items are also basically a type of multiple-choice item) doesn't fit the real-world situation except in rare situations. Almost everyone, regardless of their age, vocation, etc., is confronted daily in the decision-making process with multiple choices, BUT the choices are identified by the decision-maker and are rarely presented to the decision-maker on a piece of paper. In order to utilize the concept of multiple-choices with maximum transfer to the real-world of decision-making, the teacher should ask the student to make a decision by first identifying the major alternatives (choices); then second, to explore the consequences of each alternative; and third, to select a choice and defend the choice. In this situation, the least important part of the question is the student's choice. The most important parts are whether or not the student identified all of the major alternatives, whether or not the consequences of each alternative were correctly identified, and whether or not the student's defense of his choice followed the proper logic of the decision-making process.

> (g) The third most common *change* concerned grading. At each college at least one or more teachers used the "A", "B" or "I" (Incomplete) grading concept or a similar one emphasizing quality control. The number of teachers involved varied from only one or two in one college to over half of the faculty in another college. In addition, many teachers who couldn't quite believe that their students could learn "A" or "B" worth of their course tried "A", "B", "C" or "I".

Comments: This form of grading ("A", "B", or "I") is analogous to the concept of *quality control* or *zero defect* commonly found in business and industry. Indirectly, this grading concept had several interesting by-products. In order for a teacher to use the "A", "B", or "I" concept, they had to identify what students had to learn in order to achieve "A" or "B" worth of the course. Because of individual differences in *rate of learning* (which is ignored under the traditional approach), some students were able to complete a course much sooner than other students and some students had to take more than a quarter to finish a course. As a result, teachers were able to really individualize the instructional process. In fact, at two schools, students were allowed to register for a course in the middle of the quarter. Under this concept of *quality control*, the community colleges will really be able to offer a community service by letting interested students start any course at any time when they are ready rather than when faculty and registrars are ready. Yes, this approach does away with the present concept of a *class* because students are at all different parts of a course simultaneously. But, it is a rare event that all of the students are intellectually at the same place under the present traditional approach anyway. The major difference is that traditionally the students' learning was negatively affected by these differences. Whereas under *quality control*, these differences only affect how long a student takes to learn or what pathways the student follows in order to learn.

> (h) The seminars and departmental meetings as conducted tended to polarize the faculty on one side or the other. Very few of the faculty who attended the sessions remained indifferent towards the general concept of *systems*.

Comments: Although they constituted a minority, the faculty which developed a negative attitude towards the general concept of *systems* tended to fall into two categories. First, there were the faculty who for one reason or another didn't like the way the seminar was presented and/or the presenter. Second, there were the faculty who resented the potential of the *Systems Concepts* to be used to evaluate the ability of teachers to teach. As long as no one (including the teacher) knew exactly what students were to learn, then the design of tests and the grading of the tests (term papers, essays, projects, etc.) could be manipulated such that only the students ability to learn could be questioned. For some reason, the ability of teachers to teach in higher education has never been questioned as long as they have the proper degrees in their subject matter. Yet in elementary and secondary education, it is assumed that teachers can't teach unless they have had an increasing number of educational courses — oddly enough, in community or junior colleges, it is very difficult to identify a difference between teachers who have had education courses and teachers who haven't had any training on *how to teach* as measured by their performance in the teaching-learning situation.

>(i) Almost all of the faculty who attended the one-day seminar and the departmental meetings increased their positive attitude towards the four *Systems Concepts* (unless they already had a maximum positive attitude before the seminar) as measured on the semantic differential administered as a pretest and a posttest.

Comments: This particular evaluation instrument had a scale of 10 to 50 where a score of 10 is extremely negative, a score of 50 is extremely positive, and score of 30 is neutral. On the pretest, all of the college faculty groups had between 50 percent and 75 percent of the faculty with scores below 35; whereas on the posttest, only 10 percent to 30 percent of the faculty had scores below 35. Even most of those who scored below 35 on the posttest indicated an increase in the positive direction towards the four *Systems Concepts* as described on page 1155.

>(j) Almost every teacher who included in their *changes* the concept of letting the students know ahead of time what they were supposed to learn, experienced the same student reaction to the change — a feeling of distrust.

Comments: Students are so accustomed to the traditional teaching-learning situation which is based on ambiguity, deception, and trickery that when a teacher starts being honest with students they can't believe it.

>(k) As commonly expected, some of the teachers in the humanities tended to resist the *Systems Concepts* because they felt that the specification of objectives *dehumanized* the teaching-learning situation.

Comments: Although the specification of learning objectives in the humanities is more difficult than in some of the other areas — it can be done. Of interest, is the fact that every teacher in the humanities who is resisting the specification of learning objectives, is at the same time giving tests, grading essays or term papers, and giving course grades. Most test items are specific, measurable, and behavioral and as such are synonymous with *specific objectives.* Anytime that a student in a humanities course (or any other course) receives a grade of less than an "A" or "B", this generally indicates that a student hasn't learned *something* that the teacher thinks the student should have learned. Assuming that the teacher knows what the *something* is that the student didn't learn, is it more *human* to let the student know specifically what it is he or she didn't learn and then help the student learn "A" or "B" worth of the course or is it more *human* to let the student go on not only not knowing the *something* he or she should have learned, but not even knowing what it is they didn't learn? Unfortunately, in most cases, when students are graded down in humanities where there are no specific objectives or measurable test items, the teachers can't identify what the *something* is that the students didn't learn. To grade students down for not learning *something* when the teacher doesn't know what that *something* is, does not seem to be very *human* to me.

> (l) Contrary to what might be expected, not all science teachers are in favor of the Systems Concept even though the learning objectives in most science courses can be much more easily specified.

Comments: What makes this even more interesting is that the *Systems Concepts* in instruction very closely parallel the *scientific method* as used in research. Therefore, some of the very same teachers who lecture on the merits of the *scientific method* and who grade students down for not using the *scientific method* in their work will resist using a *scientific method* (systems concepts) in their instructional efforts.

> (m) About 90% or more of the faculty use some form of *curve grading* as defined by grading a student's achievement relative to his classmates' achievement rather than in comparison to the actual content of the course.

Comments: Although most faculty will deny that they grade on a curve, when presented with a student's achievement level, i.e., 60% achievement of a test, in two different situations (one in which the student's 60% achievement is the highest in the class and the other where the student's 60% achievement is almost the lowest in the class) they will either assign two very different grades ("A" and "F") or they will want to change the test. If a teacher makes up a test to test for the achievement of what the teacher considers important in the course and the top student only achieves 50%-60% of the test, this means that something is wrong in the teaching of the course. If a teacher changes the test (compromising on what he or she previously thought was important), then the teacher is trying to cover up for his or her ineffective teaching techniques. Most teachers who grade on the curve usually assign what the letter grades stand for after the results of the students' achievement has been identified (after a test or at the end of a course). The rest of the teachers who grade on the curve, identify the level of achievement necessary for each letter grade (95-100 is "A", 85-94 is "B", 75-84 is "C", etc.) and then design the difficulty of their tests such that the right percentage of students fall into each category. This last technique is curve grading *before the fact* whereas the former technique is curve grading *after the fact*.

> (n) Many of the faculty and administrators were worried about what the accrediting association and particularly their colleagues in the four-year institutions would think if they started using the *Systems Concepts* such that 90% or more of the students achieved "A" or "B" in all their courses.

Comments: It is a very sad comment on the affect of the accrediting associations, when the traditions of ineffective and inefficient teaching become so much a part of the educational scene that faculty and administrators are afraid of improving learning for fear of losing their accreditation. The fear of community college faculty and administrators of what their colleagues in the four-year institutions will think is based on a concept found mainly in higher education which in effect identifies the *quality* of instruction in a course or institution by equating *quality* to the percentage of failures, i.e., a course or institution in which 90% or more of the students get "A's" or "B's" must have low *standards* whereas a course or institution that fails 30%-50% or even more of their students must have high *standards*. As a result, curve grading is used in order to achieve and maintain *high standards* (without changing what actually happens in the courses.) After all, if the objectives of a course were specified ahead of time and a teacher designed his or her activities such that 90% or more of the students had success in learning all of the objectives, this would not only be indicative of *low standards*, but would also be *dehumanizing!!!*

The most important result of the project is the reaffirmation of my conviction that the real *promise* of community and junior colleges lies in their ability to throw off the shackles of educational tradition and introduce designed effectiveness and efficiency into the instructional process. In this way, the community and junior colleges can lead the way in higher education rather than continuing on as a *bastard* offspring following the dictates of their more *legal* (traditional) big brother, the four-year institutions. There are more teachers and administrators in the community and junior colleges that are sincerely and actively interested in wanting more students to learn more than in most four-year schools. There are also more innovative efforts to increase learning in the community and junior colleges than at any other level of education. The problem is that it is difficult for a single community or junior college by itself to ignore the dictates of the regional accrediting association and of nearby four-year institutions. In Washington and in other states where most of the faculty in the community colleges want to improve the teaching-learning situation, there is a very good possibility that cooperatively they could set an instructional pace for the rest of higher education throughout the nation to follow. Indirectly, their efforts could also have a very beneficial effect on the instructional patterns in the elementary and secondary schools of Washington and the country.

(2) ALTERNATE PATHWAYS TO CHANGE AVAILABLE

With the publication of this three volume series and the eventual (1976-77) filmed presentations of some of the content of the series, alternate pathways to change are available. A school district, college, or university faculty and/or administrative group that wanted to make the transition from the more traditional approach to education to some aspects or all of the Behavioral Learning Systems Approach (BLSA) could do any one of the following to learn about the BLSA concepts.

>(a) The most comprehensive and detailed pathway would be to provide each faculty member with copies of Volumes I and II of this series and one copy of Volume III for every five-ten faculty members or for each department. They should use the Active Involvement Forms for Volumes I and II as a study aid. If desired, a question and answer session could be arranged either by my coming to the school for a day or by use of long distance telephone connections. Because of the busy schedule of most teachers, it might take a month or more for the teachers to finish reading the two books and some teachers might not even get started reading

the books in that time. For faculty groups of under 50 teachers, this pathway could be the most economical and the most effective. The larger the faculty group is (over 50 teachers), the better it would be to use one of the other pathways.

(b) The second pathway would take the longest, but might involve the highest percentage of the faculty. This pathway would use the filmed presentations (when available) for an hour or so each week and would probably appeal to those faculty who might not take time to read the books. In addition to the films, copies of Volumes I and II should be available on the basis of at least one set for every five faculty members and a copy of Volume III for every ten faculty members. While on this pathway, if more faculty seem to be reading and the attendance at the filmed presentations decreases, it may be advisable to stop the films and provide more sets of books. If the attendance at the filmed presentations increases indicating that this particular faculty group prefers to learn via the films, the filmed presentations could be increased to two sessions per week. Even when the books are shared, the use of the Active Involvement Forms by each person helps to maintain continuity between reading and film sessions. As with the first pathway, question and answer sessions can be arranged either live or via telephone. This pathway could be more economical for larger faculty groups and might be preferred because there are two pathways to achieve the same goals.

(c) A third pathway would probably be the fastest, would probably cost the most and might not be any more effective than the first two pathways. Because some teachers will want to resist learning from books and films because that would suggest that their students might also learn their courses that way, there is still a need for the live presentations. This pathway would consist of one, two, or three days of large group sessions during which I would present an overview of the three books. The difference between the one, two, and three day presentations would be the detail of the overview. Obviously, in a one-day session, I would not be able to go into as much detail as I could in a three-day session. In addition to the live presentations, copies of Volumes

I and II could be provided after the presentations on the basis of one set for every five faculty members and a copy of Volume III for every ten faculty members. The books would be primarily used as reference material and reinforcement of the live presentations. Also, if after the live presentations, a group of faculty wanted to review a particular topic together and didn't want to read it, they could send for any one of the filmed presentations.

NOTE: In this third pathway, faculty members that would rather learn via the books should be permitted to do so and should be excused from the large group sessions.

Any one of these three pathways could be used to expose the faculty and administrators to the BLSA concepts. However, to increase the number of teachers making the change and to increase the degree of change they want to make, I have found it very important to follow up the presentations (any one of the three pathways) with small group and individual meetings. These should occur about a month or more after the presentations. The major function of these meetings is to help faculty apply the concepts learned in the presentation pathways to their specific subject matter area, grade level, and/or specific courses. The application of the systems concepts is accomplished by answering questions of the group and clarifying the general systems concepts from the point-of-view of the specific subject matter or grade levels involved in the small group meeting. The *practical* application of the systems concepts is accomplsihed by critiquing existing *samples* of test items, objectives and/or learning problems found in the specific subject matter or grade levels involved in the small group meeting. The following limitations of group size and time should be taken into consideration:

> (a) If all the teachers involved in a group are teaching the same course, courses and/or grade level, then there is no limit to the number of participants, but the greater the number of participants in any one group of this type, the greater the amount of time needed to work with that group. As a general guideline for scheduling, if there are less than ten teachers involved in a group, then from one to two hours should be scheduled for that group meeting. If there are ten or more teachers involved in a group, then from two to three hours should be scheduled for that group meeting.
>
> (b) If all the teachers involved in a group are teaching within the same general subject matter area or department but are teaching different courses, then the num-

ber of participants should be limited to about twenty and the meeting should be scheduled for two to three hours per group.

(c) In a small school district, college or university, where the number of teachers available for the group meetings is less than five teachers, in several or all of the groups, then it would be more efficient to combine several groups together (hopefully the combined groups still represent related areas). When there are multiple subjects involved in a small group meeting, the group size should be limited to less than fifteen and from two to three hours should be scheduled for the seminar.

Individual conferences can be scheduled and are of particular importance to a teacher or group of teachers teaching the same course who plan to make major changes in their teaching. The objective is to individualize the application of the concepts presented in the presentation sessions and in the small group meetings to the specific courses and problems of individual teachers. The application of the systems concepts is accomplished by answering questions of the teacher or teachers and clarifying the general systems concepts from the point-of-view of a specific course or instructional unit. The *practical* application of the systems concepts is accomplished by critiquing existing specific course or instructional unit test items, objectives and/or learning problems which have been developed, identified or are being used by the teacher or teachers involved in the conference. The individual conferences should be limited to one teacher or to a group of teachers who are concerned about the same course and the same instructional unit. If there are from one to five teachers, one to two hours should be scheduled for the Conference. If there are from five to ten teachers, two to three hours should be scheduled. If there are over ten teachers involved, three to four hours should be scheduled.

In contrast to the usual negative attitude towards most in-service educational seminars, the majority of the participants of the SLATE Seminars react positively. The following comments are representative of the reactions of SLATE Seminar participants on follow-up evaluation forms:

From now on, I know I will investigate the value of whatever material I intend to present to my students. I will attempt to start practicing what I have been preaching. (Faculty member — Phillips University)

I intend to throw the curve grading concept out the window. (Faculty member — Illinois Central College)

The information presented and the manner in which it was presented would be extremely valuable to thousands of teachers and persons who intend to teach. (Administrator — The Pennsylvania State University)

I returned to work with many new thoughts and ideas. In my own mind, many of my educational concepts have now fallen into place. (Administrator — Sandhills Community College)

Because of the three days which our associates and principals spent in your Seminar, we are not only closer together in educational outlook, but we are closer together as human beings as well. (Administrator — Wilton Public Schools)

I must say that I thoroughly enjoyed the Seminar and feel that I am a person who has had some of his opinions shaken up. (Administrator — Shippensburg State College)

I'll never teach the same again after this Seminar. (Teacher — Monroe School District)

I am extremely encouraged by the results of your visit. The majority of the instructors have in varying degrees, re-examined their goals and purposes, content and techniques of presentation. (Administrator — Champlain College)

I thought that the Seminar was excellent, very helpful, and the most useful Seminar I have ever attended. (Math Teacher — South Girard High School)

The concepts learned in this Seminar have developed an entirely new approach and new enthusiasm for the teaching of a course which has become a chore. (Librarian — University of Utah)

I plan to use the insights, techniques and schema acquired in the Seminar as guidelines for a task force appointed to carefully reassess our program in teacher education. (Administrator — Xavier University)

I came to the Seminar expecting to learn very little. I left the Seminar planning major changes in my teaching activities. (Faculty member — Utah State University)

During the period (1960-1975) hundreds of school districts, colleges and universities have contracted for a SLATE Seminar and have had faculty and/or administrators attend one of the scheduled Seminars. The following is a partial list of schools which have sponsored a seminar for part or all of their faculty:

SCHOOL DISTRICTS	COMMUNITY COLLEGES	COLLEGES & UNIVERSITIES
Alliance SD, Nebraska	Champlain College, Ver.	Brigham Young Univ., Utah
Anniston SD, Alabama	Catonsville CC, Maryland	Univ. of Albuquerque, New Mexico
Burlington SD, Vermont	Corning CC, New York	
Punahou School, Hawaii	Toledo CC, Ohio	Chadron State College, Nebraska
Spring Branch SD, Texas	Kenosha Tech. Inst., Wis.	
Tyler SD, Texas	Hillsboro CC, Florida	University of Minnesota
Phenix City SD, Ala.	Sullivan County CC, NY	Univ. of South Dakota
Ouachita SD, Louisiana	Brevard Jr. College, Fla.	Sacred Heart College, Kan.
Menlo Park Elem. SD, California	Meramec CC, Missouri	Univ. of Calif. at Davis
	Forest Park CC, Missouri	Univ. of South Carolina
Valley Falls SD, Kansas	Walla Walla CC, Wash.	Texas Southern University
Hazelwood SD, Mo.	Clackamas CC, Oregon	Oklahoma State Univ.
Pueblo SD, Colorado	Coffeyville Jr. & CC, Kansas	University of Wisconsin
Kerman-Floyd Elem. SD, California		Univ. of West Virginia
	Jefferson College, Mo.	University of Washington
Portola Valley SD, Ca.	Blue Ridge CC, Virginia	St. Scholastica, Minn.
Wilton SD, Conn.	Seminole Jr. College, Fla.	University of Puerto Rico
Whippany SD, N.J.	Northampton CC, Pa.	Calif. State Univ. at Fresno
Hinsdale SD, Illinois	21 of 22 Community Colleges in Washington	Loma Linda Univ., Ca.
Madison Elem. SD, Ariz.		University of Kansas
Stockton SD, California	American River CC, California	Wisconsin State Univ.
Oakland SD, California		University of Colorado
Aberdeen SD, Wa.	Shasta CC, California	Colorado Schools of Mines
Richland SD, Wisconsin	Aims CC, Colorado	Utah State University
Monroe SD, Wisconsin	13 Technical Colleges in Ontario, Canada	Univ. of Calif. Dental School
Niagra So. SD, Well., Ontario		
Frontenac Cty. SD, King., Ontario	Over 50 Nursing Schools in United States and Canada	SE Virginia Med. School, Norfolk
		Niagra University
Protestant School Board., Montreal		Texas A & M University
		Xavier Univ., Nova Scotia

For information regarding seminars, dates available, costs, etc. contact Don Stewart directly, SLATE Services, P.O. Box 8796, Fountain Valley, Calif. 92708 or call 714/962-7000.

B. IMPLICATIONS OF THE SYSTEM'S CONCEPTS AS APPLIED TO EDUCATION AND EDUCATIONAL INNOVATIONS

The most common problems encountered in trying to get faculty and school administrators to utilize various parts or all of the Behavioral Learning Systems Concept can be traced to two very basic assumptions which are consciously or unconsciously held by a majority of educators:

— learning can only take place in a classroom in a school building and
— learning can only occur directly from the mouth of the live teacher.

If and when these two false assumptions can be discarded, there are a number of implications for improving the efficiency and effectiveness of the instructional process by utilizing parts or all of the systems concept.

The most important implication concerns the role of the teacher. As long as teachers and administrators believe that students can only learn from the mouth of the live teacher, the role of the teacher is limited to the presentation of course content and the only *educational* hardware acceptable is equipment that will aid or supplement the teacher's presentation of the course content. Under the present traditional approach, few teachers have time to individualize instruction and to identify and/or solve the learners' learning problems. Once teachers and administrators accept the concepts that learners can learn away from the live teacher and that the most important goal for teachers is to help more learners learn more of whatever is important in their courses, then the role of the teacher can be changed accordingly to maximize learning effectiveness and learning efficiency. This new role would minimize the presentation of course content by the live teacher because a wide variety of *instructional* hardware can perform this role almost as well as the live teacher. The new role for the teacher would be to identify and solve learning problems which would allow the teacher to actually work with *more students more effectively* and would maximize individualized instruction. As a consequence, master and good teachers could earn considerably more money without the usual increases in the costs of education in the form of taxes or other supporting funds.

A second important implication concerns the design of school buildings and the need for traditional classrooms and laboratory space. As long as accrediting associations, state departments of education, administrators, and teachers believe that students have to be in classrooms to learn, then the major unit in any school will be the *classroom*. When these same groups finally accept the concept that learning can take place outside of the classroom, away from the live teacher, and that under the concept of *individual differences*, it is a rare occasion that 30 students will need the same learning experience (a typical classroom situation now which ignores individual differences), then the major unit in a school will be the teacher's combined office and seminar room. The major space allotment will be devoted to learning spaces such as the library, study carrells, learning resource center, etc. Because learning can take place not only out of the classroom but also out of the school, many students may prefer to learn at home and only come to the school to meet with teachers for testing, diagnosis, learning prescriptions, small group meetings, or other group learning experiences. (The school could also continue to be a center of the students' social activity). Under these concepts, an elementary or secondary school building designed for the traditional education of 2000 students may actually accommodate the instruction of 3000-5000 students of which only 1000-1500 may be in the school at any one time. Similarly, a college or university designed for 5000 students under the traditional approach may actually accommodate the instruction of about 10,000 students of which only 3000 may be at the school during any one day.

A third important implication is in reference to school districts, colleges, and universities who limit enrollment, cut or reduce special programs and course offerings, close schools, have double sessions, etc. As pointed out before, these measures which are generally instituted as a result of budget and space problems are in effect actually various forms of *public blackmail* and directly or indirectly are designed to punish the public for not voting approval of certain bond issues or tax increases. These measures are also instituted on the assumption that the schools are already operating at maximum learning efficiency and effectiveness which is very definitely not the situation in most schools. Once the false assumptions on page 1175 are discarded, many of the budget and space problems can be solved without punishing the students and indirectly the public while at the same time increasing the effectiveness and efficiency of the instructional process.

A fourth implication concerns future curriculum innovations. All too often, curriculum innovations in the past didn't make to much of an impact because the emphasis was on the content the teachers should cover rather than on the SO's of what students should be able to do as a result of the new program. Specifying the content takes away from the creativeness of the teacher and without any SO's, even the GO's can't be achieved. By specifying the desired SO's and making some materials available to the teachers, the teachers could use as much creativity as necessary in order to help all of their students learn 100 percent of the SO's and indirectly all of the GO's too.

A fifth implication is probably the best and most important advantage of the BLSA and one that will probably be resisted the most by traditional teachers, administrators, parents, and even some students. This is the concept of *open entry* and *open exit* which means that a student should be able to start a course anytime and complete it at anytime. First of all, this concept would relieve the annual flood of graduating students entering the labor market. Secondly, since there won't be classes as we know them now, students will be able to get the courses they want regardless of whether the enrollment is too small or too large.

A sixth implication concerns enrollment. As more students have success, more students will try more courses, more students will stay in school, more students will continue on in school, and more adult students will come back to school when they hear about the possibilities for success. As a result, the present surplus of teachers may disappear.

A seventh implication concerns the teacher as a professional. At the present time, professional education organizations are becoming more of a labor type union and are losing their professionalism. I think as a result of the system's concepts, the new roles for the teacher and administrators, and the actualities of educational malpractice suits, that teacher and administrator organizations are going to become more like a professional organization and less like a labor union. However, a new role of a teacher's assistant may become important in aiding the teacher do a professional job with students. These assistants may very well be considered laborers and as such will belong to a labor union.

1. EDUCATIONAL INNOVATIONS FROM THE SYSTEM'S POINT-OF-VIEW

The major reason that there are so many innovations in education is that teachers are searching for better solutions to educational problems and since few teachers have specified what it is they want students to learn, any pathway is as good as any other pathway in filling up the time that teachers and students have to spend in schools. Some innovations are tried because teachers are bored doing what they were doing. Some innovations are tried because of the public image it may give to a school. Rarely are changes and/or innovations introduced because it will solve identified learning problems and even rarer are innovations evaluated on the basis of whether or not they helped students solve their learning problems. Because of the lack of SO's and tests that match them, it is difficult to identify any increases or decreases in learning due to some innovation. And of course, the use of standardized tests which rarely relate to any SO's and the fact that it is traditionally considered bad to teach what is going to be tested solidifys the fact that most innovations won't make a difference.

However, once learning becomes the primary emphasis of schools and particularly when national, regional, state, and local minimum common core SO's are identified and teachers change their role to that of professional Instructioneers, random innovations will be reduced and subsequent instructional innovations will have a common direction of making instruction more effective and efficient for more students. Change and innovation for the sake of learning will become a way of life.

In my book, *Educational Malpractices: The Big Gamble in Our Schools,* on pp. 145-244, I commented on 30 innovations and common problems in education. I see no value in duplicating those 100 pages in this book. However, in some cases, events have occurred which suggest additional comments and there have also been other innovations and problems which I didn't comment on before which deserve comment now. This section is designed as a reference source for educators whose school is utilizing or planning to utilize one or more of the contemporary efforts to improve education that I have commented on. The objective is not to present a detailed description of a particular effort to improve education: but to point out the relationship and value, if any, of a particular effort towards increasing student learning in an instructional situation. I will also comment on the implications of appropriate system's concepts which might make a particular innovation more successful. It is assumed that the majority of readers will not want to read through all of these innovative practices and problems like one would read a chapter in some other book, but they will want to read only those that have relevance to themselves. To facilitate locating the innovations and/or problems which are of interest to the reader, a subtable of contents for the comments covered in the *Educational Malpractices* book is provided below. After that, there is a subtable of contents of the comments in this book.

A Subtable of Contents From
*Educational Malpractices:
The Big Gamble in Our Schools*

	Page
A — The National Assessment of Educational Progress (NAEP)	145
B — Elimination of Evaluation	165
C — Social Promotion	167
D — Multiple Tracking	168
E — Pass-Fail Grading	172
F — Modular Scheduling	173
G — Nongraded Schools	174
H — Over-Emphasis on Inquiry or Discovery Learning	177
I — Discipline in Our Schools: Confused and Misdirected	178
J — Preschool Programs — Head Start	183
K — Upward Bound, Job Corps, and Remedial Programs	187
L — Reading Programs	191
M — Student Strikes	195
N — Counseling and Guidance Programs	198
O — In-Service Training of Teachers	200

		Page
P —	Microteaching	202
Q —	Team Teaching	204
R —	Differentiated Staffing	205
S —	Teacher Aids	206
T —	National Teacher Corps	208
U —	Integration via Bussing, Redistricting, Etc.	211
V —	Decentralization or Local Control Over Schools	212
W —	Are Smaller Classes and Lighter Teaching Loads the Answer or the Problem?	213
X —	Financial Crisis in Education and the Shortage of Instructional Space	217
Y —	Teacher Strikes	221
Z —	Changes in School Building Design and the Utilization of Technology in Instruction	226
AA —	Accountability: A *Mole Hill* that is Going to Become a *Mountain*	229
BB —	Performance Contracting	231
CC —	The Voucher System	240
DD —	The Clamor for Humanism in Education	241

A Subtable of Contents for the Following Comments

a —	Bilingual Education	1180
b —	Alternative Schools	1181
c —	Open Education	1183
d —	Value Clarification	1187
e —	Early Childhood or Pre-School Education	1188
f —	Other Systems Approaches to Instruction	1190
g —	Career and Vocational Education	1192
h —	Community Colleges	1195
i —	Adult Education	1197
j —	Irregular Students	1199
k —	Racial Integration in Schools	1200
l —	Year-Round Schools	1203
m —	Parochial and Private Schools	1204

If you wish to skip over this unit entirely, the last section, *Questions and Answers About Utilizing the Behavioral Learning Systems Concepts*, starts on page 1205.

a. BILINGUAL EDUCATION

A long neglected aspect of individualizing instruction has been the need for bilingual education. The major drawback to the development and utilization of bilingual education has been the *Ugly American Syndrome* wherein too many Americans and especially teachers and pyschologists believed that people who didn't speak English were ignorant and had limited capacity to learn as shown by the English language IQ tests. As a result, thousands of non-English speaking children and children with only a limited English vocabulary have ended up in mentally retarded classes. The non-English speaking students and students with a limited English vocabulary who stayed in the regular classroom developed severe cases of cumulative ignorance which reinforced the teachers' opinion that these students obviously had mental limits (as long as they were taught in English). As I indicated in Volume I, p. 249, I am amazed that in 1973, the first and only state in our country, Massachusetts, passed a law that students who come from homes where the primary language was other than English had the right to learn from bilingual materials. In the rest of the states, there were some *experiments* dealing with the hypothesis *if you teach a child in the language the child understands, the child might learn more than when you teach a child in a language the child doesn't understand!*

It finally took a Supreme Court decision in 1974 to point up the problem that this is one individual difference which had been ignored along with all the rest that wasn't going to be ignored any longer. Hopefully, one of these days similar Supreme Court decisions will force traditional educators to do something about other individual differences which are being ignored. However, in spite of the decision which could ultimately affect five million children in our schools, the number being taught with bilingual materials a year after the decision is probably less than 10 percent. The delay in helping the other 90 percent is blamed on a lack of materials, trained teachers, and money. As I see it, there are really two major problems. First of all, without knowing what students would be learning in courses which are taught using English materials, it is difficult to develop matching materials in multiple foreign languages. Also, without any commonality in objectives among schools teaching the same courses, it is necessary to develop multiple versions of each of the multiple foreign language groups for each school. It would be so much easier if we had minimum common core SO's for all the courses. Then, materials could be developed in the necessary languages to facilitate the learning of those objectives and the same materials could be used in many schools.

The second problem concerns the role of the teacher. As long as teachers believe that they have to do the presenting, then bilingual materials will have to be used and taught by bilingual teachers. Obviously, this traditional approach creates a great shortage of bilingual teachers and delays the successful learning of millions of students. If teachers could accept the new role as Instructioneers, the problems could be solved much faster. If bilingual materials are developed to be used on an independent study basis. it wouldn't be necessary for the teacher to be bilingual unless the student developed a learning problem. Where there may be no or little commonality between the English version of a course and some other language version of the course, a teacher has to be proficient in both languages in order to help students in each language. However, if there were common SO's in the materials and the materials were designed for independent study (using audio tapes where students can't read in their language), a teacher could work with students of several different languages and between the teacher's low proficiency in the languages and the students low proficiency in English, they could still communicate about the common SO's.

A very important part of a bilingual program is to wean the student from a dependence upon bilingual materials. Remember in solving the learning problem of these students it isn't a situation of either teach them English first and then let them learn in English or develop materials in their language and let them learn in their own language. Although it may be necessary to have curriculum materials in a student's language in the beginning, as the student learns English, it may be possible to have materials using a mixture of English and the other language. Then a student might be able to learn in English but have a bilingual teacher available to help in solving learning problems.

In the teaching of English as a foreign language and in teaching any other language as a foreign language, the major emphasis and often the only emphasis is on the language itself. A very critical part of a bilingual program and any other foreign language program has got to be the teaching and learning of the different cultures and particularly how the culture and language affect the way a person thinks and feels.

b. ALTERNATIVE SCHOOLS

The concept of having various alternatives or pathways to fit individual differences would certainly seem to fit in the system's concepts; however, given that what students are supposed to learn has not been identified, the alternative schools are not providing alternate pathways to the same or even similar goals. Alternate schools are usually just alternate ways in which to spend the time that students and teachers are required to be in school. The choices giving to parents and students are choices in environment in which learning is an assumption. What may seem as a bad environmental choice could end up being a good learning choice and what might appear to be a great environmental choice could turn out to be a very ineffective learning choice. If we had minimum common core SO's for all courses, then the alternative schools could actually offer alternate paths to the learning of the same basic SO's.

Instead of being an aid in helping students learn what they need to know, too many of the alternative schools are similar to the *free schools* in which the major emphasis is on *do your own thing*. As long as the vast majority of our students will end up living in a social environment, to train them to *do their own thing* is very inhumane because to live successfully in a social environment there are minimum things that have to be learned and one cannot *do their own thing* when it interferes with other people *doing their own thing*. If one of our major goals of education is to help the student learn to get along with others, the teaching of selfism will not help achieve our goals, and it may very well interfere with the achievement of our goals.

In contrast to the *do your own thing* alternative, in a number of school districts, the parents are requesting an alternative school where they teach the traditional 3-R's. Parents are aware of the fact that you need to know some minimum things in order to exist in society. It can be expected that students wouldn't know what is needed because they haven't lived out in society as an adult. That is why we need teachers who can identify these minimum needs. We don't need teachers who won't admit that there are things that have to be learned. At the present time, most alternative schools are copies of the *free schools* that flourished for awhile and then floundered because of financial problems. Although these schools claim to be student-oriented, they are primarily set up by teachers who want to get paid but don't want to do anything in return. The teachers want to *do their own thing* which may very well not include helping students learn. No wonder students like them! Neither the teachers nor the students have any responsibilities. The major responsibility is borne by the parents and taxpayers who ultimately have to support the *do your own thing* students who didn't want to learn what they needed to learn to make a living and contribute to others.

Some alternative schools are designed to keep certain types of students busy until they are old enough to drop out of school. Their premise is that these students probably can't learn anyway so the curriculum is really softened by deleting SO's rather than solving their learning problems.

One of the common defenses of the alternative schools is that based on standardized tests, the students in different alternative schools don't achieve significantly different. The conclusion is that any one of the altternative schools is about as good as another. This is a valid conclusion given that no one knows what should be learned in school and that the standardized tests have little relationship to what is happening in schools and they are designed to not show a difference.

The voucher plan being tried in several places is really a form of alternative schools. The voucher plan concept was discussed in the *Educational Malpractices* book, p. 240. As an alternative under the voucher plan, if students could learn on their own out of school and away from teachers, why not let the parents or the students cash the vouchers!

c. OPEN EDUCATION

Open education is a term which is generally associated with *informal* education as opposed to *formal* education. In higher education, the term open education is applied to a variety of programs where most of the student learning occurs off campus. It can be picked up on-the-job, it can be by correspondence courses, by radio and television, by independent study, or by any combination of these pathways. In some schools, it is possible to obtain a degree without taking any formal classes on a campus. In other schools, students are allowed to take proficiency examinations and test out of only freshman and sophomore courses. There are many institutions of higher learning that are experimenting with various interpretations of the concept. I believe the impetus for open or informal education at all levels is basically that educators are realizing that students can learn on their own in or out of schools. The basic concept I can accept completely; however, the application of the concept leaves a lot to be desired. The major problem is that if teachers have not identified what it is students should learn in their courses, how is it possible to measure whether or not the students were able to learn *it* on their own? Generally, students take tests which are hidden, so students have to guess what they are supposed to learn. In the case of teacher-made tests, these are probably fairly close to what they want students to learn so the solution might be to hand these tests out as equivalent to the SO's of the courses. In the case of standardized tests, they are mostly of the *objective* type (multiple choice, true-false, and matching), so they are useless as they don't relate to standardized lists of SO's and the results are contrived ahead of time by manipulating the test items, i.e., the College Level Examination Program (CLEP) tests. Given there is no minimum common core of SO's listed for courses with common titles, there is no guarantee of any commonality in learning among students in the same course at the same school or in different schools. Also, the usual low levels of achievement found in curve grading or in pass-fail grading are found in most of the grading and evaluation practices in open education in higher education. These problems can all be eliminated, if teachers would identify their course SO's, if minimum common core SO's of common courses were identified, if the tests were designed to match the SO's, and if high quality standards were the rule such that only those learning 100 percent of the SO's received credit for the courses.

At the secondary level, open or informal education is generally associated with the free school movement or the *do your own thing* approach and is part of the current alternative school movement. As I have said many times before, this approach is generally subscribed to by teachers who for one reason or another do not want to be held accountable for student learning because they believe that many students can't learn anyway (which in itself is an inhumane thought) and they tend to also believe that to demand or guide learning is dehumanizing. These pseudo-huminists are *coping out* of their professional responsibilities. Whereas humanism is concerned with getting along with other human beings, the *do your own thing* actually develops selfism which puts the individual and his or her freedoms above other individuals and their freedoms. In a social environment, there is no room for individuals who can't or won't consider the needs and freedoms of other people.

Three premises which are integral to the secondary and elementary interpretations of the open schools movement are ones which I have mentioned as also integral with the Behavioral Learning Systems Approach (BLSA). These are:

Students know better than anyone else what they are most interested in;

Students know better than anyone else what motivates them best; and

Students know better than anyone else how they learn best.

The major problem is that these three valid and true premises are then converted into *the false statement* that students know better than anyone else *what* they should learn. I strongly agree and subscribe to the three premises; but I strongly disagree and reject the conclusion or fourth premise. Having never lived through life before, students do not know best what they should learn. This notion holds that students know more than teachers about *what* they should learn which is a subtractive rather than a cumulative view of learning and I categorically reject the notion that children are born all-intelligent and then slowly regress until they die ignorant. Teachers do know better than students concerning *what* they should learn; but they don't know better than students concerning *how* they learn best.

At the elementary school level, schools which label themselves as an *open school* vary widely as to what actually is happening in the school. Some schools are very much like the free schools or the schools of several decades ago which practiced *progressive education* in that the students are free to *do their own thing* and the teacher's job is essentially that of a librarian who provides materials and resources for the students. Some other elementary schools who claim to be *open schools*, emphasize individualized instruction wherein students have continuous progress through sets of materials to predetermined goals. A few schools are experimenting with the approach I would subscribe to wherein there are SO's set for the students to learn, but instead of a single pathway to these goals, there are multiple pathways which can be used to achieve the same goals. The students are free to pick the pathway they want or in the case of non-achievement or slow achievement, the teacher may suggest an alternate pathway.

Theodore Manolakes, University of Illinois, in the *National Elementary Principal* (Vol. LII, No. 3, Nov. 1972) stated that

> Too often our good intentions result in several years of free play and kind treatment because we have a confused notion that freedom is what children need most.

Whereas in secondary schools the teacher who subscribes to the free school concept may do so to escape accountability, in elementary schools, most teachers who subscribe to the open school as a *do your own thing* concept, sincerely believe that non-directed activities are better than directed learning. The problem is that the choice is seen as being one of two extremes: either non-directed in all activities or directed in all activities. Under the BLSA, there is an in between point in which *what* the students have to learn is directed, but *how* they learn the required SO's can be non-directed. For any elementary teacher to claim that there are no skills or knowledge that all students should learn in common before going on to secondary school is to be blind to the needs of the students. As long as the students expect to live and work in a social environment, there are certain skills and knowledge which all students have to learn. To think otherwise is a disservice to the students, their parents, and to society. In the same issue of the *National Elementary Principal* I just quoted from, Roland Barth, a principal, wrote an article in which he stated a number of assumptions which he felt were basic to open schools. One of these assumptions was that *Little or no knowledge exists that is essential for everyone to acquire.* Given that this assumption is true, wouldn't it be an interesting situation in which each child developed his or her own language such that they couldn't communicate with each other nor would they be able to learn from all those wonderful materials the teachers had selected for them to use as resources or how about even if one child decided to learn his or her own language and as a consequence became isolated from surrounding society. Barth's assumption has to be false, if in turn he provides children with English language materials and he expects the children to learn from them, then he is assuming (although not stated) that the children will *all* learn to read and write in English. If the students are going to learn from available materials, there are other basics they will have to learn. To allow the children to learn less would be to let their ignorance of basics limit their learning. An examination of some of Barth's other assumptions reveals that he is probably in agreement with the *do your own thing* philosophy of the pseudo-humanists that actually creates inhumane learning situations which are more controlled by ignorance than by intelligence.

Assumption 1 — Children are innately curious and will explore their environment without adult intervention.

If Barth really believed this assumption, he would quit his job as a principal and encourage his teachers and all educators to abandon learning to chance. Even the selection of materials to place in the classrooms represents adult intervention.

Assumption 7 — Children have both the competence and the right to make significant decisions concerning their own learning.

If these decisions are in line with *how* a child learns, I would agree; but in this case, I think Barth also means it to include *what* a child learns and in that case I would have to disagree. Competence in decision-making is not an innate characteristic or quality, it has to be learned. If Barth assumes that all children have this quality, then he is saying that all children should learn to become competent in decision making which in turn refutes his earlier assumption that there is *little or no knowledge that is essential for everyone to acquire.*

Assumption 21 — Objective measures of performance may have a negative effect on learning.

Assumption 22 — Learning is best assessed intuitively, by direct observation.

Since *objective* refers to assessment with a minimum of bias, prejudice, and feelings of the teacher towards the student and is based on directly observable evidence and *intuitive* refers to the inner feelings of the teacher and as such refers to subjective assessment which is fraught with a number of variables affecting the teacher including biases, prejudices, feelings, etc., then what Barth is saying is that assessment by teachers is better when it is affected by variables within the teacher than it is when based on observable evidence of what students *do*. But wait, in Barth's 22nd assumption, he also states that *learning is best assessed — by direct observation!* Since *direct observation* is objective, then Barth in his 22nd assumption refutes his 21st assumption. Actually, to have any assessment at all by teachers refutes his first assumption that children don't need adult intervention!

> NOTE: I am not trying to emphasize the problems in Barth's logic as much as I am trying to point out the problems of irresponsible educators who call themselves humanists and who advocate the *do your own thing* approach under the label of *open education* in order to avoid accountability. In the process, they create ineffective and inefficient chance learning situations in which non-achievement can then be blamed on the students and their external (to the school) environment. The results of this non-directional *hands-off* type of so-called *humane* education has already caused problems between students, their parents and the society around them. For a professional educator to sow the seeds of eventual conflict, discontent, loneliness, unemployment, and anti-social behaviors brought on by selfism and ignorance and then leave the students to reap the harvest of what was sown has got to be a dereliction of duty and professional negligence!

In contrast to this *cop-out* version of an *open school*, I can heartily support an *open school* in which the required SO's and minimum common core SO's have been identified and the students have to learn at least the required SO's and yet the students are free to select the vehicle for learning, the method of learning, the motivation for learning, the time needed to learn, the place for learning, and how they will use what they have learned.

d. VALUES CLARIFICATION

Sidney Simon and other *humanists* are trying to get teachers and schools to accept a concept called *Values Clarification* which supposedly helps children select their own values instead of adults imposing preconceived values upon the children. Given that there are an infinite number of values a person could have, when a teacher selects certain materials and values and omits other materials and values, the teacher is biasing the students' values in certain directions. I am not sure that teachers have the right to decide which values should be *clarified* and which ones should not be *clarified*.

Since a person's values affect how he or she progresses through life and particularly the person's relationships with other people, how is a student qualified to pick out those values which will serve him or her best through life! Given that the student will be associated with his family for life, I don't think it is such a bad idea that the student accepts and develops the preconceived values of his or her parents even though they may be in conflict with a particular teacher who they may only associate with for a year or so at the most. As I have said before in this series, for a teacher to purposely alienate a child from his or her parents and community by developing and *solidifying* values in the student which are in conflict with those held by the students' parents and community, is the same as *brainwashing* and is a disservice to the student and a malpractice as a professional.

If in the process of *values clarification and solidification*, the teacher identified the minimum common core of values which were desired by parents and the community, then the teacher helped to develop, clarify, and solidify these values, the teacher would be performing a good service for the community and the student.

If affective domain objectives are as important as many *humanist* teachers claim, then they may be too important to be controlled by teachers who are not qualified to teach affective domain SO's nor are they accorded the function of changing the values of society. If these same teachers are ineffective at teaching what they claim are the not-so-important cognitive and sensory skills of reading and writing, how could that possibly certify them as being capable to teach more important affective concepts.

e. EARLY CHILDHOOD OR PRE-SCHOOL EDUCATION

I already commented on pre-school programs in *Educational Malpractices,* pp. 183-187, but because of the increase in emphasis on pre-school education throughout the country and particularly here in California, I would like to point out a few additional problems. I had previously commented on the major problem being that the SO's and minimum common core SO's for pre-school have not been identified. As a result, it is difficult to identify what should be occurring in these schools. If once we could identify what students should know as a minimum in order to start first grade, then we could set the goals for preschool. A child that appears to be progressing satisfactorily towards these minimum goals without attending school may continue to learn at home and in the community. A child who is not showing progress should probably attend school in order to get help. The slower a student's rate of acquisition of the minimum common core SO's for preschool, the more time the student might spend in school getting help. To check on a child's progress, parents would bring their preschool children in for periodic assessments. In this way, a majority of preschool children might not be in school very often (some not at all) and preschool teachers would be able to devote a lot of time to those students who really need the help.

Although this last paragraph describes the major implication of the BLSA to instruction at the preschool level, there are two other indirect implications which are important. First, if students learn anything more by being in preschool than they would by just staying home, then they should be at higher levels of achievement than previous students have been. If the first grade teachers do not accommodate this upgrading, the preschool students will just have to sit and wait until the teacher and the rest of the students catch up. While waiting for the rest of the class, the preschool students may very well become bored, discouraged, overactive, and develop negative attitudes. This was a common problem with Head Start programs. Since the teachers didn't accomodate the advanced placement of the Head Start students, their advanced achievement over other students soon disappeared when the rest of the class caught up to them. It is very important that teachers in first grade recognize where the students are. If preschool students have learned up to one-half of first grade, then that is where the preschool students should start and continue learning. They shouldn't be locked into a class rate of learning. Obviously, the reason most first grade teachers have not given students advance placement is that they have not specified what SO's reflect first grade learning. It is very difficult to give advance placement in *something* if you don't know what the *something* is in terms of measurable learning.

The second important indirect implication of the BLSA to instruction can best be compared to the *domino theory* in which a change in one affects a number of related changes. If it can be assumed that preschool will be teaching anything that would otherwise be taught in kindergarten, then that suggests that less will be taught in kindergarten. However, what will probably happen is that some of first grade will shift into kindergarten, then some of second grade into first grade, then some of third grade into second grade, etc. In order for any effective preschool effort to be added to the instructional program without having duplication and the development of negative attitudes, there has to be planning, time, and funds available to make the subsequent changes all the way up the academic ladder. Preschool programs that are just added at the bottom without any provision for changing the other grades, are designed to be ineffective and can very well do more harm than good. In California, State Superintendent Wilson Riles has been pushing for a state supported preschool program, but no funds or effort is being made to make the necessary changes in subsequent grade levels. Huron Institute prepared a study for the U.S. Office of Education in 1973 in which they stated that three-fourths of all public school districts will be providing preschool education by 1985. How many will have made the *domino* adjustments in the upper courses by then?

Another report prepared by the Stanford Research Institute in 1974 suggested that their evidence proved that teenagers would profit more from extra funds spent on their learning than preschool children. Given that preschools have not identified the SO's of what should be learned, too much of preschool time is devoted to play rather than to designed learning. As a result, differences in learning may not be as easily identifiable, particularly if standardized tests are used. At the higher grade levels where at a single grade level there is as much as six years difference between the highest and lowest achiever due to cumulative ignorance and educational malpractices, it is relatively easy to raise the average achievement level because the students would be learning things they had been exposed to multiple times before. Contrary to what the report suggests and to what preschool advocates want, the extra funding should not go to either preschool or high school exclusively; but should be spread out to all levels to accommodate changes made by having more effective and efficient instructional activities.

A report from Russia written up in the February, 1974, issue of *Phi Delta Kappan,* pointed out that children who were more advanced at six years of age were frequently behind by seventh grade. The conclusion put forth by the report was that it was not good to push students into learning too fast because they eventually would not do as well. Of course, the study did not deal with the problem of holding the advanced student back until the others caught up. In the meantime, the advanced student has developed sloppy study habits and ultimately becomes an underachiever.

Some first grade teachers are against preschool because it will force them to upgrade what they are already teaching and that always takes time and effort. *Follow Through* was supposedly designed to help schools and teachers adapt their courses to students who had completed Head Start and other preschool programs. Sad to say, the *Follow through* program is being phased out. It could have been a significant program if it would have helped teachers identify the minimum common core SO's in the early elementary school grades so that students can be given advance placement in accordance with their achievement levels.

f. OTHER SYSTEMS APPROACHES TO INSTRUCTION

There are several systematic approaches to designed instruction which have become available during the past decade, i.e., IPI or Individually Prescribed Instruction, IGE or Individually Guided Education, Westinghouse's PLAN or Program for Learning in Accordance with Needs, IMS or Individualized Mathematics System, etc. Although most of these programs are based on many of the same concepts as the BLSA to instruction, they have some problems in common which BLSA shouldn't have. Although these programs are based on SO's, the SO's have not been identified as minimum common core learning; the teachers using these programs have not been taught their new role; the evaluation of achievement is all too often based on the so-called objective type tests (multiple-choice, true-false, and matching test items) because the scores are easy to arrive at and can be statistically handled (regardless of whether or not achievement actually occurred); generally the vehicle for learning (a single pathway) becomes the objective rather than a means to an objective; and the acceptable levels of achievement are low enough so as to allow cumulative ignorance to develop.

In order to improve on these systems, it would be necessary to get teachers to identify the minimum common core SO's and match these to the lists of SO's upon which the materials are based. Any SO's on the list of minimum common core SO's which aren't taught in the materials should be included. The tests should then be designed to match the SO's. By instituting requirements for high levels of achievement, i.e., 90 percent or more of the students learn 100 percent of the SO's, it would be necessary to develop more than one pathway for the achievement of different SO's. Given these changes, these programs could be used very successfully in achieving high levels of successful learning for all students.

As an example of the mismatch between SO's and test items found in these programs. The following not so specific So is from a unit in the Westinghouse PLAN program:

— Identify the major sources of environmental pollution and the methods of preventing and controlling pollution.

Given this objective, it suggests that the student should be able to list a certain number (unknown) of sources of environmental pollution and then describe at least one or more methods of preventing and controlling each of these sources. However, the test item used is the following:

— All of the following contribute significantly to the pollution of water except

A — industrial water   C — insecticides
B — sewage   D — automobile exhaust

As can be seen, the test item neither asks the student to identify the sources of pollution nor to describe methods of prevention and control. In fact, the emphasis of the test item is on the one choice that doesn't pollute water rather than on those that do pollute water. The fact that automobile exhaust is also a source of pollution makes this alternate choice a detractor designed to help students miss the item. The fact that automobile exhaust pollutants settle on water and are washed out of the air by rain into water makes the item one that is probably missed by about 35-65 percent of those taking the test. If the test designers had wanted the students to get this test item right, they could have made choice "D" — orange juice or some other obviously wrong answer. Then students could have gotten the item right even if they didn't know anything about pollution except that the use of so-called *objective* type test items (multiple-choice, true-false, and matching) tend to pollute the instructional materials and the evaluation procedures.

As might be expected, these systems approaches have not been proven to be superior to traditional instruction because even the internal evaluation instruments do not test for the achievement of what has been taught and learned and they are designed to prove no significant differences. The use of standardized tests for external evaluation also typically show no significant differences. But then, why should these tests show any differences? Standardized tests have a low correlation with what is taught and learned under the traditional approach and also under the systems approach.

An integral part of these systems approaches is usually a curriculum unit in a package format. This same idea has been used by itself and are labeled with a variety of names: Unipack, Learning Activity Packet (LAP), modules, etc. The idea is good and the use of these curriculum units allows for individual progress and they usually are based on SO's; however, the SO's have not been identified by a number of teachers as the minimum common core SO's so the use of any one unit is limited. In addition, the tests frequently don't match the SO's, high standards of achievement (100 percent of SO's) are not required, and usually only one pathway (the unit) is available to learn the SO's.

g. CAREER AND VOCATIONAL EDUCATION

During the early 1970's a renewed emphasis on career education was started by the U.S. Office of Education. The idea is that a majority of high school students do not go on to college, so instead of secondary schools concentrating on preparing students for college, they should also prepare each student for some type of career. Historically, formal schooling has been for the elite and any learning above the level of basic skills was considered to be superfluous for the non-college bound student. As a result, curve grading was used not only to assign grades on tests and for courses, but the results of curve grading were used to determine who should go into what programs. Those students who were at the top of the curve were viewed as college material. Those students who were at the bottom of the curve were viewed as not being educable and as such should be put into vocational training programs. Those students who were in the middle and were in the majority were also in sort of an academic-vocational limbo in which they were considered not smart enough for college and to smart to learn a vocation. The community college movement has been designed primarily for these students and has been acting as a second stage separator in that those students who are high on the curve of grades are encouraged to go on to a four year school, those students who are low on the curve of grades are encouraged to go in to blue-collar vocational programs, those in the lower half of the middle group are encouraged to go into white-collar vocational programs, and those students who are in the upper half of the middle group are still in limbo. The major problem with this whole traditional approach is that far too many educators believe that the tests which have been designed to give a curve of results actually measures the capacities of innate intelligence and that low levels of intelligence are all that are needed to work with the hands (sensory domain), higher levels of intelligence are needed to work in areas using the mind (cognitive domain), and the highest levels of intelligence are needed to work in the areas of feelings (affective domain).

> NOTE: Of continuing interest to me in the face of this intellectual *snobbery*, is the fact that many of the faculty in the highest status areas of the humanities find the workings and repair of cars, televisions, and computers too complex and they call on the ex-students, who were failed out of school because of their lack of intelligence, to repair this complicated equipment for them.

No matter what is done to change the labels of vocational education, career education will be viewed as vocational education and as such will be thought of as a low status (low mentality) program. The only way, that vocational and career education can be upgraded is to institute quality control in learning such that 90 percent or more of the students learn 100 percent of he SO's of their courses. Under this approach, there can be no designed selection via tests. Since almost all of the students will be learning 100 percent of the SO's, almost every career option is open to them. Students who select to work with their hands could just as easily have selected to work at any other career. Under these conditions, career biases and prejudices will have to diminish. Students who under the traditional approach might have preferred to work with their hands but chose the higher status four year college curriculum, can now under the BLSA, select what they really want to do because all careers have equal status as far as the mental levels of entering students is concerned.

Sad to say, although, vocational educators who train teachers to teach courses in vocational education have been saying for decades many of the things which I have said in these books, the basic concepts of the BLSA are not found in practice in most vocational courses. Most vocational teachers grade on a curve just like the other teachers and even though their courses lend themselves to the identification of SO's, not many vocational teachers have listed the SO's of their courses and consequently their written tests are frequently of little value and contribute to the low status image of the courses.

The rhetoric surrounding career education sounds great, but underneath are the same problems found in traditional vocational education. For example, Dr. Worthington, Associate U.S. Commissioner of Education, in an address to a conference in Washington, D.C., stated the following:

> Career Education is a revolutionary approach to American education based on the idea that all educational experience, curriculum, instruction, and counseling should be geared to preparing each individual for a life of economic independence, personal fulfillment, and an appreciation for the dignity of work.
>
> Its main purpose is to prepare all students for successful and rewarding lives by improving their basis for occupational choice, by facilitating their acquisitions of occupational skills, by enhancing their educational achievements, by making education more meaningful and relevant to their aspirations, and by increasing the real choices they have among the many different occupations and graining avenues open to them.

Who could be against these goals. They are like motherhood, God, country, and apple pie. In practice, I have found teachers at the elementary levels under the label of career education already making lifetime career decisions for the students based on the results of curve grading. Ideally at the elementary level, students are only made aware of the need to select a career at some point in their life and that there is an ever increasing number of careers to choose from. However, as soon as a teacher or counselor assumes that a student's intellectual limits predestine the student to lower level jobs, they stop expecting or demanding that the student learn even the basic skills. As cumulative ignorance increases, subsequent teachers are convinced of the student's limited mental abilities and as such, they steer the student into vocational or general courses which begin to limit the career options open to the student.

Since many of the careers that the students might work at have not even been identified and the students will change careers four or five times during their lives, the next step should be to teach students the process involved in career decision making and also the process involved in learning a new career once the career has been decided upon. It is not enough to just explore a specific career, students should also examine the potential working environment, potential income, and the potential standard of living. Students should also learn to identify when it is the right time to change careers because then a student could plan ahead for the change rather than wait until one career is finished before starting another. During this stage or early in the teaching of a career, the new emphasis on relating to the world of work suggests that the student actually work at a job related to his or her tentative career choice. Some employers have taken advantage of this to hire cheap help. Since the SO's to be learned while working have not been identified, the work experience is often primarily a motivational experience rather than necessarily a cognitive or sensory experience. If the teacher had the list of SO's to be learned, this list could be given to the employer and suggest that where possible the employer might see that the student learn certain appropriate SO's. As a point to remember, under the BLSA, it would not be uncommon to have students out in the world of work learning non-career oriented SO's. These students would be ones who are very practical oriented and learn even basic skills better out in the working environment. Learning in the world of work should be considered as just another learning pathway.

In the actual career training program taught in the schools, the courses are too often taught as if the students will work at the career for a lifetime. As such, a lot of facts are taught and rote memorized. Because of the high potential for change, not only from one career to another, but to different specialty areas within a career and to changes within a given specialty, the learning of career process objectives become very important. The problem is that most career and vocational teachers tend to teach and test factual SO's rather than the process SO's. There are many process SO's which are in common across different careers whereas rote memory SO's are usually different for each career.

To minimize the problem of students essentially *burning their bridges* behind them such that it would be difficult to change career choices, it should be possible to identify some minimum common core process SO's which are in common across a number of careers. Then if a student changes his or her career choice, they only have to learn the SO's which are unique to a career above and beyond that which was in common.

h. COMMUNITY COLLEGES

Community colleges probably have the greatest potential for demonstrating effective and efficient instruction because they do not have such a long history of traditional educational practices. In fact, there are probably more radical innovations going on in community colleges than at any other level of education. Despite this potential for change, most community colleges are very traditional. In my working with these colleges, the most common comment of faculty in reference to student achievement levels concerns their belief that their students aren't as well qualified as the students in the four year colleges and universities. Given this might be true, to give these students who have more cumulative ignorance and other learning problems the same text books and the same amount of time to learn the courses as the students in the four year schools is a guarantee that their learning levels will be less than the students in the four-year colleges. If the students in a community college are really less qualified, then in order to have even achievement levels that are equal to four-year students, the students would probably take longer and would probably use less difficult materials. However, if more time was given and easier materials were used, some faculty would claim that the learning levels were not equal even if the same SO's were involved.

To prove the real value of community colleges, the faculty should make an extra effort to identify the SO's of their courses and then identify the minimum common core content of these courses not only in cooperation with their colleagues at the community college level, but they should also involve their colleagues who teach the same courses in the four-year schools. In that way, a student who has achieved the minimum common core SO's of a course taken at a community college would have the same quality or depth that a student who achieved the same minimum common core SO's at a four-year school. By demanding quality control such that 90 percent or more of the students have to learn 100 percent of the required SO's, the average community college student would actually have achieved higher levels than the average four-year college students who only have to learn a *curves* worth of SO's.

Once the community college faculty have identified the SO's for their courses and have established the minimum common core SO's for their courses, they are ready to make a real contribution towards satisfying the needs of students and that is to allow for *open entry* and *open exit* such that students can start courses at any time and complete their courses at any time. This approach would also allow students to take courses they need regardless of how many students are enrolled (either too few or too many). I think these practices and policies are the real promise that community colleges can offer.

A problem which should be discussed is that community colleges make use of a lot of part time faculty. In some ways, this is an advantage in that the part time faculty frequently are working in the career or area the course they are teaching is concerned with. However, part-time faculty rarely attend inservice sessions and rarely have any training in teaching and in the evaluation of learning. This critical problem can be solved by having the faculty identify the minimum common core SO's and matching tests in the courses taught by part time faculty. Then if a part time teacher has trouble in facilitating the required levels of achievement, they can be given help by the Instructional Crisis Squad.

i. ADULT EDUCATION

For several decades at least, leaders in education, government, and in many other fields have been saying that we need continuing education for life. In a society where it is expected that people will change their jobs four or five times during their lifetime and they will have an increasing amount of leisure time, adult education can help adults accomplish at least five of their goals: to achieve higher educational goals (diplomas and degrees); to achieve higher employment goals; to achieve higher goals in the practical use of leisure time; to maintain and/or expand their abilities in their present employment; and to satisfy their curiosity and interests in their cultural life.

There has been a very high drop-out rate associated with most adult education courses. This is primarily because of the conflict between the structure and design of the courses and the needs of the adults taking the courses. Because of the demands on the typical adult's time, there are two seemingly contradictory problems. First, it is difficult for many adults to keep up with a scheduled class situation particularly where there is homework and study that has to be done before each class meeting. If something comes up, as it often does, and the adult student isn't prepared, cumulative ignorance and the notion to drop-out both begin. On the other hand, if there is no schedule, the adult student may very well procrastinate and not finish the course either.

Another common problem concerns the adult students entering level. Among younger students who are attending school on a full time and continuous basis, teachers can predict fairly accurately the spread among the students as to their entering knowledge and skills levels. However, among adult students it is very difficult to predict the spread of entering behaviors. Some adults on their own or through their work experiences have progressed much farther than their academic record indicates. Other adults may have been involved in very few, if any, learning experiences and may have actually regressed from what their academic record indicates. Because few courses are designed to start where the students are, a secondary problem arises with adult students. The younger student is more accustomed to taking courses which don't fit his starting or entering level whereas the adult student who has been out of school for awhile is not accustomed to the mismatch wherein the course starts at a place either above where the adult student is and the student is lost or the course starts at a place below where the adult student is and the student is bored. In either case, the adult student may very well decide that the class is wasting his or her time and drop-out.

Among many adults, their interest and need is not for total courses, but for certain units or concepts within courses. Since education is not generally available in such short courses, most of these adults will either try to learn on their own whatever it is that they want to learn or if they take a class, as soon as they learn what they want, they will drop out.

Given that many adult students have already spent part of their day driving to and from their work, the additional need to rush through their family meal and drive to a class becomes a little discouraging.

For these reasons, the BLSA to instruction becomes especially useful for application to adult education courses. Most important would be the need to identify what courses or units of courses the adult student wants and then to diagnose where the student is relative to the content of the course or unit and to the necessary entering levels to start the course or unit. Once this has been determined, the adult student should be able to start with a minimum, if any, gaps or overlaps between where the student is and where the course starts. From then on, flexibility is the key. For those adult students who need to have a classroom environment, they should have classrooms which are available on a scheduled basis within which they can learn on an individual basis and where a teacher is available for help. Those adult students who prefer to learn on their own and at their own location should be allowed to do so. Courses for adult students should be designed so that the students can start the course or unit at any time, and complete the course or unit at any time. This means that not only is there *open entry* and *open exit* available for courses, but also for units of courses.

For motivational purposes and also because some adults take courses to benefit from the relationship with other people, it is very important to schedule Scholarship Sessions from time to time in which a teacher, student, or someone from the community can make presentations about the content area of the courses. A part of these sessions should be set aside for small or large group discussions. Remember however, attendance to these sessions should not be a course requirement nor should tests be given on the content of these sessions.

A very critical problem in adult education concerns evaluation. Frequently, adult courses don't even have tests or if they do, the tests are very simple and are more a critique of the course than a test of what was learned in a course. The rationale behind this is that too many adults have had negative experiences with tests so why scare them away. Negative experiences with tests are the result of the traditional approach to testing. When tests are used as diagnostic tools after which the students are taught what they missed, the design of the courses can be such that testing is a very positive experience. Given that all students who finish a course or unit have to achieve 100 percent of the course or unit SO's, testing can't help but be a rewarding experience. For many adults, courses designed in accordance with the BLSA may result in the first 100 percent score they have ever received and what can be more rewarding than success.

Most manpower development and apprenticeship programs have the same problems of adult education programs and they would benefit from the application of the BLSA such that the programs more closely fit the needs of the participants in the programs.

j. IRREGULAR STUDENTS

When I speak of irregular students, I am referring to students who for a variety of reasons do not go to school regularly or who change schools frequently. This would include students who drop out of school or are pushed out and students who are children of migrant workers or other parents whose work causes them to move frequently, i.e., members of the armed services.

Although gaps in a students' attendance in an educational program might appear to cause different problems than student's whose attendance is regular but at different schools, the problems are very similar and the solution is the same. It is obvious that when a student misses school that cumulative ignorance develops and if the educational structure does not allow the student to start where he or she stopped and to make up what was missed, then the student becomes a potential drop out or push out again. Since there is only chance correlation between what is taught in one school and what is being taught in another school even in the courses with the same titles, students who change schools frequently may experience the same problems of gaps in their learning as the student who misses school. In addition, students who change schools may also experience some overlaps in courses which leads to boredom.

Once teachers have identified the SO's for their courses and particularly if they have identified the minimum common core SO's for courses with common titles, the problems for the irregular student have a potential solution. The solution will occur when the schools will allow students to progress at their own pace such that the student who is out for awhile can come back and continue learning at the point where he or she stopped and the student who moves will still be able to keep learning the minimum common core SO's even though some of the minimum common core SO's may be different as a result of a change in location. At least the students will know what they have learned so there will be no overlaps in learning and they will know what they have yet to learn so there will be no gaps in learning.

There are efforts now at trying to coordinate educational programs for children of migrant workers via a computerized system which enables educators to keep track of student records. However, the efforts tend to be more concerned with what has been presented to the students (courses taken) rather than what the students have learned. Although achievement scores are recorded in the system, they tend to be either scores from standardized tests which are relatively useless or scores on teacher-made tests which could be useful if the tests were related to minimum common core SO's but are of little value because of the lack of correlation between what is taught in courses with the same titles but by different teachers at different locations. The use of the computer offers a great opportunity to really solve the problems in the instruction of migrant children if the concepts of the BLSA are applied and if national, regional, and state minimum common core SO's are identified.

k. RACIAL INTEGRATION IN SCHOOLS

For over a decade, there have been considerable efforts to integrate or racially balance our schools throughout the nation. Research evidence has been cited by the Coleman report and others that black and Spanish-American students who are labeled disadvantaged can benefit from the association in school with more advantaged students. Other research by David Armor, Harvard sociology professor, and others suggests that the advantages claimed for integrated schooling may not really exist. The point to remember is that in most cases of research of this type, their data is based on the use of standardized tests which have little relationship with what is being taught in the classrooms. Although I am personally very much in favor of integration, I am against integration when I know the results will end up in a decrease in learning or failure for some of the integrated students. For example, consider the students who are presently getting "A's" and "B's" in a school where all or most of the students may be two or three years behind the students in some other school. If these students are now bussed to that other school, these "A" and "B" students are going to experience failure because most teachers grade on a curve, and these students do not have equal preparation. If the teachers gave them passing grades because they did not want to be labeled discriminatory, they would establish a double standard. Although this tactic might temporarily increase the disadvantaged students self-image, rather quickly both the advantaged and disadvantaged students identify the existence of the double standard and the social barriers between the two groups become even stronger than they were before in the non-integrated environment. As an extreme case of this and its results, there are school districts where Indian students attend under conditions where the Bureau of Indian Affairs is paying double for each Indian student and the school district administrators have formally or informally told their faculty that they cannot fail any Indian students because the district doesn't want to lose the money. Very quickly the Indian students realize that they can't fail, so the motivation to learn is gone. Because of the double standard, strong social barriers develop between the two groups. Since the Indian students don't have to learn anything to graduate, some of them are graduating from high school with about a second grade achievement. Of course, the traditional educator blames this on genetics and external (to the school) environment.

Most of the disadvantaged students start school one and two years behind the more advantaged student. When educators try to eliminate this disadvantage, it appears as if they are segregating the students. Any experiences or educational structure that ultimately end up showing that the disadvantaged students attain lower levels of achievement than the advantaged students, reinforces the belief by most educators that the disadvantaged are disadvantaged not only in ability and capacity, but that these limitations are genetic and hence unchangeable. This single belief is probably the most critical problem affecting race relations. However, if the extra help is given in the form of preschool (Head Start, etc.) with SO's and minimum common core SO's and with a follow up such that the students who once have gained an advantage don't have to be held back until the rest of the class catches up, then the so-called disadvantaged students may be as advantaged as the advantaged students. Instead of thinking of equal educational opportunity in which the emphasis is on equal facilities and opportunities (whether segregated or integrated), the emphasis should be on equal opportunity *for equal achievement.* Giving equal facilities to students who are different in ability and past achievement assures that the results will indicate differences in present and future achievement. Of course, giving equal facilities to different students is a step better than the previous situation wherein the disadvantaged students were given disadvantaged (lower quality) schools, materials, and teachers which practically guaranteed great differences in achievement. Pushing for *equal minimum achievement will work whether it is in separate or integrated facilities* because in order for the schools to raise each student to at least the minimum level of achievement, the necessary money, materials, and teaching personnel will have to be available in proportion to the learning needs of the students — students needing the most improvement in order to achieve the specified level of equal minimum learning will also need the most help. If it is true that the disadvantaged students learn slower and differently than the more advantaged student, then they should be given more time to learn and different materials to learn from in order to achieve the same minimum common core SO's. In order to solve many of the social problems associated with racial prejudice, it is critical to prove that differences in ability primarily affect *HOW* a person learns, these differences do not affect what a person can learn nor how much a person can learn! Equality *in achievement* of the minimum common core SO's will build stronger, more positive, and longer lasting self-images and will do more to break down social barriers and prejudice due to supposed racial (mental) difference than providing for equality in facilities. To do this, it may appear as if the concept fosters segregation, but this would only be true if learning is occurring in classes or groups and only at preschool or lower elementary school levels. Once the achievement levels are equalized or a school has true continuous progress for each student, integration can be very natural.

Previously, many of the minority group students, particularly the black students and the Spanish-American students, were accustomed to success only in their own environment. The criteria for *success* in their own environment is often quite different from the criteria for *success* in the middle class, white, protestant, midwestern American society. Many of these minority group students have either experienced *failure* personally or have observed other minority group students experiencing *failure* during attempts to find *success* in a society which represents the majority. As long as there were very limited opportunities for the minority group students to achieve *success* in the real world of the majority, there wasn't any need to achieve *success* in the academic world of the majority. With all of the changes which have been brought about by the civil rights movement, there are greatly expanding opportunities for minority group students to achieve *success* in the real world of the majority. Because of this, there is also an expanding need to achieve *success* in the academic world of the majority.

As members of the majority, it is not enough to let the minority group students enroll in our colleges and universities, particularly when we know that cumulative ignorance and curve grading will *push out* or fail the students during their first year (which psychologically is more harmful on the minority group students than not letting them enroll at all). If we are going to encourage the minority group students to enroll in our colleges and universities, then there should be an instructional design which allows the students to eliminate their cumulative ignorance and also allows for variations in learning paths because of individual differences. This instructional design or the Behavioral Learning Systems Approach (BLSA) would in effect guarantee the achievement of *success* if the minority group student really wanted it.

Some people, particularly traditional educators in higher education, have indicated a concern about the lowering of the standards for admission to the colleges and universities in order to admit the so-called disadvantaged students. Lowering the standards for admission is not that important, but lowering the standards for completion or graduation for these students is an open confession of the prejudice and bias of the establishment, because their actions prove that they don't actually believe that the minority group students can achieve the regular standards. Lowering the standards of completion or graduation is an insult to the ability of the minority group students. Instead of lowering the standards of learning for the disadvantaged students, the standards of time, materials, etc., should be changed and designed to fit the needs of the students. In order not to discriminate against other students from the majority group who also have cumulative ignorance, this instructional design should be applied and can be applied to the entire student body.

1. YEAR-ROUND SCHOOLS

As school budgets get tighter and some schools become more and more overcrowded with students, an increasingly common topic is the year-round school. There are a variety of ways which have been suggested as to how the year-round school should be scheduled and many of these plans have been implemented in one or more school districts. Although most of these plans actually do make better use of the facilities, there are increased costs in keeping the facilities in use year-round. In cases of overcrowded schools, the year-round school does in effect help to reduce the number of students in school at any one time. However, the main point to keep in mind is that no matter how much the schedule is changed, students are still expected to stay in school 180 days each year which continues to ignore the fact that students learn at different rates and need different amounts of time and materials in order to achieve the minimum common core SO's. One of the most common reasons given for year-round schools is that it would help eliminate the loss of learning which supposedly occurs over the long summer vacation which would in turn reduce the amount of time spent by teachers each fall going back over material that the students were *exposed* to the previous spring. What too many educators assume (even though they know better) is that since the students were *exposed* to the material, they should know 100 percent of it. Then when fall comes, the teachers identify that most or all of the students are no longer at the 100 percent level and have dropped to a point where the average student is only at about the 70 percent level. Consequently, it is assumed that a lot of learning has been lost over the summer. However, even a cursory glance at the spring grades of the students will show that the students were not at the 100 percent level at the end of the spring term. The students' achievement levels were more likely a curve of achievement with the average students learning at about the 70 percent level (which is where the students are in the fall). Also, if the students were really forgetting so much over the summer, this indicates several other problems: first, probably most of what was being taught must have been rote memory which can be forgotten more easily; second, if what was being taught were process objectives, they must have been irrelevant and not used much because if the students were using what they learned they would have remembered; third, think of the millions of students whose self image has been damaged by getting "D" and "F" grades in the spring for not knowing what their higher achieving classmates will forget during the next few months; and fourth, if the forgetting curve is really that sharp in a period of three months, any advantages of a high school or college education would be nullified in a year or so after graduation.

The real advantage of the year-round school is when the school year can be structured so as to allow students who need more time to learn can have that extra time. Ideally, the schools should be operated on a year-round basis such that students can progress at their own pace and take off when they feel the need to stop. In that way, students would be starting and completing courses throughout the year. I realize that the ideal is not immediately feasible in most schools; however, there are various compromises which can be tried (see pp. 221-227, Volume I). These compromises depend on built-in buffer zones during which those students who need more time to learn can have that extra time. For example, summer school can very easily be used to allow students who received "C's", "D's", or "F's" at the end of the spring semester or quarter to learn enough to get "A's" or "B's" in their courses. In the year-round school design where the students attend 45 days and then are off 15 days, it would be easy to use the 15 days as a buffer zone for those students who need more time to learn. The students wouldn't attend the full 15 days. They would only use as many of the 15 days as they needed to achieve 100 percent of the required SO's. Using this approach, it would be simple to prove that year-round schools result in significant increases in achievement.

As schools reach the ideal in which students progress at their own rate year-round, one of the best advantages will be that students will not all complete at the same time and flood the job market. Students' completion of learning throughout the year will more nearly match the employment openings which occur throughout the year.

m. PAROCHIAL AND PRIVATE SCHOOLS

This last decade has seen many parochial and private schools closing because of lowering enrollments and higher costs. In some cases, the learning environment in these schools may be bad enough that they should be closed; however, in most cases, these schools have been providing educational opportunities *as good as* and in some cases *slightly better* than the public schools. The major problem, as I see it, is that most parochial and private schools try to operate in a fashion similar to the public schools which are generally ineffective and inefficient. Of course, what has held most of these schools back from radically different structures is that they would be accused of having an inferior program, a diploma mill, and/or they might not be accredited. These accusations are based on any changes in the traditional structure of the program, physical facilities, and the supposed quality of the teachers as measured by their degrees. Rarely are any schools accredited because they can produce certain levels of achievement and rarely are any schools denied accreditation because their students didn't achieve certain levels of learning. Parochial and private schools are in a unique situation and can institute the changes suggested in these three books much easier than most public schools. If they could encourage cooperation with other local schools in the development of minimum common core SO's for each course, then the schools could use whatever methods, structure, or design they wanted to as long as they could prove that their students were learning as well as or better than the public schools. By utilizing the concepts of the BLSA, not only could these schools operate more effectively and efficiently, but they would be able to turn out students who actually know and can do significantly more than the students graduating from the public schools who are still using the traditional approach to education. As a result, parochial and private schools could become the leaders rather than the followers and they could attract more students and enjoy a much more positive image based on evidence.

>NOTE: As the elementary enrollment decreases, even public schools are closing down. By utilizing the BLSA to instruction, it might not be necessary to close these schools down. The use of the BLSA could not increase the enrollment where the enrollment is limited to a certain area, but the changing role of the teacher would enable the teachers to fill more roles which would allow the school to operate with fewer faculty, while at the same time offering the same number (or even more) courses. In addition, the schools could be used for multi-purpose laboratories and workshops, for community cultural and adult education needs, and for study spaces for those students whose home environment doesn't have space for or isn't conducive to studying.

C. QUESTIONS AND ANSWERS ABOUT UTILIZING THE BEHAVIORAL LEARNING SYSTEMS CONCEPTS

In the process of suggesting and implementing a change from the traditional approach to education to the Behavioral Learning Systems Approach (BLSA) to designed instruction, many teachers will ask questions and will want answers to their questions before going on. Some teachers will ask sincere questions in hopes that they can be answered and then they can continue to change with a clear conscience.

Over the years that I have been meeting with teachers, I think I have probably been asked most of the questions that might come up. Because it is important for any administrator or teacher contemplating or actually making changes to be able to answer these questions, I would like to list some of the most common and more important questions along with my answers. There is no particular order to these questions, so if you are interested, it might be easiest to skim through the questions and only read answers whenever you come across a question which is of interest to you.

1. Won't the student who takes a long time to learn the 100 percent feel out of place with smaller and younger students?
    a. As long as students are progressing at their own pace, the range of ages and sizes will be continuous and no one student will necessarily stand out.
    b. Where the student is physically is not as important as what the student is learning, so the student could be in a peer age or size group and yet learning from materials which match his or her learning needs.
    c. Students are usually not as conscious of age and size differences as adults are.

2. If a student is held back until he or she learns 100 percent of the SO's, what happens to the student's social and emotional growth?
    a. It is common in first grade to find a child being held back who has learned whatever he or she was supposed to learn but is considered too young socially and emotionally. Frequently, these students become so bored by repeating the same activities that their social and emotional growth regresses.
    b. Although there is sort of a design for cognitive and sensory growth in early elementary grades, there is rarely a design for affective growth. If social and emotional growth is being left up to chance anyway, then it shouldn't make too much of a difference if the student takes longer to complete the 100 percent.
    c. Since the student has to achieve the 100 percent level, the success will help build confidence and emotional growth. In helping other students learn, the student will increase socially.

When we select a good textbook for a course from among several choices, determine the portions of it for assignment and discussions, *select those problems* that involve specific principles and test over that material (for example, in a course on Intermediate Algebra) are we identifying objectives whether we have called them that or not?

   a. Yes.

4. If the systems approach were widely used in college what effect could be expected on the college income and on the total cost of instruction?

   a. If budget is based on FTE (full time equivalent) students, the income would be increased because failing students would be taught and retained rather than pushed out.

   b. Once the system is established, it might be possible to reduce the cost of instruction because of increased effectiveness and efficiency.

5. When an instructor has completed one term with three classes using the systems approach and goes into a second term with his incomplete students and three new groups of students, possibly in different courses, is his load not approximately doubled and does he not double his requirement of classroom space?

   a. There are already students in every class that are capable and would like to learn on their own in or out of class if the teachers would let them.

   b. Many students will complete the course early which will reduce student load at a time when the teacher needs to spend more time with the remaining students.

6. In past experience of the systems approach, do students who have not been in a competitive environment transfer to university classes and make adjustments to the competitive environment?

   a. In the BLSA, there is still competition in time which is not as destructive as competition in learning with its concomitant development of cumulative ignorance.

   b. Under the BLSA, the average students have to achieve 100 percent of the required SO's. As such, they will have a much better chance in a competitive learning environment than traditionally educated students who on the average may only learn about 75 percent of unknown objectives.

7. Any data on comparison of the BLSA vs. the traditional approach?

   a. Since the traditional approach is not based on the achievement of SO's, it would be like comparing apples and oranges.

    b. If standardized tests were used, the results wouldn't reveal anything because the tests don't match either the BLSA or the traditional approach.

    c. If the test used in the traditional approach really represented what the teachers wanted and the test items became the SO's for the BLSA, obviously, the BLSA would come out best because the BLSA students would have to learn 100 percent of the test items and the traditional approach would be satisfied with a curve of results.

8. In individualizing instruction, when I'm working with one student or a small group of students, what will the rest of my class be doing?

    a. That is the purpose of letting the students have the course SO's ahead of time so they can learn on their own. Just like in the old one-room school, there can be a variety of things going on at the same time. Although some teachers may not like to admit it, some students can learn without them.

9. Won't teachers tend to write and use easy SO's in order to facilitate the students achieving 100 percent?

    a. If the SO's could be kept private and no one else would see them except the teacher and the students, it could happen.

    b. By making the SO's publicly available, the teacher won't want his or her colleagues to see easy SO's.

    c. Under public conditions, there will be a tendency to make the SO's too tough; however, knowing that the students have to achieve 100 percent of the SO's, the teacher can't make them too tough. One tendency is nullified by another tendency.

    d. By having teachers work together, there is the best chance that the SO's in the minimum common core will be what they should be as far as difficulty level is concerned.

10. Shouldn't all educational levels change at the same time?

    a. The change would never take place if all levels had to do it at the same time.

    b. Just because some teachers at another level don't want to make the change to give the students more success is not sufficient justification to perpetuate the malpractices which are causing negative effects on students.

11. If I test the way I should and I can't use automatic scoring equipment, how will I find time to score all of the tests and get

them back to the students while the tests are still relevant?

    a. Remember, when students progress at their own pace, they all won't be ready for the same test at the same time.

12. Students need to live up to a schedule in the real world, so why not have deadlines in school?

    a. Setting a deadline and grading the student accordingly is evaluation not teaching. Where do we actually teach the behavior of meeting deadlines?

    b. If one of your course SO's is to give the student an assignment which is to be handed in on time ten days later, then when the student misses the deadline instead of grading the student down, give the student an incomplete and have the student repeat the process. Give the student another assignment and a deadline and if the student misses the deadline again, repeat the process until the student turns in the assignment on time and done right.

13. There is failure in the real world so why can't there be failure in school? After all aren't we supposed to prepare the students for life?

    a. To prepare a student for failure is too teach a student how to cope with failure successfully.

    b. If coping with failure is one of your SO's, develop an instructional unit in which the students have to learn "A" worth of coping with failure.

14. If a student doesn't learn the first time, how many times do you try before you give up?

    a. If a student doesn't learn a SO after repeating the learning event twice, something is wrong. Check on the prerequisites in the other domains. Try a different method or a different vehicle which may be of more interest to the student but don't change the SO.

    b. If the SO is important, don't give up. Solve the learning problem as a professional teacher should.

15. Why is it all of a sudden so necessary to have SO's? Teachers got along fine for years without them.

    a. Actually, teachers have always had SO's, they called them test items!

    b. If schools are for the elite and the function of schools is to sift out the better students, then it might be best to continue the traditional way. However, as a society, we are concerned about each and every student not just a few who can learn in spite of us.

c. As humanists, we have to help all students have success in the preparation for life and work.

16. In changing to instruction primarily based on behavioral objectives, what if the objectives are trivia, won't we lose many of the good things that are happening now?

   a. If *good things* are happening now, how do we know it? If you can prove they exist and are being achieved now, then why can't these *good things* become specified objectives such that the *good things* are taught by design rather than have them occur by chance as it is now.

   b. At the present time, since objectives are not spelled out, trivia is only discovered when the test is given and its too late to do anything about it. At least once the SO's are available, if a SO is trivia, it can be challenged by the students, parents, other teachers, or administrators and then eliminated.

   c. If the questions of justification have been asked and defended, the chances of trivia are greatly reduced. At the present time, students have no defense against being graded on their responses to test items which are trivia.

17. The behavior which we may really want may not be needed or demonstrated for many years. How can you know that any measured behaviors which are learned now will affect behaviors in the years ahead?

   a. Since we are not concerned right now with how our present approach affects behavior years away, then why evaluate the BLSA with criteria you're not using to evaluate the traditional approach.

   b. Actually the traditional approach has been evaluated on a long term basis by rates of unemployment, welfare, juvenile delinquency, etc. These problems have been blamed on the traditional approach to education. At least the BLSA could not be worse and could be much better.

   c. Its nice to worry about the years ahead, but right now hundreds of thousands of students are experiencing failure and lack of success in traditional education. They are receiving C's, D's, and F's right now — not ten and twenty years from now. Once all our students are having positive and successful experiences in schools or wherever they are learning, then it will be time to worry about the distant future — having success can't hurt them — failure can!

18. Can we normally accept the setting of objectives by *others* isn't that bordering on brainwashing?

   a. Almost every teacher that is right now involved in evaluating students are evaluating whether or not the students have done what that teacher considers *good* or *right*. But at present, most of these *good* and/or *right* things are hidden from the students. At least under BLSA, the objectives are a public list and can be challenged.

   b. Consider most objective type tests which are used at the present time in which the guiding line says *select the best answer*. According to who? Obviously, according to the teacher or author of the test! Students don't think for themselves in these tests. The successful student is the one who can out-psych the teachers.

   c. Almost every graduate student is familiar with the concept of brainwashing. It's the only way to get through and achieve graduate degrees in many departments.

   d. If teachers are going to be considered professional and be paid high salaries, then teachers should be willing to put their opinions on the line of what they think is important to learn — if teachers don't want to spell out what they want students to learn and they don't believe they have the right to impose their ideas on others — then they should quit. There is no reason for the public to pay high salaries to teachers who have nothing to contribute to the teaching-learning situation.

19. If educational objectives were really useful, teachers would have used them, after all the concept of specific educational objectives has been around for a long time, i.e., Bobbitt in 1918.

   a. The problem is that the majority of what was called specific educational objectives were not actually specific to the point of being able to measure directly for their achievement. Most of these objectives were GO's. The concept of specific measurable and behavioral learning objectives didn't really get started until the advent of programmed instruction. Even now, it is a rare event that I find teachers with lists of specific measurable objectives for their course or courses and if they don't actually have them — of course they can't use them.

b. As stated before, teachers have always had SO's in the form of their test items. They just didn't realize that their test items were the students SO's.

20. The live classroom is dynamic and in the very process of teaching and discussing, unexpected opportunities emerge for the teaching of outcomes far too numerous and complex to be specified in behavioral terms and also to identify in advance. Won't the teaching by SO's limit this?

   a. If we don't know what this dynamic, wonderful, serendipitous learning is, how does anyone know that it is occurring now!

   b. It's a matter of priority. In order to hope that these wonderful things can occur, is it humane to continue the present negative educational malpractices while waiting for serendipitous learning to occur? Wouldn't it be more humane to make sure that everyone learns by design what they should and want to and then if these chance things occur — great.

   c. Too many educators assume that the only place students ever get together and talk is in the classroom. Students do talk in other places. In fact some of the greatest serendipitous learning events probably occur out of classrooms and away from teachers and schools.

   d. Instead of being satisfied with A, B, C, D and F levels of learning, by demanding 100% learning for all students, the chances for the great serendipitous learning events to occur are increased, i.e., if a student was being exposed to an unusual piece of literature, the chances for recognizing the uniqueness of the literature would be enhanced if the student had learned 100% of the reading objectives and 100% of writing objectives and 100% of literary analysis objectives.

   e. The specifying of objectives does not say *how* a teacher will help learners learn nor *when* the learners will learn. Given course SO's, the good teacher will still take advantage of the moment to help learners learn certain SO's. In fact, knowing what it is the learners are supposed to learn and are maybe having trouble learning, actually aids the teacher to take advantage of serendipitous moments. Not knowing what is to be learned inhibits teachers and students from taking advantage of potential learning situations.

21. It may be allright in subject areas where there are predictable outcomes, but how about in the areas of art, music, or writing where creativity is the goal. To specify the product would be to kill creativity or at least inhibit it.

    a. A common mistake is to believe that the specifying of objectives only concerns *end products*. It is very possible and desirable to specify *means* or a *process* not the product. In fact in the development of the independent learner, it is necessary to help the learner be creative in both *ends* and *means*.

    b. In most of the same courses in which the teachers claim they can't specify objectives, these very same teachers evaluate students and assign grades. If there is something they are evaluating the student on, then why not be honest and spell it out. If the criteria for evaluation are too subjective to specify, then I challenge any teacher's right to assign grades (which are specific) on something they don't know what it is. That's really inhumane!

    c. Many teachers in the creative arts areas recognize that there are things that can be taught and measured (craft). If students can be taught 100% of all the measurable craft, their chances of being creative are enhanced. Not knowing the craft inhibits creativity.

    d. I am not claiming and neither are others who favor the systems concepts that everything can be put into SO's. There are many desired GO's that may never be broken down into SO's. In the meantime, there are SO's to be learned in every subject area and right now there are students in every subject area that are being evaluated as achieving less than 100% (C's, D's, and F's). Why not use the systems approach to teach whatever it is their teachers are saying the students haven't learned. After all, if whatever it is is important enough to grade students down for not achieving it, it must also be important enough to specify and to teach! To do otherwise is to try to defend being cruel and inhumane.

22. Not all — perhaps not even most — outcomes of curriculum and instruction are amenable to measurement. What is most educationally valuable is the development of that mode of curiosity, inventiveness, and insight that is capable of being described only in metaphoric or poetic terms!

a. If one doesn't know what *it* is specifically, how does anyone know that *it* is being developed now? If one doesn't know what *it* is, how do we know that it is valuable? Once we know what *it* is, why not teach *it* by design to every student (if *it* is so valuable)?

b. If we can't measure *it* it is impossible to compare *it* in quantity to what can be measured — *most outcomes.*

c. Again, given that what can't be measured is much more important and valuable, how can traditional educators justify grading students down and particularly failing students for not learning outcomes that they themselves are measuring and yet they also say are not very important nor valuable! (Inhumanity to man!)

23. If identification of all worthwhile outcomes in behavioral terms comes to be commonly accepted and expected, then it is inevitable that, over time, the curriculum will tend to emphasize those elements which have been thus identified. Important outcomes which are detected only with great difficulty and which are translated only rarely into behavioral terms tend to atrophy.

    a. If the outcomes which are specified are considered *worthwhile*, what's wrong with all students learning 100% of what is *worthwhile?* Students aren't learning that now even assuming what teachers are presently testing for is *worthwhile!*

    b. If the non-measurable outcomes are really difficult to measure or identify, how is it possible to identify or lable these outcomes as *important?* Is it reasonable to say that whatever is measurable is non-important and whatever is non-measurable is important! This attitude reflects that of a person whose own experience is such that most or all of the objectives this person has tried to specify turn out to be trite, low level, rote memory facts. It is possible to specify high level thinking type objectives, but it may be necessary to learn via designed instruction on how to do this. Few people can develop high level specific objectives on their own without any training.

    c. If the really *important* objectives are GO's, they need not disappear. That is why I recommend keeping GO's and to continually try to increase their specificity. The difference is one of priority. To take time teaching GO's at the sacrifice of achieving SO's represents gross negligence concerning the student particularly if the lack of achievement of the SO's develops cumulative ignorance and causes the student trouble in learning subsequent SO's.

24. What happen to the 10 percent in a situation when 90 percent or more learn 100 percent?
    a. It may not be 10 percent, it could be nothing, remember the criteria is 90 percent or *more.*
    b. These could be students who decide to take the "I" and just don't complete the course.
    c. These could be students that need help from counselors, guidance staff, or pychologists.
    d. Under the present traditional condition, the percentage of students learning 100 percent is very close to zero or at the most 10 percent, so 90 percent is a goal to be achieved. Possibly at a later date, this goal may be changed to 95, 98 or even 100 percent.

25. If the emphasis is on individuals how does the student learn social development skills, i.e., leadership, etc.
    a. If there are group SO's, it is designed into the learning environment.
    b. Since students are not in *classes*, it will be easier than ever to schedule non-academic activities — however if learning should occur in these activities then see (a). If no learning should occur, why are the schools doing it?
    c. Since the social development skills are not taught by design at present, it couldn't be worse under a different method.
    d. How much social development is learned in a class where the teacher is presenting and students are listening?
    e. To assume that the only place students can be in groups is in a school, is to ignore the outside world. Students constantly get together in homes, on sidewalks, playgrounds, etc.

26. Under the BLSA, in order to get students to learn 100 percent of the required SO's in all of their courses, wouldn't this considerably extend the length of time necessary for students to achieve an education?
    a. This would be true, if you tried to maximize learning without any change in the present instructional materials and modes of teaching, but by utilizing the learning systems concept in the development of whatever instructional

materials are necessary to maximize learning and by using the teacher in the teaching-learning situation where the teacher would be most beneficial for the student, the problem is not going to be what to do with the students who are taking too long, the problem is more apt to be what to do with the students who have already learned everything in a much shorter time. In fact, it has been estimated by several researchers that if we could really specify our total curriculum from kindergarten through twelfth grade, the average student could probably learn all of the required SO's in eight or nine years.